SOCIAL CHANGE

Roberta Ash Garner

DePaul University

Rand McNally College Publishing Company / Chicago

For Michael

Contents

Preface

IN THE NEXT FEW PAGES, I would like to share with the reader some of the problems and choices that concerned me during the writing of this book.

My Goals in Writing This Book

I like to think of my work as a long essay about social change, amply illustrated with case studies. It is not meant to be a review of the literature. Of course, I have relied on the work of many authors who have written about change, but I do not claim to review all of the main currents of thought on this topic. I have been selective because some perspectives are better than others in explaining the reality of social change. I have also tried to avoid name dropping —"X says such and such," "Y says this and that." I have tried to write about social change itself, not about social scientists who have written about social change.

In the same vein, I have not tried to review or compare theories of change. My book has a distinct point of view, and I feel no need to summarize other perspectives. I have tried to interpret social change using the following general principles, which I believe help us to comprehend the reality of change.

1. *All social change, including change in individuals as well as change through crisis and revolution, must be understood as change in social systems as wholes.*

2. *Our understanding of social change must be based on an examination of historical change.* A king once complained to the Greek mathematician Euclid that mathematics required too much hard computational work. The king then asked if he could study the subject without doing all the work. Euclid replied, "Sire, there is no royal road to mathematics." Nor are there any royal roads to comprehending social change that avoid the study of history. Sociology without history tends to lapse into triviality or metaphysical abstractness.

vii

To encompass social change, the social sciences must take into account time and the sequencing of patterns of human action—in other words, history. I have tried, however, to present history not as a tedious account of dates, names of kings, and battles, but as the real experiences of human beings.

3. *History and social change are both created through the clash of groups of people, often organized, within specific economic and political systems.* This in turn means that changes in political behavior and beliefs do not occur separately from economic change. The major historical changes have always involved transformation of these economic, political, and ideological systems (social formations). The most important groups in historical change are those associated with particular positions in the economy of a given social formation, vantage points from which they defend the prevailing order or struggle to bring about a new one. These groups—classes—account for the major transformations of societies. A group can be associated with a social system in a conscious and organized way, as when American businessmen defend capitalism or Portuguese field laborers expropriate landowners; but groups can also "stand for" a particular social system in a less conscious way, sustaining an old system or bringing about a new one by actions whose consequences they themselves do not fully understand or intend.

In this sense, then, "the history of all hitherto existing society is the history of class struggles." My purpose in writing about social change is to explain this statement, transforming it from a mystical article of faith (as some people regard it) into the key for the scientific understanding of long-term change.

How to Read This Book: A Detective Story

This book is arranged as an intellectual whodunit, posing puzzles in the opening chapters that are not fully resolved until Part Three. In the first chapters, we see how there are essentially no general laws of change governing processes in individuals and organizations. These processes always have to be understood in their specific historical context. Thus the study of change in individuals and organizations raises questions that can be answered only by examining change in human history as a whole, in other words, in the succession of historically determinate societies. So readers are warned not to read Parts One and Two without reading Part Three. However, like the impatient readers of detective novels, they may skip directly to Part Three. This, too, would be a mistake. One reason for arranging the book in this order is to help the reader move from the level of the familiar—individuals and organizations —to the level of historical change in whole societies because this level may seem a little more distant and difficult to understand.

What has Been Left Out?

The reader of any book should always ask what is missing. A good understanding of what isn't there is often just as revealing as a good understanding of what is there.

You will, for instance, find the crucial topic of existing socialist societies only lightly covered. There is some discussion of socialist revolutions but very little discussion about the ensuing states. This is not an oversight but rather reflects my own uncertainty about the nature and future of these societies.

Capitalist societies are easier to write about because we can always look at them from the outside and the future, from the vantage point of socialism —"looking backward" in a thought experiment. This perspective is much harder to develop for societies that are already in the midst of a transition to a socialism that we do not yet fully understand. Some societies may successfully complete this transition. Others may pursue a course that is really only an interim measure, necessary for developing their economies out of a state of underdevelopment but not leading to a genuine socialism. Still others may be already lapsing into state capitalism. All such societies have to conduct themselves as nation-states, defending national interests in situations of *realpolitik,* and this contingency also distorts their behavior. So we cannot clearly judge their progress as yet.

Scylla and Charybdis

During his wanderings, Ulysses came to the Straits of Messina where two perils confronted his ship simultaneously. On one side of the narrows was the terrible whirlpool Charybdis. On the other side, on a rocky ledge, was the monster Scylla, a giant dog-headed creature, waiting to snatch sailors off any ship that sailed too near her jaws and claws. Ulysses had to steer his ship between these two dangers.

Anyone writing about social change must also steer between two perils. On the one side is the whirlpool of subjectivism, which pulls its victims into the murky waters of the will. On the other side is the monster of economic determinism with its positivistic teeth and claws. The ship of bourgeois thought is always destroyed by one or the other danger, subjectivism or positivistic empiricism. The Marxist sails through the straits, thanks to the helmsman of dialectical thought, but not without peril.

Like Ulysses, I have chosen to sail a bit closer to Scylla, risking accusations of economic determinism in order to avoid the more subtle but deadlier whirlpool of subjectivism. This choice is my response to the situation in the social sciences in which some of the best minds seem more and more committed to one of the varieties of subjectivism. Bright young students quite often turn away—and rightly—from the trivialities of what passes as science and rigor only to find themselves drowning in the maelstrom of opinions, feelings, negotiated realities, endless reflexivities, and existential agonies. Better the risk of sailing through on the positivistic side.

On Science and Morality

The fashion among some radicals is to attack science and technology. They confuse the misuses of knowledge in a class society with the knowledge itself. They reify science or technology into a mysterious superhuman force that can and must be stopped through a celebration of irrationality. Their foolishness is the direct counterpart to the equally foolish claims of science as value free, remote from the struggle, that are made by scientists who serve the rulers. My view of science is opposed to both of these views. Science is a human activity, and as such is constrained by the society in which it is carried out. But it has the potential of freeing us from our helplessness in the face of nature and the force of our own institutions. By understanding social change, we can begin to struggle for the kind of society we want. By clarifying "what is" scientific inquiry makes possible the struggle for "what should be."

ROBERTA ASH GARNER

Acknowledgments

I WOULD LIKE TO THANK the following, each of whom contributed insights and comradeship: Mayer Zald; Bob Harmon; Bob Ogden; Larry Garner; Alix Mitchell; Peter Dreier; Dick Flacks; my colleagues at DePaul University; my friends in a number of Chicago political groups and the Chicago Marxist Forum; the people associated with Kapitalistate; and Martha Urban, my copy editor at Rand McNally. I would also like to thank my family for patience and support.

Part One

CHANGE AND THE INDIVIDUAL

"Men make their own history, but they do not make it just as they please; they do not make it under circumstances chosen by themselves, but under circumstances directly encountered, given and transmitted from the past. The tradition of all the dead generations weighs like a nightmare on the brain of the living."—Karl Marx, *The Eighteenth Brumaire of Louis Bonaparte*

Chapter
1

What Is
Social
Change?

In this chapter I shall distinguish historical change —the topic of this book—from other kinds of change. Historical change is open-ended, cumultative, and irreversible change in human activities. I shall differentiate objective change—change in human activities—from subjective change—change in the individual's understanding and consciousness. I shall show how subjective changes in the past are carried forward into the present as mental baggage or as the nightmare of the past that weighs on the brain of the living.

EVERY READER OF THIS BOOK experiences himself or herself as an individual. Change in ourselves as individual human beings seems to be the most easily observed type of change. We know that each of us undergoes many different kinds of changes: the biological changes of the daily cycle of sleeping, eating, digesting; swings in mood; maturation and aging; changes in our way of life. Some of these changes are not in themselves social change. They are changes that any living organism undergoes in some fashion. Some of these apparent changes are really not change at all, at least not in the sense of irreversible change. On the contrary, the changes in our daily cycle—getting up, eating, defecating, sleeping, and so on—reassure us that each day is a little bit like the preceding one and the next one. They are recurrent, predictable changes, and they mark a stable routine rather than an *open-ended,* somewhat *unpredictable,* perhaps *irrevocable* kind of process. It is the latter that we will focus on in this book and to which we will refer as *change.*

Different Kinds of Change

Change, in our meaning of the word, will be the kind of process that people refer to when they say "You can't go home again" or "You can't step into the

3

same river twice." You have probably experienced this kind of change yourself. Perhaps you moved away from your home town or old neighborhood and later came back and found it very different from how you had left it—inhabited by different people, living in different kinds of houses and pursuing a different way of life from the one you remembered. Or, you may find that your old neighborhood is virtually identical to the one you remember, but that *you* have changed and therefore the meaning of your old environment has changed. A house that once seemed large and comfortable now seems small and dingy; an alley that was once threatening because the neighborhood bully chased you through it now seems safe. Some of this first chapter will be devoted to the interplay between "objective" change in the environment and the "subjective" changes that take place in the individual and in the meanings that an individual assigns to that environment.

Objective Change, Subjective Change

Once more picture yourself returning to an old neighborhood. The objective changes might include such features as the following: your former neighbors have aged, and some have moved away and been replaced by people who may be markedly different in ethnicity, income, or life style; the vacant lots may have new buildings on them, but other buildings may have been torn down; trees have grown taller, landmarks have been replaced by new landmarks, the old candy store replaced by a laundromat, the restaurant's place usurped by a MacDonald's, and so on. Subjective change would include your new perspectives on that old irreplaceable way of life you remember and the way in which you accommodate yourself to the changes that you see have taken place. Throughout human life there is a linkage between changes in our physical and human environment and changes in ourselves.

Life Cycle Changes

Now, for a moment, let's go back to the recurrent biological changes that we were describing earlier. One of the most important of these is maturation and aging, in other words, the whole set of changes that we refer to as the *life cycle*. Everyone is conceived, is born, and dies. In our society (but not everywhere in the world, for many children die in infancy), the majority of those children born pass through a period of physical growth and rapid learning, especially language learning; go through a plateau phase of slower growth before adolescence; attain puberty; reach full physical strength; and eventually grow old.

For some individuals, particularly those in societies with a high infant mortality rate, this set of events may be cut short by an early death. Picture a creature with a life span enormously longer than ours, so that our life span corresponds to no more than a day of its life. For this creature, the lives of human beings do indeed form a predictable recurrent cycle, just as the lives of butterflies or mosquitoes or liver flukes seem very predictable and recurrent to us. But to each one of us as individuals, our own "life cycle" is no cycle at all but the totality of our own open-ended, often surprising, and always finite existence. Furthermore, the predictable biological changes are lived out amid essentially new, nonrecurrent and, to some extent, unpredictable *historical* change.

Historical Change

The interplay between history (open-ended nonrecurrent change) and biology (predictable cycles) shapes our experience of change. Let us return for a moment to our image of revisiting the old neighborhood. The returning visitor has undergone two kinds of change: she has become biologically older and she has undergone experiences that are unique to a given historical period. Both of these factors shape the subjective experience of change. The factor of chance, separate from both biology and history, also impinges on each individual. Our concern here, as social scientists, will be with historical change for, as we stated before, we are primarily interested in changes that are nonreversible and do not reoccur in precisely the same fashion as before. Of course, some patterns of change may recur even if the precise events do not. Each historical event to some degree shapes those that follow it in a *cumulative* manner, and it is this *sequencing* of incidents that gives history its open-ended nonrepetitive character.

Finally, by history and historical change we mean those events that are largely shaped by *human* action. Such action may not always be purposive, and the actors often may neither understand the consequences of their actions nor be able to attain their goals. The point is, however, that we are looking at processes that are set in motion by human behavior and sustained and manifested by the relationships between people. They are not biologically fixed.

Let us look at history in a simpler way. We have all heard phrases, cliches, and popular expressions that describe past periods of time: the Stone Age, the Bronze Age and the Iron Age, the Roman Empire, the Dark Ages (meaning that period when *Europeans* were not very culturally productive), the Industrial Revolution, the antebellum (pre–Civil War) South, the Gay Nineties, the Great Depression, World War I and World War II, the cold war, McCarthyism, the Kennedy era, the war in Vietnam. As we hear these words, we realize that we are talking about history, that we are talking about periods and places when life was different from what we experience now. People's behavior was in some way different. The sum total of human relationships was not the same. Technology and beliefs were different. Yet, of course, since about fifty thousand years ago, people have been virtually identical biologically to ourselves. It is this social flux, this change in relationships and action, not in the biologically defined parts of human existence, that we refer to as history.

The Phenomenon of Generations

Human beings live out their "life cycles"—their biological growth and change —against a background of historical change. Particular generations are identified by the particular cluster of historical events that characterized a period of their life. These generations do not just passively live out their biological lives against a historical backdrop; rather, their behavior helps to create the historical events themselves.

In the next few pages we shall examine how peoples' lives mesh with historical events. Again, we have all heard a number of popular expressions that assert that this meshing is an important factor in an individual's objective experiences and in the subjective meanings that he attaches to these experiences. For example, the parents of a number of the readers of this book probably "lived through the Great Depression." The stereotype of such people is that they are careful with money and perhaps fearful or insecure about their ability to maintain a comfortable income. They may want their children to learn skills that will ensure them a livelihood even during hard times. Parents of the depression era may think of themselves as having gone through "the college of hard knocks," and they may be contemptuous of young people whom they perceive as too soft or naive or self-indulgent.

Like all stereotypes, these ideas about people who entered adulthood during the depression are not necessarily true and certainly do not apply to each individual. The point is that you may find that older people look at the world in markedly different ways than you do, not because they are old but because they have lived through different historical events. The objective changes that individuals have experienced give them subjective world views that they carry with them forward in time. These world views shape their interpretations of subsequent objective events and shape their own actions. These past historical events—unique configurations of human relationships— become a kind of baggage that individuals carry with them (in their heads) into later historical situations. The events of any given historical period directly and "objectively" shape subsequent events (as we shall point out in more detail later); they also indirectly and more "subjectively" shape the future by their impact on an individual's consciousness. We will begin our analysis of change with an examination of such changes in individuals, since everyone has experienced this sort of change and can observe it rather easily.

The Impact of Historical Events

We have already discussed how historical periods define *generations,* that is, cohorts of people of roughly similar age who were particularly affected by contemporary events. In many ways this is a gross oversimplification because at any given time in a society there are always a number of people of widely varying ages. People of different ages, carrying with them different kinds and amounts of "historical baggage," may be very differently involved in and affected by the events of a particular period. For instance, when we say "the silent generation" of the fifties, we are not referring to older people who came of age in the 1930s, nor do we mean young children or teen-agers (many of whom were to be the nonquiet activists of the following decade); we are talking about younger adults between the ages of eighteen and forty. The notion of generation seems most applicable to those people who at a certain historical moment were passing out of adolescence and into adulthood and were making decisions (or letting others make decisions for them) concerning education, occupation, and family life style. Yet even this notion of generation may be challenged now, at a time when many people in early middle age or even older are reassessing their earlier decisions and changing their occupations, their places of residence, and their spouses. Perhaps *generation* itself may be a historically relative notion, meaningful in some periods and societies but not in all of them. Therefore, we have to examine what *life cycle, generation,* and *history* mean to different societies and at different time periods.

Looking Back Through Time.   Begin by drawing for yourself a timeline. The total length represents the three million years or so in which recognizably human creatures have existed. Mark off everything but the line segment that represents the last one hundred thousand years, and consider the first section. Some very important changes occurred during those first long years: humankind evolved biologically; fire was discovered and pebble tools developed; language began.

Although these biological and social events were crucial, historical change must have been virtually imperceptible from the point of view of any one individual or even band of humans. Change—probably often very traumatic and unpleasant change—must have filled the lives of Lower Paleolithic people, yet they would not have seen any direction to these changes. They probably would not have been able to say, "Our parents did it thus; now we do it differently—our way of life is different." The changes that occurred were generally random and to a large degree noncumulative. The different bands that experienced such changes were small and few and not closely connected to each other, so change spread very slowly. There were few ways of preserving knowledge of change for future generations, consequently many innovations may have been lost, being neither diffused to other bands nor very effectively passed on to later generations. Probably most changes that individuals experienced were unpleasant random accidents—injuries, brawls, death of children or relatives or friends, famines, and harsh weather.

Between 100,000 B.C. and 6,000 B.C., dramatic inventions altered this very slow process of change. One was big-game hunting, which we can date back to about 100,000 B.C. in many parts of the world. Organized hunts gave human beings better control over their food supply than they had before. This period was also marked by improvements in tools. Within the next fifty thousand years, human beings changed genetically too, to become modern *Homo sapiens.* Around 10,000 B.C. in the Near East, Southeast Asia, Meso-America, population has increased enormously. With the close proximity of groups, change is rapidly—often violently—diffused. Methods for producing goods begin to change rapidly. A large number of methods of preserving an innovation for future generations has appeared, for example, writing and, more recently, photography and electronic media. New techniques for building change into institutions have developed; social arrangements like states and armies and churches preserve changes in human relationships.

The Onset of Historical Change.   Now set your pencil on the mark at the extreme right of your timeline that indicates roughly 6,000 B.C. From this point on, change becomes rapid and markedly cumulative. The size of the human population has increased enormously. With the close proximity of groups, change is rapidly—often violently—diffused. Methods for producing goods begin to change rapidly. A large number of methods of preserving an innovation for future generations has appeared, for example, writing and, more recently, photography and electronic media. New techniques for building change into institutions have developed; social arrangements like states and armies and churches preserve changes in human relationships.

This period also marks the beginning of what we speak of as historical change. The Egyptians, Chinese, Greeks, and Romans were clearly aware of historical change. In our own day, in the industrial age, the pace of historical change is even faster than before. This book is an effort to understand the patterns and causes of historical change.

A Worker Reads History

Who built the seven gates of Thebes?
The books are filled with names of kings.
Was it kings who hauled the craggy blocks of stone?
And Babylon, so many times destroyed,
Who built the city up each time? In which of Lima's houses,
That city glittering with gold, lived those who built it?
In the evening when the Chinese wall was finished
Where did the masons go? Imperial Rome
Is full of arcs of triumph. Who reared them up? Over whom
Did the Caesars triumph? Byzantium lives in song,
Were all her dwellings palaces? And even in Atlantis of the legend
The night the sea rushed in,
The drowning men still bellowed for their slaves.

Young Alexander conquered India.
He alone?
Caesar beat the Gauls.
Was there not even a cook in his army?
Philip of Spain wept as his fleet
Was sunk and destroyed. Were there no other tears?
Frederick the Great triumphed in the Seven Years War. Who
Triumphed with him?

Each page a victory,
At whose expense the victory ball?
Every ten years a great man,
Who paid the piper?

So many particulars.
So many questions.

                                                    Bertolt Brecht

Chapter 2

Individuals and Structural Transformations

We shall look in more detail at the way in which individuals are caught up in trends or processes over which they appear to have little or no control. The examination of this material will include a definition and discussion of the concept of *structural transformation,* which is one of the most useful ways of thinking about these large-scale transformations; a consideration of the *objective* impact of these transformations on people's lives, that is, the way in which people's actual circumstances of life were changed; the *subjective* interpretations that individuals and groups gave to these experiences in order to make sense out of them; and the kinds of *action* they took in response to them. We will look at each of these points using illustrations from three historical examples: the conquest of Mexico by the Spaniards, the African slave trade, and the Industrial Revolution.

THE WRITER OF THE FOLLOWING PASSAGE was C. Wright Mills, a sociologist who wrote much of his work during the 1950s, a period when altogether too many people in American society were blind to the issues that caused their personal troubles.

Perhaps the most fruitful distinction with which the sociological imagination works is between 'the personal troubles of milieu' and 'the public issues of social structure.' This distinction is an essential tool of the sociological imagination and a feature of all classic work in social science.

Troubles occur within the character of the individual and within the range of his immediate relations with others; they have to do with his self and with those limited areas of social life of which he is directly and personally aware. Accordingly, the statement and the resolution of troubles properly lie within the individual as a biographical entity and within the scope of his immediate milieu —the social setting that is directly open to his personal experience and to some extent his willful activity. A trouble is a private matter: values cherished by an individual are felt by him to be threatened.

Issues have to do with matters that transcend these local environments of the individual and the range of his inner life. They have to do with the organization of many such milieux into the institutions of an historical society as a whole, with the ways in which various milieux overlap and interpenetrate to form the larger structure of social and historical life. An issue is a public matter: some value cherished by publics is felt to be threatened. Often there is a debate about what that value really is and about what it is that really threatens it. This debate is often without focus if only because it is the very nature of an issue, unlike even widespread trouble, that it cannot very well be defined in terms of the immediate and everyday environments of ordinary men. An issue, in fact, often involves a crisis in institutional arrangements, and often too it involves what Marxists call 'contradictions' or 'antagonisms.'

In these terms, consider unemployment. When, in a city of 100,000, only one man is unemployed, that is his personal trouble, and for its relief we properly look to the character of the man, his skills, and his immediate opportunities. But when in a nation of 50 million employees, 15 million men are unemployed, that is an issue, and we may not hope to find its solution within the range of opportunities open to any one individual. The very structure of opportunities has collapsed. Both the correct statement of the problem and the range of possible solutions require us to consider the economic and political institutions of the society, and not merely the personal situation and character of a scatter of individuals.

Consider war. The personal problem of war, when it occurs, may be how to survive it or how to die in it with honor; how to make money out of it; how to climb into the higher safety of the military apparatus; or how to contribute to the war's termination. In short, according to one's values, to find a set of milieux and within it to survive the war or make one's death in it meaningful. But the structural issues of war have to do with its causes; with what types of men it throws up into command; with its effects upon economic and political, family and religious institutions, with the unorganized irresponsibility of a world of nation-states.

Consider marriage. Inside a marriage a man and a woman may experience personal troubles, but when the divorce rate during the first four years of marriage is 250 out of every 1,000 attempts, this is an indication of a structural issue having to do with the institutions of marriage and the family and other institutions that bear upon them.

Or consider the metropolis—the horrible, beautiful, ugly, magnificent sprawl of the great city. For many upper-class people, the personal solution to 'the problem of the city' is to have an apartment with private garage under it in the heart of the city, and forty miles out, a house by Henry Hill, garden by Garrett Eckbo, on a hundred acres of private land. In these two controlled environments—with a small staff at each end and a private helicopter connection —most people could solve many of the problems of personal milieux caused by the facts of the city. But all this, however splendid, does not solve the public issues that the structural fact of the city poses. What should be done with this wonderful monstrosity? Break it all up into scattered units, combining residence and work? Refurbish it as it stands? Or, after evacuation, dynamite it and build new cities according to new plans in new places? What should those plans be? And who is to decide and to accomplish whatever choice is made? These are structural issues; to confront them and to solve them requires us to consider political and economic issues that affect innumerable milieux.

In so far as an economy is so arranged that slumps occur, the problem of unemployment becomes incapable of personal solution. In so far as war is inherent in the nation-state system and in the uneven industrialization of the world, the ordinary individual in his restricted milieu will be powerless—with or without psychiatric aid—to solve the troubles this system or lack of system imposes upon him. In so far as the family as an institution turns women into darling little slaves and men into their chief providers and unweaned dependents, the problem of a satisfactory marriage remains incapable of purely private solution. In so far as the overdeveloped megalopolis and the overdeveloped automobile are built-in features of the overdeveloped society, the issues of urban living will not be solved by personal ingenuity and private wealth.

What we experience in various and specific milieux, I have noted, is often caused by structural changes. Accordingly, to understand the changes of many personal milieux we are required to look beyond them. And the number and variety of such structural changes increase as the institutions within which we live become more embracing and more intricately connected with one another. To be aware of the idea of social structure and to use it with sensibility is to be capable of trading such linkages among a great variety of milieux. To be able to do that is to possess the sociological imagination.

(Mills, 1959:8–11)

Institutional Arrangements

The *issues* the Mills refers to are themselves only manifestations of deeper lying "institutional arrangements" (as Mills calls them) and structural changes. By structure we mean the patterned relationships that people have with each other. In the next few pages we shall be especially (but not exclusively) interested in those relationships between people and groups of people that reflect differences in power and wealth. "Institutional arrangements" implies some continuity, stability, and degree of consensus about a whole set of relationships. When we talk about an institution, we mean a set of reoccurring relationships between *groups* of people, many of them bound together in *organizations.* These institutional arrangements or relationships often operate on the basis of *power* differences (including power based on force) and often on the basis of wealth differences, and they are frequently supported by *agreement* in values and beliefs.

Remember the story of Jack and the Beanstalk: once Jack reaches the giant's house at the top, he can act outside of institutional arrangements—he seduces the giant's wife, eats the giant's food, steals the giant's gold and finally kills the giant. Could Jack behave in the same way at the king's court? Certainly not. Even if he were physically stronger than the king as an individual, Jack could only act within the limits of the institutional arrangements implied by the word *king* or *court.* (By the way, this example should not be taken to mean that all noninstitutional behavior is as rapacious as Jack's behavior toward the giant.)

In our society (and many others), we can refer to institutions such as law, the family, religion, the state, and so on. For instance, in the institution of law there are highly patterned—rigidly outlined—relationships between judges, lawyers, defendants (and plaintiffs, in civil suits), juries, the police, and prison officials. If you have ever watched courtroom proceedings, you know that there are limits on what can be introduced as evidence, on what kinds of statements can be made, on the forms of address used, and on general behavior. There may be a lot of agreement on the procedures. But even if there's no agreement —for instance, the defendant may be unfamiliar with the situation and very upset and angry—there exist specialists in the use of force (marshalls, policemen, etc.) to enforce and maintain the existing pattern of relationships.

The law represents an institutional arrangement that is extremely rigid in terms of both patterning of behavior and reliance on force. The institution of law has a national structure in that different systems of courts are related to each other through appeal procedures, constitutional law, and so on so that everyone is affected by the law. Your relations with your boss are probably more relaxed and less overtly coercive. The family represents a particularly flexible institutional arrangement with relatively little contact between families, a wide range of expected and acceptable behavior, and a "long distance" between family behavior and the introduction of organized coercion. In other words, most people disapprove of a family that has to call in the police to settle disputes.

When we look at the sum total of these arrangements in a society, we obtain a picture of the social structure as a whole. We would see that some people or groups of people tend to have important, powerful positions in several different institutions. We would see that power in one set of institutions often confers power in another set of institutions for individuals or groups. Power is vested in organizations and institutions and at least to some degree coincides with control over resources.

Structural Transformation

Institutional arrangements and social structure may remain virtually unchanged for fairly long periods of time. Individuals may lose their positions in the structure; however, this is generally not structural change unless it happens to a great many people at once. Some organizations or institutions may decline or disappear. Such changes may have many of the characteristics of structural transformations. It is sometimes hard to tell when these kinds of changes "add up" to a real structural transformation.

Distinguishing quantitative change from qualitative (fundamental) change is partly a problem of defining terms. For example, many of the institutions of modern American corporate capitalism are no different than the institutions of nineteenth-century capitalism: private ownership of productive enterprises, a labor market, and so on. But other practices seem very different: the rise of multinational corporations, the network of relationships between the private sector and the state, and so on. Is capitalism the "same" or has it undergone structural transformations? *Sometimes the nature of key resources shifts and with it virtually the entire set of institutional arrangements. Then we can safely say that a structural transformation has taken place.*

For example, we might not be sure whether nineteenth-century capitalism and modern corporate capitalism are the same system. But we can definitely see that a structural transformation lies between European feudalism with *its* agrarian productive system and class structure and modern capitalism with *its* industrial productive system and class structure. Neither the method of production, nor what is produced, nor who controls that process (class structure), nor institutional arrangements, nor culture (values and beliefs) are the same. The transition from feudalism to capitalism is definitely a structural transformation.

Understanding Structural Transformation

Sometimes these structural transformations are in large part slow and gradual. At other times, new decision-makers, new powerful organizations, and new classes appear very rapidly. When transformation occurs more rapidly, it is easier to understand what individuals experience. So we will look at two of these fast structural transformations as well as a more gradual one.

The basic point was made by Mills: Events and troubles that seem meaningless, random, and inexplicable to an individual can be understood in terms of larger structures and long-term historical processes. This is, of course, scant consolation for the victims of some of these changes. But such a view does have two advantages for the victims.

Demystification.   First, understanding structural transformation demystifies the process of change. Individuals trapped by entirely local and personal understandings of change may fall into a variety of erroneous and mystified explanations of their troubles. They may believe that their fate was "in the stars," or that their misfortunes are divine punishment for individual or collective transgressions, or are the work of the devil. History is filled with examples of groups of people who believed such explanations for what were in fact troubles that grew out of large-scale economic, political, and social change.

Another kind of erroneous explanation is to believe that it is one's own inadequacy or incompetence that has brought about one's plight. In a limited sense this may be true. During a period of high unemployment, an illiterate person who has performed only unskilled rural labor is likely to be among the first to become jobless. This is not his "fault"; however, the impact of transformations hits groups and individuals at different rates, and some people will have characteristics that make them more likely to be affected. It cannot be denied that some people have the knack of "landing on their feet," while others are more likely to be physical and/or emotional victims of the change. The point is *not* that there is no individual variation in the impact of change but rather that individual variation does not *cause* the wave of change.

Another mystified explanation of "trouble" that many people develop is that some group has caused the troubles. Such a group then becomes the scapegoat for the mystified majority. For instance, Jews have been blamed in this fashion repeatedly in European history, sometimes for causing plagues by poisoning wells, sometimes for being usurers or money lenders when in fact they were forced to act as middlemen for Gentile land-owning classes, sometimes for causing inflation or depression. In Southeast Asia, the overseas Chinese have similarly had to take the brunt of scapegoating, being blamed for troubles that were inherent in the economy of underdeveloped former colonial countries. Scapegoating is often linked with conspiracy theories in which large-scale transformations are believed to have been planned and engineered by small cliques of people. An understanding of large-scale historical processes wipes out these misconceptions that otherwise produce fatalism and/or "easy" solutions, which are necessarily futile.

A Guide to Action.   Second, correct understanding of structural change can also suggest a guide to action. In the face of structural transformation, certain kinds of action are likely either to fail or to provide only short-term amelioration. Scapegoating, for example, is unlikely to produce results of lasting benefit to any group. Other "solutions" may work, but only for small numbers of very dedicated people. For instance, communities of the descendants of seventeenth-century Protestant sectarians such as the Amish and the Hutterites have substantially succeeded in staving off the modern world, but only by intense self-discipline, unity, and individual commitment. This option is unlikely to help most people to live better lives.

A clear understanding of the many *overlapping* and *interrelated* structural transformations now under way should provide a guide not only to different kinds of action but also to their timing. To understand the timing of both the transformations and possible courses of action necessitates a historical perspective. History is not the learning of a dry series of dates and battles but an understanding of the *sequencing* of events within a larger pattern.

Examples of Structural Transformations and Their Impact on Individuals

The essence of my argument (and of C. Wright Mills') in the preceding pages is that people are caught up in historical changes that affect—often destroy— their lives. They sometimes do not understand these changes very well. They respond to the changes with a variety of strategies. Our examples are selected from a very wide array of possible cases of historical change more or less according to the following criteria:

1. The changes that are illustrated should be *relevant*. That is, they should be changes that have had some bearing on the present life situation of readers of this book. In a very abstract sense, all changes in human history are linked, but in most cases the line of cause and effect is too tenuous or too long to be useful in explaining our present situation. In other words, while the Indo-European invasion of India in 1500 B.C. is interesting in its own right, it is not very immediately useful to an understanding of the world in the present. Thus the structural transformations I have selected are those that help explain the historical roots of present-day ethnic conflict, as well as other phenomena in our society. They are part of the history of areas that have made major contributions to present conditions.

2. The examples of structural transformations I've selected illustrate how transformations in one area are related to even larger transformations, changes that have shaped the modern "world system" as a whole. Superficially, the changes I will be discussing seem to affect different ethnic groups in different geographical areas at scattered times. In fact, they are linked as part of the events that changed the world through Western expansion and the development of capitalism. Once human beings lived in a number of largely autonomous principalities and tribes—now the world is a single "system," an entity of interrelated nations and peoples within a single economy.

3. These cases have been selected to illustrate changes that lasted beyond one generation, so that the effects of the change became entrenched in the socialization of children. Language, an oral tradition, a way of explaining the world, customs, child-rearing habits—all the facets of what we call culture—had to be forged anew and transmitted to a second generation. Here we focus on changes that were carried over to a second generation.

4. The cases illustrate a variety of responses to change. The same structural transformation may be subjectively experienced differently and responded to differently. Thus, while people were involuntarily caught up in these changes, they had a range of choices for how to react. Many were not simply passive victims. Even passive victimization represents a particular *choice*. In the transformations I will describe, many people died; some responded in self-destructive ways; some practiced sabotage, including self-mutilation; some resisted violently in groups; some tried to escape; some accommodated to the change and accepted the new system of behavior and values imposed on them; some accommodated only in outward behavior and practiced an "inner" resistance or an "inner" emigration; some tried to build new institutions; and so on. Many of these responses were not individual responses but group responses. Even when people did not act in groups, their behavior was conditioned by the behavior of other people undergoing the same changes. In some sense, the title of our chapter—"Individuals and Structural

Transformations"—is nonsense; it is always individuals in *a social setting* that experience change. Even individuals who are physically isolated carry with them the frameworks for organizing behavior that they have at some time learned from others. The isolated, self-willing individual is a fantasy, particularly in the situation of structural transformations that *by definition* involve new patterns of *social relationships.*

5. The cases of change that I have selected all involve changes in structure. Clearly there generally exists gradual cultural change as well—change in feelings and beliefs. But I am not concerned here with those changes that are primarily cultural in the sense that their roots in structural change are indistinct or hard to trace. In this chapter I will be looking primarily at cases of *structural change* where there are clear-cut changes in the patterning of relationships between people and groups of people in a society as a whole.

Spanish Colonialism in Mexico

Let us begin with our chronologically oldest case, that of the Spanish conquest of Mexico. We are going to present this very sudden and fundamental change not as a series of battles or new laws, but as a number of social changes that enmeshed groups of people who responded to them in different ways.

Let us begin by placing the Spanish conquest of Mexico in its historical setting. It began in 1519 as part of the expansionist activities of Portugal and Spain, in many ways the earliest and least modern of the waves of western European expansion. Europe itself was in a period of turmoil. The Spanish conquest of Mexico is roughly contemporaneous with the beginnings of the Protestant Reformation. Both events (along with the introduction of firearms and the invention of movable type, which took place slightly earlier) mark the end of Catholic feudalism and the onset of a period of transition. In Italy this transition is manifested in the new cultural forms that we call the Renaissance —the reawakening of a secularizing humanistic spirit supposedly dormant since Greco-Roman antiquity.

The Renaissance and Martin Luther's theses were probably not in the minds of the adventurous men who seized first a number of Caribbean islands and then the Mexican mainland for the Spanish crown. The islands, discovered by Columbus in 1492, had produced little gold and very little usable labor. The Indians living on them had died within a few years of disease and brutal treatment. The conquistadores began to explore the mainland.

At first the Indians made various efforts to take these new men into their own cultural and structural framework. One of their first responses to meeting light-skinned, heavily bearded, unwashed human beings was to incorporate them into their theology, to explain them as the deity Quetzalcóatl and his followers returning from across the sea. But the religious impulse was soon harnessed to strategic ends in the constant warfare of the central Mexican city states. The Totonacs, and later the lords of Tlaxcala, became the Spaniards' allies against the more powerful kingdom of Tenochtitlán, the center of the Aztecs' hegemony. The Aztecs defended themselves well but were ultimately defeated by the Spaniards with their horses and firearms. Resistance against the Spaniards continued in the outlying areas for a very long time—until 1697 in some parts of Yucatan, and as late as the early twentieth century in the Yaqui regions of the northwest. But in the central regions, resistance was crushed within a few years.

Death of the People.   The most immediate and overwhelming consequence of the Indian defeat was death. The most likely impact of the conquest for the individual Indian was death, generally from Old World diseases and mistreatment. The smallpox epidemics of 1520, 1531, and 1545, the typhoid fever epidemics of 1545 and 1576, the measles epidemic of 1595, and the malaria and yellow fever imported from Africa—all these, combined with ill-treatment and starvation, led to an 80 percent decline of the Indian population of Middle America between 1519 and 1650 (Wolf, 1971: 231). In other words, all other changes that took place have to be understood within the framework of the single shattering change of mass death.

It may be difficult for many readers of this book to contemplate what this kind of experience means for the survivors. Perhaps you or someone you know has lived through combat duty in Vietnam or the turmoil in Europe during World War II. Such experiences may give you some insight into the physical and emotional destruction of large numbers of people in a very short time period. The modal experience, then, was death and, for a minority, survivorhood. Recent studies of survivors of the atomic bombing of Hiroshima and of the Nazi concentration camps suggest that survival in a situation of mass death brings with it the following: death imprint, in this case a jarring awareness of the fact of death and an overwhelming grief and inability to accomplish the "work of mourning"; death guilt; psychic numbing, which perhaps contributes to the deadening of affect or the fatalism that the conquerors erroneously believe are cultural traits of the conquered; a paranoid sense of being contagious, in the case of epidemics not altogether unfounded; and in the more fortunate cases some efforts—sometimes erroneous—to make sense out of the deaths (Lifton, 1968: 480, 481, 484).

Defeat of the State.   The second major effect of the Spanish conquest was the military defeat and the destruction of state-level Indian institutions. Like all human beings, the Indians of central Mexico lived in communities and within kinship and family groupings. But in addition to these levels of organization, they were organized into states. That is to say, the communities and kin groupings were part of a larger entity, an entity based not only on common customs and a sense of belonging but also on the existence of force and authority.

There were in fact a number of states in central Mexico, although the Aztec state centered on Tenochtitlán was becoming the most powerful at the time of the conquest. These states had ruling elites of nobles and chiefs. The ideology of the states—the belief system that helped to hold them together—was a religious one. Translated into action, the ideology sanctioned endless interstate warfare and the imposition of tribute in human lives (as well as goods) in order that the seasonal sacrifices to the gods could take place. As many as twenty thousand people were sacrificed in one ceremony. Although sacrifices on this scale were somewhat extraordinary, some authors suggest that human sacrifice was becoming a device to control population in the increasingly densely populated central valley. The state also directed a variety of public works, including the water-control structures around the lake of Tenochtitlán and the magnificent Aztec palaces and temples that dazzled the Spaniards.

The Aztec ruling class had at its disposal the three key components of state organization: as its *managerial* arm, a stratum of councils, lesser chiefs, and local notables of its tributary city-states; as its *coercive* arm, an elite army of jaguar and eagle knights, and a court system; and as its *ideological* arm, a unifying demanding religion and priesthood. The Aztecs did not generally conceptualize their society in these terms. Our secular analysis of the state with its rulers, managers, soldiers and judges, and priests was for them wrapped in religious imagery. At any rate, this set of institutional arrangements that we can call the Aztec state (and that appeared among other tribal groups as well) was destroyed by the Spaniards. *A "conquest" is first and foremost a destruction of a state apparatus.*

Although subject to the terrible and largely unintended death toll discussed above, the individuals, their communities, and their kinship groups remained (although in altered form, as we shall see). But the councils, the court system, the elite eagle and jaguar corps, the state priesthood, and the king—all these disappeared as social institutions within a few months of the Spaniards' arrival. What happened to them? They underwent four interrelated changes.

First, the persons who had filled the organizational positions—the soldiers, the priests, the local chiefs—were often killed or died in the new epidemics. Some died in warfare, and some were tortured and killed somewhat later in acts of resistance against Spanish rule. Thus died Cuauhtémoc, slowly burned to death by the Spaniards, and Carlos Moctezuma of Texcoco, executed by the Inquisition.

Second, the ruling classes and state functionaries that survived were integrated into Spanish rule in different ways. The ruling classes in the towns learned to speak Spanish, adopted Spanish dress and manners, intermarried with the conquerors, came to hold land worked by Indian peasants and black slaves, and became entrepreneurs. Spanish laws granted them social equality with Spanish nobles and economic parity with Spanish landholders (Wolf,

1971:244). So they were integrated into the new Hispanic ruling class, where a combination of luck and personal flexibility in religious and other cultural matters enabled them to take advantage of the Spaniards' efforts to build new institutions. Other Indian nobles, chiefly those in the countryside, simply were dispossessed and pushed down into the common mass of Indians. In some sense the stakes were higher and the risks greater for the Indian elite in the geographical and political centers: on the one hand, they were more likely to die in the turmoil of the destruction of the state than were the small-town provincial chiefs; but, on the other hand, they had a better chance of acquiring a ruling position in the new colonial system.

A third change that took place was the substitution at the state level of Spanish institutions for Indian ones. The religious orders (and the Inquisition) took over from the Indian priesthood. The Spanish court system (including its religious tribunals and its system of private justice on estates) replaced the Indian courts. Spanish soldiers kept order where once Aztec knights had ensured tribute. And above all, the Spanish conquerors (and the integrated Indian strata) maintained control of a society in the name of the Spanish crown. (The uneasy relationship between the crown and its functionaries on the one hand and the new de facto rulers and landholders in Mexico on the other hand constitutes an important chapter in colonial history that is not immediately relevant here.)

Fourth, some of the Indian state-level institutions simply disappeared without replacement. In many ways, Spanish rule over New Spain was even more localistic and provincial than Aztec hegemony had been. Three factors contributed to this increasing provincialism: the disappearance of the system of tribute in human lives to a central place of sacrifice; the terrible drop in population and the ecological destruction due to sheep-raising and altered irrigation systems; and the general financial crisis and depression in Europe. Each of these factors led to a period of "ruralism" in New Spain in which central institutions were rather weak, and the estates and their subordinate satellite Indian communities, rather than the central cities, became the focus of life.

In summary, at the level of state institutions, Spanish conquest brought four changes: widespread death of the ruling classes and their functionaries; integration of the surviving ruling classes and their functionaries into the colonial class structure; replacement of Indian by Hispanic institutions; and weakening and disappearance of parts of the state apparatus.

This discussion should also have sensitized us to the fact that one cannot write about the impact of conquest on undifferentiated individuals. *Where these individuals stood in the class and state structure of the old system was of crucial importance to how they fared in the conquest.* Those near the top experienced the most sudden and large-scale changes. If they survived, their way of life was much more altered than was that of the local subchief or the commoner in a remote rural area.

Disintegration of the Economy.   We can now turn to changes in economic institutions. The smashing of the Indian state was a necessary condition for these kinds of changes. I do not want to discuss in great detail specific economic changes but would rather indicate a general framework for discussing them, illustrating each part of the framework briefly.

First, there were changes in the basic productive activities (Wolf, 1971: 232–233). The Spaniards altered the agricultural system in at least three ways: they seized the irrigation system and expanded and altered it in such a way as to divert water away from the Indian communities and to their own lands; they introduced plow agriculture, which used the land much more extensively; and they introduced not only oxen to draw the plows but also sheep and cattle for commercial livestock-raising, with attendant entrepreneurial benefits but ecological and human disasters. These changes were in many ways parallel to changes in agriculture that were occurring throughout western Europe: the intensive, technologically simple, and more or less subsistence agriculture that used ample seasonal rotation and common lands was being replaced by land-extensive, technologically more advanced, commercial agriculture and livestock-raising that gobbled up common lands. The Spaniards also focused economic activity on gold and silver mining.

With these productive activities came new ways of organizing the Indian population as a labor force. The first impulse seems to have been to build a kind of command economy based initially on slavery and later on forced labor under terms of a royal trusteeship granted to local Spanish officials. Vast and frantic productive activities in mining and agriculture were planned in order to produce untold riches for the crown. Thus, the first experiments in establishing class relationships after the destruction of the Indian state involved the transformation of the Indians into an unfree labor force of slaves and forced laborers producing for an absolutist state.

For a number of reasons, this command economy broke down. The decline of Indian population was too precipitous. Within several decades it became apparent that neither the agricultural system nor the mines were as productive as the Spaniards had hoped they would be. The crown found it too difficult to force trusteeship on conquistadores who desired outright land ownership. Nor could the king enforce the terms of the trusteeship—that the conquistador should provide for and protect the Indians under his control in return for labor and tribute, which was sent back to the Spanish state—since the crown lacked modern means of surveillance, communications, transportation, and enforcement. Finally, the depression and inflation that hit Spain by the end of the sixteenth century prevented it from absorbing the goods that were still being produced efficiently in New Spain.

Under these conditions, the colonial command economy was gradually transformed into a more ruralistic, less state-organized halfway house between feudalism and modern capitalist commercial farming. One of the two central institutions of this new organization of class relations was the *hacienda,* the large privately owned estate with a core labor force of Indian peons. One writer has described it as follows:

> Organized for commercial ends, the hacienda proved strangely hybrid in its characteristics. It combined in practice features which seem oddly contradictory in theory. Geared to sell products in a market, it yet aimed at having little to sell. Voracious for land, it deliberately made inefficient use of it. Operating with large numbers of workers, it nevertheless personalized the relation between worker and owner. Created to produce a profit, it consumed a large part of its substance in conspicuous and unproductive displays of wealth. Some writers have called the institution "feudal," because it involved the rule of a dominant landowner over his dependent laborers. But it lacked the legal guaranties of security which compensated the feudal serf for his lack of liberty and self-determination. Others have called it "capitalist," and so it was, but strangely different from the commercial establishments in agriculture with which we are familiar in the modern commercial and industrial world. Half "feudal," half "capitalist," caught between past and future, it exhibited characteristics of both ways of life, as well as their inherent contradiction (Wolf, 1971: 237–238).

The other key institution was the Indian peasant community, with a limited supply of land. Within the community people lived in egalitarian poverty based on subsistence farming and some seasonal work for the hacienda. In the course of one person's lifetime—from 1519 to the latter part of the sixteenth century—an individual might have gone from childhood in an obscure Indian village, through slavery or forced labor as a royal ward, to old age and death in an Indian community that was probably more isolated, more provincial, and more out of touch with a cultural center than was the village of the person's birth.

Destruction of the Culture.   Finally, we can look at what these changes meant in terms of the culture. The Spaniards were quick to wipe out the Aztec religion. Its priesthood, its temples, its cult of human sacrifices, its overwhelming purpose—to maintain the daily, the seasonal, the fifty-two-year cosmic cycles—were all destroyed and replaced by Christianity. The sacrifices of the Eucharist and the martyred saints replaced human sacrifices. Spanish priests replaced the black-robed, matted-haired Aztec priests. Beautiful baroque churches stood where there had once been imposing temples.

The commoners' response was twofold. On the one hand, they dealt with this transition through *syncretism,* a convenient blending of some of the forms and motifs of Aztec theology with Spanish forms. The concept of sin appears to have existed in both cultures. Aztec personal penance and sacrifices of self-mutilation could be carried on in Counter-Reformation Catholic practices of abstinence and abnegation. Flowers, incense, elaborate buildings of worship that towered over a town and its market, and an imagery of skulls, death, and bleeding wounds were common to both. Yet amid this syncretism, which still exists in present-day Mexican popular religion, the Indians must have been troubled by doubts. Once thousands of victims were necessary to ensure the continued rising of the sun, the turn of the seasons, and the safe passage of the world through the fifty-two-year cycle—now all these events seemed to continue smoothly in a new society that failed to conduct the ceremonies and sacrifices.

Responses: Conclusions.   At this point we have picked apart the various levels of colonial impact. To understand what they meant for groups of individuals, say, in the period from 1520 to midcentury, we have to recombine them into a total picture: death and disease, the collapse of state-level institutions, forced labor in an economy geared to production of a surplus for a colonial elite and a royal court, and destruction of the unifying religious ideology.

Under these conditions the Indians reacted in a variety of ways. Most probably strove for survival of themselves and their immediate family. This necessarily meant at least an acceptance in their overt behavior of what the Spaniards demanded, once the Aztec state apparatus was defeated. It meant a hard daily round of toil and scarce food; it meant baptism and a new, still somewhat pointless cycle of Christian rites and festivals to replace the Aztec ones. For many people this harsh and largely meaningless life brought with it abandonment of the strong Aztec norms against drunkenness. By the hacienda period, a ration of pulque was part of the standard remuneration of the peon, and substantial acreage was devoted to the mescal cactus from which it is made. A small number of people took the route of resistance, a suicidal course in the central valley although not at the geographic margins. Another small number successfully integrated into the new colonial ruling class.

These have all been standard adaptations to a colonial situation, clearly visible in the Hellenistic and Roman empires. Some of the colonized people —usually of the indigenous upper classes—are either absorbed into the new ruling classes (as in the case of New Spain) or are used by the conqueror as a puppet elite. They successfully accept the new cultural forms. A second group resists change and under the proper geographic conditions (distance from the colonial administrative center, suitable terrain, etc.) can, with careful timing, hold out against military and economic conquest. Most of the population accepts the new economic structures. Culturally they develop some kind of a syncretic accommodation of religion, customs, and language. Enroute to such a syncretic accommodation, they may develop messianic movements (also of a syncretic nature and involving cultural rather than structural—military and economic—resistance). Many find the cultural imposition and the harder pace of economic activity difficult to cope with except through psychic numbing, often induced with alcohol or other depressant drugs.

To some degree many of the mass of people had not participated very fully in preconquest state-level institutions. In some cases, these state-level institutions were as foreign to them as were those of the conquerors. One set of overlords replaced another: such was the case for the Aztec and Inca tributary communities. In many cases, integration into preconquest state-level institutions was so weak that life went on much as usual for the peasantry after the conquest, with only a different content to the festivals that punctuated the yearly cycle. This was really not the case in the central valley, however, where the imposition of forced labor and the great death toll did transform daily life. Generally, after a colonial conquest the daily and seasonal round does change because the new, larger, more technologically advanced empire requires a greater level of surplus production, which is skimmed off to feed the new ruling classes, the new state functionaries, and the population of the colonial power.

We have already discussed how different strata of the Indian population underwent different changes depending partly on chance, partly on individual characteristics, and largely on its social and geographic location in the preconquest structure.

The African Slave Trade

The second structural transformation that I would like to discuss is the African slave trade and the experience of the enslaved people. In time, the slave trade overlaps the Spanish conquest of Mexico. It has similar roots in the expansion of western Europe. It had some historical origins in the conquest of Mexico because the colonial ecclesiastical authorities, especially the friar Las Casas, so deplored the terrible death toll among the Indians that they lobbied for the importation of a hardier work force—African slaves.

Despite the shared underlying causes and historical linkages the two structural changes are quite different. African slavery meant the uprooting and the transportation of millions of human beings. No feature of the physical or human environment survived the transition into slavery for the individual African. The Aztec laborer at least could still recognize his family (albeit decimated by disease), his land (albeit ravaged by livestock-raising, plow agriculture, and the diversion of the water supply), and his ancestral sacred places (although the temples were torn down and replaced by churches). The Africans were sundered from everything familiar and subjected to the most brutal treatment.

The African slave trade to the New World began in 1517 with the authorization by Charles V of Spain of the export of fifteen thousand slaves to the island of Santo Domingo, and it continued into the nineteenth century. During that period somewhere between 30 and 100 million human beings were seized. Of these, more than two-thirds died before they reached the New World plantations (Davidson, 1959:191). Most died aboard the slave ships during the Middle Passage of the triangular slave trade.[1]

The slaves were collected in the interior, fastened one to the other in columns, loaded with heavy stones of 40 or 50 pounds in weight to prevent attempts at escape, and then marched the long journey to the sea, sometimes hundreds of miles, the weakly and sick dropping to die in the African jungle. Some were brought to the coast by canoe, lying in the bottom of boats for days on end, their hands bound, their faces exposed to the tropical sun and the tropical rain, their backs in the water which was never bailed out. At the slave ports they were penned into "trunks" for the inspection of the buyers. Night and day thousands of human beings were packed in these "dens of putrefaction" so that no European could stay in them for longer than a quarter of an hour without fainting. The Africans fainted and recovered or fainted and died, the mortality in the "trunks" being over 20 percent. Outside in the harbour, waiting to empty the "trunks" as they filled, was the captain of the slave-ship, with so clear a conscience that one of them, in the intervals of waiting to enrich British capitalism with the profits of another valuable cargo, enriched British religion by composing the hymn "How Sweet the Name of Jesus Sounds"!

On the ships the slaves were packed in the hold on galleries one above the other. Each was given only four or five feet in length and two or three feet in height, so that they could neither lie at full length nor sit upright. Contrary to the lies that have been spread so pertinaciously about Negro docility, the revolts at the port of embarkation and on board were incessant, so that the slaves had to be chained, right hand to right leg, left hand to left leg, and attached in rows to long iron bars. In this position they lived for the voyage, coming up once a day for exercise and to allow the sailors to "clean the pails." But when the cargo was rebellious or the weather bad, then they stayed below for weeks at a time. The close proximity of so many naked human beings, their bruised and festering flesh, the foetid air, the prevailing dysentery, the accumulation of filth, turned these holds into a hell. During the storms the hatches were battened down, and in the close and loathsome darkness they were hurled from one side to another by the heaving vessel, held in position by the chains on their bleeding flesh. No place on earth, observed one writer of the time, concentrated so much misery as the hold of a slave-ship.

Twice a day, at nine and at four, they received their food. To the slave-traders they were articles of trade and no more. A captain held up by calms or adverse winds was known to have poisoned his cargo. Another killed some of his slaves to feed the others with the flesh. They died not only from the régime but from grief and rage and despair. They undertook vast hunger strikes; undid their chains and hurled themselves on the crew in futile attempts at insurrection. What could these inland tribesmen do on the open sea, in a complicated sailing

---

[1]On the first leg of the journey, ships carried liquor, firearms, and cotton goods from Europe to Africa, where the merchandise was traded for slaves. Loaded into ships on the west coast of Africa, the slaves were delivered in the West Indies or elsewhere in the Americas. The ships then took on cargoes of rum and raw cotton for processing in England and the continent.

vessel? To brighten their spirits it became the custom to have them up on the deck once a day and force them to dance. Some took the opportunity to jump overboard, uttering cries of triumph as they cleared the vessel and disappeared below the surface.

Fear of their cargo bred a savage cruelty in the crew. One captain, to strike terror into the rest, killed a slave and dividing heart, liver, and entrails into 300 pieces made each of the slaves eat one, threatening those who refused with the same torture. Such incidents were not rare. Given the circumstances such things were (and are) inevitable. Nor did the system spare the slavers. Every year one-fifth of all who took part in the African trade died.

All America and the West Indies took slaves. When the ship reached the harbour, the cargo came up on deck to be bought. The purchasers examined them for defects, looked at the teeth, pinched the skin, sometimes tasted the perspiration to see if the slave's blood was pure and his health as good as his appearance. Some of the women affected a curiosity, the indulgence of which, with a horse, would have caused them to be kicked 20 yards across the deck. But the slave had to stand it. Then in order to restore the dignity which might have been lost by too intimate an examination, the purchaser spat in the face of the slave. Having become the property of his owner, he was branded on both sides of the breast with a hot iron. His duties were explained to him by an interpreter, and a priest instructed him in the first principles of Christianity.

(James, 1963:7–9)

The consequence of the Middle Passage was as close to the creation of atomized individuals as is conceivable. Here all levels of human organization —family, community, and state—were stripped away. Class distinctions disappeared. Even ethnic and tribal lines blurred, often through the deliberate policy of the slavers, who believed that breaking up tribal groups would lessen the likelihood of revolt. Yet these extremely atomized slaves seemed to produce as much resistance as the more intact Indian communities. One might almost say that because of the extreme atomization revolt was more likely. Unless the Indians resisted as a tribe at the geographic margins, in which case resistance was fierce and well organized, they had to contend with their stake in their community. To fight against the Spaniards was to risk the lives of their family and neighbors. The Indians had something to lose. The patterns of intermarriage, the existence of an Indian and later a mestizo stratum in the ruling class, the imposition of Christianity—all these bridged the gap between ruler and ruled. The coercive patriarchism of the hacienda in the later period was a barrier to effective organization of resistance.

Resistance to Enslavement.   The first-generation African slave had no such commitments to a community, a family, or an emerging set of institutions. Having nothing to lose and nothing to protect, slaves resisted individually and in groups. Resistance in all forms was greatest among first-generation slaves. They had firsthand experience of freedom. They were subjected to the most

brutal treatment. They were least well integrated into the smoothly functioning structure of the slave plantation. In other words, the longer the stay in the
New World, the more likely it was that the slave had acquired a family he or
she needed to protect. The longer the stay, the more differentiation within the
mass of slaves, so that they were divided into different grades, with each grade
above the lowest being eager to protect its small advantages. The African-born
slaves were less well integrated structurally and culturally into plantation
society than were the American-born Creoles, and they were more likely to
resist.

Resistance took many forms. Some slaves committed suicide. We have
already read how some on the slave ships hurled themselves overboard. High
rates of suicide were accompanied by the related acts of self-mutilation, abortion, and infanticide, although these acts were all brutally punished. Murder
was also individualistic but not turned against the self. House slaves and
women, having the easiest access to the person of the master, often took the
lead in murder, using poison and ground glass.

Collective acts of resistance were also common and greatly feared by
slaveowners throughout the Americas. These collective acts included revolts,
in which the major purpose was the murder of the masters. More frequently
and rationally (in terms of the slave's own well-being and survival), the slaves
simply fled into the hinterland. This condition of living as a fugitive was called
marronnage. The circumstances of marronnage varied, depending on the terrain, the sparsity of settlement, the ratio of black to white population, and so
on. Where settlement was dense, a hostile white population numerous, and
supervision by white owners diligent, flight was often at best what the French
called *petit marronnage,* that is, truancy. Where there were isolated Indian
communities, slaves tried to flee to these villages and assimilate into the Indian
population. Truancy and flight to Indian villages were the courses of action
most frequently taken by slaves in the United States. Descendants of these
mixed Indian and African slave communities still exist throughout the South.
Often extremely poor, these people are inclined to identify themselves as
Indians.

Throughout the Caribbean and the Latin American mainland, conditions were generally more favorable toward Maroons (fugitive slaves). Here
they developed many large well-organized communities. In some areas, such
as the Guianas, the hinterland was remote enough and a sufficiently large
number of the fugitives shared a common African background that substantial
features of an African way of life could be recreated under relatively peaceful
conditions. For instance, the Djuka, Boni, and Saramaca "Bush Negroes" of
the Guianas were able to re-establish many of the cultural features of their
Ghanaian homeland although only at a tribal or community level, without
most of the West African state-level institutions. In other areas, such as Bahia
in northeastern Brazil, the British and French Caribbean, and Mexico, the
Maroon communities had to be more oriented toward constant warfare. They

also had internal problems because of the relative scarcity of women and the problems of incorporating and socializing new members. Thus many Maroon communities were more like armed camps than stable villages; most were engaged in prolonged wars against the white settlers. Even so, in Jamaica, for instance, Maroon communities continue to exist as distinct entities.

The collective resistance of blacks against the white plantation-owning ruling class was most fully realized in the Haitian revolution. The half million slaves of the island revolted in 1791 during the turmoil in the French colony that was set off by the French Revolution (James, 1963:ix).

One scholar has formulated a hypothesis for predicting the incidence of slave revolts: "Large-scale, monopolistic slave systems with a high rate of absenteeism (among the owners) will, geographical conditions permitting, exhibit a high tendency toward slave revolts" (Patterson, 1973:289). This hypothesis is a summary of the operation of a number of interrelated conditions:

1. Where the slave population greatly outnumbers that of the master class.
2. Where the ratio of local to foreign-born slaves is low.
3. Where the imported slaves, or a significant section of them, are of common ethnic origin.
4. Where geographical conditions favor guerrilla warfare.
5. Where there is a high incidence of absentee ownership.
6. Where the economy is dominated by large-scale monopolistic enterprise.
7. Where there is weak cultural cohesiveness, reinforced by a high (male:female) sex ratio among the ruling population (Patterson, 1973:288).

(Condition 7 implies that no effort had been made to integrate the slaves into European culture, that they were not treated paternalistically, and that they were seen exclusively as means toward the end of making money in a commercial venture.) These conditions prevailed more extensively in the Caribbean and Latin America than in the United States, where *social* and *economic* conditions were less favorable to sustained and large-scale revolts.

Resistance to Acculturation.   Even those slaves who did not engage in collective or individual acts of overt resistance resisted acculturation. Again, this cultural resistance was most visible in Latin America, where the late duration of the slave trade brought a constant influx of African-born persons, and where blacks generally constituted a larger percentage of the population.

In Haiti and much of Brazil, for example, African religions (with Christian overlays) are essentially the national religion, variously referred to as candomblé and macumba in Brazil and vodun in Haiti. These religions involve the worship of a complex pantheon. The gods are largely of Fon (Dahomean),

Yoruba (Nigerian) and, less prominently, Central African and Angolan origin. They are sometimes linked with Christian saints. For example, in Bahia in northeastern Brazil, worshippers identify St. George with Oshoshi, the god of the hunt; St. Jerome with Shango, the god of thunder; the Immaculate Conception with Yemanjá, the goddess of the sea; Sts. Cosmas and Damian with Ibeji, the divine twins; and so on.

In Haiti and Brazil, these religions are institutions with hierarchies of priests and priestesses, temples, drummers, novices, and a rich material culture of costumes, magical objects, paintings, and so on. The strength of African traditions and the relative isolation of Afro-American culture from European culture in these regions is apparent in the vitality of this religion. This cultural tradition exists in a much-attenuated form in other areas of the New World, often surviving more as folk beliefs extensively mingled with European superstitions than as a true religion. The practitioners are no longer a well-organized group of priests and priestesses but rather individual fee-for-service professionals in magic, spiritualism, healing, and advice-giving. Thus, we find the remains of African religion practiced as obeah in the English Caribbean and as voodoo in New Orleans and elsewhere in the United States, and blended into Catholic practices in the *santeria* cults of Puerto Rico and Cuba.

Where the slave system was so paternalistically meddlesome and integrative that African religions were crushed, only the music, folktales, some oral traditions of poetry and joking-and-insult formulas (the "dozens"), and the maintenance of an African-influenced dialect survived. In these circumstances, often the only resistance possible was to protect one's feelings and thoughts by day under a pretense of sullen stupidity so that they could be voiced and enjoyed at night in the privacy of the slave quarters. The slaveholder, and after him generations of white schoolteachers, bosses, and sociologists, were fooled by the silence, by the "verbal and cultural deprivation" of the Afro-American in the daytime white-man's world. As C. L. R. James (1963:17–18) remarks:

> Yet those who took the trouble to observe them away from their masters and in their intercourse with each other did not fail to see that remarkable liveliness of intellect and vivacity of spirit which so distinguish their descendants in the West Indies to-day. Father du Tertre, who knew them well, noted their secret pride and feeling of superiority to their masters, the difference between their behaviour before their masters and when they were by themselves. De Wimpffen, an exceptionally observant and able traveller, was also astonished at this dual personality of the slaves. "One has to hear with what warmth and what volubility, and at the same time with what precision of ideas and accuracy of judgment, this creature, heavy and taciturn all day, now squatting before his fire, tells stories, talks, gesticulates, argues, passes opinions, approves or condemns both his master and everyone who surrounds him." It was this intelligence which refused to be crushed, these latent possibilities, that

frightened the colonists, as it frightens the whites in Africa today. "No species of men has more intelligence," wrote Hilliard d'Auberteuil, a colonist, in 1784, and had his book banned.

Thus we see that the apparent individualistic atomism of the slaves was only superficial. On the one hand, socialization into African cultures had been strong enough that these traditions could survive even through slavery. And on the other hand, as soon as slavery was imposed, it created a common set of interests, solidarities, and conditions that forged the slaves into groups that could offer various forms of resistance. Where these two types of social integration coexisted—in other words, where people from the same tribe were enslaved together—revolts were particularly likely. But everywhere, slaves developed a society and a culture of their own, in part African and in part a culture of survival and resistance. The vitality and overt resistance of this culture varied from location to location, for the masters, no more than their slaves, were not isolated individuals. Slaves were confronted by different social structures in different locations. These structures varied in terms of the dimensions suggested by Patterson and set the conditions for revolt and other forms of resistance. *The choice to acquiesce, to celebrate a secret religion, to kill oneself or one's master, to sabotage, to flee, to revolt—these were choices made by individuals but always by individuals carrying with them a particular culture, interacting with others on the plantation, and exposed to a common set of limiting structures and conditions in the regional plantation economy.*

The Industrial Revolution and the Experience of the Laborers

The dwindling of the sick and dying Indian labor force necessitated the importation of a new labor force—African slaves. And commercial cotton farming, based on black labor, in turn provided the raw materials for the British cotton industry that spearheaded the take-off into modern industrialism. Thus the consequences of each of our major structural transformations are linked to the next set of changes, as antecedents. The set of changes we will be discussing in this section are the changes usually referred to as the Industrial Revolution. I would like to present this crucial structural transformation primarily as a series of changes in social relations.

Preconditions. These changes in relationships took place between 1780 (some might say 1760) and 1840. They came about only because certain preconditions existed, above all in England. One was the *existence of commercial farming*, beginning as early as the sixteenth and seventeenth centuries. Commercial farming and livestock-raising were necessary conditions for industrialization for three reasons. First, only if there was a productive and technically efficient farm system could enough food be raised to feed a substantial nonfarm population of industrial workers. Second, the money to be made in commercial farming and livestock-raising provided a substantial amount of the capital necessary for the development of manufacturing. Third, commercial farming and livestock-raising (especially sheepherding) was imposed by land-owning classes, forcing the farmers off the land. The main mechanism of this forced emigration from rural areas was the enclosure system. In the enclosure system, land previously devoted to subsistence farming, small commercial farming, and the commons (communally owned land) came under the control of commercial sheep raisers who expropriated the previous users and turned their acreage over to sheep. Thus a destitute population of potential industrial laborers was created, along with a source of food and raw material and a supply of capital.

A second precondition of industrialization was the *capture of the state machinery* in the late seventeenth and early eighteenth centuries by those strata of society that were interested in commercial ventures at home and abroad. The state supported enclosures and other coercive aspects of the switch to commercial farming. It also provided support for manufacturing ventures, such as the provision of ports, waterways, and so on. As yet the state was not specifically committed to manufacturing rather than agrarian commercial interests, but in any case it was committed to economic development.

A third precondition was the existence of a *supply of coal and iron* that could be used in manufacturing and in the production and operation of machinery, railways, and ships.

The fourth precondition was *the existence of an industry that could provide the initial thrust for the take-off into industrialization; this was the cotton industry.* It was the ideal industry for expansion. There was a vast domestic and foreign market for cheap cotton goods, including Africa, Latin America, and India, which had been systematically deindustrialized. Cotton manufacture easily absorbed simple and effective new machinery—the spinning jenny and spinning mule and, shortly thereafter, the power loom. The industry had a vast and rapidly expandable raw material source—the cotton fields of the southern United States, where slave labor and the westward thrust of the frontier produced a supply that increased much more rapidly than did the supplies of raw material that depended on European commercial farming. E. J. Hobsbawm, a leading historian of the Industrial Revolution, comments:

> Colonial trade had created the cotton industry, and continued to nourish it. In the eighteenth century it developed in the hinterland of the major colonial ports, Bristol, Glasgow, but especially Liverpool, the great centre of the slave trades. Each phase of this inhuman but rapidly expanding commerce stimulated it. In fact, during the entire period with which this book is concerned slavery and cotton marched together. The African slaves were bought, in part at least, with Indian cotton goods;

but when the supply of these was interrupted by war or revolt in and about India, Lancashire was able to leap in. The plantations of the West Indies, where the slaves were taken, provided the bulk of the raw cotton for the British industry, and in return the planters bought Manchester cotton checks in appreciable quantities. Until shortly before the "take-off" the overwhelming bulk of Lancashire cotton exports went to the combined African and American markets. Lancashire was later to repay its debt to slavery by preserving it; for after the 1790s the slave plantations of the southern United States were extended and maintained by the insatiable and rocketing demands of the Lancashire mills, to which they supplied the bulk of their raw cotton (Hobsbawm, 1962:52).

Thus, the set of changes that we call the Industrial Revolution is itself based on *preceding changes in social relationships,* not only on new materials, productive techniques, and inventions. *Commercial farming, the role of the state, the development of a foreign market in colonies and economically weak nations, the slave-based cotton industry—all these reflect changes in the nature of relationships between groups of people.*

Now let's look at the structural changes—the large-scale changes in relationships—that make up the Industrial Revolution.

Decline of the Craftsworker.   The first of these structural changes is the transformation and decline of the prevailing system of craft production. In eighteenth-century England, craft production was based on the relationship of a contractor or "master" to a number of craftsmen. The latter were not strictly speaking wage workers. Many of them owned their own equipment—for instance looms—and set their own pace of work. Their livelihood in this "domestic," "putting-out," or "cottage" system depended not so much on the sale of their labor for a fixed period of time to a factory owner as on the production of a finished product under working conditions of their own arrangement. Sometimes the master-workman relationship was complicated by multiple layers of subcontractors who farmed out various subparts of the production process. In turn, the chief contractor might arrange the sale of the product through a series of middlemen. Thus production was organized as a series of small ventures involving workmen who were primarily artisans and even petty entrepreneurs in their own right.

It is important not to idealize the condition of the workers under this system. On the one hand, they often did own their tools, set the pace of their work, and involve themselves in all or, at any rate, a substantial part of the production of a finished product. In these respects they were vastly better off than the factory laborer who owned no machinery, had to work long hours at a pace he could not control, and worked at only a small, monotonously repeated part of the process. On the other hand, the craftsman (or woman) in the cottage system had to put up with the same fluctuations in the price of and demand for the finished goods as the factory worker; he was thus just as hard hit by economic depression. The craftsworker had two major protections against exploitation by contractors. One was tradition, which was more and more frequently and freely violated in the late eighteenth century and in what was left of the domestic system in the early nineteenth century. The second was machine wrecking. Machine wrecking, far from being an irrational effort to halt the inevitable process of mechanization, was a reasonably useful method of exerting leverage on the masters by intermittent shows of strength and of enforcing solidarity on workmen who could not possibly scab when the machinery itself was inoperative (Hobsbawm, 1964:11).

A final point must be made about this whole set of relationships between artisans, artisan-entrepreneurs, and entrepreneurial contractors: these institutional arrangements were already a first step toward modern capitalist organization of production. Like commercial agriculture based on slavery in the New World, the contracting arrangement of the eighteenth-century "domestic" system of production is one of the halfway houses between feudal and guild production on the one hand and modern capitalism on the other. From the viewpoint of the individual laborer, they were of course quite different; induction into plantation labor was sudden and traumatic, whereas the transition from feudalism to the "domestic" system to factory labor in England tended to be more gradual.

But gradual as the process was, by the 1840s much of the transitional domestic contracting system had disappeared. The first step in this transformation was the rapid decline in artisans' wages. Underemployment and unemployment brought on by economic upheaval and increased mechanization forced the artisans to undercut each other's wages. By the first decade of the nineteenth century in the weaving trade, for example, the independent producers who owned their own equipment—the "little makers"—began to decrease. Both power looms and handlooms were increasingly owned by merchant manufacturers who located them in one place—in factories. Sometimes the owner of a power-loom factory supplemented his income by putting out work to independent handloom workers during periods of high demand (Thompson, 1963: 281, 285).

The skilled craftsmen in the first decades of the nineteenth century had three choices: to accept factory work (for which they had to compete with women, children, and ex-farmers), to accept relief (which, as we shall shortly see, was a terrible alternative), or to accept a falling standard of living. Most "chose" the third because of the unattractiveness of the first two options and the general force of inertia. During the eighteenth century, craftsmen in the textile industry enjoyed a position of modest well-being: most had little garden patches, decent housing, simple furniture (chests, clocks, chairs, bedsteads, and candlesticks), adequate food, and enough time and money for a moderate amount of beer drinking. Textile workers of the nineteenth century became sunk in misery (Thompson, 1963:289).

The New Factory System.   Meanwhile a new set of relationships (and attendant living conditions) appeared in British manufacturing—the factory system. In the factory system, the factory owner owned all the equipment used in production. These *means of production* were located in one place, the factory. The factory owner hired people to come into the factory and produce goods for him using the machinery and tools in the factory.

The factory owner tended to be an entrepreneur on a much larger scale than was the contractor in the "putting-out" system. Factory owners were drawn from the ranks of successful commercial farmers as well as from among the most ambitious and lucky of the entrepreneurial contractors. The ones who succeeded did so through a combination of chance and those personality traits that we have since come to believe are virtues: freedom from the "grip of custom and tradition"; a puritanical self-righteousness that protected them from both kindheartedness and the vices that would have made them lazier and more lighthearted; a strong practicality; and a desire to invest wealth rather than "squander" it on consumer luxuries or generosity. They were men who ruthlessly enforced labor discipline in their factories. For every owner who turned his mill into a harem, there were several who did their best to enforce Puritan morality among their workers, even firing those women who bore illegitimate children. Prodigality was not their strong point; indeed they came to refer to orgasm as "spending." Their women have been described as "stupid, uneducated, impractical, theoretically unsexual, propertyless, and protected" (Hobsbawm, 1962:226). The personalities of the successful men were to some extent the result of changes in child rearing practices—the shift toward efforts to mold a child into an adult with a certain type of character. They were also often products of certain religious traditions—largely pietistic Protestant of one sort or another.

The workers were subjected to two altogether new types of relationships —factory discipline and the sale of their labor power in a market. Of factory discipline, Hobsbawm (1962:247) writes:

> . . . it was unfree, under the strict control and the even stricter discipline imposed by the master or his supervisors, against whom they had virtually no legal recourse and only the very beginnings of public protection. They had to work his hours or shifts, to accept his punishments and the fines with which he imposed his rules or increased his profits. In isolated areas or industries they had to buy in his shop, as often as not receiving their wages in *truck* (thus allowing the unscrupulous employer to swell his profits yet further), or live in the houses the master provided. No doubt the village boy might find such a life no more dependent and less impoverished than his parents'; and in Continental industries with a strong paternalist tradition, the despotism of the master was at least partly balanced by the security, education, and welfare services which he sometimes provided. But for the free man entry into the factory as a mere

"hand" was entry into something little better than slavery, and all but the most famished tended to avoid it, and even when in it to resist the draconic discipline much more persistently than the women and children, whom factory owners therefore tended to prefer. And, of course, in the 1830s and part of the 1840s even the material situation of the factory proletariat tended to deteriorate.

The "Free" Labor Market.   In other words, the purpose of the system was exclusively to harness human labor to the production of goods in the way that would best produce the most output at the lowest labor costs. This aim brought with it stringent discipline, extremely long work hours, all loss of control over workplace and work pace, and child labor. The factory owner was able to enforce discipline because he owned the machinery, because he had the coercive power of the state available in case of unrest, and because he operated in a labor market that worked in his favor. He no longer had to deal with artisans selling products. The free labor market became the central mechanism for allocating labor power; that is, it was (and still is) an institution in which the majority of people *sell their own labor power* to an employer in order to sustain themselves. This was a method of obtaining labor power that was quite distinct from serfdom, peonage, slavery, state-organized forced labor, and other "unfree" forms, where labor power is not sold by the laborer. It is also distinct from the contracting system in which finished goods and not labor power are the commodity that is sold in the market, and it is different from fee-for-service systems (such as a private medical practice).

The labor market was free only in a relative sense, that is, when compared with slavery or serfdom. In fact, it was supported by armed force (to crush efforts at workers' uprisings) and by changed relationships between the poor and the state. At the same time the labor market was becoming the dominant institution for providing labor to the owners of enterprises, the welfare system was also being transformed. During the transitional period prior to 1832, the Speenhamland laws were in effect. Briefly summarized, these laws guaranteed a minimum wage as long as the poor did not leave their parish. After 1832, the only relief measure that existed was the prisonlike workhouse. Given this choice, most people opted for the "free" labor market. The new welfare system not only expressed and supported new relations between employer and employee, but also wiped away the traditional constraints that attached people to their parish, reduced their geographical mobility, and tied them to their squire.

Consequences: Living Conditions and Ideology.   The factory, the labor market, the collapse of traditional and transitional welfare relationships—all opened the way to the growth of industrial cities and to a decline in living standards. As in the case of the conquest of the Indians and the enslavement of blacks, one of the leading personal consequences of this structural transformation was death. Some of the industrial cities had higher death rates than birth rates, and they generally had higher death rates than did the surrounding countryside. Infant and child mortality rates were extremely high: around 40 to 50 percent for spinners in Manchester in the 1830s, for example. The average age at death varied markedly for different class groups. For instance, in Liverpool it was thirty-five, twenty-two, and fifteen, respectively for gentry, tradesmen, and laborers, while in Manchester, the average age at death for the same groups was thirty-eight, twenty, and seventeen, respectively (Thompson, 1963:330).

Along with death came epidemics, ill health, and child neglect.

Mothers, for fear of losing their employment, returned to the mill three weeks or less after the birth: still, in some Lancashire and West Riding towns, infants were carried in the 1840s to the mills to be suckled in the meal-break. Girl-mothers, who had perhaps worked in the mill from the age of eight or nine, had no domestic training: medical ignorance was appalling: the parents were a prey to fatalistic superstitions (which the churches sometimes encouraged): opiates, notably laudanum, were used to make the crying baby quiet. Infants and toddlers were left in the care of relatives, old baby-farming crones, or children too small to find work at the mill. Some were given dirty rag-dummies to suck, "in which is tied a piece of bread soaked in milk and water," and toddlers of two and three could be seen "running about with these rags in their mouths, in the neighbourhood of factories" (Thompson, 1963:328).

Most appalling of all was child labor. Although child labor had been used in the "putting-out" system, in the factory system and free labor market it became totally brutal. Unfortunately, it also became economically "rational." Again, the human impact of this institution is best described by the victims —in this case, child miners—and by contemporary observers.

The reports of the Children's Employment Commissions of 1842 showed new-model Boards of Guardians, in Staffordshire, Lancashire and Yorkshire, still getting rid of pauper boys of six, seven and eight, by apprenticing them to colliers, with a guinea thrown in "for clothes." The boys were "wholly in the power of the butties" and received not a penny of pay; one boy in Halifax who was beaten by his master and had coals thrown at him ran away, slept in disused workings, and ate "for a long time the candles that I found in the pits that the colliers left overnight." The mixture of terror and of fatalism of the children comes through in the laconic reports. An eight-year-old girl, employed for thirteen hours a "day," to open and close traps: "I have to trap without a light, and I'm scared. . . . Sometimes I sing when I've light, but not in the dark; I dare not sing then." Or seventeen-year-old Patience Kershaw, who discussed the merits of different employments: ". . . the bald place upon my head is made by thrusting the corves [baskets for carrying coal]; my legs have never swelled, but sisters' did when they went to mill; I hurry the corves a mile and more under ground and back; they weigh 3 cwt. . . . the getters that I work for are naked except their caps . . . sometimes they beat me, if I am not quick enough. . . . I would rather work in mill than in coalpit (Thompson 1963:334–335).

Living conditions and diet were miserable, and there is considerable evidence that they became even worse during the Industrial Revolution (Thompson, 1963; Hobsbawm, 1964:64–125).

These experiences of the laborers have been partially veiled from our eyes. There are many reasons for the invisibility of their suffering. It is unfashionable to write history in an outraged or polemical fashion. "Value-free" history describes the experience of the new industrial working classes in generalized abstract terms. The exciting takeoff into expanding productive capacity has dazzled historians to the point of being blinded to the actual impoverishment and loss of freedom associated with early industrial growth. While the volume of goods and machinery increased in quantity and in diversity, the lives of people became duller, more regimented, more impoverished intellectually and culturally, and more stultified by monotonous work. Thus, while the average New Guinea highlander labored about 1,000 hours a year to make a living in subsistence slash-and-burn agriculture and pig-farming, the average worker in early Victorian England toiled 3,500 hours (Harris, 1971:218).

"Labor-saving" advances in mechanization *increased* human labor as well as making it more monotonous. There was no ownership of the tools of production much less control over the pace of the work. Thus, *the increase in production does not seem to have benefited the laborer; his ability to produce more in a mechanized industrial system of production was not returned to him in the form of more leisure time but was appropriated for the wealth of others and the expansion of the system.* These effects of mechanization were possible because of the new relationships between groups of people that we have discussed as the heart of the Industrial Revolution.

The new relationships were clothed in an appropriate and attractive new language. Most of us are familiar with the process by which unpleasant structural realities are referred to by innocent-sounding code words. Often the originators of these code words come to believe that the words describe a reality; for instance, *disadvantaged* and *urban renewal* have come to stand for "poor and black" and "removal of poor blacks from the central city by a coalition of the government and private developers."

In the nineteenth century, two types of vocabulary were developed to deal with the structural changes we have described. One was religious, and attemped to reconcile workers to their earthly fate and to extol discipline and a work ethic. The other was a secular liberal ideology that used words like *laissez-faire, freedom,* and *free choice,* and the concept of the atomized individual making choices in a marketplace to cover up the reality that all these "free individuals" in "free" markets were really representatives of two groups of people: one, the factory owners, who imposed a labor market favorable to their own entrepreneurial success on the second group, the workers, who had to sell their labor power to the capitalist entrepreneurs. Laissez-faire did not mean that things took their natural course (a meaningless idea) but that the state supported private enterprise and the modern labor market, protecting these institutions against a variety of alternatives, such as a return to craft production or a leap forward to socialism.

Responses.   The English working class did not peacefully and wholeheartedly accept either the ideology or the new structure. The gradual nature of the transition often made it hard for individuals to decide where to "draw the line," however. Unlike the enslaved blacks, the workers lacked a definite traumatic moment of change, a distinct period of previous happiness to serve as a benchmark, an obvious enemy whom they could hold responsible. Nevertheless, responses covered the range we have discussed before. Self-destructive flight into alcohol or opiates was a widespread response: "Drink is the shortest way out of Manchester." Others accepted the new ruling-class ideology and, unlike the slave, found they could rise into the ranks of the middle class. Still others accepted ruling-class goals by becoming docile workers.

Some workers openly rebelled in a variety of ways, depending on time and place. Sporadic and generally unsuccessful revolts occurred in the early decades of the nineteenth century and included machine-breaking (e.g., the Luddites caused widespread damage to textile machinery in the English midlands between 1811–1816), demonstrations, and uprisings. These activities were followed by two related and more carefully organized movements: the Chartist *political* action of the 1830s, aimed at securing working-class people at least a role in the state (through universal manhood suffrage, the secret ballot, pay for members of Parliament, and so on); and the trade-union movement, aimed at changing, or at least ameliorating, the relations between the producer and his employer.

As was true of individual slaves, many working-class English may not have taken part directly in these resistance movements, but they did take part in building a culture of resistance and survival that fueled the actual movements. Like the Afro-American culture, this working-class culture was composed of many bits and pieces.

One element was the tradition of religious dissent. Many working-class people belonged to Protestant churches and sects that were outside the official Church of England. They shared a religious language and religious hopes. Sometimes religion made them more conservative, when anger and despair at their living conditions were undercut by counsels of meekness and preparation for heaven. But sectarian religion could also radicalize people and give them valuable experiences in building working-class institutions. For example, early trade-union organization was directly modeled after the Primitive Methodist Church organization. Waves of radical agitation paralleled in time and place the expansion in the ranks of Methodism (Hobsbawm, 1964:32). Working-class culture in England drew strongly on sectarian religious organizational experience, style, and imagery in its radical as well as conservative forms.

A second element of working-class culture was rationalist, secularized, politically oriented Jacobinism, a political heir of Enlightenment thought. This element is predominant in the thought of the American Revolution. It confirms the importance of political action, of self-government, of the creation of political institutions in which everyone participates and that therefore serve the people rather than the oppressive elite. This component of working-class culture was perhaps stronger among the remaining artisan stratum than among factory workers of rural origin. It drew upon and contributed to the remarkably high level of literacy and political debate in this stratum.

A third component of working-class culture was the experience of hunger and exploitation, of being crowded into industrial slums, of a general wretchedness. Above all else, these experiences contributed anger and hate and a sense of the division of society into "them" and "us." Sometimes the heroes in this culture were drawn from the legends of thieves and outlaws, from those who stole from the rich with a gun just as the rich were stealing from the poor with a pen. The easy transition between banditry and revolt was even stronger at the margins of the industrial world than it was in England—in southern Italy, Sardinia, Spain, Russia, Brazil, the Scottish highlands, the American South (Hobsbawm, 1969). In these areas crime was still a viable alternative to accepting the culture and exploitation imposed by the upper classes and the state. In England, becoming a bandit or criminal was rapidly collapsing as a route of working-class resistance. The years during which the factory system and the free labor market were imposed on workers were also precisely those years in which London became the first city in the world to have a modern police force and relatively safe streets. "Safe streets" meant, at least in part, that the crimes of the poor were turned against each other rather than against the middle class. We should not glorify working-class crime lest we forget that in slums like London's East End and the Gorbals district of Glasgow (as well as in American slums and ghettos) the principle victims were usually other poor people, and the net effect was probably to brutalize rather than to politicize the working-class population. Nevertheless, banditry, crime, and their more mild and widespread form—youth gangs—are vital parts of working-class culture.

A fourth component was hedonism. It was a carry-over from preindustrial village life with its round of holidays, merrymaking, and casual sex. Working-class hedonism competed with the puritanism preached by the religious sects. Working-class hedonism offended the middle class, which tried to stamp it out in various ways and to replace it with discipline, modesty, and sobriety. Hedonism helped the working class to resist cultural oppression, but it may also have interfered with building disciplined working-class organizations. Hedonism contributed conviviality, generosity (or prodigality), strong kin ties, a rowdy "youth culture," and a strong sense of community and solidarity.

The fifth component of working-class culture was experience in the movements themselves. The movements were successively Luddite, Chartist, trade-union, and later Socialist. The tactics included machine-smashing, political demonstrations, workplace organizing, and the formation of a mass party. In England (as in most other industrialized countries), these movements failed to destroy the state apparatus, although for periods of time they captured and modified it. But in the process, the movements gave a coherence and direction to at least some components of working-class culture.

To Understand the Present and Future

We have examined three structural transformations—three that were crucial in shaping the experience of major ethnic groups in this country and of the country as a whole. In each discussion we used a slightly different approach to understanding the events. In the first (the colonization of Mexico), we looked at the destruction of one society and the creation of another in terms of changes in the different systems of behavior—political, economic and cultural—that characterized the societies. In the second case study (African slavery), we examined the structural transformation primarily in terms of the responses that individuals and groups in particular settings made to the structural transformation. In the third case study (the Industrial Revolution), I tried to concentrate on the changes in relationships that constituted the structural transformation. Each of these approaches could have been used for each of the other case studies. I have deliberately used several different approaches to show that there is more than one way of analyzing a structural transformation. But a number of themes are shared by all the examples.

1. The structural transformations involved changes in a variety of different features of people's environments: in their interpersonal relationships, in their economic circumstances, in their relationship to political institutions, and in their culture or way of life.
2. The changing relationships were between groups of people, not between isolated individuals. New relationships between *groups* appeared: between Spanish landowners and Indian peasants, between white masters and black slaves, between factory owners and factory workers.
3. The structural transformations all involved change in the organization of productive activity ("work") and in the social relationships surrounding this activity.

4. The structural transformations all created "personal troubles." Everyone experienced them as personal troubles; some were also able to see them as social issues.

5. People generally did not passively accept or absorb these changes. They acted in response to them and, in acting, altered the course of the transformation. Many revolted and resisted. Resistance did not just mean an effort to turn back the clock (clearly a futile effort) but an effort to build new institutions that could meet human needs. Even if movements of resistance could not be formed, people developed cultures of survival and resistance. Nevertheless, many people died and others succumbed physically and psychologically to despair, sickness, apathy, drink, and drug abuse. The cultures of resistance and survival were retained even beyond the period of structural changes and became part of the "cultural baggage" of the groups.

Can we learn from these different types of analysis of historical situations and from the common themes anything that may be useful to us in understanding our own time? With the knowledge of hindsight, we can see the larger structural changes that trapped people in the past. Can we do the same for the structural changes that we are now undergoing, changes in which we are necessarily actors as well as observers?

First of all, this historical discussion should make us look at *structure* and *changes in structure.* In other words, to understand the present, we should ask ourselves *what is the nature of relationships between individuals and groups of individuals, and how are these relationships changing?* This question is perhaps too abstract to answer. We might therefore focus specifically on the *nature of work and on the relationships involved in work.* Combining these two approaches we might find, for example, the following to be the case: Relationships that focus on the sale and purchase of goods and services are among the most important relationships in our society. The sale of labor power is one of the most important of these commodity relationships. Because labor power is a commodity, we might decide that our society is markedly different from the hacienda and slave societies that we discussed. But does our society differ from English society at the beginning of the Industrial Revolution? First, we would want to look at which groups in our society are involved in production. Is there a group that does most of the work, that sells its labor power? Is there a group that owns the mines, large farms, machinery, and products and that controls the process of production? Insofar as the answer is yes, our society is a capitalist society like nineteenth century England. Are these relationships changing?

Another area in which we would look for answers to the question Where are we headed? is in the *nature of the state.* We saw how in the Industrial Revolution, the state—specifically, the British government—had an important role in the growth of new relationships and new institutions through its welfare policies, its support for manufacturing, and its imperial activities. Similarly, the state in our society can be expected to shape our lives through its foreign policy, its welfare policy, its regulatory agencies, its monetary policy and other intervention in the economy, and so on. We should try to distinguish policies that shift from administration to administration from those that seem very stable or change in a steady cumulative fashion over a period of several decades. For instance, the general commitment of the federal government to create a favorable climate for big business has not changed since the late nineteenth century, although specific monetary, tax, or regulatory policies have changed. To fully understand the role of the state, one would have to look not only at the federal government but also at state and local government, at state and local police forces and national guard units, and at various private bodies that wield power and are linked to public institutions—for instance, large foundations, unions, the major news media, and think tanks like the Air-Force-affiliated RAND Corporation, and so on.

The final set of forces that we need to understand in order to analyze present trends in our society is *culture and ideology.* Here, as when we examined the state and the organization of work, we would need to look at trends in the dominant or official sectors—the media, the arbiters of taste and fashion in the consumer markets, the school system. But we could also look at "nonofficial" culture and its uneasy relationship to official culture. For example, we would want to examine trends in working-class culture—its erosion by the middle-class-oriented media, the recent rise in wildcat strikes and intraunion dissension, the phenomenon of the long-haired greaser, the impact of working-class suburbanization. We would have to look at trends in ethnic subcultures—black, Latin, European ethnic, and so on. We would have to look at a variety of ethnic communities and see the blend of ethnic culture, working-class culture, and middle-class culture.

Eventually, we would have to repeat this analysis of economics, politics, and culture for the world as a whole to avoid being caught by surprise—as the Aztecs were—by the spillover into our society of events taking place elsewhere. While all this would be the work of a lifetime, it would be the only way of understanding the forces that shape our lives. As long as sociology remains a microdiscipline, primarily concerned with interpersonal behavior, the family, and the neighborhood, it is doomed to miss an understanding of what shapes these microenvironments and the lives of the individuals who live in them.

References

Davidson, Basil.
   1959   The Lost Cities of Africa. Boston: Little, Brown.

Harris, Marvin.
   1971   Culture, Man and Nature. New York: Thomas Y. Crowell.

Hobsbawm, Eric J.
    1962   The Age of Revolution: 1789–1848. New York: World Publishing.
    1964   Labouring Men: Studies in the History of Labour. New York: Basic Books.
    1969   Bandits. New York: Delacorte Press.

James, C. L. R.
    1963   The Black Jacobins. New York: Random House.

Lifton, Robert J.
    1968   Death in Life. New York: Random House.

Mills, C. Wright.
    1959   The Sociological Imagination. New York: Oxford University Press.

Patterson, Orlando.
    1973   "Slavery and slave revolts: A sociological analysis of the first maroon war, 1665–1740," in Richard Price (ed.), Maroon Societies. Garden City, N.Y.: Anchor Books.

Thompson, E. P.
    1963   The Making of the English Working Class. New York: Random House.

Wolf, Eric R.
    1971   "The Spanish in Mexico and Central America," in George Dalton (ed.), Economic Development and Social Change. New York: Natural History Press.

Chapter
3

Change in
Individual
Consciousness
In this chapter I shall explore some
of the processes by which subjective change—change in individual consciousness—occurs. I
shall first suggest a framework for describing these processes. Next I shall describe some
major stages in this change. Throughout the chapter I shall endeavor to show that the nature
and circumstances of the change processes themselves are changing.

AN UNDERSTANDING OF HOW INDIVIDUALS CHANGE must include the following elements:

1. The concepts we use must be able to take into account the unfolding
of a person's own life. These concepts must recognize how people's behavior
reflects both their current situation and the "baggage" of beliefs, habits, dispositions, values, and personality traits with which they have burdened themselves in past experiences. Thus the concepts must recognize that people move
through a sequence of states or experiences in their lives. Each new experience
is assimilated into a framework of behavior that is based on the past experiences. At the same time, the new experience affects the "baggage" of the past
experiences. It forces some kind of reorganization of these experiences.

2. The concepts we use to analyze individual change must simultaneously take into account the continuity in human life and the irreversible
movement of history. Humanity does have an unchanging core of drives and
capabilities: we eat, sleep, copulate, think, and talk. Yet the biological basis of
human behavior is such that it substantially frees us from "nature." Nature
itself gives us the capacity to create our own future to a very large degree.
Important ingredients of this capacity are ability to speak, the long period of
childhood, the year-round sexual receptivity of the human female, and certain
physical traits, such as upright posture, an opposable thumb, and a large

cerebral capacity. All of these capabilities add up to a substantial freedom from instinct and a reliance on other human beings to define needs and goals. The fact that it is "human nature" to be "unnatural," that is, to be self-defining and relatively free from instinct, means that human behavior is largely shaped by the structure of society at any given time. This structure of society in turn reflects past events of human history. Thus change in individuals is not a repetitive, unvarying set of processes but is altered by historical change.

In other words, an understanding of change in individuals has to take into account the flow of time itself—the particular situation of the individual in the unfolding of his or her own life and in the flow of history.

Consciousness and Structural Transformations

In this chapter we will be concerned primarily with the processes by which the individual moves from one state of consciousness to the next in the setting of historical change (or structural transformations). There are certain types of individual change, of moves from one phase to the next, that have very little to do with structural transformations. For example, I am not particularly concerned with child-rearing, job changes, and other parts of an individual's career in themselves, torn out of their historical context.

In the last chapter, I approached this issue by examining the impact of structural transformations on people. The structural transformation was like a cross-section in time, a great slash across the lives of the affected individuals. I looked at a historical discontinuity and saw how it affected large numbers of people caught up in it. Now I would like to ask what kinds of processes occur within individuals when they are caught up in the structural transformation. I shall look at discontinuities in their thoughts and feelings. In the last chapter, I treated the discontinuities from the viewpoint of external objective changes in the structure of society. In this chapter, I want to see what these discontinuities mean for the subjective state of individuals. We shall refer to this state as consciousness. To observe these processes in individuals, I shall temporarily put the objective structural changes into the background and bring the individual experiences into the foreground. But this emphasis is only temporary. The subjective approach, by itself, makes no sense if we want to understand the large picture of historical change.

How do people experience, comprehend, and respond to changes in their environment? We can think of changes in consciousness as the result of changes in rewards and punishments. Change in individuals takes place through changes in their immediate environment. The immediate environments are structures of rewards and punishments for certain types of behavior. Behavior that is rewarded or punished includes not only outward actions but also the creation of frameworks of belief and meaning. Individuals learn interpretations or meanings because they are rewarded for doing so and punished for not doing so. But rewards and punishments are usually hard to identify. What constitutes a reward or a punishment is itself learned and is usually rather complicated.

In a few situations, rewards and punishments are extremely simple and tangible. On the slave plantation or in the concentration camp, starvation, beatings, torture, and death are the punishments; food, adequate shelter, and the remission of beatings are the rewards. The rewards and punishments produce work and obedience. But no human being enters a situation without bringing cultural baggage from past situations. Even in extreme and tightly controlled situations, previously learned meanings affect responses. For instance, in Latin America, Moslem Africans like the Mandingo and Hausa were more rebellious than other slaves, perhaps because of the militancy of Islam in Africa. Few environments have as clear and simple a structure of rewards and punishments as did slavery. In most settings, rewards and punishments are complicated and often inconsistent. Individuals are subjected to a variety of rewards and punishments whose affects often work at cross-purpose. The outside observer is hard put to predict the response of individuals in this structure.

The actual change in consciousness involves a change in the meanings that a person assigns to everything in himself and his environment. These meanings are usually shared with other people. All interpretations of reality must be sustained by relationships with other human beings. The interpretation of the world does not take place in isolated individuals. It always takes place in individuals who are or have been in interaction with other individuals. When the relationships change or break down, the interpretations that the relationships sustained become problematical. According to Berger and Luckmann (1966:chap. 3), the rapidity with which interpretations change when relationships change depends on several factors:

1. The degree to which the meanings were learned in childhood (It is easier to switch jobs than to switch dialects.)
2. The seriousness of the meanings and their closeness to the core of the self (It is easier to switch beer brands than to undergo a sex change.)
3. The extent to which the changing environment is altered in a planned, systematic, consistent, and closed way (Patty Hearst's sudden conversion to the Symbionese Liberation Army's philosophy of terrorism was possible in the intense, closed environment that was set up by her kidnappers.)

This framework emphasizes that social change includes change in vocabulary and in meaning. In some sense, a structural change is not complete until it induces individuals to think and talk in new ways.

Changes occur not only in words and unverbalized thoughts but also in the unconscious, a sector of the personality where wishes and ideas exist that are not perceived during the normal waking state of awareness. Change may also affect the organization of bodily drives, particularly the sexual drive, which is most influenced by social forces. Thus we see that very profound changes alter persons' verbalized thoughts, their bodies, and their "personalities," that is, the way all their dispositions, habits, body images, interpersonal behavior, and conscious or unconscious longings are put together. However, these changes in individuals and their immediate situation do not take place in random or haphazard fashion. They tend to be caused by the larger structural transformations. The structural transformations change and disrupt personal situations; they alter the way in which all forms of behavior are rewarded or punished, consciously or unconsciously, by other people in the person's environment. Thus they alter the individual's actions and frameworks of meaning. Most people are not fully aware of these changes; they are unaware of how these changes occur within themselves and of how they are caused by structural transformations.

Change Processes

There is a large body of literature on individual change processes. Some of it describes childhood socialization, the first learning experiences of a person's life. Some of it describes attitude change later in life. Attitude change is relatively superficial change in small fragmented parts of a person's world view. Attitude change has been of special interest to sociologists and social psychologists in the U.S. because of its relationship to the practical problems of advertising and political campaigning. Attitude-change studies are directed toward finding out how best to sell a commodity or to package a candidate. Only a very small segment of the potential buyer's outlook or personality is affected in this process; moreover, the change is reversible. These attitude changes don't add up to any fundamental structural change in the society; they just mean higher sales of a particular brand of soap or a more or less liberal politician in office.

The individual change that is of interest here is the change that accompanies structural transformations. It is this type of subjective change that is meant by the term *consciousness,* not the attitude change involved in switching soap brands. This kind of profound individual change has the following characteristics: it accompanies reorganization of the individual's life situation as a result of and in response to the structural transformation; it profoundly affects the individual's personality and world view—in other words, the individual's whole being; it is irreversible in the sense that while the change may be undone, it cannot be forgotten. To be a backsliding Christian or an ex-Communist is to have to deal with a fact about oneself that does not trouble a person who has simply changed detergents.

There is a sequence of stages in these major changes in people's consciousness, stages through which individuals move in altering the totality of their understanding of themselves, of their everyday life, of their society, and of their world. In actuality, however, the stages I am about to describe may be telescoped; they may occur virtually simultaneously.

Deroutinization

Deroutinization is the breakdown of habits and dispositions that were developed within a preceding structure. The old ways no longer work. The rewards and punishments that sustained them disappear. The personal contacts that nourished them drop away. Sometimes these changes happen very suddenly, as in the case of the European conquest of tribal groups or the African slave trade, for example. Sometimes the collapse of routines is more drawn out and gradual, as during the period of industrialization. Not all breaks in routine are part of historical change. Some breaks only defuse the desire for change. Festivals of all kinds have traditionally served as releases from routine. Festivals do not lead to demands for more change but rather dissipate tensions and streamline the existing order. Letting people "blow off steam" has been the conservative function of festivals like the orgiastic Roman saturnalia, the rituals of rebellion in the East African kingdoms in which the king is insulted and humiliated by his subjects, Mardi Gras, football weekends, and so on. These should not be confused with the long-term, open-ended breaks in routine associated with major structural transformation.

Some people live an exceptionally deroutinized life. For them, change is so constant a condition that major structural changes are lost amid the constant flux of new jobs, new personal contacts, new cities, new rounds of life. Some very poor people and some very marginal people—drifters on Skid Row, bikers, cafe society—may arrange to live their lives in so deroutinized a way that deroutinization ceases to be an effective catalyst for involvement in social change. Some people—like refugees in a war zone or the very poor—may enter a prolonged and an ultimately paralyzing state of deroutinization entirely involuntarily.

One of the tendencies of modern capitalism is to place many people in situations where their lives are in continual flux: new jobs, new clothes, new gadgets, new lovers, new spouses, and new houses make life a dizzying whirl of change and disposable relationships. This condition has been called "future shock." Like refugees or the very poor, people in a state of future shock may be too deroutinized to sort out major structural changes from the chaos of their everyday life. Like the deroutinization of tension release, the deroutinization of future shock inhibits rather than promotes political action.

So, like many other situations, deroutinization is inherently ambiguous. It can potentially paralyze people, but it can also potentially stir people to action. Therefore we cannot generalize about all deroutinization, but must look at specific historical instances. Also, deroutinization is not only a result of structural transformations, but it is also a response to them. Initiative for changes in reward structures and for deroutinization may originate from below as well as from above. Primarily powerless people can initiate change that disrupts "normal" reward and punishment routines. A very good example of such change is Mrs. Rosa Parks's refusal to sit in the "colored" section of a Montgomery, Alabama, bus in 1955. With that action she shattered years of habit that had been externally imposed on southern blacks. The lunch counter sit-ins and freedom rides (integration of intercity buses and waiting-room facilities) that followed were similarly largely a grass roots movement to destroy the routine behavior of segregation; these activities originated in churches and on college campuses.

At one level, this deroutinizing behavior was caused by the industrialization and urbanization of the South, by the increasing education of the black population, and by the greater exposure of southern blacks to the legal equality of blacks and whites in the North, all of which was related to the penetration of northern capital into the southern economy. The rewards and punishments that had enforced black docility broke down in the South following World War II because such rewards and punishments only worked in an agrarian society. At another level, the deroutinization not only was a product of a structural transformation but also hastened the coming of new patterns of behavior. Bus boycotts, lunch counter sit-ins, and freedom rides accelerated the pace at which southern life-styles and experiences came to resemble northern ones.

Sit-down strikes by factory workers are another example of deroutinization. In a sit-down strike the workers seize a factory and hold it until management accepts their demands. This was a common tactic in the late 1930s, when sit-down strikes were an important part of union drives and the only way that workers could win union recognition in some industries. On the one hand, the sit-down strikes were a largely spontaneous reaction to certain structural changes that occurred in the 1930s: the speedup of factory work as employers tried to keep profits high during the Depression; the crowding into factories of workers who had been forced off the land by the Depression and who experienced factory work for the first time. On the other hand, the sit-down strikes also created new ways of responding to these changes and helped to build the large industrial unions. The sit-down strikes occurred as unplanned and uncoordinated ways of changing factory routines that spread throughout the whole society, in waves of simultaneous behavior. Within each factory the workers who occupied it created a new social world in which worker solidarity was rewarded rather than punished, as it had been by management. The unions that grew from these sit-down strikes helped to improve the workers' lives, even though some of them subsequently became oligarchical and conservative.

A final example of deroutinization is the wave of disturbances that took place at European and American universities (and, in Europe, at factories as well) in the late 1960s. These disturbances were caused by the structural changes of advanced capitalism that brought together large numbers of young people in institutions to be processed in interchangeable batches for training as the "manpower" required by employers. In the United States, this situation was exacerbated by the war in Vietnam and the threat of the draft. The response was growing unrest and finally deliberate violations of routine by the workers and students. For instance, during the 1968 sit-in at Columbia University, the students' seizure of the buildings interrupted the routines of campus life. The mechanisms of grading, assignments, lecture attendance, and so on that were part of the routine could no longer operate very effectively. The breakdown of internalized constraints that kept students functioning in expected roles, the breakdown of external constraints, such as grades, that kept them in these roles, and the breakdown of routine all occurred more or less together. Each of these breaks was not so much a breakdown of routines as a suspension of one routine and its replacement by a different form of human relationship.

The modern media often help spread the techniques of deroutinization so that waves of disturbances occur throughout a country without central coordination. Nineteenth-century social scientists of conservative bent, being inclined to view patterns of grass-roots behavioral change as a pathology of the social order, liked to refer to this phenomenon as a contagion. It is also referred to as spontaneity.

Sometimes disruptions in routine and changed rewards structure are more carefully planned and coordinated on a larger scale. For instance, the repeated efforts of left-wing parties in Europe to organize a general strike—a strike of all workers that would lead to such widespread disruption of societal routine that the government would fall—represent an attempt to develop an overall strategy for the disruption of routine. Terrorists have repeatedly attempted to create deroutinization (and thereby topple the state) by isolated acts of violence and destruction, but this method has hardly ever succeeded.

In a revolution, both spontaneous and organized disruptions of routine and changes in reward structure occur. For example, before the Chinese revolution, landlords dominated the countryside. They and the corrupt magistrates punished peasants for late rents or for signs of independence. During the revolution, peasant associations were established with the help of Communist party organizers. Formed primarily by poor peasants, these associations took power in each community. They took land away from the landlords and the rich peasants and redistributed it to the poor peasants and landless laborers. These actions were part of a completely new system of rewards and punishments. The poor people in the countryside—the vast majority in China—now set standards of behavior. The old routines of extorting rent ended; new routines of village life, work, and decision-making were established by the peasants. With these changes in routines, rewards and punishments, and the distribution of power and land came a change in consciousness. Just as the peasants freed themselves from the yoke of the landlords, so they freed themselves from fear, apathy, docility, superstition, and the "idiocy of rural life."

Cross-Pressures and Marginality

Related to deroutinization as a force for uprooting people from their accustomed lives are marginality and cross-pressures. In traditional societies, reward structures are few and consistent. For example, the landlord, the father, the husband, the priest, the old village women—all exercise similar pressures for docility and conformity on a peasant woman. But in a modern society, pressures from different groups are at odds with each other. For example, your parents want you to have a steady well-paying job and to marry someone in your own ethnic group; your peers want you to be a generous and carefree friend; your teachers want you to study hard; your boss wants you to be productive and obedient; the media admonish you to buy consumer goods. These goals may be at least partly incompatible with one another.

The contradictory cross-pressures on behavior that appear in a modern society destabilize and deroutinize behavior. More and more people find themselves in marginal situations, pressured by two or more substantially different reward structures and interpretations of reality. The black student in a white college, the working-class youth at an Ivy League school, the college graduate working in a factory, the country boy looking for a job in the city, the child of an ethnically or religiously mixed marriage—all are examples of marginal individuals. Marginality may make a person more insightful and aware of the workings of the society; it makes behavior less "taken for granted." Modern capitalism has produced many deroutinized, cross-pressured, and marginal individuals because it has institutionalized rapid change and brought together large ethnically diverse populations.

Geographical Marginality.   Leaders of political movements have sometimes come from geographically marginal areas. For example, Napoleon was a Corsican. As such, he was raised in a culture distinct from mainland French culture and was subjected to social barriers that were not faced by mainland people. Stalin was a Georgian, one of the ethnic minorities in the Caucasus region of Russia. Hitler was born in Austria, not Germany. Marcus Garvey, the leader of a mass movement among black Americans in the 1920s, was a West Indian. Gramsci, the leading theoretician of the Italian Communist party before World War II, was a Sardinian, not a mainland Italian.

Geographical marginality, *if it is indeed a factor,* could have several different kinds of interrelated effects. First, it might increase feelings of resentment and partially repressed rage, since persons from marginal regions have often been discriminated against both by the inhabitants of the core region and by outside invaders who occupied the marginal areas. Second, being born into a marginal area sometimes conferred bilingualism (in a distinct language or a dialect) and biculturalism on the individual; thus such a person was more likely to grasp alternatives to the cultural and structural status quo than were those individuals who had been immersed in only one way of life. It certainly cannot be asserted that geographical marginality was a characteristic of all prominent political leaders. For each leader from a marginal area there are many who were born and raised in central regions. Data on the Nazi leadership suggest some overrepresentation of geographically marginal men, but again this is an area in which careful historical research is necessary (Lasswell & Lerner, 1965: 238–240, 288–291).

Social and Cultural Marginality.   It becomes even harder to make a case for the role of social and cultural marginality in change processes, since these types of marginality are more difficult to define. Social movements do seem to include a disproportionate number of women or ethnic minorities compared with the population at large or with the state apparatus under routine conditions. These groups sometimes have less to lose and more to gain from social change. Also, movements for change may provide outlets for organizational skill that minority members are not allowed to express in routine activities. Thus, we may find that people who belong to ethnic minorities that are excluded from powerful positions in the state realize their potential in movements. This was the case of Jews in revolutionary Russia and central Europe, and of blacks in America, as well as of colonial peoples everywhere. Women may also play outstanding roles in social movements, whereas they have been almost universally excluded from the exercise of power and organizational initiative in status quo society.

As I've already remarked, however, deroutinization and marginality by themselves do not inevitably lead to action. On the contrary, they may create apathy and paralysis. Or they may produce only waves of spontaneous contagious behavior that can destroy old institutions but that, by themselves, do not create a new society. If only deroutinization and marginality prevail without instilling a vision of a new society, those affected tend to drift with a structural transformation without making an effort to direct its course. In the next section, I shall discuss how visions of a new social order become implanted in individuals.

Conversion Experiences and Resocialization

A conversion is any sudden and clearly identifiable switch in a person's interpretation of the world and of herself. Sometimes a person converts from one coherent, clearly developed set of interpretations to another equally coherent and organized set. Sometimes the change is from the rather internally inconsistent and unorganized cognitive state of most people to a coherent and organized one. To a greater or lesser degree, any change in consciousness is like a conversion.

These remarks imply that the sets of interpretations available to people in a society differ in their sharpness, coherence, internal consistency, and intensity. Most people do not carefully examine their beliefs. They are relatively unconcerned whether the beliefs they express at one moment in the course of one activity are consistent with their beliefs or behavior at another time. They do not strive for consistency, and they rather automatically compartmentalize different types of meanings. For example, in church, people may wholeheartedly sing a hymn about how the hills shall be leveled and the valleys raised, but on Monday, at work, they may be involved in planning a construction project that replaces low-income housing by middle-or upper-income homes.

Some people in any large society adhere to very distinct and intense frames of references, however. They seek a high degree of consistency between their beliefs and their actions; they tend to interpret whatever they experience in terms of a single frame of reference. These interpretive frames of reference include values, beliefs, attitudes, styles of behavior, and vocabularies. Some people may be directly socialized into such a view. Thus a child may grow up as a Hasid or a Pentecostal Christian or a Jehovah's Witness. Other people may be exposed to the frame of reference but not fully accept it until later in life. Still others may have a late and sudden conversion experience.

Phases of Conversion

Conversion experiences—that is, sudden and decisive adoption of a new, distinct frame of reference—seem to involve several phases.

Exposure. At first there must be some exposure to the new frame of reference and to the people who are its carriers. This exposure may be routinized and casual; for example, one's neighbors or coworkers might belong to a Pentecostal church. Or it could be hostile, as in the case of Paul's original contacts with the first Christians: "And Saul, yet breathing out threatenings and slaughter against the disciples of the Lord, went unto the high priest, and desired of him letters to Damascus to the synagogues, that if he found any of this way [i.e., Christian], whether they were men or women, he might bring them bound unto Jerusalem" (Acts 9: 1–2). Here the future convert made his initial contact with the new community in order to repress the new ideology and practices. Sometimes the future convert's initial contacts with the group may be involuntary and hostile, as in the case of American POW's in Korea. However, there can be no conversion to a new frame of reference until some of the vocabulary has been learned. The new teachings are learned but not yet internalized. The words, gestures, and attitudes have become familiar but not yet accepted as one's own.

Internalization. In the next phase of the conversion experience—the dramatic conversion itself—this internalization begins to take place. The reality of the new frame of reference replaces the reality of the old frame of reference. This experience may be very painful. The tension between the two competing frames of reference may be almost unbearable. Sometimes it may be expressed in bodily symptoms—visions, paralysis, temporary blindness, and so on. Again the example of Paul is a good illustration: "And as he journeyed, he came near Damascus: and suddenly there shined round him a light from heaven: And he fell to the earth, and he heard a voice saying unto him, Saul, Saul, why persecutest thou me? . . . And Saul arose from the earth and when his eyes opened he saw no man: but they led him by the hand and brought him into Damascus. And he was three days without sight and neither did eat nor drink" (Acts 9: 3–9).

Similarly in the lives of prophets and religious leaders, long periods of sickness and somatic symptoms may precede the actual commitment to a new ideology. For instance, Theresa of Avila, the sixteenth-century Spanish mystic and religious organizer, was sick and partially paralyzed for many years before the onset of her visionary and political powers. Throughout the world, from Zululand to the Arctic, shamans ("witchdoctors") are called to their vocation by a variety of physical symptoms as well as by other signs. Young Luther struggling with his decision to be a monk suffered from convulsive fits as well as attacks of depression. Wovoka, the prophet of the Indian Ghost Dance cult, began to prophesy after suffering "brain fever" and lying in a coma for several days, during which time he felt himself travel into the sky. Joan of Arc was encouraged by her voices and the visions of saints to undertake her campaign against the English in France.

It is not particularly useful to dismiss these experiences by using the jargon of psychotherapy to describe them. This type of explanation is sometimes used to debunk the experience and the frame of reference it ushers in. But it is more intellectually honest to see the physical symptoms not as evidence of derangement but as signs of emotional and intellectual tension. Persons thus afflicted are able and talented people. Their later organizing work or tribal leadership belies the notion that they are mentally incompetent. The voices that many people hear in such moments of conversion are projections of the new ideas that they have been exposed to, that are not yet quite their own, not yet fully internalized and are therefore perceived as disembodied external agencies.

The relationship between comprehension of the new frame of reference and bodily tension and discomfort can also operate in reverse. Not only can the intrusion of a new set of interpretations induce bodily symptoms, but weakening or otherwise extraordinary treatment of the body can be used to make the person more receptive to the new ideology. This is well understood by religious practitioners who use fasting or other ascetic means to induce very intense experiences of a kind different from their routine everyday experiences. It is also used in institutions of thought reform or rehabilitation in which poor diet, lack of sleep, and other sources of intense discomfort are used to weaken an individual's commitment to one frame of reference, to make him more impressionable and open his mind to an alternate frame of reference. Some kinds of drugs may be used in a similar fashion. It is important not to ascribe new ways of looking at the world solely to the properties of the drugs but rather to the joint impact of drugs and the personal and historical context in which they are used and in which their effects are interpreted by others.

The breakdown of sexual repression may also be a key bodily experience that accompanies new concepts and political action. In themselves, the sex drive and the unconscious can be harnessed to the prevailing social order. Sexual freedom is not necessarily related to political action. On the contrary, energy and tension that might otherwise have been given political expression are harmlessly drained off into personal gratification and sexual play. Better access to birth control can make the bed, along with liquor, drugs, and television, one more apolitical route out of working-class miseries. Yet sexual gratification also has a subversive potential. It provides a moment of pleasure that destroys the discipline and repression of factory work, housework, office work. Sexuality destroys the usual organization of time. Time is now organized to suit the demands of employers or the state. By attacking this flow of time, sexuality attacks a social order based on the use of human beings' time for ends that are not their own. However, the role of sexuality in building a new order must be evaluated in terms of the reorganization of human relationships and consciousness that accompanies it; it is not solely an issue of individual pleasure (Marcuse, 1955; Robinson, 1969).

Reintegration. The most important phase of the conversion experience is the reintegration of meaning, using the new frame of reference. This phase necessarily involves other people directly. The preceding phase, the peak experience itself, is sometimes experienced alone (like Saul on the road to Damascus). But the conversion experience must be interpreted by other people of that persuasion. The new believer must learn a variety of new gestures, words, and norms —a complete way of life. And he must be surrounded by people who will confirm the worth of his new choice, protect him against backsliding, and integrate him into a new community. The New Testament provides numerous examples of the importance of human relationships in consolidating conversions. For example, here is a passage from the story of the conversion of an Ethiopian official:

> And Philip ran thither to him and heard him read the prophet Esaias and said, understandest thou what thou readest?
> And he said, *How can I, except some man should guide me* [italics mine]? And he desired Philip that he would come up and sit with him (Acts 8:30–32).

In the example of Paul's conversion, a Christian named Ananias seeks out Saul shortly after the latter's vision on the road and explains to him the meaning of the vision within the Christian frame of reference:

> And Ananias went his way, and entered into the house; and putting his hands on him said, Brother Saul, the Lord, even Jesus, that appeared unto thee in the way as thou camest, hath sent me, that thou mightest receive thy sight and be filled with the Holy Ghost.
>
> And immediately there fell from his eyes as it had been scales: and he received his sight forthwith, and arose, and was baptized.
>
> And when he had received meat, he was strengthened. Then was Saul certain days with the disciples which were at Damascus.
>
> And straightway he preached Christ in the synogogues, that he's the Son of God (Acts 9:17–20).

In some cases the conversion process may be intensified when the interpreters of the new frame of reference also control the same kinds of sanctions that parents used in primary socialization—control over food, sleep, defecation, and so on. The more the interpersonal aspects of the conversion can be made like childhood socialization, the more likely it will be that the new frame of reference will have the centrality and intensity of those meanings learned in childhood.

These interpersonal processes could be conceptualized in the language of rewards and punishments that I introduced earlier. As is always the case when human beings rather than rats or pigeons are involved, the rewards and punishments are complicated and largely composed of social approval or disapproval, especially as the approval or disapproval works on earlier learned layers composed of experience with parents and childhood peers.

Consolidation Techniques.   The operation of rewards for accepting the new frame of reference is often built around several mechanisms. One involves some degree of physical and social isolation from one's old associates. This strategy for consolidating conversions was particularly well developed in various religious communes. For instance, the Shakers (a religious and communal sect in nineteenth-century America) sang:

> Of all the relations that ever I see
> My old fleshly kindred are furthest from me.
> So bad and so ugly, so hateful they feel
> To see them and hate them increases my zeal.
>
> > O how ugly they look!
> > How ugly they look!
> > How nasty they feel!

But—my *gospel* relations are dearer to me,
Than all the flesh kindred that ever I see. ...

O how pretty they look! ...

(Kanter, 1972: 90.)

The Shakers, like other communal sectarians, restricted contacts with the outside world. Some scrubbed their houses thoroughly after outsiders visited them. The breach may be very painful: thus Jesus told his followers to leave their fathers and mothers.

A second mechanism may be the development of a feeling of mutual hostility between oneself and "outsiders" or "old associates." Every coherent ideology will include some concepts for debunking the alternate frames of reference. Both cognitively and in terms of overt behavior, this hostility may be painful and difficult: "I come not to bring peace but a sword."

Finally, a new frame of reference is consolidated within the convert's new community by the reconstruction of the individual's biography (Berger & Luckmann, 1966:159). The old way of life, with its beliefs, experiences, and significant others, is reinterpreted in the new frame of reference. The old life is seen as miserable, oppressed, unaware, and sinful, depending on the new frame of reference. Thus, for instance, converts to various Christian sects see their former life as dominated by the Devil or as laden with sin. "Testifying" includes this discussion of past behavior and problems. People in the Chinese thought-reform schools, the May 7th schools, learn to see the operation of the bad habits of prerevolutionary society in their previous life: petit bourgeois individualism, liberalistic condoning of oppression, incorrect comprehension of the social order, and so forth. They are required to write an autobiography in which they analyze these problems and trace their origins. Persons in psychoanalysis reconstruct their past in the language appropriate to the psychoanalytic framework.

Sometimes this reconstruction of the past is a prelude as well as a follow-up to changes in frames of reference. For instance, in such situations people are encouraged to see the routines of their present life as problematical —sinful, oppressed, and so on. Or, they are encouraged to reconstruct certain experiences in terms of a new framework. For instance, Party cadres encouraged Chinese peasants to hold "speaking pain to recall pain" sessions in which the peasants become aware of their shared oppression and learned to see this oppression as a condition that could be changed. In rap groups in the feminist movement during the 1960s and 1970s, women described their experiences of abortion, rape, job discrimination, and sexual exploitation. Thus they came to see their condition as shared and remediable. These kinds of reconstructions of the personal past tend to transform what seem to be individualistic failings or misfortunes into a shared experience of injustice (Turner, 1968).

Content of Conversions

The conversion experience itself is a very old phenomenon. But the content of the conversions change. As the structure of human society has changed over the course of history, so has the content of conversion experiences changed. It is now less mystified. We understand that conversion experiences are caused by changes in social conditions and personal experiences. In fact, we know how to alter immediate environments in such a way as to bring about change in meanings. But the changes brought about by these techniques often wear off when the individual has to continue living within the existing social structure. The rehabilitation of the addict or criminal through group therapy is meaningless if the individual is returned to the larger society with its poverty, street culture, discrimination, and brutalization. The peak experiences of people in therapy or in encounter groups are often not very compatible with the realities of day-to-day existence in capitalist America. Sometimes people who have been through these kinds of thought change create little insulated worlds for themselves where they can be shielded from the larger society—movements and sects, communes and retreats. In the Maoist revolution in China, on the other hand, the alterations of small environments and local systems of behavior were part of the revolution, of a complete change in social structures.

Fortunately, we can develop an understanding of the larger changes within which these individual and small-group experiences occur. We can understand the larger changes in the following way:

1. These changes are not reversible or cyclic. Change in human history is cumulative and unidirectional. We cannot play the movie of history backwards, nor can we retrace our steps and "take the other fork in the road."

2. Society changes in the sense that structures change. Structures are relationships between clusters of activities. Long-term change is not change in isolated institutions or in unrelated events or in single individuals. Rather, it is change in the total pattern of human activity. Conversions, attitude changes, and all other transformations of individual consciousness must be understood as small elements of these transformations of the total pattern.

3. As we shall see later, the fundamental structure is that set of relations that cluster around the activities that humans carry out to insure their physical survival and well-being—the mode of production. The mode of production determines the pattern of relationships between other kinds of activities.

In the next few chapters we shall present changes in individual consciousness as one phase in the process whereby humans make their own history, by their own choices, although these choices are always posed by circumstances not of their own choosing. The metaphors of human society contained in past comprehensive frameworks—the visions of reincarnations, divine cosmologies, messianic ages, second comings, and natural orders—can be replaced by a systematic understanding of the totality of change.

Individual Change and Mobilization for Social Action

So far we have talked about processes that occur within people—processes of change in personality and ideas. Unless this *intra*personal change leads to change in *inter*personal relationships, especially to change in organizations and institutions, it is incomplete or unconsummated. There are a number of wisecracks that capture the difference between internal change and change in actions. For instance, after World War II, some people in Europe claimed that although they had neither fled from the Nazis nor joined the resistance movements, they had experienced an "inner emigration" or an "inner resistance" —in other words, they had not accepted the Nazi frame of reference and had remained inwardly opposed to the Nazis. These phrases soon came to be used sarcastically, however; "inner emigration" and "inner resistance" really meant no opposition at all. A sign on the desk of a CIA official expressed a similar point of view: "Don't worry about their hearts and minds as long as you've got them by the balls." In other words, as long as any overt action can be crushed, the attitudes of the people don't matter to those in power.

My concern in this section, then, is how people who have undergone partial or extensive change in their frame of reference—"change in hearts and minds"—come to participate in action and even accept formal membership in a movement. I shall later explore this question from the point of view of organizations that want to recruit members or mobilize people for action; here I want to look at these issues from the point of view of the individual.

Participation in Movements

When do people join a movement? A partial answer is that they do so when they are encouraged by people they know. For most persons, the support of others is an important factor in their decision to join a movement or to act in other ways to alter the conditions of their lives. Very often this support is mutual. Some people undergo changes in beliefs but they remain isolated and uninvolved in action. Action for change implies disruption of routine. Most people will overtly disrupt routines after they have learned how to do so in a group setting and have some assurance of group support for such behavior.

A writer on mass strikes describes these preconditions of worker solidarity for the strikes. Note how these are possible in a society in which many workers are crowded together in a factory and much less likely where workers are separated from each other, as were craftsmen in the "putting-out" system or farmers on isolated homesteads.

The Mass Strike Process

If, as Rosa Luxemburg wrote, mass strikes form "a perpetually moving and changing sea of phenomena," how is it possible to make sense of them? What ties together the disparate local, national, and general strikes, occupations, street fights, armed confrontations, and other actions we have seen arise during these peak periods of social conflict?

Let us start by isolating three related processes: the challenge to existing authorities, the tendency of workers to begin taking over direction of their own activities, and their development of solidarity with each other.

These processes begin in the cell-unit of industrial production, the group of those who work together. As Elton Mayo discovered in his study of factories,

> In every department that continues to operate, the workers have— whether aware of it or not—formed themselves into a group with appropriate customs, duties, routines, even rituals; and management succeeds (or fails) in proportion as it is accepted without reservation by the group as authority and leader.

The development of these work groups was studied in 1946 by the Committee on Human Relations in Industry at the University of Chicago. In a number of factories in the Chicago area, they found that most work groups established a "quota" beyond which the group expects that no individual worker will produce. The new employee was systematically "indoctrinated" by the work group. The work group "expects him to conform to its system of social ethics." This system was backed by the workers' knowledge that management would use higher production by one of them to speed up everyone else. As one worker expressed it, "They begin by asking you to cut the other guy's throat, but what happens is that everybody's throat is cut, including your own." The workers worked intensively for a short time to meet the quota, then used the remaining free time as their own.

> Much of the time accumulated in this fashion was used "shooting the breeze" or reading newspapers in the toilet. The observers, however, believe . . . that the greater part was spent in "government work." Such work included making the "illegal" devices and fixtures which served as short-cuts in production, repairing parts damaged by men in other departments so that repair tickets might be avoided, and making equipment for their automobiles and homes. Most workers did not like to be idle for too great a time, but all preferred "government work" to production work.

The workers saw the cooperation and sociable relaxation created by such action as valuable in themselves. As one put it, "Sure, I think most of us would admit that we could double our take-home if we wanted to shoot the works, but where's the percentage? A guy has to get something out of life. Now my little lady would rather have me in a good humor than have the extra money. The way it works out none of us are going to be Van-Asterbilts so why not get a little pleasure out of living together and working together."

The work groups also created their own ways of getting the work done, contradicting those of management. The scheduling of work was often reorganized so that machine operators could eliminate extra time setting up the work. Each work group had special cutting tools, jigs, and fixtures, usually made on "government time," through which operations could be performed in a fraction of the time allowed for them. As the study concluded,

> Such restrictive (and, from management's point of view, illegal) devices make necessary a system of social controls imposing, upon the individual, responsibility to the group. Essentially what results is an informal secret organization . . . workers employ a social ethic which requires that each individual realize his own goals (social and pecuniary) through cooperation with the work group.

It is in these groups that the invisible, underlying process of the mass strike develops. They are communities within which workers come into opposition to the boss, begin acting on their own, and discover their need to support each other and the collective power they develop in doing so. The end product of this process is precisely the rejection of management as "authority and leader," and the transformation of the work group into what one industrial sociologist described as a guerrilla band at war with management.

Although the unofficial actions of these groups generally go unnoticed and unrecorded, we have been able to catch glimpses of them from the cooperative action of the railroad workers in each town in 1877 to the wildcat strikes and informal control of production by factory workers during World War II.

The large-scale struggles of periods of mass strike develop out of the daily invisible and unrecorded skirmishes of industrial life in normal times. Clayton Fountain, later a U.A.W. official, but at the time an auto worker so untouched by unionism he was still willing to cross picket lines, describes such a conflict at a Briggs auto plant in 1929, one of the quietest years for industrial conflict in American history:

> According to the theory of incentive pay, the harder and faster you worked, and the more cushions you turned out, the more pay you received. The employer, however, reserved the right to change the rules. We would start out with a new rate, arbitrarily set up by the company time-study man, and work like hell for a couple of weeks, boosting our pay a little each day. Then, bingo, the timekeeper would come along one morning and tell us that we had another new rate, a penny or two per cushion less than it had been the day before.
>
> One day when this happened we got sore and rebelled. After lunch the whistle blew and the line started up, but not a single worker on our conveyor lifted a hand. We all sat around on cushions waiting to see what would happen.
>
> In a few minutes the place was crawling with big-shots. They stormed and raved and threatened, but our gang stood pat. We just sat on the cushions and let them rant and blow. When they got too abusive, we talked back and told them to go to hell. We told them that the Briggs plant was run by a bunch of rats who did nothing but scheme how to sweat more

production out of workers and that we didn't care a damn how many of us they fired; we just weren't going to make any more cushions or backs at the new low rate.

We didn't belong to a union and we had no conception of organiza ˈ tion. There were no leaders chosen by us to deal with the angry bosses; we all pitched into the verbal free-for-all with no epithets barred. Some of the workers threatened to take the bosses outside and beat the hell out of them—in fact, they had a damn good notion to do it right then and there inside the plant.

Finally, after about forty-five minutes of confusion, the bosses relented. They agreed to reinstate the previous piecework rate. With this assurance, we went back to work. Looking back, I can see that, in a small and disorganized fashion, we tasted the power of the sitdown strike on that far-away day in the Briggs plant in 1929.

This miniature revolt and innumerable ones like it, unknown to all but those directly involved, form the submerged bulk of the iceberg of industrial conflict, of which the headline-making events of mass strikes are the visible tip. Because workers do not direct production, they find it is directed to their disadvantage—in a way that tries to hold down their income, extract more labor, and increase the power of the employers over them. Against this, as in the example above, workers are forced to fight back, thus discovering their own power.

Out of the day-to-day conflict in the workplace, the sense of exploitation revealed in inadequate wages, and the general resentment against subordination, develops the sentiment for a strike. As the Interchurch World Movement's *Report* on the 1919 steel strike put it,

> It cannot be too strongly emphasized that a strike does not consist of a plan and a call for a walkout. There has been many a call with no resultant walkout; there has been many a strike with no preceding plan or call at all. Strike conditions are conditions of mind.

Whether triggered by a relatively trivial incident or by a strike call, at some point in the accumulation of resentment workers quit work. Already this is a kind of revolt, as Alvin Gouldner put it, "a *refusal to obey* those socially prescribed as authorities in that situation, that is, management."   (Brecher, 1974:283–287)

Figure 1 diagrams this kind of mobilization for action.

Sometimes personal relations stand in the way of disruption of routine. We know that plantations with paternalistic local owners had fewer slave revolts than did the large, monoculture, absentee-owned plantations. Similarly, in Latin America and Southeast Asia, tenant farmers are less likely to participate in mass political movements than are plantation workers (Stinchcombe, 1961; Zeitlin, 1967). The plantation workers live in a setting where they develop personal relationships with each other, with people like themselves. The tenant farmers have relatively fewer contacts with each other and relatively more with the landowner or *patron;* these relationships are paternalistic.

Figure 1

Mass Strike Process

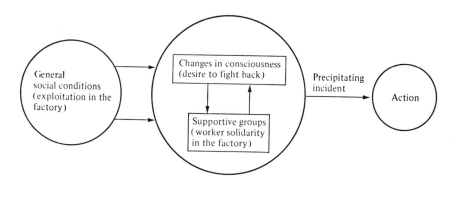

The patron knows his tenants personally. He is kind to them in a condescending way. He helps them out with small favors as long as they remain docile. In fact, the patron is interested primarily in collecting rents, and he has harsh sanctions to back up his power. Unlike factory workers or plantation laborers who can confront their boss in a body, the tenant farmer is geographically isolated from other tenants. The tenant is alone with the patron at precisely the moment of payment collection (or other crucial contact) at which he could refuse to accept the imposed routines.

Many modern urban workers—bank tellers, secretaries, salesmen, telephone technicians, hospital aides, policemen, teachers, and so on—are somewhere between the tenant farmer and the factory or plantation worker in terms of their isolation from one another on the job. Unlike rural workers, however, many modern urban workers do not have a common culture or a traditional place of residence. They live scattered throughout the city and suburbs, are recruited from many different ethnic groups and subcultures, spend relatively little time on the job, and are often geographically very mobile. So in some ways there is even less opportunity for workplace solidarity among them than among tenant farmers. Effective unionizing and workplace organizing of white-collar and service workers is only beginning. It seems to be happening faster in countries like Italy, where there is less cultural and ethnic diversity than in America.

Recruitment Tactics

Different recruitment tactics are related to general differences between movements. In some movements, individuals are attracted into a very tight *primary-group* structure. In a primary group, people know each other well, have strong personal attachment to each other, and come to interact with each other informally and as complete human beings. When a primary group is part of a movement, we can refer to it as a *cell.* In a cell-based movement, people will often be willing to make very large changes in their lives for each other. The costs of such disruption in routine and punishment by outside authorities are offset by the strength of primary-group ties. These primary-group processes can be seen among the early Christians, the Weathermen collectives, and the Pentecostal churches. Each of these groups faced great external hostility. Each had a very strong and distinct world view and strong group loyalty. Group strength was based on weakening of ties with outsiders, on emotional support of others, and on various rites or customs. The sacrament of the Eucharist bound cells of early Christians together. The Weathermen collectives used customs such as sharing clothing and randomly assigning sexual partners to strengthen group feeling and weaken individualistic tendencies. Some of this strong group solidarity appeared during sit-down strikes in the 1930s and in university sit-ins in the 1960s.

A different pattern of interpersonal processes in recruiting appears in movements that are based on social networks or social circles. Networks and circles are groupings of people who share interests and life-styles and who know each other or have acquaintances in common. Thus, for example, in many large American cities people who are in psychoanalysis form this sort of a circle or network; so do people who are involved in cross-country motorcycle racing or square dancing or socialist politics. Generally these networks are not consciously involved in change, although they may often contribute to life-style and attitude changes. But sometimes they transform themselves into pressure groups that actively push for reforms or other kinds of changes. Some movements for change may deliberately develop a network type of organization. People are brought into the movement through personal contact, but these contacts are more tenuous and less intense than the personal relationships involved in primary-group or cell-like movement structures.

Particularly weak forms of network-type movements are based on recruitment through mailing lists (where there is essentially no personal contact) or casual mobilization for participation in short-lived crowd behavior (like demonstrations rather than sit-down strikes). These mailing-list and ad hoc crowd behavior recruitment patterns contributed to the weakness of some recent American movements: for example, the Joe McCarthy "movement" in the early 1950s and some of the activities of the American Left in the 1960s. A movement to which people are recruited by network contacts is less dependent on strong personal ties than is a cell-type movement. It may be less able to count on its members making sacrifices for the movement; however, personal tensions are less likely to disrupt it.

The most important category of people that can be drawn into a movement are those groups that play a crucial role in the production of a society's goods and services. The unified action of these groups can change very fundamental aspects of the society. These groups (or classes) can alter the course of a society in a way that most interest groups cannot.

At this point we have really reached the limits of our analysis of change in personal behavior. By starting to talk about movements, we are really moving into a new topic, organizations. We have repeatedly seen that any analysis of change that looks only at how change affects individuals and at how individuals change is necessarily inadequate. An analysis of individuals and change necessarily has to look at processes outside of individuals—processes that take place in societies as a whole (the structural transformations I discussed earlier) and processes that involve organizations.

Changes in Change Processes

As I pointed out earlier, we must take into account changes in the nature of the change processes themselves. What are these changes?

1. A large number of people now want to involve themselves in change and have ceased to see themselves as only passive victims of change.
2. We have better concepts for comprehending change than in the past. That is, we have reached a more advanced state of consciousness, in which we can understand how social change occurs. These changes in consciousness are in turn related to three structural changes:

    a) There are now more people subjected to marginality, deroutinization, and experiences shared by large numbers of people crowded into the same environment as a result of the tremendous upheavals associated with modern capitalism. Capitalism has crowded people into cities and factories, brought together diverse ethnic groups, and created a world economy. It has destroyed isolated local ways of life and made huge populations interdependent and uprooted.

    b) Capitalism and its accompanying technologies (such as the media, transportation systems, and military and police power) and political institutions have greatly decreased the time lag between decisions and their effects, between the beginnings of a structural transformation and its impact on the population as a whole.

    c) Modern history has brought with it a special kind of discontinuity —the revolution—and this discontinuity in turn creates and reflects the more advanced consciousness, the knowledge and the desire to participate in making history.

There are also times in human history when more people take part in change, consciously as well as passively. In general, since the revolutions of the late eighteenth century in France and America, more people have aspired to become actors in historical change rather than merely acted upon. The ideas of citizenship, revolution, and the "rights of man" that emerged from the American and French revolutions indicate this growing desire to participate in the making of history. This participation becomes even more evident in the Russian and Chinese revolutions, in which for the first time the desire for the conscious planning of institutions is extended to the economy. The revolutions themselves are the fullest expression of this modern impulse to make history. Both spontaneously acting masses of people and organizations step forward to refuse to support old routines, to smash existing institutions, and to build new ones. As Lenin, the leading theoretician and practioner of the Russian Revolution, remarked:

> ... Revolutions are the locomotives of history, said Marx. Revolutions are festivals of the oppressed and the exploited. At no other time are the mass of the people in a position to come forward so actively as creators of a new social order, as at a time of revolution. At such times the people are capable of performing miracles, if judged by the limited, philistine yardstick of gradualist progress. But it is essential that leaders of the revolutionary parties, too, should advance their aims more comprehensively and boldly at such a time, so that their slogans shall always be in advance of the revolutionary initiative of the masses, serve as a beacon, reveal to them our democratic and socialist ideal in all its magnitude and splendour, and show them the shortest and most direct route to complete, absolute, and decisive victory (Lenin, 1962: 113).

In the past few people had coherent ideas about their society. They took most of its features for granted. They lived their everyday life in an unquestioning manner, with the assumption that their lives would be unchanging. They experienced change primarily in bits and pieces, with little or no understanding of how the whole of society has changed in the past or how it might change in the future. Thus when a major change hit them, they usually did not understand it. They acted out of what they believed to be necessity, whether that action was suicide, apathy, or revolt. They acted in accordance with the pressures in their immediate environment that were generated by the collapse of the old structure. Most people were cornered in their local time and space. They could not see the source of the events that affected them. The time lag between the events that accompany a structural transformation and the impact of these events on most individuals was fairly long and contributed to mass ignorance of what was happening. Now more people are beginning to think about the direction of change. It is no longer only intellectuals and politically active elites who think about the society as a whole. Millions of ordinary people are trying to comprehend historical processes.

Even more important, our understanding of change is itself becoming clearer, better, less mystified. In every society, in every age, some people have tried to understand change. But these understandings have tended to be mystified. Changes in human behavior have been attributed to the mysterious workings of supernatural forces. For instance, in medieval society, the rigid lines between nobles and serfs were explained as a manifestation of divine will. In Hindu society, the caste system was explained as part of the supernatural order of the universe.

Another way of mystifying society was to assert that the present order of society was stable, unchanging, and "natural." Thus, for example, in early nineteenth-century capitalism, free enterprise was believed to be the "natural" form of an economy. All these beliefs covered the way the society really worked. These mystified ways of understanding society were not simply deliberate self-serving fabrications of the ruling classes and intellectual elites of those periods but were reflections of their experience of the structure of their societies. We now have the conceptual tools for a better understanding of historical processes. In other words, although the processes within the individual that I described are recurrent in the sense that many people in different times and places have gone through them, the causes and consequences of their occurrence are different each time and have changed in an irreversible way over the course of history.

We now have two major tasks before us. One is to get a better understanding of organizations, since these are important actors in the structural transformations. Deroutinization means deroutinizations in organizational as well as individual habits. Organizations manage and promote conversion experiences; in turn, some converts become leading figures in creating new organizations. Mobilization for action is usually mobilization by an organization that defines the terms and goals of the action. So to understand change, we must look beyond the individual to the level of organizations. The second part of this book will address itself to this question.

Finally, we shall have to look at the structural transformations themselves, at the course of history. A look at history is the task of Part Three. In that section, I shall no longer look at structural transformation from the point of view of the individual trapped in change—the worm's-eye view of the world —but shall try to present concepts that will give an eagle's view of the entire landscape of structural change.

References

Berger, Peter L., and Thomas Luckmann.
  1966   The Social Construction of Reality. Garden City, N.Y.: Doubleday.
Brecher, Jeremy.
  1974   Strike. New York: Fawcett World Library.
Kanter, Rosabeth M.
  1972   Commitment and Community. Cambridge, Mass.: Harvard University Press.

Lasswell, Harold D., and Daniel Lerner (eds.)
  1965   World Revolutionary Elites. Boston: MIT Press.

Lenin, V. I.
  1962   Collected Works. Moscow: Foreign Languages Publishing House.

Marcuse, Herbert.
  1955   Eros and Civilization. Boston: Beacon Press.

Robinson, Paul.
  1969   The Freudian Left. New York: Harper and Row.

Stinchcombe, Arthur L.
  1961   "Agricultural enterprise and rural class relations." American Journal of Sociology
          67:165–176.

Turner, R.
  1968   Unpublished paper. Los Angeles: UCLA.

Zeitlin, Maurice.
  1967   Revolutionary Politics and the Cuban Working Class. Princeton, N.J.: Princeton Uni-
          versity Press.

Chapter
4

Methods of Studying Change in Individuals

In this chapter, I am going to discuss how change can be studied at the level of the individual. I shall identify some commonly used methods and indicate sources for further reading.

STUDYING PEOPLE as though they were unchanging is much easier than studying change. Asking people to "freeze" for a snapshot is easier than making a home movie. But we know that the frozen gestures and pasted-on grins of the people in the family album are not what they are really like. The photograph is not a good representation of reality. Even though the work of some photographers may be very beautiful and technically perfect, it is too static to capture the feelings of motion and change that we all experience. In the same way, many techniques of social researchers are very polished and refined but are not particularly good for studying change. In the next few pages, I shall suggest how some of these techniques can be adapted to studying change.

The Survey

A survey is a technique for obtaining information by asking individuals (usually referred to as subjects) a number of questions either in a personal interview or through a written questionnaire. The questions are planned in advance by the researcher, and there is relatively little leeway in posing or answering them once the questions are decided upon.

Let us look in more detail at the use of surveys to study change. In order to see change (or lack of change) in individuals' opinions or reported behavior, we need to *compare* data collected at two or more points in time. If we collect such data only once, we either cannot reach any conclusions about change or we have to compare it with some other type of data collected at another time.

The Panel Study.   A series of at least two surveys designed to study changes occurring between survey times is called a *panel.* In panel studies, the same individuals are included in the two surveys. This type of arrangement is necessary if the researcher wants to study the processes of change in a person's life. For example, in the mid-1960s, a colleague of mine conducted a survey of high school students in an industrial suburb of Chicago, placing special emphasis on the students' plans and goals. In the early 1970s, she contacted the *same* sample to see if they had realized their goals and how their new situation affected their view of themselves and their relationships with their families and high school peers. This kind of panel study is an excellent way of observing what happened to an individual's feelings, plans, and reported behavior over a period of time. The disadvantage is that the researcher must wait the entire elapsed time to complete the survey, so these studies take a long time. Furthermore, tracking down the individuals for the second interview may be very difficult and costly.

Repeated Cross-Section Survey.   A less difficult (and also less information-producing) survey design is the repeated cross-section. In this design the researcher repeatedly samples a specified population without aiming to include precisely the same individuals. For example, my colleague could have conducted a survey among East Chicago high school seniors in 1965 and then, in 1972, conducted a survey of a sample of East Chicago young adults who had graduated from the high school in 1965, without insisting on questioning the same individuals. This study would have told us something about aggregate patterns of change; for example, we could find out how many people actually finished college compared with the number who planned to. But it would tell us little about how given individuals had experienced these changes. Furthermore, while contacting the second sample would be much cheaper and easier than tracking down specific individuals, such a survey would really produce misleading results. For instance, we would miss all those people who had moved out of East Chicago, and those might be precisely the ones undergoing the greatest kinds of change. In other words, this kind of study is useful only if not too many people "drop out" of the sampled population between the surveys.

One-Shot Survey.   Least satisfying of the ways to study change by survey methods is the one-shot survey in which past opinions or behavior are reconstructed through the subjects' answers. For instance, in several child-rearing studies, mothers of four or five year olds were asked how they had toilet trained or weaned the child. Their answers were affected by forgetfulness and changes in their opinions. But the researcher had no way of distinguishing correctly reported behavior from incorrectly reported behavior.

Studying Cause and Effect.   Survey research presents special problems when it is designed to study change in terms of cause and effect. Often we would like to understand change in terms of the effects of some factors (the *independent variables*) on other phenomena (the *dependent variables*). A well-designed panel study allows us to draw conclusions about causality. In order to reach these conclusions, a study should have the following design: (1) there should be two groups, initially similar (for instance, both selected by random sampling from the same population); (2) one group only is exposed to the possibly causal factor; (3) the groups are then compared with the expectation that the one exposed to the factor ("the cause") will be in some way different from the other group.

It is difficult and often unethical to establish an experimental situation of this sort for studying human beings. We can sometimes approximate the situation, however. For instance, there is a well-known study of how the political and economic attitudes of young women changed as a result of their attendance at Bennington College (Newcomb, 1943). The women's similar political attitudes was the dependent variable in this study, while the four years at Bennington was the independent variable. As a control, data was also gathered from students of similar background who attended Williams College and Skidmore College. According to Newcomb's findings, more of the women at Bennington developed liberal and radical political and economic views than did the students from the other two institutions. Therefore, we can conclude that something about the Bennington experience caused the attitude change.

The reader will probably already have noticed some ways in which the Bennington study is not as conclusive as a laboratory experiment. For one thing, Newcomb did compare Bennington women with students of similar background who attended other colleges, but he did not control the process of college choice. Women who chose to attend Bennington might already have been quite different from their peers, even though superficially similar in their initial political attitudes. The Bennington experience could thus have merely "brought out" differences of much earlier standing and not really changed anyone. Newcomb's main evidence on this point was the finding that the longer a woman was at Bennington (measured by college class), the more liberal and informed she was. The gradual and cumulative nature of the change suggests (but of course does not prove) that the institution caused the change rather than merely triggering a characteristic of the women themselves that had already been at work in their decision to go to Bennington.

Use of a Control Group.   The question of whether an institutional arrangement—the army, a reform school, a college, a college course, a social welfare
agency—really *changes* individuals has perennially concerned groups in
charge of such arrangements. The best way to answer this question is through
a panel study with a control group. Two otherwise indistinguishable groups
are exposed to different situations and then compared again, with the expectation that those exposed to the program will have changed more than or in ways
different from the group that is not exposed. The Bennington study approxi-
mates this design but falls short because we cannot be sure that the two groups
were really similar initially. Any study in which the two groups were established by volunteering or some other form of self-selection is subject to question. For example, if college seniors in the liberal arts had different political
attitudes than seniors in commerce, it would be misleading to conclude that
the difference in curriculums produced the difference in attitudes. More likely,
students who chose liberal arts rather than commerce were different in the first
place.

To establish the initial similarity or difference, we need a panel design:
we have to see what the groups were like at the beginning as well as the end
to see if change took place during the intervening period. We have to have
random assignment to the two groups. These research-design problems plague
not only studies of program impact but also studies of migration. We know
that urbanization and migration are very important causes and consequences
of social change, particularly of the kind of aggregated individual change that
we have been discussing in this part. But generalizations about these processes
are constrained by the fact that we are not sure whether migrants (to a city,
a region, or another country) are a highly self-selected group. They are certainly self-selected in some ways, but we don't know with respect to exactly
what characteristics. Intelligence, aggressiveness, marginality, mental instability, class status in the initial setting, and so on are possible candidates.

Age and Generational Factors.   Another problem to which we need to be
sensitive in survey studies of change is the difference between age factors and
historical-generational factors. For example, a survey study may report that
older people are more disapproving of premarital sexual relations than are
younger persons. Is that because they are *older* (at a different stage in the
biological life cycle) or because they have undergone different sets of historical
experiences? To answer this question, we would need to conduct panel studies
to see if within succeeding generations these attitudes changed with age.

Some Reservations about Survey Studies

In general, survey studies of change can be very useful subject to two
reservations:

1. The surveys that tell us the most about change are those with the following design: the panel study (*a*) involves at least two groups (a control group and a group exposed to a possible causal factor); (*b*) includes a before *and* after survey; and (*c*) retests the same individuals. All other research designs are in some way less satisfactory either in studying causality or in getting some insight into change processes. Considerations of time, money, special problems and concerns, and so on may dictate only partial fulfillment of these criteria. But as a reader (and as a researcher), you should be aware of possible shortcomings.

2. Surveys are useful for examining individual changes, especially changes in *aggregates* of individuals. They are relatively less useful for studying changes in social structure and in the frames of reference embedded in language. Survey studies tend to tell us little about how clites initiate change, although we may learn how such changes affect masses. Surveys are not particularly useful for studying organizational change or the historical structural transformations. They are useful for looking at some life-style changes and changes in beliefs and attitudes. They are not very useful for looking at largely unconscious processes.

Collection and Analysis of Documents

Another way to study change in individuals and groups is to look at material that they have produced in their own frame of reference. I've already pointed out how, in a survey, considerations of quantity and comparability swamp the opportunity to let the respondents "speak for themselves." Even if the questions call for open-ended answers, the very fact of asking the question focuses the respondents' attention on issues that they might not normally care about. But groups and individuals also produce material that they select and organize as they see fit. Such material gives the researcher insight into what was on the minds of the people who produced it—how they perceived their own experiences and how they felt about them. Anthropologists, social psychologists and, above all, historians routinely use these materials. Sociologists need to learn from these disciplines.

All these materials have certain features in common. The categories or concepts that are used to organize the material tend to be the subjects' and not the researchers'. Thus the materials have a richness and liveliness to them that make them more interesting than questionnaire responses in many ways. However, they also create serious problems in coding and quantifying the data. For instance, the researcher often has no control or only very limited control over the selection of respondents. Although these characteristics are shared to some degree by all documentary materials, I find it useful to discuss life histories separately from other documents.

Life History

A life history is an individual's autobiography. From it we can learn about all the kinds of change discussed in this book. It is an excellent source of information about the impact of historical transformations on individuals. Historians and anthropologists have relied on the life history as a mainstay of their craft. The life history is an excellent way of giving a voice to people living in times or cultures far distant from our own.

Some life histories are spontaneously produced—they are then more like memoirs, reminiscences, diaries, literary autobiographies, or "confessions" of the kind written by St. Augustine or the French philosopher Rousseau. In some cultures, old people like to produce such documents in oral or written form. People who have had an exciting life and are fortunate enough to enjoy a leisurely, comfortable old age may be particularly likely to spontaneously create such material. But life histories can also be elicited by the student of human behavior. The advantage of the elicited life history is that the researcher can select a "typical" or reticent member of a group and avoid learning only about outgoing, talkative people. Elicitation minimizes but does not eliminate the problems of self-selection and poor sampling that plague the collection of life histories.

Life histories are fairly difficult to collect and analyze. You must draw your respondents into your project. They must understand the importance of revealing to others what their lives were like and what their experiences meant to them. The great life histories in anthropology were often collected over a long period of time, in a relationship of close cooperation and growing friendship. In my opinion, they should always be published under joint authorship and not under the name of the collector alone (as, unfortunately, is generally the case) because they really represent the work of the respondent more than that of the researcher. A good collector can, however, contribute to the quality of the life history by directing its course with questions and by editing it to remove repetitions, as well as by analyzing it.

Analysis also presents problems. In its original form, the material, while very rich, may be bulky and repetitive. The life history probably must be edited and shortened to make it more readable. Some researchers code the material into categories, themes, or frequent word choices; or they perform some other form of content analysis on it. This procedure makes the data easier to analyze and summarize, but it may destroy some of the value of the document—its richness of detail, its revealing use of language, and its presentation of a unique human being's experiences. Analysis focuses around concepts such as child-rearing customs and psychosexual development, language and meanings, past historical conditions and the impact of culture change, and individual idiosyncrasy and the operation of chance in the course of the people's lives.

Other Documents

Other kinds of documents also provide insights into the understandings that individuals have. In some societies, these documents are created by people working in special institutions geared to creating and distributing beliefs and meanings. In our society, for instance, these institutions include television and radio broadcasting, newspapers and magazines, book publishing, advertising, public relations and speech-writing, the visual arts, and the recording industry. In the United States, a relatively few people produce and package beliefs and meanings for the majority of the people. Through the use of modern technology—electronic media, recordings, printing, and so on—a product is made that is sold for a profit to millions of consumers. In the past, priests and scribes had a similar role in producing and distributing beliefs and meanings to the mass of the people.

Alongside these experts and their institutions, there may exist a more "spontaneous" production of documents—personal letters, diaries, graffiti, children's rhymes, and singing or painting for personal enjoyment. In small simple societies without class distinctions, there is no difference between the "official" culture and the folk culture, as there is in class societies. Both types of documents can be analyzed for insights into how the beliefs and shared meanings of a society have changed. Collections of songs, political speeches, children's rhymes, diaries and letters, films or media broadcasts, newspapers, and so on can be used to see how tastes, values, beliefs, and "official" as well as "folk" culture have changed.

The most serious problem in using such materials to study change is that we often do not have adequate information about the conditions under which the materials were produced or about the impact they had on the consumers. It is clear, for instance, that the changing themes of American movies since the 1930s reflect changes in American society. But the catch is in the word *reflect*. As long as we focus only on the style and contents of the films themselves and not on the organizations that produced them or the mass of individuals who consumed them, we will have difficulty in understanding why and how the changing movies reflect the changing society. Nevertheless, they are an important indicator of how beliefs and shared meanings are established or altered. Sometimes such documents may be the only clues we have to social change in a past society. All these documentary data free the researcher from the prison of the present. Through them the past can be reentered; hence their inherent importance to the study of social change.

Observational Techniques

Close, direct, prolonged contact with a group is an excellent way to find out about the group and to study changes in it. Observation can range from pure observation with virtually no interaction (as when a group is observed from behind a one-way window in a laboratory) to participant-observation, in which the observer becomes a member of the group. Among the advantages of observational techniques are:

1. The chance to observe actual behavior rather than rely on a verbal report about it
2. The chance to observe interactions over time
3. The chance to observe ongoing *processes*
4. The chance to develop an understanding of the group's own meanings (an advantage that observational techniques share with the use of documentary data, and which sets both off from surveys)

Each of these advantages makes observation and participant-observation a very powerful method for studying change.

The most serious objection to participant-observation is that it has a severely limited time span. While the process of change can be observed over time by observational techniques, the time spans involved are usually weeks or months. Since many processes of change take years and even decades to unfold, observational techniques cannot capture their full extent. Observational techniques trap the observer in the present. While such techniques are excellent for observing interactions over short periods of time, they are necessarily confined to microprocesses currently occurring. The "micro" nature of observation-participation makes it useful for seeing how a structural transformation has an impact on individuals or small groups, but we cannot use it very easily to understand these transformations in terms of world history. In other words, a danger in participant-observation is that it draws the researcher into the same constricted time perspective that most people are unfortunately trapped in.

Reference

Newcomb, Theodore M.
  1943 Personality and Social Change. New York: Dryden Press.

Part Two

ORGANIZATIONS AND CHANGE

Change cannot be understood by studying only individuals. Individuals change in response to changing social conditions, and the causes of these changes lie outside the individual. Individuals are not necessarily completely passive in the process of change. However, insofar as they direct its course, they usually do so as members of a group, possibly of the special kind of group called an organization. In this part, therefore, we shall broaden our scope from the individual to the group level.

Chapter 5

The Nature of Organizations

In this chapter, I shall introduce the concept of an organization, a special kind of group with goals and structure. I shall also define a number of terms that help us to understand organizations.

WHEN YOU WERE A CHILD, you may have belonged to a club of some kind. I am not referring to the rather stuffy and dull clubs that the school offered but to the clubs that you created with your friends. Since you had very little choice about the membership and behavior of your family or school, the peer group, club, or gang that you belonged to was probably the first group that you could help to create. Some of your peer groups were very casual and unplanned. Sooner or later, however, you probably decided to give yourselves a name, to find a clubhouse, to select leaders, and so on. You may have decided to keep some people out, and you may have set up initiation rites or entrance tests. At that point, you had transformed a casual peer group into a grouping that had most of the characteristics of an organization.

What Is an Organization?

Let me state the defining features of an organization more formally:

1. An organization is a group. In other words, when I use the word *organization,* I am referring to a collection of *people* who behave in certain ways. An organization may also own land or machinery or other material objects, but these are not part of the organization in the same way that the human beings are.

2. An organization has an internal patterning of behavior. The people who are in the organization act toward each other in certain ways that are

79

relatively recurrent and fixed. People in the organization expect each other to behave in these ways and to continue that behavior over a period of time. The patterning of behavior *may* include differences in power: some people may be able to get others to do what they want, but not vice versa. But differences in power are not a necessary feature of organizations.

3. An organization has an identifiable boundary. Some people are in it and other people are not. Related to this characteristic is the characteristic that people recognize the organization as such. There are some exceptions to this —clandestine organizations take care to remain unrecognized—but generally the organization is thought of as an entity.

4. Finally, most organizations have a set of goals or a purpose. At one time people came together to build the organization in order to accomplish some aims that they could not have accomplished otherwise. Sometimes the initial goal is lost or replaced by other purposes.

Applying the Criteria

Let's see what happens if we apply these defining characteristics to some groupings in American society. Certain groupings that we can think of are very clearly organizations.

Business Firms.   Businesses obviously are organizations. They are groups of people (along with capital; capital goods such as machinery, office space; and so on). The group members are arranged in relatively permanent patterns. In other words, there are identifiable tasks and positions that can be filled by different people—for instance, there may be owners, managers, an office staff, production workers, and so on. The firm has identifiable boundaries: owners, managers, and workers are *in* the organization; clients have contacts with the organization across this boundary but don't really belong to it. A firm has at least one clear purpose, namely, to make a profit for its shareholders. Usually this purpose is accomplished by fulfilling a secondary purpose, namely, to make goods or to sell services.

Social Movements.   A second type of grouping is also very clearly an organization. This type consists of groupings that are formally constituted parts of a social movement. We will refer to them as social movement organizations. For instance, in the 1960s, there was a clearly visible civil rights movement, which consisted of many people feeling and acting in certain ways—against segregation and discrimination. Some of the people who felt and acted for the goals of integration and widened opportunities for black people joined specific groups that had names and recognized leaders. CORE (Congress of Racial Equality), SNCC (Student Nonviolent Coordinating Committee), and SCLC (Southern Christian Leadership Conference) were social movement organizations within the civil rights movement. They had goals (integration, an end to discrimination). They had boundaries in the sense that some people were members and some were not. They had an internal structure or patterning of relationships, that is, they had leaders and decision-makers who coordinated their activities nationally and regionally as well as locally.

A large number of people participated in civil rights activity without belonging to the movement organizations. They did so as members of churches or as unaffiliated individuals. Similarly, the antiwar movement contained only a limited number of movement organizations—Student Mobilization Committee, the Draft Resistance, Clergy and Laity Concerned, the Eugene McCarthy campaign organization, and so on. Even more than the civil rights movement, the antiwar movement was built on unaffiliated, spontaneously acting individuals and local informal groups rather than on formal organizations.

Voluntary Associations.   A third kind of organization that, as a rule, fairly clearly meets the defining characteristics is the voluntary association. Voluntary associations are groupings whose members come together to accomplish some purpose of their own choosing, including conviviality. Membership in a voluntary association is not automatically assigned at birth but is deliberately decided upon. Nor is membership in a voluntary association necessitated by the need to make a living, as is becoming an employee. The Rotarians, the local PTA, and the Sexual Freedom League are all examples of voluntary associations. The social movement organization is really a special type of voluntary association, one that is particularly purposeful and particularly concerned with institutional arrangements, either to preserve them or, most commonly, to change them.

An interesting and especially important type of association is the occupational organization. There are many different kinds of occupational organizations: unions, which are intimately tied to the job and directly control entry into the occupation; powerful groups like the American Medical Association, National Association of Manufacturers, and the American Psychological Association, which indirectly affect entry of individuals into occupations and also act as lobbying bodies; and politically weaker groups like the American Mathematical Association, which act more as a forum for the exchange of ideas. The most powerful of these groups can bring strong sanctions to bear on members, nonmembers within the occupation, employers, and government agencies. In many ways, they are not *voluntary* associations at all because membership is necessary, or at least advantageous, for entry into the occupation. The less powerful groups have no sanctions available and basically only provide a framework for intellectual and sociable meetings.

Government Agencies.   A fourth type of organization is the government agency. Government agencies perform the task of managing the society as a whole. From the point of view of the individual employee, such agencies are not unlike business firms. Working as a secretary or an accountant or a statistician for a government agency is not much different from working at such a job for a profit-making firm. In societies with separate private and public sectors, the purposes of government agencies are different from the purposes of business firms. Business firms are supposed to make profits; government agencies are supposed to attend to tasks that are necessary to maintain the society in its present form. The agencies and other organizations that are part of the government are one of the components of the state, the single overriding managing apparatus for the whole society. The Internal Revenue Service, the Department of Defense, local public schools, metropolitan transit authorities, and state universities are all examples of government agencies in the United States.

This description of four types of organizations represents only a small sampling of all the possible kinds. It is neither an exhaustive nor a mutually exclusive typology of organizations. Some extremely powerful organizations, such as the Roman Catholic Church, do not fit neatly into any of the categories. Others may fall into more than one category. Actually, these categories really only make sense in a modern capitalist society. They do not apply to other types of societies. The purpose of this listing was only to give the reader some examples of organizations.

Some Empirical Questions

By now the reader should be aware of the problems of classifying organizations into typologies. Such typologies may be useful for getting an overview of the many different kinds of organizations that exist. However, like all typologies for social phenomena, they gloss over important empirical questions. These questions require historical and comparative data that a typology can only point to, but never adequately incorporate. For instance, we need to ask what kinds of societies actually include organizations at all? In some hunting and gathering societies, the only organization that exists is the extended family or clan. It has many characteristics of an organization, but most social scientists distinguish the family from organizations whose members are not related by kinship ties. There are other societies in which all adult males belong to a decision-making group, a "club" that meets regularly in the men's house. Is this sort of patterning of relationships an organization? Some tribal societies have multiple men's groups (and sometimes also women's groups) that at least partially cut across kinship lines and in which membership is at least partially voluntary; such are the "secret societies" of a number of North American Indian groups and some African tribes. These secret societies appear to be more like our concept of organizations than are clans or other groupings in otherwise undifferentiated societies.

Relationship to State. Another historical and comparative question that we need to ask is, What is the relationship of a society's organizations to the state? In some societies, most organizations may be formally outside the government. For instance, in the United States, business firms are linked to the government in many ways, but they are not formally part of it. Similarly, voluntary associations such as social groups, churches, local citizens groups, and professional organizations are not part of the government. In other societies, both economic enterprises and "voluntary associations" are very directly a part of the state. They are created by and responsible to the government or a political party in charge of the government. In the Soviet Union, for example, we can still distinguish economic enterprises that make goods from agencies that provide services, and both of those from associations that mobilize people for general activity for the state (like youth groups). A good many of the distinctions used in typologies of organizations are blurred, however, because all these organizations are created by and are a part of the state. In fascist states like Nazi Germany and Fascist Italy, private profit-making enterprises are distinct from the public sector, but "voluntary associations" are transformed into state-created organizations like the Hitler Youth or the powerless workmen's associations.

The maximum distinction between state organizations and the rest of society—the "civil society" of private firms and voluntary associations—was probably attained in nineteenth-century England and America. There the state pursued a laissez-faire policy, a policy of not intervening in capitalist development. The state protected private property and contracts, put down labor unrest, and provided armed forces, roads, ports, canals, and so on. But the state did not intervene greatly in the internal decision-making of business, nor did it sponsor voluntary associations on its own. The belief that there is and should be a large sector of civil society persists in modern America. It is built into our use of the word *government,* which implies a relatively *limited* and *clearly defined* set of organizations for managing the society. In other societies, instead of *government,* people are more likely to use the word *state,* with all that word's connotations of wide scope, penetration into civil society, and great power. Our continued use of the concept of government has to some extent blinded us to the recent interpenetration of government organizations and the organizations of the civil society in our country.

International Organizations. So far our empirical problems with the concept of organization have centered on the blurring between different types of organizations *within* a society. We will also have to be cognizant of the existence of organizations that span several societies. The Roman Catholic church has been an excellent example of such an organization for many centuries. We are now seeing an increasing number of such organizations in the form of multinational corporations, large profit-making firms that have divisions or subsidiaries in many different countries. ITT, Unilever, Aramco, General Motors, and IBM are examples of such gigantic entities. Most of them are owned primarily by citizens of the advanced industrial capitalist countries; but, at the time of this writing, the oil-rich Arab nations are beginning to produce investors of their own. In some sense, the multinationals are only a special form of the private profit-making firm that I discussed earlier as a common type of organization. However, their existence in different nations means that special new relationships between corporations and states are developing.

Political Parties.   Another particularly interesting and powerful form of organization is the political party. Political parties form a kind of bridge between voluntary associations, which they often resemble in their local internal patterning, and the state, which they sometimes use as the vehicle for maintaining their power.

In considering the Roman Catholic church, the multinational corporations, and the political parties of modern states, we have come a long way from your neighborhood gang. Yet all have an internal patterning of behavior, definable boundaries, and some sense of purpose or shared goals. In the next section, I shall introduce some more concepts that will be useful in discussing organizations and change.

Organizational Patterns

In this section, I shall introduce concepts that will be useful for discussing organizations, define each one, and give some illustrations for it.

Structure

Structure is the patterning of social relationships that we referred to earlier. The simplest way of thinking about structure in an organization is to look at the organizational chart. It will show you who can give orders or information to whom, who directs or supervises whose work, and so on. The chart will tell you what the *formal* structure is like. The informal structure may be quite different. While in the formal structure the lieutenant gives orders to the sergeants, informally, in reality, the sergeants do what they please. Structure does not always mean differences in power. For example, you could draw your family tree, which is a picture of a structure. But in a family tree, the relationships are ones of sexual union and parenthood, not primarily of power. In discussing organizations, however, we are often interested in power relationships.

The word *structure* implies some degree of stability or recurrence in the relationships. If a structure exists, we can more or less predict what the relationships will be like at a later date if we know what they are like now. Structure also implies that people's behavior is shaped in ways that have relatively little to do with their personality. In other words, as long as they are "in the structure," they act on the basis of the patterned behavior that is expected of them; they carry out roles. Thus, the assumption is that whether Robert McNamara or Donald Rumsfeld or you are secretary of defense, the requirements of the job tend to overwhelm the personal characteristics of the incumbent.

Some people prefer not to think about structure at all but to picture human relationships as being in constant flux, with the patterns created anew every time people interact with each other. From this point of view, structure has no real existence. It exists only insofar as people agree to behave toward each other in a certain way and to continue to behave in this way whenever they are in contact with each other. The agreement can be imposed by physical force or material incentives as well as by shared beliefs and values. In some sense, to view structure as nothing more than the repetition of certain patterns of behavior in interactions is less of an abstraction than to think of structure as the stable patternings of relationships. However, the concept of structure provides us with a shorthand way of talking about all the interactions at once. Without the concept of structure, it would be extremely cumbersome to detail all the different kinds of interaction that take place. Also, the concept of structure draws attention to the tendency for these interactions to be repeated again and again.

Structure does not necessarily mean rigidity or *formal* patterning. For instance, the so-called unstructured classroom may actually have a very rich and complicated patterning of behavior. It may, in fact, be more structured than the conventional "structured" classroom in which all the children are in an undifferentiated subordinate relationship to the teacher and are discouraged from working with each other. The stability and recurrence of the patterning of relationships in a structure make the concept somewhat difficult to use for talking about change. We will explore this problem further below.

Power

I've already remarked on the fact that very often in organizations the relationships involve a difference in power. I did not give a formal definition of this word, but I used it to mean the ability to make decisions or the ability to give commands. One sociologist has defined power as the ability to accomplish one's goals regardless of opposition (Weber, 1947:153).

Differences in power can have many sources. In very simple tribal societies or among children, strength, intelligence, and verbal ability confer power. Stronger persons can make the weak obey; the quick thinkers and fast talkers can force their aims on others in the group. In primitive societies, a leader's strength and wit must contribute to the group's survival in order for that person to remain a leader; the struggle for survival under harsh conditions provides a quick test of a would-be leader's competence.

In larger societies in which control of resources is differentiated, power is not usually in the hands of the most able. Rather power is located in particular structural positions. People attain these positions through a combination of luck, birth, and the right personality characteristics for succeeding in organizations. A very incompetent or inappropriate power holder can be forced to resign—as happened in the case of Richard Nixon, for example. But the tests of leadership tend to be less severe and less frequent in complex organizations than among children or savages. Furthermore, those who hold power through their position in a structure tend also to have access to an apparatus of enforcers that keeps them in power.

There are a number of mechanisms by which power holders stay in power. One of them is sheer physical force. For instance, the Roman emperors of the last centuries of the empire stayed in power only as long as they had the support of their guards; the elite cadres of the armed forces could make or break the emperor. Material incentives are also an important mechanism for staying in power; the president of General Motors stays in office only if he can continue to provide large stockholders with reasonable dividends. The Chicago ward boss must continue to do favors for his constituents and deliver votes to the political machine.

At this point we need to distinguish the stability of the individual in a position of power from the stability of the position itself. In many cases, incumbents come and go but the office continues to be a position of power. There are limits to the extent to which an office outlasts its incumbents. A very incompetent president can weaken the presidency vis-à-vis Congress. A series of emperors who are only creatures of the guard will tend to cause a shift of effective decision-making to some more stable and reliable branch of the state, provided the haphazard imperial succession does not weaken the state altogether.

Often when an office outlasts its incumbents, it is backed up not only by force or material incentives but also by legitimacy. Essentially, legitimacy means that the exercise of power is seen as right or moral by those over whom it is exercised. This special kind of power—legitimate power—is known as authority. Legitimacy is the lubricant that oils the machinery of power, so that every decision does not have to be backed up by a beating or a payoff. Legitimacy and authority convert the reward/punishment currency from the hard cash of beatings and payoffs into the soft money of internal constraints and the search for approval. Concentration camps, prisons, and penal colonies are run on the currency of beatings, torture, food and cigarette bartering, and sexual payoffs. However, most societies most of the time use not only better material rewards but also large amounts of consensus and a sense of legitimacy. Many people in most societies accept the legitimacy of the structures in which they have little power. They accept authority.

Hierarchy

A hierarchy is a structure in which there are at least two levels of power (and usually more). This diagram represents the simplest possible hierarchy:

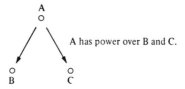

A has power over B and C.

Hierarchy usually also implies that there are more people with less power at each level. Hierarchies thus tend to have a pyramidal shape. (So, for instance, a slave with two masters, while clearly in a situation of unequally distributed power, would generally not be considered to be in a hierarchy.)

We often think of organizations as having a hierarchical structure. This is frequently, but by no means universally, the case. For instance, the Protestant Pentecostal movement is not organized as a hierarchy at all, but as a headless multisegment structure like this:

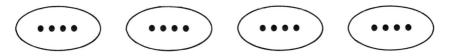

These segments are to some degree linked by a coordinating body, but the coordinators have virtually no power over the local branches (Gerlach & Hines, 1973: 233). Other Protestant denominations also have nonhierarchical structures in which there is more power in the local bodies than in the national coordinating body. This nonhierarchical structure also appeared to some extent in social movement organizations of the early and mid-1960s, such as SNCC and SDS (Students for a Democratic Society).

On the other hand, most business firms and government agencies *do* have hierarchical structures. Power flows from the top down. At each level there are more employees with less power. It is important, however, *not* to confuse hierarchy with structure or organization. Many people who think of themselves as antistructure or antiorganization are really antihierarchy. They are not objecting to a stable pattern of relationships or to some kind of recurrent way of making decisions in a group; they just don't want it to be from the top down in pyramidal fashion.

Bureaucracy

A bureaucracy is a special kind of organization. In addition to having the general features of an organization—structure, boundaries, and purposes—a bureaucracy has the following features:

1. It is a hierarchy. Power flows from the top down. At each level, superordinates can give commands to subordinates but not vice versa. Information can flow in both directions.
2. The behavior of its members is governed by rules that persist regardless of the incumbent in the position. Thus, a bureaucracy can last long beyond the lifetime of any one of its members. Such has certainly been the case with the Roman Catholic church. The word *bureaucracy* is derived from the word *bureau,* meaning office. In other words, power is vested in the office, not in particular individuals. Written rules and records ensure routinization.
3. Officeholders tend to be selected by appointment based on their meeting formal, universally known requirements. If people are elected to offices, or are appointed to them on the basis of payoffs and political favors, or are selected according to "who they know," the organization is not a bureaucracy in the strict sense. Officeholders are full-time workers (Weber, 1958: 196–198).

Figure 2 may help clarify the relationships between these different types of groupings. Following are some examples of each type.

Figure 2

Relationships Between Different Types of Groupings

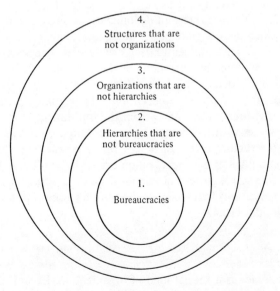

4.
Structures that are
not organizations

3.
Organizations that are
not hierarchies

2.
Hierarchies that are
not bureaucracies

1.
Bureaucracies

Circle 4: Structures That Are Not Organizations. I've already talked about the fact that human relations can be patterned without meeting all of the defining characteristics of an organization, although we are really in a troublesome region here. For instance, entire tribes or societies, families, clans, social networks, all adult males in a tribe—all of these groupings involve some structure, but they are generally not thought to be organizations. In part, they do not have purposes; yet can one say that the economic survival and procreation aims of families in most societies are any less clear or pressing than the purposes of Rotary clubs or Moose lodges? In part, nonorganizational structures have vague boundaries. For example, social networks or circles, such as people in psychoanalysis or parents of children in free schools, lack strong internal patterning and sharp boundaries. Since all human activities to some extent involve patterned relationships, purposefulness, and boundaries, the lines between organizations and other groupings are somewhat vague.

Circle 3: Organizations That Are Not Hierarchies. There are a great many of these. We have already mentioned several—the Protestant Pentecostals, SDS in the midsixties, and so on. Tribal "secret societies" are another example, for decision-making in them tends to be evenly distributed and by group consensus. In other words, tribal organizations and a good many voluntary associations and movement groups tend to be nonhierarchical organizations. Often this lack of hierarchy is not at all accidental but a deliberate effort to create an organization that is different from the generally prevailing hierarchical ones. For example, the Protestant sectarians wanted to build organizations that would not be hierarchical in the same way that the Roman Catholic church and the established Protestant denominations were hierarchical. Along with a rejection of established theology went a rejection of established organizational forms. The rejection of hierarchy was also a deliberate policy of American social movement groups in the 1960s as well as of nineteenth-century European anarchists.

Some organizations may have incipient hierarchies, in which a relatively small number of people are beginning to monopolize power. Some large urban youth gangs represent such a transitional form, in which decision-making is no longer diffuse but falls into the hands of a president or a minister of defense.

Circle 2: Hierarchies That Are Not Bureaucracies. A common type of non-bureaucratic hierarchy is the organization built around a charismatic leader, an individual who is believed to have extraordinary powers. The structure of such organizations is pyramidal; power is concentrated at the top. But power is not based on offices, rules, and formal entrance requirements. Rather, it flows out of the charismatic leader. Close contact with the leader confers power on an inner circle; the inner circle in turn bestows it on successive layers of the faithful. Authority here rests on magic. The corresponding rewards and punishments are a desire to be in contact with an entity believed to be sacred and a fear of being cast out from the extraordinary presence. The interracial Kingdom of Peace movement built around Father Divine, whose followers believed him to be a personification of God, is an example of a movement with hierarchy but relatively little bureaucracy. The Black Muslims, which focused on Elijah Muhammad, are another example. So is the movement that has developed around Guru Mahara-ji. Sometimes these hierarchies have only a dimly perceived central figure; charisma flows entirely from an imaginary being. For instance, in Krishna consciousness (familiar to most of us through shaven-headed, saffron-robed, street-corner mendicants), the organizer, an Indian swami, is not well known and the focus is on the Hindu deity Krishna. The hierarchical form of all these movement organizations is fairly similar, with layers of members differentiated by different degrees of commitment.

Circle 1: Bureaucracies. The Roman Catholic church, the large corporations, and most government agencies are all examples of bureaucracies.

Figure 2 is, of course, an oversimplified picture of the situation. In fact, there are many borderline phenomena. Some off-the-main-line organizations either combine elements of all the types or have some idiosyncratic features that make them very hard to classify. None of these types is entirely stable. Many types of organizations are in transition from one to another form. Each type is susceptible to characteristic changes. We will examine these in greater detail in Chapter 6. Here a brief listing will suffice.

— Nonhierarchical organizations face strong internal pressures to assume a hierarchical centralized form. The tendency to succumb to such pressures has been referred to as the "iron law of oligarchy."
— Hierarchical charismatic organizations have to face the death (or sometimes apostasy) of the charismatic leader. They tend to turn into bureaucracies in which rules and the authority of the office replace charisma as the source of authority. Such organizations become routinized, if they survive at all.
— Bureaucratic organizations tend to be very stable. Rather than suffer an outwardly visible collapse or transformation, they frequently remain apparently intact but lose the ability to fulfill their initial purpose. They become entirely focused on surviving in a structurally unchanged form, on maintaining themselves as organizations even if they no longer will or can accomplish their goals.
— Each of these transformations of movement structure *can* occur. Whether it does or not depends not only on internal strains but also on the environment of the organization.

Organizational Environments

Changes in organizations are the result not only of internal processes but also of pressures from the organization's environment. The boundaries of an organization are one of the places at which the environment affects the organization. Boundary problems may take many forms.

Membership. One kind of boundary problem is the issue of membership. Sometimes people want to join an organization but the members of the organization want to keep them out. Tension and, in some cases, change result. An influx of new people can bring about change: "Happy Acres Country Club just hasn't been the same since they started letting Bulgarians in." The new people may really cause the changes by their behavior. Or the organization may simply be changed by the presence of new members regardless of their actual behavior.

 If an organization successfully resists an influx of new members, the very effort of resistance will change the organization. It will develop special mechanisms for keeping people out, and some members will have to devote their energies to this new goal. Mechanisms of exclusion may include the following: elaborate tests that appear to be fair but in fact screen out the threatening group; apparent compliance with the new members' demands, but actually developing ways to "cool them out" by making them feel uncomfortable or by giving them the least attractive tasks; changing the formal charter of the organization, for instance, by turning it from a public body into a private one that does not have to accept new members.

 All of these devices for resisting new members will be familiar to anyone who is involved in integrating women or Third World people (blacks, Chicanos, Asian-Americans, etc.) into organizations. From the viewpoint of the old membership, the organization—be it a firm, a school system, a university, a club, or whatever—is in a no-win situation. If it accepts the new groups, its character is altered. If it resists their demands, it begins to change as more of its members' energies have to be devoted to resistance. Furthermore, in some societies, an organization also risks sanctions from the larger environment— for instance, cutoffs of federal funds for noncompliance with affirmative action women-and-minority-hiring quotas.

 Often organizations try to work out compromise strategies in which a few of the most "acceptable" or assimilated of the new group are "allowed" in. Some of these are subsequently "cooled out" and the rest put into special token slots. Record-keeping may be suitably fudged to demonstrate compliance. For example, in a firm that must comply with affirmative action policies, the firm avoids integration in the following way:

> All our jobs were filled by advertising the vacancy in local suburban newspapers. Our location's hiring area established by law encompasses ten suburbs, of which only one is as much as 27 percent nonwhite. There is no form of transportation to the suburb from the more heavily nonwhite central city. Thus, few applicants are nonwhite. Then at the year's end, the applications are combined and a claim of nonwhite apathy in seeking jobs is claimed and is supported by manipulated proof. . . . A

few blacks or Latinos may be placed in conspicuous higher paying jobs to satisfy the on-the-spot inspections called "locational compliance reviews" (Hawk, 1974).

Boundary problems involving membership can also take the opposite form—people may want to drop out when the organization wants them to stay in. High schools and universities may have high dropout rates. Factories may have high turnover rates. Movement groups may have trouble keeping their members. These problems in membership loss are often the product of changes in the larger environment rather than just the product of organizational features. A whole type of organization—schools, factories, social movement groups—may be affected by high dropout rates because of societal trends. Within a given type, however, specific organizations may have especially severe attrition rates because of the characteristics of their members or because of their own policies.

Sometimes high dropout rates are not a problem for an organization at all, but are a deliberate strategy for maintaining the status quo. For instance, public colleges may have to take in large numbers of students but will then arrange to have large classes and impersonal exams to flunk out what the administration considers excess numbers. MacDonald's Hamburgers deliberately encourages a high turnover rate among its employees because high turnover makes it virtually impossible for employees to organize into a union. In this way wages are kept low (Vega, 1973).

Clientele.   A different set of boundary problems for organizations are those involving clients rather than members. Clients and customers are those people who rely on an organization for goods or services and who would like to make the organization accountable for the quality of these goods and services. Specifically, clients want fast delivery, high standards, appropriate responses to complaints, and the ability to change organizational policy when it is not to their advantage. Many organizations resist one or more of these client demands. A powerful organization may be able to resist them effectively, depending, of course, on the power of the clients.

Organizations develop various mechanisms for shielding themselves against clients. They may make themselves rather inaccessible; for instance, the phone numbers of schools in the Chicago public school system are unlisted. Organizations may withhold information from their clients so that their performance is difficult to judge. Often they have resources, such as money and legal counsel, that their clients do not have. Throughout the sixties and early seventies, we have seen repeated movements to force organizations to be more accountable to their publics. This demand was one part of the agenda of movements for university reform, welfare rights, community control of schools, and consumer protection.

Other Organizations. One of the most important features of an organization's environment is other organizations. Individual members, would-be members, or clients cause the most serious boundary maintenance problems when they are organized.

Organizations also have relations with other organizations in areas other than defense and resistance. They may cooperate or form coalitions. In this process, the organizations may cooperate by dividing the labor so that each organization carries out tasks that the others can't or won't do. In the student antiwar movement of the middle sixties, for example, an uneasy cooperation existed between the Student Mobilization Committee, which organized large demonstrations; the Draft Resistance, which was oriented especially toward individual protestors; the various draft counseling centers, which provided alternatives for the less committed; and Students for a Democratic Society, which offered the theoretical analysis and the overall perspective.

Researchers often use the concept of interlock to study coalitions and other kinds of organizational linkages. An interlock is an overlap in members, especially members of the elite of organizations. The definition of interlock might be extended to include friendships or past overlapping memberships.

The existence of interlocks suggests interdependence or common interests. Interlock data are relatively easy to store in a computer. Although there are some problems in charting clusters of interlocks in an easy-to-understand way, interlock data can provide valuable information on urban power structure or clusters of related firms. For example, see Figure 3. Each line in Figure 3 represents an interlock, a person on the board of directors or in a top executive position for each pair of organizations. They could also represent linkages of friendship and kinship, past overlapping memberships, or the holdings of trusts or large stockholdings. The three large encompassing circles represent clusters of interrelated firms and institutions.

Obviously, Figure 3 represents only a fragment of a larger picture. We can see how three clusters of organizations emerge. Linkages to government agencies would involve research on informal ties as well as formal interlocks.

Organizations may also compete with one another. This is the usual state of affairs for many small firms in a market situation. To some extent, movement organizations also compete with similar organizations for members and resources. For example, the National Organization of Women competes with other feminist groups for funds and members; it also cooperates to some degree in attaining feminist goals and putting feminist issues on the national agenda. The feminist movement as a whole can be seen as competing with other types of organizations for the time, energy, and money of women. For example, these other organizations may include other movement groups (the environmentalists, black groups, or Socialists) as well as even more "distant" organizations, such as the voluntary associations (the PTA, Hadassah, the Rosary Society) or cosmetics and detergent companies. With these latter types, little cooperation is likely. Organizations in any kind of a market or quasi-

Figure 3

The Organizational Power Structure of "Zenith"

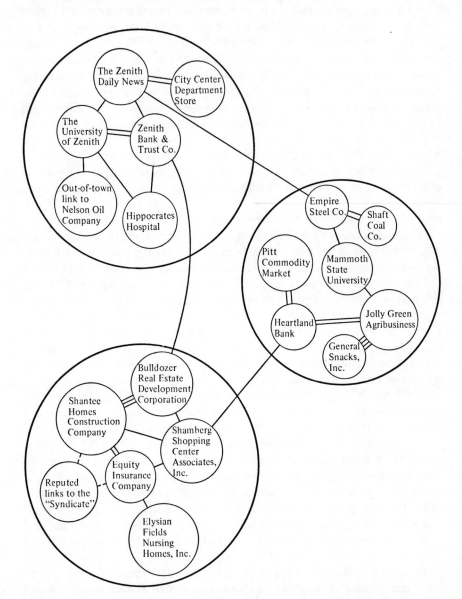

market environment of competition and coalition have to decide how much to differentiate their "product." The aim is to have a "product" that is unique and distinctive, one that will win definitely committed adherents as opposed to one that is similar to competing "products," which may gain a possibly larger but more wishy-washy following.

Incorporation is another possible type of relationship between organizations that occurs among both firms and voluntary associations or movement organizations. Among firms, this process is often referred to as a merger. Among movement groups, it may be known as infiltration or "boring from within," as members of one movement group try to take over another one. For instance, in 1969, members of a left-wing group called Progressive Labor tried to take over SDS by stacking the national convention. While unable to capture SDS, the PL group managed to force a factional split (Sale, 1973:555–574). This kind of incorporation is often followed by factional splits, where people who don't like the merger break away from the new organization (as did the Weathermen and some other groups after the 1969 SDS convention).

Regulation is another interorganizational relationship. One organization may have power over another and be able to control its purposes, boundaries, or internal structure. Sometimes the regulated organizations may actually be more powerful than the regulating body. For example, somewhat uneasy relations exist between the Food and Drug Administration and the pharmaceutical companies, between the Federal Communications Commission and the broadcasting networks, and between the Federal Aviation Agency and the airlines.

Each time one of these interorganizational relationships emerges, the organizations are changed in some way. Organizations are not only concerned with environments of members, clients, and organizations, they also have a larger environment consisting of (1) the climate of the society as a whole, (2) the structure of the society as a whole—its distribution of wealth and power —and (3) the state. In very large part, these aspects of the larger environment are manifested in the organization's relationship with its more immediate environment of clients, members at the boundary, and other organizations. For instance, we have already seen how the state has an impact on organizations (especially private firms) through its various regulatory agencies. In other words, the state itself is very largely composed of organizations and thus affects other organizations in this manner.

The general climate of the society can affect organizations through both aggregate individual behavior and the emergence of new organizations. Let's say you open a massage parlor in a town that is strongly opposed to commercialized sex. On the one hand, aggregate individual decisions will affect your organization: your massage parlor may have few customers. On the other hand, new counterorganizations may become part of your organization's environment: your massage parlor's manager may have to contend with angry demonstrators from the Anti-Vice League. The state itself—in the form of the police department—may impinge on your organization. Of course, local climates of opinion may not correspond to national trends. An organization may change in response to both local environmental changes and larger societal ones, which may pull it in opposite directions.

The organizational environment, like the microenvironments of individuals, can also be conceived of as structures of rewards and punishments. As long as we think of an organization as a fairly cohesive entity, we can think of its behaving in response to these rewards and punishments.

Organizations and Everyday Life

Organizations shape the lives of most of us. Organizations determine where we work, how much money we make, what we eat, where we live, for whom we can vote, how we travel, what we learn, what we can buy, and when and where we die. In a modern society, almost every instant of our day is shaped by the large organizations of the society.

The conditions of our employment are set by large organizations— businesses, government agencies, unions, private nonprofit organizations. If we decide to start a small business instead, its operation is contingent on a market both for the goods we buy and those we sell. Often the raw materials markets are dominated by a few large firms. Furthermore, the business is subject to government regulation. If we are poor or disabled, the conditions of our life are set by government welfare agencies. The fee-for-service system of health care in the United States determines the nature of health care we receive and perhaps also the time and place of our death.

Some details of our life are under our own control. We *can* make choices in personal matters like friendships and between certain rather narrow consumer options—whether to spend our money on travel or clothes, for instance. These are *personally* important details, no doubt, but they have little effect on the organizations themselves. They represent only narrow choices. Of course, people in simple traditional societies have only narrow choices also. If anything, their range of options is even narrower than ours. The point is *not* that we have no choices, but that our choices are constrained by organizational policies and structures. The choices of Eskimos (before European contact) were not constrained by organizations but by the harshness of nature and the opinions of their personal acquaintances.

Organizations shape our choices. They are also our links to a larger world. By our participation in organizations, we are linked to people whom we shall never see face to face. The products we make at our workplace meet these people's needs. The agencies, legislatures, and party machinery of the state tie us to people with similar interests and subject us to the interests of more powerful groups. A society without organizations, other than face-to-face groupings or informal networks, remains simple; its people remain isolated.

If we live in a society of organizations, we can effect change only by building new organizations ourselves or by changing the existing ones. The isolated individual is generally powerless against an organization. Isolated members of an organization have a hard time pressing their demands against their own organization; therefore, unions had to be built within companies. Clients find organizations irresponsible; therefore, they form counterorganizations, hold sit-ins in organizational offices, press demands, and initiate class-action suits. Individuals find the state and the society oppressive; therefore, they band together in reformist and revolutionary movements. In a society dominated by organizations, isolated individuals who try to fight the system have little hope of success unless they build organizations to back them up (Kesey, 1962). To an increasing extent, structural change in an organizational society comes about only through new organizations. *Organizations are the machinery for changing complex societies.*

References

Gerlach, Luther P., and Virginia H. Hines.
   1973   Lifeway Leap. Minneapolis: University of Minnesota Press.

Hawk, Frank.
   1974   "Affirmative action programs and institutional deviance." Unpublished paper. Chicago: DePaul University.

Kesey, Ken.
   1962   One Flew Over the Cuckoo's Nest. New York: Viking Press.

Sale, Kirkpatrick.
   1973   SDS: Ten Years Toward a Revolution. New York: Random House.

Vega, Jeff.
   1973   Personal communication regarding MacDonald's Organizing Project.

Weber, Max.
   1947   The Theory of Social and Economic Organization. New York: Oxford University Press.
   1958   From Max Weber. Edited and translated by H. H. Gerth and C. Wright Mills. New York: Oxford University Press.

Chapter 6

Change in Organizations

This chapter will focus on changes that affect an organization as a whole: changes in its goals, routinization of charisma, institutionalization, and birth and growth.

FOR THE PURPOSES OF THIS CHAPTER, I shall assume that an organization is a unit or an entity. I shall look at organizations as though they were organisms struggling for survival and growth. This organismic way of thinking about an organization as an entity is really very misleading. Organizations are groups of people, and different people within an organization actually have very different goals and interests from each other and from the organization as a whole.

To think of an organization as an entity or organism usually means to think about it in the same terms that the most powerful groups within the organization think about it. For instance, if you think of a company as a profit-making enterprise, you are accepting the goals set by stockholders and top management. Workers in the company are not primarily concerned with profits, but with their wages and salaries. From the point of view of the workers, the organization is not like an organism. Rather, the organization is primarily a means to their making a living, and its profit goals are not directly connected to their own goals. From the point of view of stockholders and top managers, the organization is a single entity with a single goal—profit. To them the demands of workers or customers are pathologies that interfere with the organism's smooth functioning.

There is nothing wrong with temporarily accepting a unitary or organismic view of organizations; certain kinds of processes can most coherently be analyzed from this perspective. However, we must be careful not to accept the unitary view as the only one. And we need to be aware that the unitary view of an organization tends to be the one held by its most powerful members. If we accept such a view to some degree, we legitimate their power and purposes.

Goals and Organizational Change

Many of the changes that take place within an organization are changes that assure its continued survival, in other words, changes that maintain boundaries, sustain at least some semblance of its initial purpose, and retain the overall features of its internal structure. Obviously, these relatively abstract characteristics can be kept only if some practical contingencies are met: the organization must be able to continue attracting resources, including members, funds, and so on. To a large degree, the continued flow of these resources becomes one of the prime reasons for keeping the organization going. Individual members require the resources for their own survival and therefore want the organization to continue because it is the vehicle by which they collect these resources.

Goal Displacement

The transformation of an organization in order to insure its survival is usually referred to as organizational maintenance and goal displacement. *The original goals of the organization are displaced by the goal of organizational maintenance or organizational survival.* Let's look at a well-documented example, the Townsend movement. The Townsend movement was started in the 1930s in California as a response to the desperate plight of many old people in that state. Townsend and his followers formulated a number of demands centering on government-supported pensions, and they began to organize old people into local groups that worked to further these demands. When the federal government instituted the social security system, the chief purpose of the Townsend Plan was accomplished, although perhaps not in the form envisioned by Townsend. But the local clubs did not disappear. Instead, the movement organization found two new goals—sociability and commercial activity. The local groups became clubs in which the old could congregate to talk and play cards. The organization began to market potions and remedies. The original goal of pressing economic demands was nullified by changes in the organization's environment; however, the organization continued to exist with new goals for a number of years. On the one hand, its specific constituency (old people) and its local roots made it a reasonably effective way of marketing products. On the other hand, it met deep-seated needs for activity and companionship among its members (Messinger, 1955).

We can see similar processes of goal displacement at work in a voluntary association like the March of Dimes. This organization began in a form that was almost movement-like. It could draw on the charisma of Franklin D. Roosevelt, who was himself a victim of polio, to rally extensive volunteer help and financial support for research into the prevention of polio. It could also draw on the fear and hope of many people during the forties and fifties, when seasonal polio epidemics crippled large numbers of children. When the polio vaccine was developed and polio became largely a disease of the unvaccinated poor, the March of Dimes was left with no goals and a very effective organizational structure. Subsequent efforts to channel this structure into raising money for birth-defect research seem to have been only moderately successful. Still, the organization's name and some of its membership and structure continue to exist.

A less benign example of goal displacement is afforded by some government agencies. For example, some urban school systems seem unable to fulfill the usual goals of primary and secondary education. They have very high dropout rates. Their graduates are sometimes virtually illiterate. Each year that children spend in these systems lowers their achievement relative to other children on national measures of reading, writing, and arithmetic skills—the basic skills whose inculcation can be said to be the major official goal of public education. Yet despite this failure to meet stated goals, the organization continues. Partly it serves other unstated goals, such as keeping unemployable young people "off the streets" or providing employers of its graduates with proof of their obedience or, at least, docility. Largely, however, the organization's main goal has become its own survival, regardless of the needs of its clients. A large variety of devices assure its survival: sheer physical inaccessibility, manifested in unlisted phone numbers, locked doors, and protective layers of secretaries and receptionists; the use of physical force against the unruly among the "pacified" population of young people, manifested, for instance, in the stationing of policemen in some urban high schools; the establishment of committees and research commissions to swallow up and stall the demands of students or community groups; the growth of extremely strong unions to protect teachers' rights within the existing structure. This system grinds down genuinely well-intentioned efforts to teach within the structure and at the same time prevents any substantial changes.

Similar kinds of processes seem to occur in prisons, mental hospitals, and welfare agencies. Like urban schools, these organizations are caught between two millstones: on the one hand, their environment is one of extreme scarcity —they are usually badly underfunded by the state. On the other hand, they have to deal with clients who are both unruly and powerless. (Probably they are unruly in large part because they are powerless, having only the power to disrupt organizational routines and not to achieve their own goals.) In this situation, the organization—that is, the staff—struggles to survive by maintaining the routines of the organization sufficiently to keep the flow of funds going and to prevent destruction of the structure either from above or below.

The language of rewards and punishment is useful for conceptualizing these processes. The staff of an organization can usually protect itself from disruption from below, from inmate/clients, by punishment through physical force and by relatively simple material rewards. The staff itself is kept in line by the desire to keep its own material rewards—wages and salaries—flowing through the organization. Decision-makers at the top of the organization (some of whom may be formally outside its boundaries) usually see their own interests served by the preservation of routines. Usually they will permit the organization to survive provided the client/inmates do not get out of hand or the organization raises the cost of interference excessively high. The latter strategy is quite common; we are probably all familiar with cases in which top administrators were forced to resign because they tried to "rock the boat," that is, to attack and reform the organizations they controlled. Organizations counter such top-down disruptions of routine by noncompliance with orders, by complaints to yet higher authorities, by exaggerated compliance, and by using client/inmate disruptions as evidence against those who interfere.

A fourth example of goal displacement is provided by the Young Men's Christian Association. The YMCA started as an organization that brought evangelical Christianity to young urban men, often lower-level white-collar workers of rural background. It provided them with "wholesome" activities and fellowship in an urban setting fraught with vice and loneliness. By the early decades of the twentieth century, this pattern of urban immigration, acculturation to the city, and strong commitment to evangelical religion was shifting. Decision-makers in the YMCA responded to these shifts in the larger environment by emphasizing sports and crafts activities for lower-middle-class white urban families and de-emphasizing the religious aspect. Membership and funding remained high, and the organization continued to be viable. Following World War II, many Y's found themselves stranded in neighborhoods that were filling up with low-income blacks. To some extent, the YMCA has been able to again shift its goals to service this new client population. But the shift has not been easy, since it has entailed changes in funding sources as well as changes in the values and behavior of the staff (Zald & Denton, 1963).

We've now looked at several different cases of goal displacement in organizations. Each one was somewhat different, depending on the characteristics of the organization and of the larger environment. In the cases of the Townsend movement, the March of Dimes, and the YMCA, the environment itself shifted, forcing the organizations to find new official goals in order to attain the overriding goal of survival. In the case of schools, prisons, and other organizations with rather powerless clients, the organizations were inherently not well equipped in terms of resources or internal structure to service these clients. Thus these organizations proceeded to substitute organizational functioning and survival for the original service goals.

Goal Inflexibility

A second kind of process of organizational change may be called goal preservation or goal inflexibility. Goal preservation is goal displacement turned upside down. *In this process, the organization clings to the original purpose even when it no longer makes sense in a changed environment.* The organization then undergoes loss of resources and changes in membership. The nature of its participation in the larger society also changes. The Women's Christian Temperance Union provides an excellent example of changes accompanying goal inflexibility.

The WCTU reached its peak of influence and membership as a voluntary organization during the Progressive era, 1900–1916. It was part of a larger movement, broadly thought of as the Progressive movement. This movement pursued a number of goals: among them were the Americanization of non-WASP immigrants, the amelioration of the quality of life for the working class, the improvement of consumer goods and public services, the end of corruption and corporate rapaciousness, and the streamlining and professionalization of government. The Progressive movement was in no way radical in that it did not attack fundamental American institutions such as capitalism or class inequality. Rather, it breathed a spirit of middle-class reform. It instituted city-manager-type urban governments to replace corrupt ethnic machine politics, backed pure food and drug laws, worked against child labor, built settlement houses to acculturate immigrants and, in general, stood for wholesome middle-class efficiency against both business corruption and working-class vice.

One wing of the Progressive movement was especially concerned with the way in which poor people—particularly non-WASP poor people—turned to drink. The reformers saw liquor as an obstacle to the thrift, hard work, and regular habits that they believed would bring the urban working class into a middle-class way of life. Temperance and ultimately prohibition of alcohol were important parts of their program for improving living standards. The Women's Christian Temperance Union attracted activist women of a type similar to those who worked on child labor laws, recreational facilities, and so on. But the society itself changed. With the rise and fall of Prohibition, the WCTU was left stranded with goals that had lost their meaning. An increasingly urbanized America did not share the WCTU's attitudes toward liquor. Temperance and other middle-class virtues no longer appeared to be realistic routes out of the working class. Unionization and changes in the economy itself brought about more decisive changes in working-class life than any individualistic virtues could.

For a number of reasons inherent in the characteristics of the WCTU's leadership and in the way it kept control of the organization's internal structure, the organization could not shift its goals. Basically, the internal constraints, or ideological "baggage" of the leadership, overwhelmed pressures to respond to more immediate rewards and punishments from the environment. The WCTU failed to redefine its goal away from complete condemnation of alcoholic beverages to goals such as the rehabilitation of individual alcoholics. Such a redefinition would have opened to it the cooperation and resources of groups like Alcoholics Anonymous or various governmental drug and alcohol abuse programs. Instead, the WCTU maintained a highly moralistic and indignant stand. Its membership among the more cosmopolitan urban middle-class women virtually disappeared. It shrank to a hard core of primarily small-town Protestant lower-middle-class women. A leadership group of this background was able to tighten its hold on the structure (Gusfield, 1966).

These patterns of goal inflexibility and consequent loss of resources, declining membership, and tightened structure are particularly characteristic of movement organizations because in this type of organization ideological rewards can override material rewards. A company that behaved so inflexibly would generally go out of business. Movement groups require less material feedback from their environment. Processes similar to those in the WCTU have operated in the Industrial Workers of the World (an anarcho-syndicalist labor-organizing group) and some of the left-wing parties in the United States. Ideological purity is maintained at the cost of losing a broad base.

Routinization of Charisma

A second process of organizational change is routinization of charisma. I've already commented on the fact that some organizations are organized around a charismatic figure—a leader believed to have extraordinary powers. When such a leader dies or is discredited, the organization may also die. However, a whole series of mechanisms exist to maintain the organization. Almost all of these involve the loss of the sense of magic or of the extraordinary provided by the original leader. The routinization of charisma refers to this loss of an enchanted feeling. The organization is saved, but its special glow is lost.

Establishing Succession

One mechanism for routinizing charisma is to establish some kind of succession. For instance, the charismatic leader's children or other relatives may succeed to the leadership position. Muhammad's father-in-law and other kinsmen succeeded him as the leaders of Islam. The institution of the caliphate, in which the caliph was seen as the deputy or representative of Muhammad, routinized this essentially dynastic kinship-based succession. The transformation of charisma into traditional dynastic succession is a very common solution to the routinization problem. Often kinsmen will have some of the personal characteristics of the charismatic leader. In any case, kinship-based succession fits quite well into the patterns of many traditional societies. In our own society, we can see some traces of this type of routinization of charisma in the fortunes of the "Kennedy clan."

Different forms of succession are also possible. The new leader does not necessarily have to be related to the charismatic leader. Nonkinship patterns of succession appear in both Buddhism and Christianity. The pope is selected by the cardinals generally from among their own number or from among other high church officials. The Dalai Lama and the other rulers in pre-Communist Tibet were selected by councils of monks. When the Dalai Lama died, the powerful clerics sent out a committee to find the child who represented his reincarnation—the body into which his soul had been reborn. Such a child had certain special features: leopard-skin speckling on his back, prominent ears, marks on his body indicating a second pair of arms, and so on. Essentially the myth of reincarnation and the search for the child were the ideological fictions that justified the power of an inner circle of monks, corresponding in many ways to the college of cardinals that select the pope.

Succession is generally orderly, since it is in the interests of the decision-making group to have a smooth and legitimate transfer of power. There have been, of course, exceptions to orderly succession. During the late fourteenth century, there were rival popes, each claiming the mantle of legitimacy and supported by different rulers according to their political interests. Incidentally, the pope seems more likely than the Dalai Lama to act as a decision-maker in his own right; he is less a creature of the selecting body than is the obscure infant who is identified as the Dalai Lama. These mechanisms of nonkinship selection seem particularly suited to societies in which one or both of the following conditions hold: there is a celibate clergy, as in Tibet and Catholicism after 1100, so that religious and political activity are already to some degree divorced from kinship ties; and there is a belief in reincarnation, as in Tibet, which provides a myth for the reappearance of charismatic power.

Frequently there is an uneasy tension between kinship and nonkinship patterns of succession. This would seem to be the case among the Hasidim, a sect of Jewish mystics. Hasidic communities of the faithful were organized around charismatic figures, the *tzaddikim* (singular *tzaddik*). To a large extent, charismatic power was very short lived. Many of these communities did not outlive their *tzaddik,* many new *tzaddikim* sprang up, and the centers of Hasidic activity shifted rapidly around eastern Europe. Occasionally, kinship succession—from father to son—was present. And sometimes a new *tzaddik* could emerge from among the disciples.

Diffusing Charisma

Another pattern for routinizing charisma is to try to extend charisma to all members of the organization; this diffusion is justified by a myth or symbol. In early Christianity, the appearance of the Holy Ghost to all the disciples at Pentecost represents this sort of diffusion of extraordinary powers, as does the sacrament of the Eucharist in the contemporary church. The divine inner light that the Quakers saw in every human being is also diffused charisma. This sort of diffused charisma seems to correspond well to a democratic, decentralized, cell-like structure. Gerlach and Hines (1973) refer to this as an acephalous (headless) segmental structure. It can be found among Quakers, in the Protestant Pentecostal movement, and in early Christianity. This sort of diffused charisma involves less routinization than the other ways of dealing with the absence of the single charismatic leader.

Bureaucratization

A final common way of routinizing charisma is bureaucratization. It can accompany other forms also, as can be clearly seen in the case of the Roman Catholic church with its apostolic succession (an only partially bureaucratized structure) and its large bureaucracy. In bureaucratization, the charisma virtually disappears, although the extraordinary powers of the leader are perhaps still used to justify the rules and regulations of the bureaucracy.

Institutionalization

Very closely related to routinization and goal displacement is the process of institutionalization. In the very early stage, shortly after its birth (a process that we will discuss later), an organization may not yet have stable patterns. Its internal structure may be in flux, its boundaries expanding and ill-defined, its relationship to the existing organizations of the society problematical. Over time all these issues may be resolved, and the new organization becomes a stable feature of the organizational landscape. Other organizations recognize and accept its presence, and its internal structure develops some continuity. Such an organization may be said to be institutionalized. In state-level societies, an important feature of institutionalization may be recognition by the state. Some organizations are more rapidly institutionalized than others—for instance, in our society, business firms (even if they later go out of business) tend to gell internally more rapidly and be externally recognized more readily than, say, hippy communes.

From Sect to Church

One of the most famous statements about institutionalization concerns the sect-church dichotomy. Troeltsch (1931), a German Protestant scholar, examined the way in which Protestant denominations arose. They began, he found, as sects—small, intense, informal, sometimes with charismatic leaders. Their internal structure was charismatic or egalitarian, almost never bureaucratic. Commitment was intense and so was persecution, in many cases. Adult baptism and ecstatic practices ensured that members participated in a religious experience rather than only passively belonged to a congregation. Members knew each other personally. The radical wing of the Reformation (Hutterites,

Mennonites, Anabaptists, Levellers, Diggers) and the non-Anglican denominations in England (Quakers, Baptists, Methodists, as well as scores of smaller sects that sprang up during the seventeenth and eighteenth centuries) began in this form.

A number of the sects—*but not all of them*—became churches. They grew large; they became bureaucratized; they developed a professional clergy to replace the lay leadership—often female—of the sect; membership became a status that people were born into rather than one they assumed joyfully and self-consciously; commitment correspondingly diminished. Sometimes the church even became the established denomination of the state, funded by tax money, its clergymen paid state functionaries, its doctrines taught in the public schools, and membership in it a prerequisite for government employment. Yet when conditions were right, the church could bring forth a new round of sects, some of which would die out or be crushed, some of which would remain small encapsulated sects, and some of which would in turn become churches.

Similar processes have occurred within Buddhism. However, Roman Catholicism and, to a lesser extent, Islam and Judaism have tended to remain more unified with more church structure and relatively fewer sects. (The reasons for these differences are too complex to investigate here. They depend not only on the initial structure of the religion itself but ultimately on the structure of the societies in which they exist. Furthermore, there is variation by society within the religion—Islam, for example, has different characteristics in Java, North Africa, and Iraq.)

Some people have gone so far as to postulate successive cycles of structure (institutionalized organizations) and nonstructure (emerging sectlike intense organizational forms) as a general feature of most societies (Turner, 1969). I am inclined to be skeptical of this view. But without embarking on grandiose cyclical theories, one can agree that shifts from emergent sectlike organizations to institutionalized churchlike ones, which may later factionalize and spin off new sects, are frequent features of organizational change. It is not a universal law, however, and a good many counterexamples can be found. For instance, many of the seventeenth-century Protestant sects have remained quite sectlike, while the Roman Catholic church, both before and after the great schism of the Protestant Reformation, has been quite successful at forcing innovators to keep their new organizations within the church, subject to papal authority, as new orders rather than as separate sects.

Within the State

The processes of institutionalization can be observed in state organizations as well as in movements and voluntary organizations. For instance, in its early years, the Peace Corps had a sectlike atmosphere of enthusiasm strongly tinged with the charisma of John F. Kennedy. By the middle 1960s, amid the external conditions of the war in Vietnam and growing disillusionment with the American empire, it lost many of these characteristics and became one more government agency. Similar processes took place in the various "war on poverty" agencies. Where charisma and ideological hoopla are less part of the establishment of an agency, institutionalization sets in even faster, although there is necessarily some lag during which relationships with other agencies, clients, and so on have to be routinized.

Organizational Growth

A fourth process of organizational change is growth. Not all organizations are committed to gaining new members. Some are, however. For these, recruitment drives are very important. I have already discussed some of these processes from the point of view of the individual being recruited. As stated earlier, three ingredients are usually necessary: (1) objective conditions such that the organization makes sense to the potential member; (2) correspondence between the potential member's frame of reference and that of the organization (which is, of course, most likely to occur when the objective conditions match the organization's analysis); and (3) interpersonal recruitment processes. To some extent, a very great strength in any one of these factors can outweigh weaknesses in the others. For instance, an organization with an analysis of objective conditions that is as patently absurd as that of the Guru Mahari-ji can still draw many members because the organization's frame of reference corresponds well to the fantasies of some young people in this society and because it has effective recruitment mechanisms.

Growth Despite Failure

There are some amusing and extreme examples of the growth of movement organizations despite—even because of—gross absurdities in their ideology. One of the best known is a flying saucer cult that was studied by a group of social psychologists. In this instance, the cult had prophesied the end of the world on a certain date. When the cataclysm failed to materialize, cult members reinterpreted their failure to mean that humanity was being given "one more chance," and they began to proselytize harder than ever. Sometimes, when faced with a discrepancy between "the facts" and the movement's frame of reference, members are more willing to reinterpret what has happened than to abandon the movement (Festinger, Riechken, & Schachter, 1956).

The Sabbataian heresy in seventeenth-century Judaism provides a similar example. A Jew of Smyrna, Sabbatai Zevi (1626–1676), at the age of twenty-two declared himself to be the Messiah. According to Scholem (1961:290), Sabbatai's message was given little serious consideration in the

Jewish communities around the eastern Mediterranean to which he traveled during the next years. In 1662, however, his cause was taken up by a young Jewish scholar, Nathan of Gaza, and word of Sabbatai's messianic mission began to spread throughout the eastern Mediterranean and into northern Europe. Already in this phase of the movement, Sabbatai's often bizarre and offensive behavior, far from diminishing his following, was taken as a sign of his extraordinary nature that transgressed and thus transcended the bounds of the normal and lawful. Taking note of Sabbatai's growing popularity, the Sultan imprisoned him in Constantinople. Under duress (which may have included the threat of torture and threats against the Jewish community), the self-proclaimed Messiah renounced Judaism and converted to Islam.

Sabbatai's apostasy set off. waves of frantic argument and activity throughout the Jewish communities in Europe and the Near East. Many people gave up their messianic hopes, but others remained convinced that Sabbatai was the Messiah. They abandoned their earthly possessions in triumphant anticipation of the Kingdom of Heaven on earth. They subjected themselves to mortifications, including prolonged fasts, the eating of nettles, and exposure in the snow, according to some accounts. They even hailed the terrible persecutions that Gentiles were inflicting on the Jews during this period as evidence of the imminence of the apocalypse.

Why did not Sabbatai's apostasy—his conversion to Islam—put an end to Sabbataianism? Why did some of his followers find their faith confirmed by this act? First, objective conditions were right. European Jews were undergoing persecution and were searching desperately for a better life. They preferred to pursue messianic dreams rather than face a bleak reality, even if it meant denying that reality. Second, the apostasy itself actually confirmed the faith of some of the Sabbataians, because it fit in with a Jewish mystical tradition that the Messiah would first plumb the depths of evil, that his behavior would seem repulsive, bizarre, and wicked. Sabbatai had already shown himself to be a strange and sometimes offensive person. His apostasy, the most heinous act a Jew could commit, sealed the certainty that he was fulfilling the prophecy about the Messiah's behavior.

> Sectarian Sabbataianism was born when many sections of the people refused to accept the verdict of history, unwilling to admit that their faith had been a vain illusion fondly invented. There was the alternative possibility of faith in an apostate messiah, but it had to be bought at the price of the naive innocence of the original faith. To believe in an apostate messiah was to build one's hope on foundations of paradox and absurdity that could only lead to more paradoxes (Scholem, 1973:690).

But the seventeenth century was indeed a time of wild intellectual experiments, of upheavals and movements among both Jews and Gentiles, who were painfully stumbling along the path from medieval stability to modern society.

In other words, under the right objective conditions, movements can grow when they promise to fulfill their members' dreams, even when these dreams are inappropriate maps of the social, political, and economic world.

Predicting and Measuring Growth

The complexity of these processes makes prediction about growth difficult. For example, labor and political organizers would like to know the relation between fluctuations of the business cycle and participation in unions or left-wing movements. Unfortunately, the patterns are not at all clear. For instance, the depression of the late 1830s seemed to dampen the early growth of unions in the United States and to arrest the growth of workingmen's parties. The prosperity of the post–Civil War period was accompanied by intense misery among many newly urbanized workers and by high levels of labor unrest. The depression that began in the late 1880s and continued through the 1890s triggered a period of labor organizing and unrest that did not really tail off until World War I and the 1920s. On the whole, the 1920s were fairly quiet. But in the Great Depression of the 1930s, unionization gained rapidly, especially in the latter half of the decade. In other words, the business cycle *alone,* considered apart from conditions in specific industries and the policies of movement organizations, and apart from the general patterns of historical change, is a *poor* predictor of labor movement growth.

The growth of business organizations must be measured by a different kind of indicator than membership. For instance, volume of sales or net return on investment are perhaps useful indicators. To some extent, growth (or decline) may be a result of trends and policies in the larger environment. Since the late nineteenth century, our government has made efforts to insure a climate for corporate growth. For example, considerable parts of U.S. foreign policy reflect the state's support for the expansion of markets for American products and a favorable climate for American investments abroad (Williams, 1972).

When corporations are extremely large and have a monopoly or oligopoly status within their industry, they have the capacity to control their environment. They are no longer like an organism that has to react to environmental changes. They can shape the environment to support their growth. For instance, they can control markets in various ways:
1. By vertical integration, that is, by expansion into the production of raw materials and into marketing and distribution (For instance, the large food-processing corporations have spawned agribusinesses— large corporate farms—and have established supermarket chains. Thus they no longer have to contend with the vagaries of the market in produce, nor with the actions of wholesalers and retailers.)

2. By advertising, a device to create consumer wants and thereby markets, which are therefore to some degree predictable
3. By special "cost plus" contracts with the government that guarantee a return on investments and evade the uncertainties of the market (Galbraith, 1967)

Smaller firms cannot assure themselves of stability and growth in this manner. However, specific company policies can contribute to organizational growth. The change in individual smaller corporations in competitive parts of the economy is quite different from the growth and increasing dominance of large oligopolistic corporations in terms of consequences for the society.

Growth in government agencies has followed different patterns. We will later discuss the growth of the state as a whole. Here we will more or less confine ourselves to individual agencies, although the two phenomena are very hard to distinguish. Growth of the state has meant that more resources are available for the growth of each agency. In general, growth in a state organization could be measured by the size of its budget, by the number of its employees, and by the increase in its output, which might include characteristics such as the number of clients serviced.

Patterns of Growth

There are no uniform laws of growth for organizations. Patterns of growth vary depending on the larger historical setting, the type of organization in question, the rewards the organization offers its members and clients, and the organization's specific purposes and policies. For example, on the one hand, we can point to organizations like the Hutterite communes, which tend to fission when they reach a membership of about one hundred. The communes are communities of a Christian sect that after centuries of persecution and wandering in Europe and Russia has settled in the northern plains area of Montana and Canada. The Hutterites have an extremely high birth rate and, as a result of good health care, a very high rate of population growth. To sustain their close-knit social structure, they encourage fissioning of communes and the formation of new settlements. Each Hutterite settlement therefore remains fairly small, with strong personal ties, collective nonbureaucratic decision-making, and control over individual behavior through informal peer pressure. For the Hutterites, growth means the establishment of new communes, each of which is more or less a replica of the fairly simple structure of the others, rather than growth and internal differentiation within each commune.

The same pattern of what might be called segmental growth—growth by adding on new, fairly small, more or less identical segments or cells—appears in the Pentecostal movement. Members are encouraged to start new Pentecostal groups rather than to swell the size of existing groups. Each group can maintain its internal patterning of face-to-face contact, egalitarian decision-making, and an intense sense of communion. The movement as a whole grows by the addition of small rather undifferentiated segments, very loosely linked together. In the case of the Pentecostal movement, this pattern of growth is associated with doctrinal "looseness." Local groups can more or less establish their own interpretation of the movement's religious teachings. There is no central coordinating body, and thus there is no central doctrine or "line" that gets imposed on the local groups. The rewards of this movement, like those of the Hutterites, are primarily ideological and interpersonal—a strong sense of rightness, hope for salvation, release of tension through intense ecstatic religious experience ("speaking in tongues," shaking, singing, and so on), participation in decision-making, and a strong sense of group membership.

At the other extreme of patterns of organizational growth in our society are the giant corporations. For them, growth means internal differentiation and an increase in the number of levels of supervision. They grow by adding new divisions and by merger with other, often rather different, corporations. For instance, both of these processes are visible in the large auto manufacturers. The automakers develop separate divisions partly by increasing their internal division of labor (Fisher Body appears as a separate suborganization within GM *specialized* for making car bodies), or by creating somewhat undifferentiated segmental subdivisions (Vega plants are separate from but parallel to Chevrolet plants within GM), or by adding new suborganizations through mergers (many of the long-standing divisions of GM were once separate companies). The suborganizations are themselves hierarchical and internally differentiated; they are not like the simple egalitarian cells of the Pentecostal movement. General Motors—unlike the Pentecostals—has multiple coordinating and supervising layers. There is a clearly defined top to its hierarchy (although the divisions and local plants participate in lower level decision-making on a limited range of issues).

Material rewards are the primary motivational glue that holds the giant corporation together. Some members of management may be intensely loyal to their company; still, compared with the Pentecostals and other movement groups, material rewards overwhelmingly outweigh interpersonal and ideological rewards at all levels of the corporation, from stockholder to assembly-line worker. As long as material rewards flow, organization members are willing to make sizable concessions in terms of personal satisfaction and participation in decision-making (although not unlimited concessions, as the recent wildcat strikes and rebellions at the Dodge plants, the Lordstown Vega plant, and so on demonstrate). Thus we see that the reward structure of General Motors permits growth with hierarchy and internal differentiation, just as the reward structure of the Pentecostal movement is linked to fissioning and undifferentiated segmentalizing growth. *These examples help illustrate the statement that there are no general laws of growth that all organizations follow.*

The larger environment as well as an organization's internal structure, goals, and rewards shape growth patterns. Resource bases for organizational growth may expand or dry up. Potential members may increase or decrease. Finally, the technology of transportation and communication puts some limits on the size and internal structure of organizations. Actually, however, these limits are perhaps more flexible than one might think—traditional empires such as the Chinese, the Roman, and the Byzantine remained remarkably coherent and centrally administered without modern communications systems. Also, the great trading companies of early capitalist expansion, such as the East India Company and the Hudson Bay Company, controlled vast amounts of wealth without modern communications and record-keeping.

The Birth of Organizations

Organizations are rarely created out of nothing. Rather, they grow out of other organizations or more informal groupings. The examples that follow demonstrate three characteristics that are often a part of the birth of an organization:
1. Organizations are born as a response to changes in the political and economic climate.
2. Organizations are started by people who have had experience in other, similar groupings.
3. Sometimes important organizations begin as factions of preexisting organizations.

Beginnings of the American Political Party System

The U.S. Constitution specifies the formal framework of representative government. It does not specify how people are to compete in elections. The process of fleshing out the formal framework with actual competition for office was one of the sources of the American political party system. A second, more fundamental source of the party system was the factions and different interests among the American people. The factions existed before the formal constitutional framework was established. But that framework provided one arena in which the factional disputes could be fought out. In particular, competition for office provided short-run goals for the diverse factions. In the long run, they had different and conflicting ideas about the distribution of wealth and power in the United States, about support for the revolution in France, and about whether the United States should be a country of small farmers and craftsmen or powerful manufacturers and factory laborers. But these long-run conflicts could be expressed in a short-run routinized competition for votes.

Thus in the origins of American political parties, there were two strong contradictory pressures: the pressure to turn the party into a vehicle for imple-

menting the interests and world view of the faction from which it sprang, and the pressure to turn it into a vehicle for gaining votes and winning elections. The last decade of the eighteenth century and the first two decades of the nineteenth century are the period during which these pressures shaped the American political party system. Thereafter, of course, the party names and particular interests they reflected changed, but the basic structure was established.

Class Bases. The more egalitarian or left-wing faction of the revolutionary organizations gave rise to the Democratic-Republican societies as its organizational expression. Support was based extensively, but not exclusively, on workmen and "mechanics" (Link, 1942:93), who, as a group, outnumbered other occupations in the membership of the societies. Leadership and personnel of the Democratic-Republican societies overlapped the leadership of urban associations of workers such as the mechanics, master sailmakers, and coopers societies. Farmers represented a second major group that contributed to the Democratic-Republican societies. Sailors and maritime workers were a third.

Modern analysis of membership lists support the Democratic-Republicans view of themselves: "It must be the mechanics and farmers, or the poorer class of people (as they are generally called) that must support the freedom of America." Their opponents said of their meetings that they were attended by "the lowest order of mechanics, laborers and draymen" (Link, 1942:94). Yet the most wretched strata of American society—blacks and white indentured servants—were not represented in the societies, whereas intellectuals, doctors, and inventors were. So, too, were certain manufacturers who were independent of British trade as well as some commercial sugar and tobacco farmers who were worried about British competition. Speculators who made fortunes in the land boom in western Pennsylvania and Kentucky, who "discerned no incompatibility between hoarding land, collecting rents, and driving off 'squatters,' and at the same time indulging in high talk of equal rights and equal liberty" were also among the members (Link, 1942:78).

Like the Democrats of our own day, the organizational vehicle was not pure in its commitments. It became an umbrella group for a variety of interests whose values were often incompatible even if they could agree on a rhetoric of equal rights, liberty, and support for the French Revolution. In any case, the Democratic-Republican societies did not attack private ownership of land or other productive property. They did not want a few rich men to dominate the government and run it for their own benefit. They did not want a small handful of the very wealthy to gain control of productive property—land and workshops—and reduce the rest to the status of employed laborers. By and large, they wanted to have as many people as possible own moderate amounts of property.

The other major faction was smaller, less diverse, more united in its values and life-style. The antirepublicans were primarily the rich and wellborn. They were merchants with ties to Britain. In addition, they included what

Jefferson called "nervous persons" who were afraid of the masses, of disorder, and of popular participation in government. Intellectuals were numbered among this faction, as were many ministers because of the anticlerical and even atheistic image of the Democratic-Republicans. The conservatives established a national organization of Federalists, as well as local associations and chambers of commerce. Most important, the press was largely in the hands of Federalist owners (Link, 1942:189).

Organizational Background.   In modern history, virtually no organization appears out of nowhere. Most new organizations are in fact offshoots of other organizations or are created by people who have had experience in other organizations. This continuity of organizational goals and personnel, even if names and formal structures change, characterized the formation of the American political party system. The Democratic-Republican societies were in many respects a continuation of the Sons of Liberty. The Revolution left a legacy of local organizations of militiamen, mechanics, and farmers who had participated in revolutionary organizations. In the years after the Revolution, these bodies (sometimes calling themselves Regulators or Associators) pushed for state constitutions that included widespread suffrage (as opposed to stringent property qualifications) and easy credit (a perennial demand of debt-ridden farmers and small entrepreneurs). The Constitution disappointed them because it reduced the role of small property owners in political participation. The Federalist presidents seemed to represent the ascendancy or aristocratic moneyed interests who favored an aloof government.

Revolution in France.   The French Revolution of 1789, and its turn leftward in 1793, provided a wider ideological focus around which these dispersed societies and organizational leftovers of the Revolution could revitalize their role and attack Federalist control of political office. The issue of the French Revolution became a symbolic battleground for economic and political factions in the United States. The French Jacobin Clubs—the breeding grounds of the French Revolution—provided a model, which American radicals self-consciously followed. The old radical clubs and a number of new ones (about forty in all) first turned to the task of political education, to inform their neighbors of what was happening in France.

Piggybacked onto this international ideological concern were local interests, class interests and opposition to the Federalist administration. The clubs worked to cooperate with France, often even to attack British holdings in North America and to support French insurgents in these areas (such as Quebec). These projects did not produce any outstanding results. The Democratic-Republican societies in seaboard cities harassed British vessels. In some towns, food for relief in France was collected. Many societies were primarily study groups, reading works about France or the writings of Tom Paine or Joseph Priestley, the English scientist and political radical. By the end of the

1790s, the Democratic-Republican societies provided the beginnings of a party structure by means of which Jefferson would oust the Federalists from the presidency. The clubs and popular societies effectively organized for support of Jefferson in 1800. Even Alexander Hamilton, "the master mind of the Federalists," grudgingly complimented the organizational ability of the "mobocrats," as he called the Democratic-Republicans (Link, 1942:207).

Conclusions: The Dynamics of the Growth of Parties.   Figure 4 depicts the transformation of revolutionary groups into political parties. These transitions were gradual. There was an overlap in personnel and in the general class basis of the radical political organizations of the 1760s (before the Revolution) and those of the 1790s (just before the emerging party system brought the Jeffersonians to power). The class interests were primarily those of small entrepreneurs—farmers and independent artisans—but larger coalitions could be built, for two different reasons: (*a*) the broader ideological international issues could unite people with dissimilar local interests, and (*b*) the competition for public office and the desire to oust the Federalists from control provided a common bond for different groups.

Figure 4

Transformation from revolutionary organization to political party

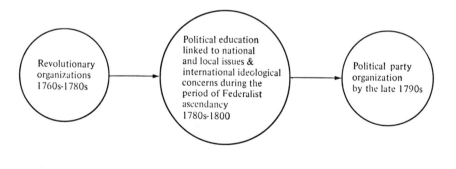

During the years of Federal ascendancy, the Democratic-Republican societies were more involved in political education than in political action, but under favorable circumstances could switch from one to the other. During this "latent" period, personal contact and written expression were important activities in preparing the organizations for their later role in elections. The media provided the forum in which the ideology of egalitarian, politically active small property owners could confront the Federalist ideology of limited political participation and control by large merchants and manufacturers. Although the Federalists controlled much of the press, the Democratic-Republicans expressed their ideology in rallies, broadsides and other "underground media," and personal contacts.

Finally, events abroad had an important effect domestically. The French Revolution was the ideological touchstone—Americans were either for or against it. Local and national factions used the French Revolution as a symbol —as an expression of the way in which the domestic cleavages were part of a larger picture of conflict between classes in the societies located in or colonized by western Europe. The Jacobin clubs of revolutionary France provided a model for American political activity, so that it was fed not only by its own tradition and continuity but also by the French style of organization. Ultimately both sets of organizations—French and American—shared common roots in the economic, political, and ideological changes of the late eighteenth century (Hofstadter, 1969). Thus all of the following factors were important in the growth of the American party organization: the national class structure, the experience of organizing the American Revolution, the international situation, the impact of the French Revolution, the role of media and political education, and the "spoils of victory" to be gained in winning office.

Unions in the 1930s

> Mellon pulled the whistle,
> Hoover rang the bell;
> Wall Street gave the signal,
> And the country went to hell.
>
> Popular Depression jingle

In this section, I shall describe briefly the start and expansion of industrial unions during the 1930s in the United States. Unions had existed in America since the nineteenth century. By the 1930s, they had succeeded primarily in organizing skilled workers in crafts and railways, and some groups of workers, such as miners and garment workers, who had been bound together by strong ethnic ties or the traditions of their isolated, specialized, or hazardous occupations. Often there was little solidarity between the unions. Within the shipping industry, for example, different types of workers, such as marine firemen, sailors, cooks, and longshoremen, failed to support each other's strikes (Brecher, 1974:191). When the layoffs and speedups of the thirties came along, when employers fired workers and forced the remaining ones to work harder, the existing unions gained many new members. Union organizers made efforts to create industry-wide rather than craft-specialty unions.

The Industrial Unions.   The labor organizing of the 1930s received its impetus from several sources: from a group of labor leaders within the craft-oriented American Federation of Labor (AFL), who in the mid-1930s split off to form the Committee (and, shortly, the Congress) of Industrial Organizations (CIO); the rank and file itself, who understood that victory at the local level, in plants and firms, required industry-wide organization and a more militant style; and, the American Left, which provided some professional organizers, considerable enthusiasm, and a larger vision of where union organizing might go. The formal organizational efforts came from the union leaders and the Left. However, the union-organizing drives would not have taken place without the actions of the rank and file, who responded to the conditions of their workplaces.

The CIO began formally in 1935. A strategic factor in its birth was the changing political climate. President Roosevelt, in preparation for the 1936 campaign, interpreted public opinion as a mandate to turn politically left. Along with other legislation, a bill proposed by Senator Robert Wagner (D-N.Y.) was passed that spelled out mechanisms for holding elections to determine who would represent workers, and prohibited unfair labor practices, such as discriminatory discharge of union members. In other words, this bill gave legal standing to union organizing.

At the AFL convention in the summer of 1935, a group of union officials from the United Mine Workers; the Typographical Workers; the Mine, Mill and Smelter Workers; the Oil Field, Gas Well and Refinery Workers; and a number of clothing and textile workers' unions met and formed the Committee for Industrial Organization. During 1936 and the early months of 1937, the AFL moved to suspend these unions and expel all their delegates. One of the causes for the split was AFL fears that industrial (as opposed to craft) unionizing would cut into the jurisdiction and autonomy of the AFL unions. But underlying this immediate cause was AFL distrust of unskilled and semiskilled workers and their young militant leadership. Furthermore, unlike the AFL, the CIO wanted government support for the labor movement.

Thus by 1937, the government legislation and the national-level union organization were present. The vehicle for the union drives was ready. What was needed to set it in motion were local-level organizers and the workers themselves. The latter were ready to act. The continuing depression and efforts by employers to cut wages, lay off workers, and speed up production sparked a wave of sit-down strikes.

The Sit-Down Strike.   In this type of strike, the workers not only refuse to produce but also seize the plant and equipment. A striker in the February 1936 Akron rubber strike remarked: "The two outside agitators in this strike are

Goodyear hours and Goodyear wages." The sit-down strike was extraordinarily important in the growth of unions. The workers demonstrated that only their labor made production possible. By taking control of the tools and plant where production occurred, they reasserted the control over tools that most workers had lost during the Industrial Revolution. But their new control over the plants was not a futile nostalgic harkening back to the days of the individual craftsman. The new assertion of control was a collective effort, in which each striker understood that all workers depended on each other for loyalty and maintenance of strike discipline.

This collective effort was also exciting in its own right. One striker at GM commented, "The guys with me became my buddies. I remember as a kid in school reading about Davy Crockett and the last stand at the Alamo. That's just how I felt. Yes sir, Chevy No. 4 was my Alamo" (Brecher, 1972:244). The sit-downers sang, made up songs, danced, and felt a sense of happiness and purpose. One wrote, "We are all one happy family now. We all feel fine and have plenty to eat. We have several good banjo players and singers. . . ." Another wrote, "I am having a great time, something new, something different, lots of grub and music." The families of the strikers and other people who manned the outside support committees also felt this new sense of purpose and excitement. One wife commented, "I found a common understanding and unselfishness I'd never known in my life. I'm living for the first time with a definite goal . . . just being a woman isn't enough anymore. I want to be a human being with the right to think for myself" (Brecher, 1972:245). The sit-down strikers maintained order among themselves. They set up committees on food, information, and contacts with their outside support committees, sanitation, education, and defense; and each worker was expected to serve on at least one committee. As a group, they secured the defense of the factory and prepared homemade weapons in case they were attacked by troops or "law and order" vigilantes. They cleaned the factory, showered daily, and maintained a quiet zone for rest and sleeping.

The sit-down strike was essentially nonviolent on the part of the strikers. They seized property, but they did not attack people. The companies had to initiate violence in order to recapture the plants, thereby risking the destruction of their own equipment and creating an unfavorable public reaction to violence.

The sit-down strike spread from the Goodyear plant to the automobile industry. After some hesitation on the part of CIO president John L. Lewis, the CIO backed the newly founded United Auto Workers. In some ways, the sit-down strike was too spontaneous, autonomous, self-reliant, and from the bottom up for union officials to be entirely pleased with it. From the auto industry—particularly the massive 1937 sit-down strike at the Flint General Motors plant—the sit-down spread throughout the country. As many as a half-million workers in transit systems, restaurants, offices, small factories of every type, five-and-dime stores, sanitation departments, hospitals (where services were maintained for patients), workshops for the blind, and cemeteries were involved. Students, prison inmates, and welfare recipients also have used the tactic. As Brecher (1972:261) remarks:

> The sit-down idea spread so rapidly because it dramatized a simple, powerful fact: that no institution can run without the cooperation of those whose activity makes it up. Once the example of the sit-downs was before people's eyes, they could apply it to their own situation. On the shop floor it could be used to gain power over the actual running of production. In large industries it could be used for massive power struggles like the GM strike. In small shops it could force quick concessions.

The wave of sit-down strikes, which peaked in March 1937, ebbed for a number of reasons. Union recognition was won and concessions were made. Employers soon acted preemptively and preferred voluntary negotiations with union leaders to running the risk of a tumultuous sit-down strike. Thus, for instance, some of the companies in the steel industry accepted top-down unionization and bargaining with "responsible" labor leaders. Even so, steel unionization took a toll of workers' lives in violence against strikers in Illinois, Ohio, and Pennsylvania. Eventually the war turned the efforts of the nation and of the unions to new activities. Routinization beset the CIO as it had the AFL. But for awhile—in 1936 and 1937—the drive to organize industrial unions had meshed with the experiences, demands, and actions of hundreds of thousands of workers to produce a movement of great power and lasting effects.

Change in Social Movement Organizations

Social movement organizations face special internal problems. Because they are committed to changing the society, they must remain active and flexible. In many cases, social movement organizations are committed to being democratic and encouraging a high level of participation among the members, but they have few tangible rewards to offer their members. Usually they cannot promise members a high salary; often they cannot provide any income for members. They may even have difficulty in collecting enough resources to keep the movement organization going at all. Thus movement organizations are under constant pressure to become more conservative, more oriented toward maintaining themselves as organizations, and more oligarchical (run by a small clique).

Conservatism, the priority of organizational maintenance, and oligarchy tend to go together. The process may take place something like this: Even in a democratic social movement organization, a small number of people may do most of the work and planning. In effect, they come to run the organization. They manage the resources—dues, donations, and so on—that are paid into it. They control the flow of information within the organization. They speak for the organization and arrange contacts with the rest of the society. Eventually this group comes to see its own identity, purpose, and even livelihood tied up with the organization. The leaders come to fear that the organization may be destroyed or altered in such a way that they will lose their position within it. Thus the organization's original goals for social change are replaced with a new goal—keeping the organization strong and stable. Sometimes this switch in goals is accompanied by greater conservatism. If the social movement organization really "rocks the boat"—acts to alter or disrupt the existing distribution of wealth and power within the society—it may be destroyed by the authorities, its leaders jailed or harassed, and its resources cut off. Therefore, the leaders orient the organization toward less disruptive, threatening, or radical activity; they want to make sure that nothing the organization does could lead to its end.

Finally, the leaders may also change the internal structure of the organization to ensure that they will continue to have power within it. Bureaucratic appointment may replace the election of officers. Procedures or rules that make the rank and file feel powerless and apathetic may be introduced. This process of goal displacement, oligarchization, conservatism and rank-and-file apathy was first observed by Robert Michels (1949), who was involved in European Socialist party politics. Michels observed how parties that had been committed to change and democratic organization, both internally and for the whole society, gradually turned conservative and came under the control of a small clique that maintained its hold on the party. He asserted that these changes in organizations happened regularly enough to suggest "an iron law of oligarchy." The iron law of oligarchy can also be observed in many American unions that began as militant working-class organizations but became highly bureaucratized, run by small cliques of union officials (some of whom had never been on the shop floor) and aimed at streamlining and regularizing rather than overthrowing management's hold on the workers.

Are there conditions under which the iron law of oligarchy does not hold in a social movement organization? We can identify a number of such conditions. For instance, a movement organization may not be committed to having a mass base and a democratic organization. It may begin as a small, tightly knit, highly committed group of professional activists. The organization accepts as members only those people who would become the leaders of the movement. Thus from the start, it does not have to contend with rank-and-file apathy. Since this type of movement organization does not have to recruit and retain a large mass membership, it can remain somewhat insulated from shifts in public opinion. It can mobilize a large number of people when the time is ripe, when the situation in the society changes in such a way that the organization can attain its goals. Until such a time, its small size, tight structure, and highly committed membership make it relatively insulated from pressures to become more oriented to the status quo and more accommodating to outside pressures.

Unlike the mass organization, the small, highly committed organization does not so easily become conservative and bureaucratized. The best examples of this type of structure are the revolutionary socialist vanguard parties like the Bolsheviks, the Chinese Communist party, and so on. At the core of these parties are cadres of full-time revolutionaries. At certain crucial times, these cadres may mobilize and direct a mass base; but during "drab and peaceful" times or periods of repression, the movement organization can continue to exist without mass support.

Without going so far as to establish a cadre organization, a movement organization can institute practices that reduce the tendencies to conservatism, oligarchy, and goal displacement. For example, a cell structure can be established in which the units of the movement organization are small and egalitarian. The cells may be either loosely coordinated or virtually uncoordinated. The Protestant Pentecostals and some of the New Left groups of the late 1960s reflect this structure. The movement grows by adding new cells rather than by drawing new people into the bottom of a hierarchy. Sometimes movements splinter and factionalize unintentionally, with similar consequences for their internal structure and continued radicalism.

Another organizational device to hold back the iron law of oligarchy is to rotate leaders systematically. Terms of office can be kept short, officeholders can be prevented from succeeding themselves, recall can be used effectively. Local officials can be forced to move to new locations to prevent their building up a local machine to keep them in office. The Student Nonviolent Coordinating Committee used some of these devices in its civil rights work in the South during the 1960s.

In the face of large-scale changes in the climate of the whole society, however, these organizational devices are at best holding tactics. Like a lungfish that hibernates in the mud until the river rises again, only the cadre organization can really survive periods of apathy or repression. The mass organizations tend to succumb to the iron law. Segmentalized mass organizations either lose segments until they are reduced to essentially cadre organizations or they don't survive at all.

The iron law is not always in effect, however. The crucial factor in changes within a movement is the organization's relationship to its environment, that is, to the society in which it operates. Organizations do not have a "life cycle" or "natural history" of their own, operating independently of their environment. To understand how and why social movements change, one has to examine the particular historical situation in which they exist (Zald & Ash, 1966).

Record-Keeping

Organizations have generally been acutely aware of the change processes that I have been discussing in the preceding pages. Unlike isolated individuals and individuals in unorganized groups, organizations try to take steps not to be caught unawares by change. They develop ways of measuring the impact of environmental change on the organization and of gauging changes in the organization itself. An important part of the internal structure of most organizations is some way of measuring, recording, and interpreting change.

Information-processing within organizations is an important activity: it keeps organizational elites informed about what is happening within the organization (for instance, a company's records of absenteeism or quitting are a measure of worker morale that can be used by management to determine labor policy); it is used to interpret the organization's activities to a wider public (many movement organizations maintain newspapers); it is used to monitor changes in the organization's environment (caseload records in a welfare agency or student enrollments in a university are indicators of changes in the organization's environments). Later we shall be concerned with organizational information-processing for two reasons: first, control of information becomes a weapon in the *intra*organizational struggles that I shall discuss in the next two chapters; second, organizational records are an important source of data about organizational change for the researcher. Here I am primarily introducing the notion of record-keeping and information-processing in organizations to show that most organizations try to be aware of changes and to measure them in some way. Organizations are much more conscious of change processes than are isolated individuals.

There are a great many ways to measure and record changes in an organization's condition. For thousands of years, agencies of the state have made inventories of available resources, including human manpower. Ancient Egypt kept records of supplies and captured treasures; the Bible is full of lists of captives, armaments, and temple furnishings; the Romans carried out a census as well as made inventories of materials; the Domesday Book of William the Conqueror records a survey of English wealth carried out to provide information for taxation. To the historian, these lists are records of the material culture of the society and of the strength of its state organizations.

Modern organizations—particularly large corporations and branches of the state—have developed a variety of sophisticated accounting schemes. The introduction of computers and various microstorage devices has made possible the storage and processing of vast amounts of data within organizations. Cost-benefit analysis has become a currently fashionable tool for assessing an organization's condition. Sometimes the indicators of costs and benefits are invalid or meaningless. Cost-benefit analysis often leads to very narrow, easily quantified definitions of "costs" and "benefits." Efficiency tends to be measured in dollars and cents.

The storage and manipulation of organizational records can never be better than the data-collection process itself. When American officers in Vietnam pressured their subordinates to demonstrate that the Americans were winning, phony body counts became the data used for sophisticated systems analysis. The ultimate debacle of this system of data collection and information-processing came in 1972, when large numbers of North Vietnamese equipped with tanks penetrated the electronic sensing net of the demilitarized zone and appeared in South Vietnam. As computer programmers say, "Garbage in, garbage out." The conclusions can never be better than the data.

References

Brecher, Jeremy.
1974   Strike. New York: Fawcett World Library.

Festinger, Leon; Henry W. Riecken; and Stanley Schachter.
1956   When Prophecy Fails. Minneapolis: University of Minnesota Press.

Galbraith, John Kenneth.
1967   The New Industrial State. Boston: Houghton Mifflin.

Gerlach, Luther P., and Virginia H. Hine.
1973   Lifeway Leap. Minneapolis: University of Minnesota Press.

Gusfield, Joseph R.
1966   Symbolic Crusade. Urbana: University of Illinois Press.

Hofstadter, Richard.
1969   The Idea of a Party System. Berkeley: University of California Press.

Link, Eugene P.
1942   Democratic-Republican Societies, 1790–1800. New York: Columbia University Press.

Messinger, Sheldon L.
1955   "Organizational transformation: A case study of a declining social movement." American Sociological Review 20(February):3–10.

Michels, Robert.
1949   Political Parties: A Sociological Study of the Oligarchical Tendencies of Modern Democracy. Translation by Eden and Cedar Paul. Glencoe, Ill.: Free Press.

Scholem, Gershom G.
1961   "Sabbataianism and mystical heresy." Pp. 287–324 in Major Trends in Jewish Mysticism. Third edition (paper). New York: Schocken Books.
1973   Sabbatai Zevi: The Mystical Messiah, 1626–1676. Bollingen Series, no. 93. Princeton, N.J.: Princeton University Press.

Troeltsch, Ernst.
1931   The Social Teachings of the Christian Churches. London: Allen and Unwin.

Turner, Victor W.
1969   Ritual Process: Structure and Anti-Structure. Chicago: Aldine.

Williams, William A.
1972   The Tragedy of American Diplomacy. Revised second edition. New York: Dell.

Zald, Mayer N., and Roberta Ash.
1966   "Social movement organizations: Growth, decay and change." Social Forces 44(March):327–341.

Zald, Mayer N., and Patricia Denton.
1963   "From evangelism to general service: On the transformation of the YMCA." Administrative Science Quarterly 8:214–234.

Chapter
7

Innovations
and Power
Struggles

In this chapter, I shall examine the kinds of changes that take place in organizations as a result of conflict between factions in the organization. In many cases, these factions represent groups within the larger society; the conflicts in the larger society are fought out within the organizations. I shall conclude the chapter by suggesting that productive enterprises can be effectively taken over and run by production workers with little or no managerial supervision.

IN PAST CHAPTERS, I have discussed organizations as though they were unified entities, pursuing goals that the members have agreed upon. This conception of an organization is perhaps a fairly valid view of groups such as Hutterite communities or the cells of the Pentecostal movement. But most organizations do not have such internal consensus. Various kinds of conflicts exist within them. These conflicts always concern power. In some organizations, these disputes are not over structure and goals at all but involve competition for powerful positions. In other organizations, factional disputes represent different interests, different goals, and different ideas about the internal distribution of power. In this case, the conflict can bring with it change in the sense of alteration in structure.

Of course, this distinction between incumbency conflicts and substantive conflicts within an organization is more analytical than practical. People who are competing for power tend to rephrase their rivalry in terms of issues and interests to build up a following, even when they are essentially indistinguishable from their antagonists. Many fights that are little more than power struggles over who gets control of key positions and resources are disguised as struggles over important substantive issues. On the other hand, what appears to be personal rivalry may develop into a dispute that really changes the organization's policy or power structure.

The intraparty struggles in the Russian Communist party during the 1920s and 1930s, for example, reflected Stalin's successful effort to obtain power and crush his various rivals—Trotsky, Bukharin, Zinoviev and Kamenev, and so on. In part, these dissensions were only struggles between individuals and their followers for positions of power. But these struggles were tied to different strategies for Soviet development. Each faction accused the other of selling out the revolution, of wishing to pursue disastrous policies in agriculture, and so on. Each faction appealed to substantive issues and interests in order to gain support among wavering party members. Finally, what began as a struggle involving elements of personal rivalry, veiled in ideological terms, ended up in the institutionalization of definite policies with very decisive material consequences—the collectivization of agriculture, the emphasis on industrial expansion, the killing of the kulaks, and so forth. Thus, the boundaries between interpersonal competition, interpersonal competition disguised by appeals to substantive issues, and real substantive factionalization over policies and structure are often indistinct.

The most interesting intraorganizational disputes are those between the top power holders in an organization and those with little or no power. First, these struggles are most likely to involve divergent stands on politics and structural issues and are very likely to produce transformations of the organizations. Second, these conflicts most probably reflect differences in power and control over resources within the society as a whole: *the organization becomes the arena in which these larger conflicts are fought out.* Third, when these intraorganizational conflicts occur in organizations that carry out the productive activities of a society—the production of goods and services—these conflicts have an especially far-reaching significance.

In this chapter, I want to look at conflict and change in organizations from two different perspectives. First, I shall look at it from the point of view of organizational elites, discussing their goals, their dilemmas, and their strategies so that the reader will be more able to recognize them in the future. Second, I shall look at conflict and change from the perspective of those who have little power in the organization.

The Origin of Power Differences in Organizations

Basically, there are two sources of power differences in organizations—processes within the organization and the carryover into the organization of power differences in the larger society.

Inequality in Society

The latter situation is simpler to summarize. Some organizations reflect power and wealth differences in the larger society. In some cases, such organizations may even be designed to perpetuate these differences. In any event, they have no particular commitment to egalitarianism. This sort of intraorganizational power difference is characteristic of business enterprises and the agencies of the state. In Part Three of this book, we shall discuss at much greater length how differences in power and wealth emerged in society as a whole. Here it suffices to state that these inequalities are built into businesses and state organizations. In businesses, we see clearly the distinction between employees, supervisory workers, top management, and stockholders. By and large, when we talk about power holders in a business, we shall be referring to owners and upper management. Supervisory workers (office supervisor, foreman, etc.) are themselves employees and have essentially no power of their own—that is, they do not participate in decision-making but only serve to keep lower level workers in line. These power differences within a firm reflect the differences in the larger society between those people who own productive property (capitalists) and those whose living depends on being employed—on selling their labor power.

The organizations of the state in a capitalist society also reflect inequality in society but in a more subtle way than the business firm. The upper reaches of government bureaucracies are filled by powerful political figures who may even have direct ties to corporate power. The middle levels of government bureaucracies are filled by professionals, including professional managers and bureaucrats, who carry out rather narrowly defined tasks with their sphere of expertise. Often these professionals are trained to accept the downward flow of power in the bureaucracy. On the whole, they do not question or make policy, although they may indirectly influence it by their control over information that top policymakers need. They may also influence policy by the way in which they interpret and implement decisions. At the bottom of the bureaucracies are employees who are not very different in life conditions from the working class in the private sector. The clients of the bureaucracies are very diverse. Some, like prisoners, mental patients, or welfare recipients, are very powerless and are often drawn from the poorest and most unorganized people in the society. Others, like the "clients" of the Internal Revenue Service, the regulatory agencies, and the Federal Reserve System, may represent the most powerful private interests.

Oligarchization

Voluntary associations and social movement organizations, on the other hand, do not always have the built-in power differences that are carried over from the larger society into firms and state organizations. In these organizations, inequalities emerge through internal processes and environmental pressures. As I noted in the last chapter, even those organizations that are committed to an egalitarian internal structure may become hierarchical and bureaucratized under the "iron law of oligarchy." Robert Michels (1949) first formulated this iron law of oligarchy after observing the Social Democratic (Socialist) parties of central Europe during the early years of the twentieth century. Michels saw how parties that were committed to democratic decision-making became increasingly dominated by a small group, an oligarchy. He argued that this process was inherent in the structure of a large democratic party. First, an internal division of labor appeared in which some people gained control over the organization's monetary resources and its various information-processing activities (its newspaper, its files, and so on). This control gave these people power and made them able to fend off efforts to oust them from these positions. To some extent, the power holders wanted to keep these positions because they did not want to go back to the kind of work they had been doing before they became party functionaries. Thus, the people involved in certain key party functions became an oligarchy, and by virtue of their control over these functions were able to maintain their power.

Michels also argued that oligarchization in a previously egalitarian mass party made the organization more conservative because the oligarchy did not want to risk its position by "making trouble" in the larger society. A similar charge has been leveled against Communist parties in Latin America and Western Europe (Debray, 1967). The oligarchical functionaries in charge of these parties do not want a revolution. They are content to cooperate in electoral politics because they can continue to enjoy their status in the party and live off its financial resources. Therefore, these Communist parties made little effort to help the guerrilla struggles of Che Guevara in Bolivia and of other armed revolutionaries elsewhere or to support the 1968 French worker-student uprising. Such charges have also been made against American union leaders who, having become oligarchical functionaries, use the union to support them in a comfortable middle-class way of life instead of pressing militant demands. As I have argued already, not all voluntary associations or movement organizations are uniformly subject to the iron law of oligarchy. Nevertheless, it is one of the processes by which inequality appears in such organizations.

Structurelessness

A second and similar process by which inequality can appear is through lack of structure. An organization can be committed to equality in theory. In *fact,* people with more time, more energy, certain personal or social characteristics, and/or stronger ideological commitments take over. They attend policy-making meetings more often, talk more at these meetings, stay at them longer, put in more time on organizational activities, and informally come to dominate the organization. The other members find it difficult to stop this take-over because there are no formal mechanisms for selecting leaders or for sanctioning those who informally take power. A participant in the women's movement comments on what she calls the "tyranny of structurelessness."

Contrary to what we would like to believe, there is no such thing as a structureless group. Any group of people of whatever nature that comes together for any length of time for any purpose will inevitably structure itself in some fashion. The structure may be flexible; it may vary over time; it may evenly or unevenly distribute tasks, power, and resources over the members of the group. But it will be formed regardless of the abilities, personalities, or intentions of the people involved. The very fact that we are individuals, with different talents, predispositions, and backgrounds makes this inevitable. Only if we refused to relate or interact on any basis whatsoever could we approximate structureless— and that is not the nature of a human group.

This means that to strive for a structureless group is as useful, and as deceptive, as to aim at an "objective" news story, "value-free" social science, or a "free" economy. A "laissez faire" group is about as realistic as a "laissez faire" society; the idea becomes a smokescreen for the strong or the lucky to establish unquestioned hegemony over others. This hegemony can be so easily established because the idea of "structurelessness" does not prevent the formation of informal structures, only formal ones. Similarly "laissez faire" philosophy did not prevent the economically powerful from establishing control over wages, prices, and distribution of goods; it only prevented the government from doing so. Thus structurelessness becomes a way of masking power, and within the women's movement is usually most strongly advocated by those who are the most powerful (whether they are conscious of their power or not). As long as the structure of the group is informal, the rules of how decisions are made are known only to a few and awareness of power is limited to those who know the rules. Those who do not know the rules and are not chosen for initiation must remain in confusion, or suffer from paranoid delusions that something is happening of which they are not quite aware.

For everyone to have the opportunity to be involved in a given group and to participate in its activities the structure must be explicit, not implicit. The rules of decision-making must be open and available to everyone, and this can happen only if they are formalized. This is not to say that formalization of a structure of a group will destroy the informal structure. It usually doesn't. But it does hinder the informal structure from having predominant control and make available some means of attacking it if the people involved are not at least responsible to the needs of the group at large. "Structurelessness" is organizationally impossible. We cannot decide whether to have a structured or structureless group, only whether or not to have a formally structured one. Therefore the word will not be used any longer except to refer to the idea it represents. *Unstructured* will refer to those groups that have not been deliberately structured in a particular manner. *Structured* will refer to those that have. A Structured group always has a *formal* structure, and may also have an informal, or covert, structure. It is this informal structure, particularly in Unstructured groups, that forms the basis for elites.

Because elites are informal does not mean they are invisible. At any small group meeting anyone with a sharp eye and an acute ear can tell who is influencing whom. The members of a friendship group will relate more to each other than to other people. They listen more attentively, and interrupt less; they repeat each other's points and give in amiably; they tend to ignore or grapple with the "outs" whose approval is not necessary for making a decision. But it is necessary for the "outs" to stay on good terms with the "ins." . . .

Since movement groups have made no concrete decisions about who shall exercise power within them, many different criteria are used around the country.

Most criteria are along the lines of traditional female characteristics. For instance, in the early days of the movement, marriage was usually a prerequisite for participation in the informal elite. As women have been traditionally taught, married women relate primarily to each other, and look upon single women as too threatening to have as close friends. In many cities, this criterion was further refined to include only those women married to New Left men. This standard had more than tradition behind it, however, because New Left men often had access to resources needed by the movement—such as mailing lists, printing presses, contacts, and information—and women were used to getting what they needed through men rather than independently. As the movement has changed through time, marriage has become a less universal criterion for effective participation, but all informal elites establish standards by which only women who possess certain material or personal characteristics may join. They frequently include: middle-class background (despite all the rhetoric about relating to the working class); being married; not being married but living with someone; being or pretending to be a lesbian; being between the ages of twenty and thirty; being college educated or at least having some college background; being "hip"; not being too "hip"; holding a certain political line or identification as a "radical"; having children or at least liking them; not having children; having certain "feminine" personality characteristics such as being "nice"; dressing right (whether in the traditional style or the antitraditional style); etc. There are also some characteristics that will almost always tag one as a "deviant" who should not be releated to. They include: being too old; working full time, particularly if one is actively committed to a "career"; not being "nice"; and being avowedly single (i.e., neither actively heterosexual nor homosexual).

Other criteria could be included, but they all have common themes. The characteristics prerequisite for participating in the informal elites of the movement, and thus for exercising power, concern one's background, personality, or allocation of time. They do not include one's competence, dedication to feminism, talents, or potential contribution to the movement. The former are the criteria one usually uses in determining one's friends. The latter are what any movement or organization has to use if it is going to be politically effective.

The criteria of participation may differ from group to group, but the means of becoming a member of the informal elite if one meets those criteria are pretty much the same. The only main difference depends on whether one is in a group from the beginning, or joins it after it has begun. If involved from the beginning, it is important to have as many of one's personal friends as possible also join. If no one knows anyone else very well, then one must deliberately form friendships with a select number and establish the informal interaction patterns crucial to the creation of an informal structure. Once the informal patterns are formed, they act to maintain themselves; and one of the most successful tactics of maintenance is to continuously recruit new people who "fit in." One joins such an elite much the same way one pledges a sorority. If perceived as a potential addition, one is "rushed" by the members of the informal structure and eventually either dropped or initiated. If the sorority is not politically aware enough to actively engage in this process itself, it can be started by the outsider pretty much the same way one joins any private club. Find a sponsor, i.e., pick some member of the elite who appears to be well respected within it, and actively cultivate that person's friendship. Eventually, she will most likely bring you into the inner circle.

All of these procedures take time. So if one works full time or has a similar major commitment, it is usually impossible to join simply because there are not enough hours left to go to all the meetings and cultivate the personal relationship necessary to have a voice in the decision-making. That is why formal structures of decision-making are a boon to the overworked person. Having an established process for decision-making ensures that everyone can participate in it to some extent.

Although this dissection of the process of elite formation within small groups has been critical in perspective, it is not made in the belief that these informal structures are inevitably bad—merely inevitable. All groups create informal structures as a result of interaction patterns among the members of the group. Such informal structures can do very useful things. But only Unstructured groups are totally governed by them. When informal elites are combined with a myth of "structurelessness," there can be no attempt to put limits on the use of power. It becomes capricious.

This has two potentially negative consequences of which we should be aware. The first is that the informal structure of decision-making will be much like a sorority—one in which people listen to others because they like them and not because they say significant things. As long as the movement does not do significant things, this does not much matter. But if its development is not to be arrested at this preliminary stage, it will have to alter this trend. The second is that informal structures have no obligation to be responsible to the group at large. Their power was not given to them; it cannot be taken away. Their influence is not based on what they do for the group; therefore they cannot be directly influenced by the group. This does not necessarily make informal structures irresponsible. Those who are concerned with maintaining their influence will usually try to be responsible. The group simply cannot compel such responsibility; it is dependent on the interests of the elite.

(Freeman, 1972)

Deliberate Centralism

A third process by which movement organizations and voluntary associations become inegalitarian is the deliberate decision to do so. Some become bureaucratic, believing this form to be efficient, especially for administering a large organization. Full-time movement professionals are hired. Others, as I have already described, begin as charismatic organizations, which implies an inegalitarian structure. Still others—the Leninist revolutionary parties, for example—organize themselves by the principle of "democratic centralism." Party decisions are made by an inner core of largely full-time, fully committed movement members who set party policy and communicate the line to various outer groups of supporters. The latter may be encouraged to provide information and feedback to the central group, but they have no formal control over its decisions. Obviously, this form of structure can be varied, depending on how the central group is selected—whether elected or self-appointed.

Innovation from the Top Down

When power holders in an organization want to innovate, they are faced with a basic dilemma. They must overcome resistance to change among subordinates without whetting an appetite for change that might threaten their own power. Power holders see change from two analytical perspectives: (1) acceptance and resistance to change (How can we get subordinates to accept changes that are advantageous to us?) and (2) containment of change (How can we control the process of change so that we are not threatened by it?).

Overcoming Resistance to Change

Let's begin our discussion of this dilemma of organizational power holders by citing a well-known study, the research conducted by two sociologists of the "human relations" school, Roethlisberger and Dickson (1939), at the Western Electric plant in a Chicago suburb. This study is often reprinted or summarized in introductory sociology texts as a model of sociological discovery, in particular, the discovery of the importance of primary groups within an organization.

The major purpose of the study was not to learn abstractly about primary-group relations but to help Western Electric (a subsidiary of the Bell Telephone System) increase the productivity of its workers. Management wanted the workers to produce more. The workers limited their output. Even though they were paid on a piecework basis, that is, paid according to the amount they produced, the workers did not produce as much as they could have if they worked at top speed. They deliberately kept their output below the maximum level. The restriction of output kept management from trying to speed up production (by changing the piecework rates) and from using the higher productivity as an excuse to lay off workers. In other words, from the point of view of the workers, the restriction of output was a perfectly rational policy; they accepted a take-home pay that was less than the maximum possible in order to preserve a reasonable work pace and to protect themselves against layoffs. Restriction of output was not simply an individualistic choice; the group of workers agreed to it and used various informal sanctions to enforce it on each other. Rate-busters or "speed-kings" (people who worked too fast) were looked down upon, as were laggards whose output fell below informally set standards.

Restriction of output and group sanctions against rate-busters are widespread phenomena in organizations where the relatively more powerless members do not share the goals of the organizational elite. For instance, workers want to make a living and students want to get a diploma, while management wants profits and teachers want to instill knowledge. When the lower level members have goals that are identical to those of the elite and are very strongly held, group norms about restriction of output and mutual support break down and individualistic competition sets in. Undergraduates in premed programs are notorious for their individualistic competition for grades and their low degree of cooperation with each other. Some instructors identify individualistic competitors as "good students." The official organizational reward structure in this case has overwhelmed the reward systems of subgroups.

Elites can also use ideological incentives to destroy subgroup solidarity and restriction of output. In the Soviet Union, during the years of the push to industrialize and increase agricultural output, the state gave special recognition and rewards to workers, called Stakhanovites, who were exceptionally hard-working and prodigiously productive—"rate-busters" from the point of view of their fellows who preferred a more reasonable work pace. Reward structures interact with the personal characteristics and culture that workers bring to the workplace to produce different amounts of worker solidarity.

The kind of urban working-class culture that developed in western Europe after the Industrial Revolution and among immigrants to the United States stresses worker solidarity and supports restriction of output. Other cultures and socialization patterns do not. For instance, rural Protestant farm backgrounds are correlated with relatively higher output and less support for worker solidarity, unionization, and output restriction. This cultural difference was observed both within a factory and on a regional basis: northern companies have been eager to relocate to the South where the labor force is more rural, more docile, and less unionized. The differences between rural Protestants and other workers may be partially due to cultural norms of Protestantism, with its emphasis on hard work and individualism. However, rural origins and the structure of farm work probably account for even more of the difference than does religion, since in Protestant countries with a long-standing urban factory system, patterns of worker solidarity have also emerged. The isolation of the farmers and their individual dealings with the wholesalers or landlords prevent them from immediately adopting norms of solidarity that urbanized factory workers have.

The middle classes in industrialized countries also lack traditions of restricted output such as those of factory workers (and slaves). Middle-class children believe that individual effort and maximum output will provide the maximum material and personal rewards. However, these beliefs may now be breaking down in the face of a changed employment situation that offers fewer jobs for college graduates than previously.

Entire societies (as well as subgroups within a society) may have norms of solidarity and against competitiveness. For the Eskimo or the Bushmen of the Kalahari Desert in Africa, the harshness of the climate makes sharing, generosity, and cooperative effort a condition of survival. A number of native American groups, such as the Hopi and other Pueblo societies, also have strong sanctions against competition. When white authorities forced them into schools, they appeared to be apathetic, slow, and silent because they did not accept the individualistic competitive displays that the classroom situation imposes on children.

Strategies for Increasing Productivity

Increased productivity is one of the changes that organizational elites would like to impose on other members of the organization. They can elicit this response in a number of ways:

1. One strategy is *recruitment;* only those cultural groups that have weak traditions of solidarity and strong traditions of individual effort are taken into the organization. For example, textile mills can move South, out of New York and New England, to draw on a nonunionized labor force.

2. Organizational elites can introduce a *reward structure* that favors increased output. This can be accomplished in a number of ways: *(a)* Strong ideological incentives can be offered, as in the case of the Russian Stakhanovites. Workers can be convinced that increased productivity is for the good of the whole society. *(b)* Actual material payoffs can be increased to the point where they overwhelm worker solidarity. Many professional workers are so highly rewarded in terms of salary, fringe benefits, working conditions, and free time that there is no particular immediate reason why they should restrict their output or unionize. Such has been the favored position of many university professors, accountants, salaried lawyers, and other employed professionals, at least until very recently. Similarly, hard work and good grades have more tangible payoffs for many students than do student solidarity and restricted academic output. *(c)* The furthest development of a reward structure that favors high productivity occurs when the organizational "masses" are rewarded in the same way as the organizational elite. This device is most evident in profit-sharing plans, which at least to a limited degree give the lower levels of a firm the same *kind* of reward (although in lesser amounts) that top management and stockholders get. Since the 1968 uprising, the French government has pushed for profit-sharing as a method of curbing labor unrest. *(d)* Organizational elites can use rewards of intrinsic satisfaction to increase productivity. This strategy is becoming increasingly common in many plants, where work is structured so that workers have to cooperate, make decisions, and oversee a large process instead of only repeating one minute action. The Volvo auto plant in Sweden and some parts of IBM production are usually cited as examples of efforts to make work more interesting.

3. Organizational elites can try to increase output and destroy solidarity by increasing *punishments* rather than rewards. Very high levels of punishment—deprivation of food, sleep, and shelter; beatings and killings; torture; and so on—can break down the bonds that tie inmates/slaves/workers to each

other. They become physically and psychologically dependent on their guards and are willing to do anything to save themselves regardless of its effect on their fellows. Whether productivity can be very high under such conditions is a matter of debate. For instance, historians are arguing whether or not slavery in the antebellum South was economically productive, whether slaves could have been used to industrialize, and whether slavery was really as morale-destroying as has been suggested in the past (Genovese, 1965; Fogel and Engerman, 1974). Levels of productivity roughly comparable to those of employed workers seem to have been attained by slave laborers in the Nazi rocket industry (Speer, 1970). This experience and the productivity of Soviet scientists held in special camps during the Stalinist repression suggest that even technically sophisticated work can be done under a primarily punishment system.

4. Organizational elites can use a combination of rewards and punishments to manipulate group structure and turn solidarity toward their own ends. We have already discussed this strategy in the context of changes in an individual's frame of reference. It can also be used to increase the output of whatever it is that organizational elites want to maximize. This strategy is used in the Marine Corps to build units with a strong group solidarity harnessed to the organizational goal of fighting. It is used by penologists to break down solidarity among prisoners and to reconstitute this solidarity in the service of the goals of the institution.

5. Organizational elites can use *technology* to increase output. In discussing the Industrial Revolution, I pointed out how power machinery, located in a single place (the factory), was able to standardize output and remove workers from control over the pace of production. Machinery can force a pace of work that cannot be countered by worker solidarity or by cooperation to restrict output. This great advance—from the point of view of the factory owner—reaches its fullest development with the assembly line. Its pace, and therefore the pace of production, is almost entirely out of the hands of the workers. Their only power is the power of disruption. Automated technology, although less exhausting and brutalizing than assembly-line work, also has a pace that is largely not set by workers at the site of its operation but by managers and programmers. Increasing productivity by the introduction of new machinery has the added advantage that it can be made to seem impersonal and inevitable. Some people are fooled by the argument that "the computer has decided such and such." Through the use of computers and related information-processing devices, elites are able to increase their control over productivity by centralizing information and other processes of management.

The conflict over increased productivity is most marked in a profit-making private firm, where the interests of the elite (shareholders and management) are most obviously not identical with those of the production workers. Productivity is particularly simple to measure in such a firm. Profits, wages, and working hours provide quantifiable measures of how well the goals of different subgroups are being achieved. Working-class traditions of worker solidarity and resistance to management's goals are relatively straightforward and easy to observe. All of these factors make the private firm an ideal place to observe elites' efforts to increase productivity and workers' responses. In other types of organizations, this process is less easily quantified, less clearly defined in its goals, and more "contaminated" by ideological commitments and rhetoric. In other words, in other organizations the interests of the elite and the mass are not so clearly at odds; the pie is not so limited and narrowly defined as in the private firm. Also, the production of goods and services in the private sector is the key activity of an industrialized capitalist economy and provides a model for other organizational activities in the society.

Now we can begin to better understand those famous Western Electric studies. The purpose of the studies was to see how "human relations" within an industry stood in the way of increased productivity, and how they could perhaps be manipulated to increase output.

While the increased output of an organization's stated goals is generally the kind of change that elites want to bring about, they may also occasionally want to tamper with the structure. Elites may make structural changes when they feel threatened or as an intermediate step toward increased productivity. They may want to make changes that will allow the organization to run more smoothly. Many of the strategies that I've discussed for increasing productivity also hold for making other kinds of changes. A few additional ones can briefly be listed:

1. Outside consultants may be used to carry out unpopular changes. They can be credited with special expertise in assessing the organization's problems and at the same time be blamed for unpleasant shake-ups. For instance, consulting firms that specialize in the firing of executives are beginning to appear.

2. Specialists in instituting limited change may be hired for full-time staff positions.

3. Organizational record-keeping and information-processing can be changed to create an appearance of substantive change, a common practice in police work.

Containing Change

By and large, organizational elites are more interested in stopping or containing change than in initiating it. They tend to want limited change that increases productivity, reduces the power of resisting groups, leaves their own power intact, and does not destroy the organization. How do they go about limiting or stopping change that goes beyond acceptable boundaries, that is, change that diminishes their own power decisively, brings new groups to power, redefines the goals of the organization, and/or destroys the organization entirely? Corporations during periods of labor unrest, universities in the

1960s, the American army during the war in Vietnam, and inner-city schools —all provide some interesting examples of these kinds of effort to contain conflict and change.

Resources.   First, let's see what resources organizational elites have available.

1. Organizational elites generally have some control over the flow of information. They usually are in possession of files. They are the recipients of information from various parts of the organization. In other words, they have access to means of collecting and storing information. Therefore, they tend to have a more global view of the organization than other groups in it. Organizational elites also control the flow of information *to* as well as from members. They have a printing press, a mimeograph machine, an intercom system, a staff to type and mail memos, and so on. This control over the means of communication gives them the opportunity to distribute their own interpretation of events, to disseminate their own ideology. This distribution of interpretations can be directed both to organization members and to outside audiences.

2. Organizational elites generally control incoming funds. This control also gives them control over material rewards to members.

3. Organizational elites generally have better access to the means of violence. As I shall discuss later, the state monopolizes the use of violence in most societies. In order to settle intraorganizational conflict by means of violence, the elites of most organizations must convince the state to intervene on their behalf through the use of the police, military, national guard, and so on. For example, during the labor unrest of the late nineteenth century, many companies were able to persuade the president or a governor or mayor to send in troops or police to end the disturbances. University presidents in the 1960s sometimes permitted police or troops on the campus. School administrators sometimes ask urban police departments to post policemen in the school to keep order. Obviously, organizational elites are in a better position to obtain the help of state violence than are their organizational opponents. Elites have more contacts with the top levels of the agencies of violence and in general share with them certain assumptions about preserving order. In addition, the organizational elites may hire special nonstate specialists in violence, such as the Pinkertons. The Pinkertons are a private police force that was established during the nineteenth century to control labor unrest. When an organizational elite resorts to violence, it often tries to define the objects of the violence as "outsiders" or "outside agitators." To admit that violence had to be used *within* the organization could have long-term disruptive consequences. The organizational members opposed to the elites may also use violence. Strikers beat up scabs and fight against troops and company guards. Because they generally do not have access to state-monopolized *legitimate* violence, the opposing members are more easily made to *seem* violent and disorderly. The elites who have access to state violence find it easier to make its use *seem* legitimate and warranted by the occasion, even when they actually initiate the use of force.

4. The final resource of organizational elites is authority. Legîtimation of their ability to give commands to organizational members is related to their first resource, ideological strength. But much of their authority does not need to be constantly legitimated by ideological appeals. It is built into the routines of the organization. Groups that want to change an organization necessarily have to disrupt—or at least change—routines. However, people are inclined to continue routines and habits unless there are very strong rewards or punishments to limit change.

Tactics.   There are a multiplicity of tactics of social control that use administrative procedures. I shall select and illustrate a few:

1. The organizational elite can accept demands for change and can create a committee to implement them. The processing of demands through a committee slows down change, often until initiators of change leave the organization. For example, at a meeting of a Chicago area state-established health care commission, a woman started to shout that her son bled to death because ambulance service was so inadequate. The health care planning body immediately established a committee to study ambulance services, which a year later filed a report.

2. The organizational elite can call in an outside expert to study the feasibility of the demanded changes. The expert is selected and paid by the organizational elite. He has no power to make them implement the changes he recommends. For example, a sociologist is hired by an agency to evaluate its services to the handicapped; his evaluation and recommendations are not acted upon.

3. The organizational elite can create a pseudostructure with no decision-making power to act as the vehicle of dissident groups' demands. After black students complained about the curriculum and living conditions at an elite women's college, an advisory group of black students and faculty was established. Unlike the research committee in the first example, an advisory group can immediately recommend actions, but it has no power other than the moral force of its advice.

4. The organizational elite can permit dissidents to join organizational decision-making bodies and then move key decisions out of these bodies. For instance, after the 1968 rebellion in French universities, students gained representation on various university decision-making councils. According to one observer, these councils promptly lost most of their power; decisions were made informally or in meetings without student representatives by the same groups that had made the decisions before the reforms.[1]

5. Organizational elites can manage meetings set up to discuss demanded changes. They can call meetings at times and places inconvenient for the rank and file. They can set the agenda. And they can control the flow of the meeting through skillful use of *Robert's Rules of Order.*

---

[1]Michelle Patterson, University of California, Santa Barbara, 1974: personal communication.

6. Organizational elites can weed out ringleaders. Elites can use their managerial skills and authority to get rid of troublemakers either by co-opting them or by firing them. Co-opting ringleaders can involve putting them into powerless leadership positions, paying them to remain quiet, or actually bringing them into the organizational elite. Another variation of this tactic is to label outspoken rebels with a term that makes them unacceptable to other rank-and-file members. For example, in a university, administrators can call professors organizing a union "unprofessional." In the military, dissenting officers can be accused of conduct "unbecoming to an officer." In the health-planning organization mentioned earlier, the organizational elites would say of an outspoken troublesome member, "She talks crazy." The label "crazy" would then tend to discredit the woman's statements (Berry, 1974).

7. Organizational elites can transform substantive issues into procedural issues. The rebellious rank and file makes a series of substantive demands. The organizational elite responds with a variety of stalling tactics that involve considering the procedures for making demands rather than the demands themselves. For example, the demanders may be told that they must go through "legitimate channels." Going through legitimate channels may be impossible; in fact, the rebels may already have tried this tactic and found it ineffective. Or they are told that a special procedure will have to be established to process their demands, which are thereby delayed (a tactic that includes the establishment of committees or investigatory bodies). In general, this tactic forces the rebels to discuss the question of procedure rather than the substantive issues, which are ignored by the elite.

8. Organizational elites can accept as an individual demand what is, in fact, a group problem. For example, a rank-and-file member, backed up by her fellows, demands redress of a grievance. Her demands are met (sometimes immediately, sometimes after prolonged conflict) by the organizational elite, but the favorable decision is *not* applied to anyone else in this situation. If others wish the same redress, they must go through the same procedures and conflicts. The organizational elite thus transforms shared problems into individual troubles. Public issues become personal misfortunes. In the legal system (not, strictly speaking, an organization) the device of the class action suit exists, in which a legal action is taken in behalf not only of the individual plaintiff but of all people with the identical problem or grievance—for instance, everyone who owns a brand of car that has a leaky exhaust pipe. Recent Supreme Court rulings have limited the power of class actions by insisting that all persons in the "class" be notified and by setting a floor on the magnitude of damages involved.

The concept of resisting change by partial incorporation, and the concept of limiting change by stabilization and routinization of pressures from below are broader, more analytical ways of interpreting these containment tactics. Partial incorporation refers to the fact that many of these tactics add up to the strategy of accepting some substantive innovations in order to preserve the overall structure and goals of the organization. In other words, the demands of the rebellious groups are "partially incorporated" into organizational policies but not to the extent that they replace or fundamentally alter the goals of the organizational elites. (Conservatives tend to see this process as a subversion; liberals hail it as a compromise; radicals decry it as a sellout.)

The tactics are also part of a major strategy to stabilize demands for change and channel them into routinized structures. Thus protestors in an organization are almost always told by elites to make their demands known through "legitimate channels." When they refuse to do so, elites hasten to create new structures that will routinely handle, within the existing goals and power structure, rank-and-file demands. A critical view of American unions sees them as bodies through which worker demands can be met by corporations without overturning the institutions of private ownership of productive enterprises or the employer-employee relationship. In other words, unions that accept these institutions gain better wages, hours, and grievance procedures for workers. Worker organizations like the Industrial Workers of the World ("Wobblies"), which aimed at worker control of industries as well as short-term improvements, were crushed. Unions routinized conflicts between workers and management, and they made such conflicts more limited and predictable.

The tactics that organizational elites use to crush, limit, or stabilize demands for change from below clearly vary with the type of organization. For instance, the elites of a manufacturing firm whose workers come from a strong working-class culture; face a lifetime of ill-paid, brutalizing, sometimes physically dangerous work on an assembly line; and are accustomed to everyday violence will tend to use different control tactics than will the elites at a college with upper-middle-class students who are only there for a four-year stay. Prison and inner-city school administrators will tend to use more violence in their control of change than will organizations in which middle-class people try to maintain some semblance of gentility and cooperation. Tactics also vary with the larger societal climate.

Innovation from the Bottom Up

In the preceding section, I discussed how organizational elites try to initiate changes that will maximize their goals and how they resist changes that are initiated from below. I pointed out how much of what is taught in personnel management, sociologically oriented business administration, and "human relations in industry" programs are essentially these two major types of strategy. In this section, I want to discuss strategies for initiating change from below. These strategies can be summed up in a single sentence: Organize, build groups with solidarity, and do not face organizational elites as isolated individuals.

Before examining this conclusion in more detail, we need to put into a larger context the process of innovation from the bottom up. First, we need to remember that power *within* an organization roughly corresponds to power in the society as a whole. *Power within organizations is based on access to resources outside of organizations.* This generalization does not hold all the time, but it is usually the case. Keeping this remark in mind, we can develop a better understanding of what innovation from the bottom up is all about.

Motives for Change

Why do people in an organization want to change it? First, they often want material benefits, such as higher wages or shorter working hours. They want safer work conditions. They want work to be less boring and more interesting. In other words, workers want to change organizations in order to improve working and living conditions.

Second, in order to assure these benefits, the workers may have to change the structure of the organization and attain more power in it. They do not want the benefits to be handouts from organizational elites. They want to be certain that they can continue to enjoy the benefits regardless of the whims or moods of the elites. So they have to change organizational routines. For example, collective bargaining and grievance procedures are ways in which unionized workers assert their power to take part in setting their work conditions in an organized way.

Third, some people like to increase their power in an organization for its own sake. They do not like to feel helpless or apathetic. They see participation in decision-making as an important value in itself. They would agree with the ancient Athenian who ridiculed the man who withdrew from politics into private life. Our word *idiot* derives from the Greek *idiotes,* meaning private self; the idiot is the man who cannot look beyond his personal needs to the larger whole.

Finally, a fourth goal is to take over and transform the organization itself. People in an organization want to use the resources of the organization —money, equipment, contacts, and so on—for a new set of purposes in the society. They want to harness the organization to some larger set of goals for the whole society. This is one of the reasons why social movements seek to "bore from within" in certain organizations.

The goals of innovation from below can also include resistance to change. We have already seen how organizational elites try to increase productivity. Change is also vital to a modern industrial society, hence change is institutionalized. The large corporations and the state force changes on people whether they want them or not. The market forces consumers to buy new products or fashions because the old ones are no longer available, or because they were built to fall apart, or because they are out of style. Corporations expect their employees to uproot themselves and move, at the company's behest. Corporations impose new technologies on their workers. Workers are subjected to work speedups and layoffs. In this situation, the demand for the cessation of change can be very revolutionary.

Even in societies whose elites are less passionately committed to change than ours, revolutions against elites often begin as opposition to change. They begin as efforts to safeguard existing rights. We shall examine this fact later in our chapter on revolutions. Here we can focus on the phenomenon within organizations. For instance, unionization in the 1930s often began as an attempt by workers to protect themselves against management-initiated changes like the speedup of the assembly lines or the imposition of new piecework rates. White-collar employees, such as professors, may now begin to unionize, at first to protect such traditional privileges as tenure or light course loads and only much later (or possibly never) to bring about new institutional arrangements. Groups that begin by resisting change often find that they can accomplish this goal only by initiating other changes—in the structure and goals of their organization.

Obstacles to Change

What are the obstacles to action initiated by the bottom levels of an organization? The elite usually has the following advantages in power struggles against the rank and file: More clearly defined goals, and better access to rewards and punishments (including payoffs) and to media publicity and legal violence. Also, the elite tends to be united in its goals and tactics. Rank-and-file opposition may be a heterogeneous coalition that has trouble coordinating its efforts. Organizational elites are skillful at encouraging confusion about goals and tactics in their opponents.

While some administrators become specialists in finding co-optive types of reform, some organizational elites believe that any concession brings in its wake further demands. They favor a "get-tough" or "nip-it-in-the-bud" policy, which often involves promptly crushing by violence or other punitive sanctions any efforts at change. For example, the University of Chicago, when faced by the same kinds of disturbances that shook Columbia University, responded by refusing to negotiate with the demonstrators and by expelling forty of them. Of course, the structure of the two universities was quite different, as was the racial composition of the demonstrators. Different strategies grow out of different situations—there does not exist one uniform recipe for all occasions for either elites or rebels.

One of the main obstacles to change in organizations is routinization; members are enmeshed in organizational routines and the routines of everyday life. Not only does the organization set these routines through its authority system, but people are also socialized to expect organizations to be routinized.

This expectation is especially strong for business firms, somewhat less so far state organizations and voluntary associations. We are trained in school to expect routines and authority. When we enter the school, we give up our rights over our time and our activity, rights that primitive peoples and young children take for granted and that school dropouts and some highly privileged professionals and artists seek to recapture. One of the functions of schooling is to prepare us for the routinization and authority of organizations that we join later. This expectation that to enter an organization means to give up excitement, control over the pace of our activities, and peer-group democracy is most developed for employing organizations, especially corporations and government bureaucracies.

The belief that workers must give up all these values while on the job is a piece of cultural baggage that they bring to their employing organization in modern industrialized societies. The labor force must be disciplined. The discipline is first imposed on most people through the school system. The individual member's acceptance, which permits the organization to enmesh him unquestioningly in its routines, is sustained partially through rewards and punishments and partially through socialization, that is, by internalized interpretations learned in the past.

Ways to Initiate Change

Three steps are necessary to create change in an organization: disruption of the previous organizational routines, alteration of the reward structure, and creation of new routines (including new positions of authority and new rules and regulations). Where there is a vacuum of authority, organizational rebels can build a new organization. Building this new organization is a spiraling process. Sometimes the initial disruption of routine is accidental. Sometimes it is caused by a counterorganization. In any case, the rebelling rank and file must build its own strong counterorganization to fill the breach left by the disruption of routines. New kinds of structures have to be created in order to alter the reward structure and sustain the changes. Changes in routine that are made without the backup of an organization with power to provide rewards and mete out punishments are difficult to preserve against the old organization's reward and punishment system.

In 1912, for instance, the anarcho-syndicalist IWW (Industrial Workers of the World) won a victory through a large strike in the Lawrence, Mass., textile mills. Within a few months, however, many of their hard-won wage demands were allowed to lapse. The local strike leaders were fired from their jobs (Dubofsky, 1969). This outcome was partly due to the open, decentralized, unbureaucratized structure of the IWW that made it an excellent organization for initiating changes in routine but not particularly well suited to sustaining its gains. This argument and illustration should not be taken to mean that loosely structured, nonhierarchical (or nonbureaucratic) organizations that rely heavily on the spontaneous actions of those whom they are trying to mobilize cannot succeed in transforming the organizations they seek to change. But changing an organization by building a strong counterorganization is easier than changing an organization without such a base of operation.

Control from Below: Worker Self-Management

The most extreme form of rank-and-file control of an organization is worker control over a productive enterprise. Some examples of worker control demonstrate that workers can run an organization and produce for society's needs without supervisors and foremen, unequal wages, or a hierarchy of command. Elected decision-makers replace the old management structure, and a narrow wage scale corrects the former wage inequality. An economy of worker-controlled plants still has to face problems of national coordination, however. The following examples explore the concept, possibilities, and limitations of worker control.

How might productive enterprises function if they were run by their workers? Worker control is a logical extension of efforts by rank-and-file members to gain more power in an organization. Some people like to argue that worker control is not feasible because most people wouldn't work if they weren't supervised. In fact, there have been experiments in worker control, and most of them seem very encouraging. The most limited experiments have taken place in private industrial firms in Western Europe—for instance, at the Saab and Volvo automobile plants in Sweden. The enterprises are profit-making and have a management structure and a supervisory hierarchy. The worker-control experiment is very limited; workers organize themselves as a team to build a car. They definitely exercise more responsibility and have a more interesting and varied job than do American automobile workers. However, the Swedish workers are still supervised by management. They do not have a voice in what the plant should produce or in how plant earnings should be used. In most capitalist countries, workers in "work enrichment" experiments still produce only for private profit.

Worker control in Yugoslavia is more fully developed and better integrated into the national economy. Within each plant and department there are elected councils of workers that make decisions about production. These councils largely take the place of management, although technical experts still play some role in such decisions. At the level of the work team, all workers join in day-to-day production decisions and in the distribution of income available to it. There are also regional councils that include both workers and community members and which make some decisions about municipal and regional development. Nationally, the economic system functions partly through planning by the Communist party and partly by "market socialism," an application of the effects of supply and demand to nonprofit, publicly owned economic enterprises. In other words, at the national level, the Yugoslavian economy is not worker controlled.

One of the most complete systems of worker control existed in 1936 in Catalonia, a region of northeastern Spain bordering the Mediterranean Sea and adjacent to France. Catalonia has long been a stronghold of the anarchist movement. Anarchism gained strength during the nineteenth century in several areas, such as Spain and Italy, that were beginning to industrialize or were indirectly affected by industrialization and commercial farming. Spanish anarchism did not mean"each man for himself, and the Devil take the hindmost." Rather, the movement emphasized the ability of peasants and workers to organize themselves collectively to carry on the work of production and to treat each other with justice and respect. The anarchists believed that capitalists, landlords, and state officials oppressed and exploited the mass of people. The anarchists favored the development of small-scale, participatory, non-hierarchical organizations. Supported by the mass of Catalans, the Spanish anarchists had paramilitary units standing ready to follow the advice of Enrico Malatesta, the Italian anarchist: "Seize a town or a village, render the representatives of the state harmless, and invite the population to organize itself freely."

In 1936, the moderate-left government of Spain had failed to improve the conditions of the impoverished mass of workers and peasants, and the country was beset by a series of strikes. The right wing, including large portions of the military, seized this opportunity to revolt against the government. In the turmoil that followed, different groups seized different parts of the country. In Catalonia, the anarchists came to power. They were not just a small movement that acted as spokesmen for the interests of the workers. Rather, to say that the anarchists came to power meant that the vast majority of people in Catalonia seized control of factories, landholdings, and public services. The small elite of landholders, large business owners, and managers were killed or fled. Many technical experts, such as engineers, fled as well.

Incautacion—seizure of a firm by the workers formerly employed in it—was the fate of 70 percent of the firms in Catalonia. The following types of enterprises were taken over in Barcelona, the leading city: railroads, gas and electric utilities, newspapers, movie theaters, hotels and restaurants, local transit services (streetcars, buses, and the subway), and most large industrial firms, including an oil company and two large automobile manufacturers (Ford-Iberia Motor Company and Hispano-Suiza). In general, these enterprises were run by elected committees. The wage scales were tightened but not eliminated. In other words, the large differences in pay between technicians and less-skilled workers were diminished but not completely leveled. This goal was usually accomplished by setting a ceiling on wages and bringing up the pay of the most disadvantaged groups. However, the anarchists failed to eliminate the differential between men's and women's pay. These general processes were worked out in slightly different form in different enterprises.

For example, at Ford-Iberia, the plant was run by an elected committee of 18 members, of whom 12 represented the 478 full-time and part-time production workers and 6 represented the clerical staff. This committee included members of two distinct left-wing parties. It set a ceiling on pay, but generally maintained existing wage scales. The pace of production was somewhat slowed, although the general organization of the work process was not substantially altered. In the public works firm, the wages of six hundred workers were increased, the position of foreman eliminated, and leadership carried out by elected representatives.

The movie theaters of Barcelona were all consolidated and run by an elected committee of seventeen, who were paid the same wages as the other theater workers. A ceiling on wages was set. Each worker got a month and a half of annual vacation leave, drew full salary during sickness or layoffs, and 75 percent of full salary in case of disability. All "profits" of the movie theaters were used to build schools and clinics.

Similar processes of peasant control emerged in the countryside. Peasant collectives supplied food to the cities. In Barcelona, a special food committee was set up to handle food and meal services. To some extent, money was eliminated in that any person with a union card—that is, evidence of being a worker—got free food. Beggars disappeared from the streets of Barcelona because everyone was guaranteed a minimum living standard.

In the manufacturing firms, services operated smoothly, although perhaps at a somewhat more leisurely and humane pace than before. Most people felt a sense of purpose and understood quite clearly that the success of their experiment and the survival of Catalonia necessitated continuing to work. The belief that supervision by management is always necessary to enforce production was shown to be quite erroneous. Under the conditions of expropriation, where there is worker control, a sense of purpose, and a regional history of commitment to the principle that "you don't need a boss," workers could and did organize themselves to produce for the common good. Within two days of the seizure of enterprises, public services functioned normally.

In the streets as well as in the workplaces, the city of Barcelona was quiet and orderly. Violence was not in the hands of the army—a specialized organization—but in that of the militias, armed groups of ordinary citizens. The city and region were administered by local assemblies of workers who elected delegates to regional coordinating bodies. An Austrian historian described the appearance of the city in August 1936.

Barcelona, 11 P.M.
Again a peaceful arrival. No taxi-cabs, but instead old horse-cabs, to carry us into the town. Few people in the Paseo de Colon. And, then, as we turned round the corner of the Ramblas (the chief artery of Barcelona) came a tremendous

surprise: before our eyes, in a flash, unfolded itself the revolution. It was over-whelming. It was as if we had been landed on a continent different from anything I had seen before.

The first impression: armed workers, rifles on their shoulders, but wearing their civilian clothes. Perhaps 30 per cent. of the males on the Ramblas were carrying rifles, though there were no police, and no regular military in uniforms. Arms, arms, and again arms. Very few of these armed proletarians wore the new dark-blue pretty militia uniforms. They sat on the benches or walked the pave-ment of the Ramblas, their rifles over the right shoulder, and often their girls on the left arm. They started off, in groups, to patrol out-lying districts. They stood, as guards, before the entrances of hotels, administrative buildings, and the larger stores. They crouched behind the few still standing barricades, which were competently constructed out of stones and sand-bags (most of the barricades had already been removed, and the destroyed pavement had been speedily restored). They drove at top speed innumerable fashionable cars, which they had expropri-ated and covered, with white paint, with the initials of their respective organiza-tions: CNT-FAI, UGT, PSUC (United Socialist-Communist Party of Catalonia), POUM (Trotskyists), or with all these initials at once, in order to display their loyalty to the movement in general. Some of the cars simply wore the letters UHP (Unite, proletarian brothers!), the slogan glorified by the Asturias rising of 1934. The fact that all these armed men walked about, marched, and drove in their ordinary clothes made the thing only more impressive as a display of the power of the factory workers. The anarchists, recognizable by badges and insignia in red and black, were obviously in overwhelming numbers. And no 'bourgeoisie' whatever! No more well-dressed young women and fashionable señoritos on the Ramblas! Only working men and working women; no hats even! The Generalitat, by wireless, had advised people not to wear them, because it might look 'bour-geois' and make a bad impression. The Ramblas are not less colourful than before, because there is the infinite variety of blue, red, black, of the party badges, the neckties, the fancy uniforms of the militia. But what a contrast with the pretty shining colours of the Catalan upper-class girls of former days!

The amount of expropriation in the few days since 19 July is almost incredible. The largest hotels, with one or two exceptions, have all been requisi-tioned by working-class organizations (not burnt, as had been reported in many newspapers). So were most of the larger stores. Many of the banks are closed, the others bear inscriptions declaring them under the control of the Generalitat. Practically all the factory-owners, we were told, had either fled or been killed, and their factories taken over by the workers. Everywhere large posters at the front of impressive buildings proclaim the fact of expropriation, explaining either that the management is now in the hands of the CNT, or that a particular organization has appropriated this building for its organizing work.

In many respects, however, life was much less disturbed than I expected it to be after newspaper reports abroad. Tramways and buses were running, water and light functioning. At the door of the Hôtel Continental stood an anarchist guard; and a large number of militia had been billeted in the rooms. Our driver, with a gesture of regret, explained that this obviously was no longer an hotel but a militia barrack, but the manager and the anarchist guards at once retorted that not all the rooms were occupied by militia-men, and that we could stay there, at somewhat reduced rates. So we did, and were well cared for, as to food and service.

All the churches had been burnt, with the exception of the cathedral with its invaluable art treasures, which the Generalitat had managed to save. The walls of the churches are standing, but the interior has in every case been completely destroyed. Some of the churches are still smoking. At the corner of the Ramblas and the Paseo Colon the building of the Cosulich Line (the Italian steamship company) is in ruins; Italian snipers, we are told, had taken cover there and the building had been stormed and burnt by the workers. But except for the churches and this one secular building there has been no arson.

These were the first impressions. After a hasty dinner I went out again, in spite of warnings that the streets would not be safe after dark. I did not see any confirmation of this.

(Borkenau, 1963:69–70)

In the short run, the experience of an entire society organized according to principles of worker control was extraordinarily successful. In the long run, the revolutionary gains were lost largely because of the external pressures of the civil war. Increasing amounts of effort had to be put into fighting the Spanish Fascists under Franco. The Catalans allowed some of their new institutional arrangements to be undermined by the demands and needs of the central government; for example, the militia units were integrated into the regular army and a police force was established. Finally, in May of 1937, after a period of tension and the murder of a number of political leaders, the central government sent in four thousand soldiers to occupy the city. An uneasy truce eventually set in, but what was left of anarchist worker control of a whole region was destroyed when Franco came to power.

References

Berry, Steven.
  1974 "Ideology and organization in a health care planning agency." Unpublished Master's thesis. Chicago: DePaul University.

Borkenau, Franz.
  1963 The Spanish Cockpit. Ann Arbor: University of Michigan Press.

Debray, Regis.
  1967 Revolution in the Revolution. Translation by Bobbye Ortis. New York: Monthly Review Press.

Dubofsky, Melvyn.
  1969 We Shall Be All: A History of the Industrial Workers of the World. Chicago: Quadrangle Books.

Fogel, Robert W., and Stanley Engerman.
  1974 Time on the Cross. 2 volumes. Boston: Little, Brown.

Freeman, Jo.
  1972 "The tyranny of structurelessness." The Second Wave 2(no.1). Reprinted in Ms. 11 (July 1973):76–78+.

Genovese, Eugene.
  1965 The Political Economy of Slavery. New York: Random House.

Michels, Robert.
    1949   Political Parties: A Sociological Study of the Oligarchical Tendencies of Modern Democracy. Translation by Eden and Cedar Paul. Glencoe, Ill.: Free Press.

Roethlisberger, Fritz J., and William J. Dickson.
    1939   Management and the Worker. Cambridge, Mass.: Harvard University Press.

Speer, Albert.
    1970   Inside the Third Reich. New York: Macmillan.

Chapter
8

Organizations
Causing
Change
In this chapter, I shall show how very powerful organizations can alter the structure and activities of a whole society. A number of such organizations are described, especially very large companies and revolutionary organizations that seized state power.

I HAVE ALREADY MENTIONED that the everyday life of people in modern societies is shaped by organizations. Organizations set the routine by which we pace our day, make our living, and use our spare time. These organizations are the firms or agencies that employ us; the enterprises that distribute our food, clothing, shelter, travel, and entertainment; and the public bodies that provide our water supply, regulate land use, oversee our behavior, and tinker with the economy. These different organizations are more loosely coordinated in our society than in those societies in which they are part of the state. Given the concentration of power in organizations and their pervasive control over the routines of everyday life, changes in these routines are most decisively made by other organizations. Organizations are a major agent of change in modern societies.

The aggregated choices of individuals are another major source of change. The two are related to each other in complicated ways. On the one hand, individual changes and individual choices gel into organizations through the action of enterprising individuals. For example, general antiwar sentiment in the 1960s found a voice and an organizational vehicle in the antiwar movement. In the nineteenth century, the common experience of millions of people forced to find employment in factories produced the labor movements of the period. On the other hand, organizations create individual sentiment and force individuals into new routines. During the 1960s, the armed forces (a large organization) drafted thousands of young men, changing their routines and their experiences—changing, in fact, their whole lives. Private firms produce and advertise new products and encourage aggregate private decisions to buy these products. Some of these aggregate individual decisions may in turn have a far-reaching impact. For instance, the mass production and marketing of automobiles from the 1920s on changed the nature of American society in almost every detail; road construction, gasoline consumption, residential patterns, courtship customs are only a part of the large-scale and pervasive change caused by the market distribution of automobiles.

Sometimes the organizations that initiate changes in private lives are very large. They may have a monopolistic or near-monopolistic position in the society. The armed forces and the present-day Detroit-based automobile companies are examples of organizations that have a dominant position in the society. Other organizations that affect private lives may be much smaller, more numerous, and less able to shape their own environments. Their behavior may in many ways be closer to that of private individuals in terms of their role in social change. Their decisions are more like the aggregated decisions of individuals than like the decisions of the monopolistic giant corporations and national government bodies. Motels and restaurants that are unaffiliated with national chains, small retail "mom and pop" stores, and local school districts are examples of such smaller, weaker organizations. In their impact on people's lives, corner candy stores are organizations that are virtually identical to individuals or households; they certainly have more in common with individuals than they do with giant organizations like General Motors, the Pentagon, and CBS, which can change the behavior of millions of people and have a great deal of control over their environment.

In this chapter, I would like to look primarily at those organizations that have the power to change societies. This power involves the ability to alter the private lives of the people in a society and also the ability to create, terminate, or alter other organizations. I would like to illustrate my discussion with four examples of organizations that substantially affected social structure in at least one society:

1. The great trading companies that were the first major vehicles of northern European expansion into the rest of the world
2. The radical organizations that engineered the American Revolution
3. The Bolshevik—the name implies "majority faction"—wing of the Russian Social Democratic Labor Party that became the major vehicle of the Russian Revolution in the fall of 1917
4. The multinational corporations of modern capitalism

Each of these organizations emerged at a time of social change and unheaval. Each provided a focus for these changes so that myriads of individual choices merged into a common, decisive direction. After summarizing the four examples, I would like to use them as the basis for some generalizations.

The Great Trading Companies

From the fifteenth century to the present, the countries of western Europe have transformed the rest of the world. This transformation came about through direct military conquest, ideological change, and economic dominance. A variety of organizational forms have been involved, including state-supported military action, settlement by individuals under the protection of the state, and the commercial ventures of large private companies. In this section, I would like to describe primarily the action of the companies during the early and middle years of European expansion. The companies were largely English, Dutch and, to some extent, French. The Spanish and Portuguese carried on their expansion through the direct action of the crown and, at the local level, the activities of adventurers, priests, and independent traders. The resulting system was characterized more by plunder than planning.

The English and Dutch began their empires through large trading organizations. These were private bodies operating with the support and protection of the state. The English East India Company and the Dutch East India Company were started in 1600 and 1602, respectively. On the one hand, these companies were chartered by their governments and granted a monopoly of trade with the East Indies; thus, their governments bestowed on them special rights. On the other hand, within the territory of their charter, they functioned like a state themselves. For example, the English East India Company made and enforced laws governing its workers overseas and defending its own holdings. No ship of the Royal Navy entered the waters east of the Cape of Good Hope; these waters were the territory of the company. The "East Indiamen" —the ships of the company—were outfitted for war as well as for trade. English ships carried more than twenty guns and were capable of fending off pirates, local princes, and the Dutch and Portuguese. On land, the company hired troops recruited from the Indian population. Similarly, the Dutch company employed troops, made and enforced regulations in the ports and territories it controlled, and negotiated with native rulers.

The regions of south and southeast Asia were more or less split between the British and the Dutch. The latter had established control over the Spice Islands (Indonesia) by the middle of the seventeenth century. The English had to accept Dutch hegemony in the Spice Islands, but they began to expand their base in India—in Madras, in the area around Bombay, and soon in Bengal.

Impact on Southeast Asia

Unlike Spain, the East India companies did not primarily extract large amounts of nonrenewable mineral resources from their areas of trade. (Chinese and Japanese silver and Japanese copper were acquired, however.) Their major goal was to obtain spices, tea and coffee, and cloth—in other words, largely tropical plant products. Some of this extraction simply involved the companies in ongoing native trading patterns. But these patterns were soon changed in several ways:

1. Trade with the European companies flooded the local markets with gold and silver (obtained initially from Spanish colonies in the New World). This wealth created a native elite of regents and, in the East Indies, Chinese merchants. The traditional peasant economies began to be drawn into a world market. The new local ruling classes also included native princes, who added participation in profit-making to more traditional religious and political control. In many parts of Southeast Asia, however, the emerging non-European bourgeoisie and petty traders were Chinese. In some areas (such as Amboina in the East Indies, where the Dutch maintained a clove monopoly), they were Christianized natives. Thus class relationships were changed by contact with the companies and by the influx of gold and silver.

2. The companies changed agricultural patterns by introducing large-scale commercial agriculture based on plantations. Traditional crops like cotton (in India) and certain spices were grown on these plantations. The Europeans also introduced new crops—coffee, sugar, and opium. The farmer who had largely produced for subsistence, barter, and payments to a traditional ruler became a worker tied to commercial crops through a system of tribute, labor service to native princes, slavery, or wage employment. Thus the trading companies changed the life conditions of the peasants of southern Asia as well as the agricultural and ecological patterns of the area.

3. The trading companies also altered the patterns of crafts production. At first they established "factories"—for instance, the cotton factories of Coromandel in southern India. I put the word *factories* in quotes because these establishments were not factories in the modern sense, with power machinery. Rather, they were enlargements of native crafts establishments in which more of the proceeds than formerly were routed away from the workers to the companies. These establishments produced cloth according to specification, with different quality levels, printed designs, and bleaching methods for the Indonesian, Chinese, Japanese, European, and African trade. Eventually, however, European policy toward Asian industrialization changed. The factories were abandoned and native crafts were replaced by European-made goods to provide an outlet for European manufacturing concerns. So the trading companies affected the craftsworkers as well as the peasants.

4. The trading companies opened the gates for actual colonial expansion in southern Asia. By the end of the eighteenth century, these regions had been transformed into colonies, that is, brought under direct military and political control of the European power.

Impact on Europe

The other half of the trading companies' dual impact was felt at home.

1. By opening up trade in Southeast Asia, the East India companies made available to Europeans new foodstuffs and new materials, thereby changing the quality of life. Pepper and other spices were used to preserve foods, hence the food supply became more dependable. Better food preservation was one of the factors that contributed to the declining death rate and growing population in Europe during this period. The introduction of other tropical products made available to people—especially the emerging middle class—a greater variety of food, clothing, and mild stimulants. Thus began the long process of increasing people's expectations about the variety and quantity of goods available to them. The so-called revolution of rising expectations—the mass demand for more consumer goods and new kinds of consumer goods—had begun in northern Europe.

2. The great trading companies both reflected *and* stimulated the growth of a wealthy commercial stratum in northern Europe. At first, money was raised for each separate voyage, which forced the company to undertake repeated fund-raising efforts and exposed the investors to great risk and complete loss if the ship were wrecked or seized by hostile forces. In 1657 in England, a permanent investment fund, the "New General Stock," was established to finance all future ventures.

> For thirty years after the Restoration, the profit on the original stock averaged first 20 and later 40 percent, per annum. The market price of £100 stock touched £500 in 1685. There was no need to increase the amount of the original stock, since the Company was in so strong a position that it could borrow short loans at very low interest, sometimes 3 percent, and reap enormous profits with these temporary borrowings.
>
> The great wealth derived from the Eastern trade therefore remained in a few hands, chiefly of very rich men (Trevelyan, 1942:220).

This situation had a number of direct and indirect consequences. One political result was that the merchants of the great trading companies supported the Roundheads—the forces against the crown—during the English Civil War in the middle of the seventeenth century, because the king did not favor their eastern monopoly. As late as the end of the eighteenth century, the mercantile interests—the wealthy men relying on state protection of their trade—played an important role in the American Revolution because they forced the crown to make policies that harmed American entrepreneurs. The Boston Tea Party was a protest against British efforts to force the Americans to accept British East India Company tea at prices that undercut those of American merchants.

British efforts to establish a fur monopoly west of the Alleghenies that would be closed to Americans was also a grievance of the colonial revolutionaries against the crown.

The mercantile community (of which the British East India Company was a part) destroyed Irish commerce and manufacturing. The Irish were not allowed to manufacture or export any goods that might compete with those the English were trying to sell in foreign markets. Scottish trade was also curtailed, although not quite as drastically, and many Scots resorted to smuggling. Thus the mercantile companies were an important element in the uneven development of the British Isles and in the reduction of Ireland to an underdeveloped agrarian society.

Finally, the East India trade increased the supply of gold and silver in the northern European countries because, although the precious metals were exported to pay for wares, these goods were resold in other foreign markets for several times their original price. With this flow of bullion came rising prices as well as increased resources for investment in commercial agriculture and, eventually, manufacturing. I don't have the space to develop in detail the very interesting monetary history of Europe in the late seventeenth century. Suffice it to say that the flow of gold and silver into northern Europe had a variety of important consequences in both economic and political life.

The most important effect of the overseas trade initiated by the great trading companies was the beginning of a world economy, an economy that linked Mexican silver; Indonesian coffee, sugar, and spices; Indian textiles and opium; Carribbean rum; Eastern saltpeter and Western firearms; and African slaves. At the heart of this gigantic trading empire stood the countries of northern Europe (and, to a lesser extent, their offshoots in North America). The mercantile trading companies were important organizations in the creation of this European-dominated worldwide system. They were not the only component of it, of course. The Spanish armies and adventurers in the New World, various smaller trading organizations, the European governments themselves, and collaborationist native princes—all contributed to its establishment. But the great trading companies tied it together and transformed a system of simple plunder into a long-term stable part of a profit-making capitalist economy.

Relationship to Modern Capitalism

Some people might argue that the mercantilist companies were a dead branch on the family tree of capitalism. They would claim that only competitive capitalism, freed from state protection, could develop into modern industrial capitalism. I would like to question this assertion in two ways.

First, I think we tend to overestimate the "freeness" (from the state) of postmercantile capitalism. In England (and even more so in France and elsewhere in the countries of northern Europe) the government had an uninterrupted policy of supporting private ventures and of committing itself to economic development, dating back to the mercantile period. Admittedly, the forms of this support shifted from the granting of monopolies in the seventeenth century to more subtle measures, such as providing ports, canals, and the armed power of the state, by the late eighteenth century. The principle of support was long-standing, however.

Second, even if the mercantile ventures did not directly spawn the later, more modern capitalist ventures of the late eighteenth and early nineteenth centuries, they indirectly made them possible by creating the European-dominated world economic system. The capitalist development of the English textile mills would have been very different if the mercantile ventures had not stimulated the world textile market, the large-scale cultivation of cotton, and (more indirectly) the African slave trade. These worldwide commercial nets were spread in the period of the great trading companies, even if they did not reach their full potential until the beginnings of industrial development.

The trading companies are thus one example of organizations that have changed history—and the everyday lives of masses of people.

The Organization of the American Revolution

Many historians have selected one of two approaches to the American Revolution: either they have treated it as a chapter in the history of ideas, emphasizing the faith in representative government and national self-determination that fueled it; or they have treated it as a chapter of military history, emphasizing the campaigns and strategies of the war for independence. Here I would like to emphasize a third aspect of the Revolution, namely, the way in which there emerged large-scale insurgent organizations that coordinated colonial resistance to the British.

These insurgent organizations were the means by which the general beliefs and ideas of the colonists were put to work for an armed cause. The ideas and sentiments arose from the shared experiences of the colonists, from the social conditions in which they lived. But before they would defend these sentiments and interests in a war, they had to create organizations that would define short-run goals, propose strategies, force people to make choices, and mobilize men and resources. These organizations became a dual structure of power, a countergovernment to the English authorities in many localities. They issued commands, appealed to sentiments, interpreted events, and meted out rewards and punishments in such a fashion that people came to accept their power instead of that of the British. These organizations of the Revolution spread geographically and evolved over time.

Expansion

Linking local insurgent groups in the colonies was one important task. Otherwise confrontations with the British might well have remained local incidents. There could have been a large number of such local hostilities, demonstrations, and incidents without a revolution if there were no organization to spread the news and coordinate resistance. This task was complicated by the slow means of communication and transportation. Also, the colonies developed unevenly in their support for independence. The city of Boston, Massachusetts generally, and Virginia had undergone experiences that created a larger body of sentiment and stronger local organizations in favor of independence. So a task of the revolutionary organizations had to be the search for support in the colonies with less revolutionary fervor.

Evolution

The revolutionary organizations had to change their own structure in order to keep up with the changing events. We shall shortly see how they were able to evolve from small local bodies of committed persons into three other kinds of organizations—military and paramilitary units (the militias and Minutemen), an all-colonial coordinating body (the First Continental Congress), and units that acted as local authorities (the Committees of Safety).

The history of the organizations of the American Revolution begins with the New England–based Sons of Liberty, the Stamp Act Congress, and the Committees of Correspondence. These organizations were formed in response to British restrictions on the prosperity and economic development of the colonies, primarily the Stamp Act (1765), which imposed a tax on newspapers and legal documents. This act was especially onerous for the northern colonies in which there were many lawyers, printers, and merchants. Other acts imposing duties on a variety of commodities preceded and followed the Stamp Act. American Colonists were incensed by these taxes. Outraged colonists organized local groups—the Sons of Liberty, for instance—that refused to pay the duties, demonstrated against English officials appointed to collect them, destroyed the stamps, and so on. The local groups were loosely linked through the Stamp Act Congress. The Stamp Act proved unenforceable and was repealed. The Sons of Liberty, however, continued to exist. These were local groups composed of both merchants and substantial numbers of artisans and workmen. The various radical groups maintained contact through Committees of Correspondence, which Sam Adams started in 1772. Thus began coordination of resistance against British authority.

Independence was not yet the goal; rather, the new organizations demanded a more autonomous position within the British Empire, as well as an end to specific taxes and regulations that the British continued to try to impose on the colonies. When the British crown supported the East India Company in its efforts to flood the American market with tea at prices undercutting those of American importers, a group of Bostonians dumped the tea into Boston Harbor. The Boston Tea Party, which occurred in December 1773, was followed by punitive measures against the city of Boston. In the spring of 1774, the port of Boston was closed. Also, British soldiers were to be garrisoned in the colonies to put down disturbances. Called the "Intolerable Acts," these punitive measures were met by widespread support for the Bostonians throughout the colonies. Local actions included the burning of a copy of the acts and the collection of large quantities of food to be sent to Boston. The Committees of Correspondence helped to spread—and interpret—such news and to organize the actions.

Paralleling the actions of the radical organizations, the legitimate wielders of authority in at least some of the colonies pursued an increasingly militant course. The Virginia House of Burgesses (a legislative body) supported the proposal of a general intercolonial congress, as did the Massachusetts House in June 1774. Fifty-five delegates met for the First Continental Congress in Philadelphia in September. Some no doubt hoped that this body would reach a moderate compromise. Indeed, the Congress was not wholly outside the structure of colonial authority; it did have the support of moderate groups and included a fair number of moderates who opposed independence. But in the First Continental Congress, the radicals won out.

In the beginning the Congress seemed pretty evenly divided between the radicals, who wanted action, and the moderates—Adams called them "trimmers and timeservers"—who preferred petitions. The radicals seized the initiative and held it. They won two initial victories: the choice of Carpenter's Hall, rather than the State House, as the meeting place, and the election of the Philadelphia radical, Charles Thomson, as secretary. Then came a decisive test.

Hard on the heels of Gage's expedition to seize gunpowder on Quarry Hill, outside Boston, delegates from every town and district of Suffolk County, which included Boston and environs, met at Woodward's Tavern in Dedham, and there, on September 9, passed a series of resolutions which had been drawn up by Joseph Warren. Riding night and day, Paul Revere, who gallops through the Revolution like a centaur, brought these Suffolk Resolves to Philadelphia on the seventeenth. There was a sharp debate; then Congress adopted them and thereby endorsed them. "This was one of the happiest days of my life," wrote John Adams. "In Congress we had generous, noble sentiments and manly eloquence. This day convinced me that America will support Massachusetts or perish with her."

What elated Adams, alarmed the conservatives. Their leader was Joseph Galloway, a rich Philadelphia merchant and lawyer long active in colonial politics, speaker of the Pennsylvania Assembly, and a man of parts. On September 28 Galloway introduced his famous Plan of Union, a plan designed to give the American colonies something like dominion status in the empire. "Among all the difficulties in the way of effective and united action in 1774," wrote John Adams, "no more alarming one happened than the plan presented by Mr. Joseph Galloway." After a sharp tussle the plan was defeated by a vote of six to five, and subsequently expunged from the minutes of the Congress. . . .

With the Galloway Plan out of the way, Congress settled down to business and endorsed in rapid succession a series of notable state papers. On October 14 came the Declaration and Resolves, which included a declaration of the rights of the colonies. Four days later Congress adopted the Association which has some claim to be considered the first true American union: it provided for nonimportation, nonconsumption and a cessation of slave trade. Other papers included an *Address to the People of Great Britain,* drafted by young John Jay of New York; an *Address to the Inhabitants of Quebec,* and a *Petition to the King,* both largely the work of Dickinson. . . .

Within a few months assemblies, conventions, or town and county meetings of eleven colonies had approved or ratified the proceedings of the Congress. The New York Assembly rejected ratification; that of Georgia did not get a chance to act on it.

(Commager & Morris, 1958:46–47)

By the time it had adopted the Contintental Association, the Congress had become an extralegal body. It had decisively thrown in its lot with the radical organizations. The Continental Congress recognized its revolutionary role by including in the Association the Committees of Safety, groups that were to enforce the nonimportation and nonconsumption agreements against English goods. The Committees of Safety also circulated news of British and American actions during the ensuing months. Finally, the Committees of Safety were one of several groups that worked to organize a revolutionary army. They were aided in this undertaking by the spontaneous organizing of militia units and paramilitary groups such as the Minutemen in Massachusetts and the Fairfax County (Virginia) committee of planters, who were instrumental in strengthening the Virginia militia and making it independent of the British.

The reader should bear in mind that the colonists had generally been armed, that maintaining local militias was a long-standing practice, and that no vast disparity in military technology existed between the British and the revolutionaries. In other words, the nucleus of a revolutionary army already existed and was at least partially supplied. Thus the committees of Safety and other organizing bodies had the task of turning the militias against the British and of coordinating their actions rather than that of building an entirely new fighting force. Even so, contemporary commentators saw the revolutionary army as undisciplined and very poorly outfitted compared with the British regulars (Commager & Morris, 1958:153–156).

From the task of successfully preventing British imports, the Committees of Safety turned to the social-control problem of dealing with the Loyalists. About one-third of the colonists were Loyalists, another one-third were supporters of the revolutionary cause, and the last one-third were not definitely committed to either side. Commager and Morris (1958:333) describe the treatment of the Loyalists:

> The very strength of loyalism in America condemned it to persecution. Had the Loyalists been few in number, weak and disorganized, the Patriots might have ignored them, or have contented themselves with making sure that they could do no harm. But they were numerous and powerful, strong enough at times to take the offensive against the Patriots and endanger the success of the Revolution. It was not, therefore, surprising that even before Independence the Patriots moved to frustrate, intimidate, punish and, if possible, wipe out loyalism. In the fall of 1774 the Provincial Congress of Massachusetts denounced Loyalists as "infamous betrayers of their country," and the Continental Congress in setting up the Association called for a "committee in every county, city and town . . . to observe the conduct of all persons touching this association . . . to the end that all foes to the rights of British America may be publicly known and universally contemned as enemies of American liberty."
>
> It was in fact these self-constituted committees of safety—often the successors of the earlier committees of correspondence and the Liberty Boys—that were the instruments for intimidating Loyalists. Such groups could not be easily controlled, nor was there any assurance that they would operate with a nice regard for justice, or that they would not, on occasion, confuse loyalism with conservatism or Anglicanism, or use their extralegal authority to indulge personal or class grudges. Most of the early violence—breaking windows, whipping, tarring and feathering —was perpetrated by members of these committees and their friends and hangers-on.
>
> Very soon, however, the provincial legislatures gave at least an appearance of legality to the proceedings of these committees. State after state passed test laws, required ostentatious proof of devotion to the Patriot cause, and imposed penalties against loyalism, active and passive alike. In a broad way these laws limited freedom of speech and freedom of movement, disfranchised, suppressed, quarantined or banished Tories, and made adhering to George III a crime punishable by confiscation of property and, in extreme and aggravated cases, by death.
>
> The treatment of the Loyalists was harsh, but harshness has almost always characterized the treatment of those who were on the wrong, or losing, side of a revolution. From the point of view of the Patriots, the Loyalists were traitors and therefore worse than open enemies. Nor can the judicious historian deny that the Patriots had considerable justification for their attitude and their actions. Loyalists were numerous enough to be dangerous; they did in fact give aid to the enemy; many were spies

and informers, many more sold food and supplies to the British; thousands fought in the British ranks.

In a formal sense, with the Declaration of Independence the revolutionary organizations became parts of a new state. In actuality, of course, the establishment of a new state was accomplished only through a prolonged war. My purpose here is not to give a chronology of the American Revolution. I have only briefly summarized some of the events leading up to the war in order to be able to make some general comments about the evolution, tasks, and effects of the revolutionary organizations:

1. The revolutionary organizations evolved unevenly, appearing first in those parts of the society that were most directly exposed to unfavorable conditions. In particular, they appeared first in New England.

2. Once started, the revolutionary organizations very rapidly attracted to them men who grasped the larger implications of this discontent with unfavorable conditions. But the ideologues and organizers could not force the pace of events. The rather quiet years between the passage of the Stamp Act in 1765 and the Boston disturbances of the early 1770s support this view. The revolutionaries could seize the time—shape the actions of men responding to changes in their conditions—but they could not singlehandedly bring about such actions.

3. The first revolutionary organizations were local and acted locally. But very soon larger organizations developed, best illustrated by the Committees of Correspondence. Structurally, they linked the local groups; ideologically, they provided a larger picture and a sense of participation in a larger enterprise. Eventually they could involve people in causes that were not immediately their own and did not affect the routines of their personal everyday lives. This role in the creation of the "larger picture" is suggested by the rallying of towns like Baltimore; Philadelphia; Kingston and Durham in New Hampshire; Windham and Farmington in Connecticut; and Essex County, Virginia (to name only a few) to the cause of the blockaded Bostonians.

4. The revolutionary organizations consolidated the tasks of coordination and propaganda by the establishment of a central body, the Continental Congress. With the establishment of this body, a spiraling feedback process was begun. Representatives nurtured in the local radical organizations blocked the moderates and pushed the Congress toward their own goals. At the same time, the Congress began to provide central direction for the local radical groups.

5. From propaganda and coordination of local unrest, the central organizing groups moved to two new tasks: *military action* and *social control.* The origins of both lay in preexisting local bodies. The state militias already existed. The local radical groups had already asserted new systems of power against the British by demonstrating and rioting. The revolutionary groups now had to weld the militias into a national army, and they had to expand and legitimize

the system of local social control through the Committees of Safety. The latter had the delicate task of disrupting old routines—for instance, ending the purchase of English-imported goods—while simultaneously establishing new authority. On the one hand, they had to mobilize the hesitant and timid to alter their habits and behave in ways that resisted the British; on the other hand, they had to restrain rowdy and purely localistic disturbances. Above all, they had to create a situation of polarization. People had to choose whether they would follow the authority of British officials or the authority of the revolutionary organizations.

The American Revolution benefited from the preexistence of militias and from the weakness of British authority and British social control. The British crown was thousands of miles away. British officials were few. Outside of its army, the British had a very poorly developed apparatus of social control. Compared with a modern regime, it had few patronage jobs, few informers, few secret police, few loyal specialists in violence. There were a substantial number of Loyalists whom the Committees of Safety had to convert or, more frequently, silence or exile—often brutally, as we have seen. But the Committees did not have to cope with many professionals in counterrevolution, at least not by modern standards.

Under the economic, political, and technological conditions of the late eighteenth century, the organizations of the American revolutionaries were effective vehicles for mobilizing the colonists.

The Organization of the Russian Revolution

> Just as a blacksmith cannot seize the red hot iron in his naked hand, so the proletariat cannot directly seize the power; it has to have an organization accommodated to this task. The coordination of the mass insurrection with the conspiracy, the subordination of the conspiracy to the insurrection, the organization of the insurrection through the conspiracy, constitute that complex and responsible department of revolutionary politics which Marx and Engels called "the art of insurrection." It presupposes a correct general leadership of the masses, a flexible orientation in changing conditions, a thought-out plan of attack, cautiousness in technical preparation, and a daring blow (Trotsky, 1957:169).

The Russian Revolution occurred at the meeting place of two lines of organizational change: the collapse of the state institutions of imperial Russia and the evolution of Russian revolutionary organizations. As in the case of the American Revolution, these changes occurred only as the economic and political circumstances of the society changed and, with them, the life experiences of groups of individuals.

That changes in objective conditions as well as organizational structure were important prerequisites for a revolutionary seizure of state power is suggested by the fate of preceding generations of Russian revolutionaries. There had been peasant uprisings during the sixteenth and seventeenth centuries. But as serfdom became more rigid in the late eighteenth century, large-scale peasant revolts ceased. In any case, the early revolutionaries had not had well-defined goals of seizing the state.

By the 1820s, there was upper-class agitation for a constitutional monarchy. As the literate strata grew to include more people of poor and middle-class background, and as Russia was affected by western European socialist and anarchist ideas, movements for change took a turn to the left. The "generation of the fathers" demanded liberal changes, such as the establishment of a constitutional monarchy, representative institutions, the gradual abolition of serfdom, and so on. After midcentury, the "sons" began to hope for an increasingly radical mobilization of the vast mass of Russians. In the 1870s, radical intellectuals went "to the people"—that is, tried to organize the peasantry and to educate it politically. The peasants—many of them recently emancipated serfs—did not respond favorably. A second generation of radicals in the 1880s turned to terrorism. Their deeds, which included the assassination of the czar, contributed to a reactionary period in the late nineteenth century. By the beginning of the twentieth century, Russian radicals were impressed by two points: (1) the need for a better organizational vehicle than either that of the "to the people" movement or of the terrorists, and (2) the emergence of a Russian stratum of factory workers and artisans who had more in common with European proletarians—and were hence more promising material for Socialist movements—than did the peasants.

Having recognized the weakness of the populist and terrorist movements, however, and having placed strong emphasis on the emerging urban and small-town industrial workers, the Russian radical movement still debated a number of questions: In terms of strategy, was building a strong trade-union movement the best way to begin revolutionary change? Could revolutionary change come about through the ballot box—in other words, should socialists compete with liberal and conservative parties in institutions of representative government (which were extremely weak in Russia compared with western Europe)? Finally, how could the fragmented, locally oriented bits and pieces of a revolutionary movement (which in 1900 consisted more of circles and networks than of an organization) become an organization?

Lenin, who was then in exile in Siberia, proposed a particular set of answers. Neither trade-union work nor electoral campaigns was to be the primary orientation of revolutionary activity. The organizational structure should be tight, closed, and based on full-time, highly committed members, in other words, on professional revolutionaries. These cadres were to educate workers politically. They were not to hold back in expressing their socialist ideas but should lead the workers to an understanding of the whole society, beyond local economic problems. In this task a newspaper was essential to spread ideas, to serve as a focus for organization, and to coordinate local work. Finally, in a despotic state like czarist Russia, a revolutionary organization had to be secret and tightly organized. The organization would be democratic through its "complete, comradely mutual confidence among revolutionaries" rather than through open meetings or elections, which would incapacitate it in czarist Russia. In *What Is To Be Done?* Lenin summarized these views as follows:

> I assert: (1) That no movement can be durable without a stable organization of leaders to maintain continuity; (2) that the more widely the masses are drawn into the struggle and form the basis of the movement, the more necessary is it to have such an organization and the more stable must it be (for it is much easier then for demagogues to sidetrack the more backward sections of the masses); (3) that the organization must consist chiefly of persons engaged in revolutions as a profession; (4) that in a country with a despotic government, the more we *restrict* the membership of this organization to persons who are engaged in revolution as a profession and who have been professionally trained in the art of combating the political police, the more difficult will it be to catch the organization; and (5) the *wider* will be the circle of men and women of the working class or of other classes of society able to join the movement and perform active work in it (Lenin, 1967:199–200).

Shortly after the publication of this statement, the Russian state embarked on two "great undertakings that required the active participation of the masses" (Garner, 1974:173), namely, the Russo-Japanese War of 1904 and World War I. The czarist government did not fare well in either conflict. In the Russo-Japanese War, territory was lost. Peasants who had been mobilized as soldiers began to experience a larger existence than that of their fields and villages. The war was followed by a small-scale revolution, which hastened the establishment of some of the institutions of a constitutional monarchy as well as instances of violent repression. Political parties multiplied—most of them liberal or mildly socialist rather than revolutionary.

Organizations of all kinds began to appear as expressions of local political activity. Although mostly stimulated by the events of 1905, some of these voluntary associations had been started in the 1890s as a consequence of industrialization more than of any specific political impetus. Many of these were organized by the various political parties. Some, such as the institutions of city government, were organized by region and residence. Others, such as the trade unions, the *soviets* or worker councils, the groups of professional men loosely affiliated with the center parties, and the consumer cooperatives founded by liberals and moderate socialists, were economic and occupational bodies. But this development of varied interest groups and private organizations came too late to save the czarist regime. Moreover, the landowners, the emerging industrialists, and the czarist government opposed even these limited reforms. Those in power clung to their efforts to control the society through the large state bureaucracy alone. They interpreted the efforts of political parties, cooperatives, uncensored media, local government, and so on as attacks on their undisputed control of the society. They failed to see that in western Europe and North America societal stability was not tied solely to the state but depended on a host of private and voluntary organizations. As one political scientist has remarked:

> In Russia the political resources of the ruling class were concentrated in a single institution: the state apparatus. Political parties, particularly mass political parties, were virtually nonexistent; the countryside had only primitive forms of political organization at best; the national economy was relatively independent of the international market; and the operations of the state's administrative machinery were centralized in one or a few cities. In short, the network of "private" institutions necessary for the legitimation of the ruling class in the eyes of the ruled classes did not exist.
>
> These circumstances dictated a revolutionary strategy . . . of "frontal attack." Once an "organic crisis" opened a "breach" in a sociopolitical terrain of this nature, a direct assault on the state could lead to revolutionary success. Everything would depend on the revolutionary force's capacity to act with lightning speed in organizing its cadres and throwing them into the breach, which had created a favorable political-*military* situation. With the overthrow of the state apparatus, the power of the ruling class was reduced to nothing and the revolution's objective realized. This was the strategy followed by the Russian Bolscheviks, and it accounted for their success. . . .
>
> As opposed to the sociopolitical terrain in Russia, "in the West there was a proper relationship between state and civil society, and whenever the state began to shake one could perceive at once the sturdy structure of civil society. The state was only one forward trench, behind which there was a strong chain of fortresses and bunkers." Revolution in the West required, then, the construction of an opposing array of trenches and fortifications capable of sustaining class warfare under conditions that precluded a frontal assault on the state apparatus (Garner, 1974:174–175).

After 1905, this overconcentration of power in the state apparatus could perhaps still have been remedied by a more astute elite. But with Russia's entry into World War I, any such reconstruction became impossible. Russia's armies marched from catastrophe to catastrophe. The instabilities of Russian society were intensified by the process of state mobilization and the uprooting of peasants and workers to serve as soldiers. The superstitiousness and general idiocy of czar Nicholas II, and especially of the czarina, hastened the collapse of the state. In February 1917, this collapse came through the spontaneous strike of the workers in Petrograd (Leningrad), the capital city, and the refusal of various units of the armed forces to restore order.

The following months—in many respects, the following several years— saw a crisis in state institutions in which a variety of organizations fought to become the wielders of power. The goal was to become the organization that monopolized armed power and that could also gain enough support, or at least passive acquiescence, to establish routines of administration and everyday life. In short, the organizations strove to seize the state. The Bolsheviks succeeded. They were the organization for which Lenin had provided the blueprint in his treatise *What Is To Be Done?*

What steps did the Bolsheviks take after the collapse of the czarist government to gain state power?

1. They waited long enough for the masses of people to see the inability of the moderates (who came to power in February) to settle the two most pressing issues—peace and land distributions. For a number of reasons, the moderates were not ready to agree to unfavorable peace terms with Germany. The troops continued to starve and die. The war brought with it inflation and profiteering in the cities. The Provisional Government, which was dominated by the moderates, did not institute land reform. Without this act they could not expect any loyalty from the peasants, regardless of what support they might have from other strata, particularly the small urban middle class.

The government of the moderates, committed to representative institutions like those of western Europe, evoked no sympathy from the peasants and workers. Representative democracy was a superfluous luxury to people whose immediate desires were an end to the war, better food and shelter, and access to land. Insofar as the Bolsheviks promised peace and a redistribution of wealth, they were preferred to the moderates. Thus at the level of ideology and mass attitudes, the Bolsheviks (and other left-wing parties) had more support than the moderates, at least in the sense that the majority of Russians were not interested in risking their lives in armed support of the moderates.

Various writers have told of the disruption of routine that swept the country in 1917, despite the surface air of calm in the everyday lives of the rich, and many have described the force of the Russians' desire for peace and better living conditions. The following account was written by the American journalist John Reed.

September and October are the worst months of the Russian year—especially the Petrograd year. Under dull grey skies, in the shortening days, the rain fell drenching, incessant. The mud underfoot was deep, slippery and clinging, tracked everywhere by heavy boots, and worse than usual because of the complete break-down of the Municipal administration. Bitter damp winds rushed in from the Gulf of Finland, and the chill fog rolled through the streets. At night, for motives of economy as well as fear of Zeppelins, the street-lights were few and far between; in private dwellings and apartment houses the electricity was turned on from six o'clock until midnight, with candles forty cents apiece and little kerosene to be had. It was dark from three in the afternoon to ten in the morning. Robberies and housebreakings increased. In apartment houses the men took turns at all-night guard duty, armed with loaded rifles. This was under the Provisional Government.

Week by week food became scarcer. The daily allowance of bread fell from a pound and a half to a pound, then three-quarters, half, and a quarter-pound. Toward the end there was a week without any bread at all. Sugar one was entitled to at the rate of two pounds a month—if one could get it at all, which was seldom. A bar of chocolate or a pound of tasteless candy cost anywhere from seven to ten rubles—at least a dollar. There was milk for about half the babies in the city; most hotels and private houses never saw it for months. In the fruit season apples and pears sold for a little less than a ruble apiece on the street-corner. ...

For milk and bread and sugar and tobacco one had to stand in *queue* long hours in the chill rain. Coming home from an all-night meeting I have seen the *kvost* (tail) beginning to form before dawn, mostly women, some with babies in their arms. ... Carlyle, in his *French Revolution,* has described the French people as distinguished above all others by their faculty of standing in *queue.* Russia had accustomed herself to the practice, begun in the reign of Nicholas the Blessed as long ago as 1915, and from then continued intermittently until the summer of 1917, when it settled down as the regular order of things. Think of the poorly-clad people standing on the iron-white streets of Petrograd whole days in the Russian winter! I have listened in the bread-lines, hearing the bitter, acrid note of discontent which from time to time burst up through the miraculous goodnature of the Russian crowd. ...

Of course all of the theatres were going every night, including Sundays. Karsavina appeared in a new Ballet at the Marinsky, all dance-loving Russia coming to see her. Shaliapin was singing. At the Alexandrinsky they were reviving Meyerhold's production of Tolstoy's "Death of Ivan the Terrible"; and at that performance I remember noticing a student of the Imperial School of Pages, in his dress uniform, who stood up correctly between the acts and faced the empty Imperial box, with its eagles all erased. ... The *Krivoye Zerkalo* staged a sumptuous version of Schnitzler's "Reigen."

Although the Hermitage and other picture galleries had been evacuated to Moscow, there were weekly exhibitions of paintings. Hordes of the female *intelligentzia* went to hear lectures on Art, Literature and the Easy Philosophies. It was a particularly active season for Theosophists. And the Salvation Army, admitted to Russia for the first time in history, plastered the walls with announcements of gospel meetings, which amused and astounded Russian audiences. ...

As in all such times, the petty conventional life of the city went on, ignoring the Revolution as much as possible. The poets made verses—but not about the Revolution. The realistic painters painted scenes from mediæval Russian history—anything but the Revolution. Young ladies from the provinces came up to the capital to learn French and cultivate their voices, and the gay young beautiful officers wore their gold-trimmed crimson *bashliki* and their elaborate Caucasian swords around the hotel lobbies. The ladies of the minor bureaucratic set took tea with each other in the afternoon, carrying each her little gold or silver or jewelled sugar-box, and half a loaf of bread in her muff, and wished that the Tsar were back, or that the Germans would come, or anything that would solve the servant problem. . . . The daughter of a friend of mine came home one afternoon in hysterics because the woman street-car conductor had called her "Comrade!"

All around them great Russia was in travail, bearing a new world. The servants one used to treat like animals and pay next to nothing, were getting independent. A pair of shoes cost more than a hundred rubles, and as wages averaged about thirty-five rubles a month the servants refused to stand in *queue* and wear out their shoes. But more than that. In the new Russia every man and woman could vote; there were working-class newspapers, saying new and startling things; there were the Soviets; and there were the Unions. The *izvoshtchiki* (cab-drivers) had a Union; they were also represented in the Petrograd Soviet. The waiters and hotel-servants were organised, and refused tips. On the walls of restaurants they put up signs which read, "No tips taken here—" or, "Just because a man has to make his living waiting on table is no reason to insult him by offering him a tip!"

At the Front the soldiers fought out their fight with the officers, and learned self-government through their committees. In the factories those unique Russian organizations, the Factory-Shop Committees, gained experience and strength and a realization of their historical mission by combat with the old order. All Russia was learning to read, and *reading*—politics, economics, history —because the people wanted to *know*. . . . In every city, in most towns, along the Front, each political faction had its newspaper—sometimes several. Hundreds of thousands of pamphlets were distributed by thousands of organizations, and poured into the armies, the villages, the factories, the streets. The thirst for education, so long thwarted, burst with the Revolution into a frenzy of expression. From Smolny Institute alone, the first six months, went out every day tons, car-loads, train-loads of literature, saturating the land. Russia absorbed reading matter like hot sand drinks water, insatiable. And it was not fables, falsified history, diluted religion, and the cheap fiction that corrupts—but social and economic theories, philosophy, the works of Tolstoy, Gogol, and Gorky. . . .

Then the Talk, beside which Carlyle's "flood of French speech" was a mere trickle. Lectures, debates, speeches—in theatres, circuses, school-houses, clubs, Soviet meeting-rooms, Union headquarters, barracks. . . . Meetings in the trenches at the Front, in village squares, factories. . . . What a marvelous sight to see Putilovsky Zavod (the Putilov factory) pour out its forty thousand to listen to Social Democrats, Socialist Revolutionaries, Anarchists, anybody, whatever they had to say, as long as they would talk! For months in Petrograd, and all over Russia, every street-corner was a public tribune. In railway trains, street-cars, always the spurting up of impromptu debate, everywhere. . . .

And the All-Russian Conferences and Congresses, drawing together the men of two continents—conventions of Soviets, of Cooperatives, Zemstvos, nationalities, priests, peasants, political parties; the Democratic Conference, the Moscow Conference, the Council of the Russian Republic. There were always three or four conventions going on in Petrograd. At every meeting, attempts to limit the time of speakers voted down, and every man free to express the thought that was in him.

(Reed, 1967:11–15)

2. The Bolsheviks organized effectively in the various groups that made up the political system after the February 1917 collapse of the czarist government. Some of these groups were relatively long standing, including the soviets (the councils of peasants, workers, and soldiers), the trade unions, shop committees, and local government bodies. The Bolsheviks became a majority faction in many of these bodies, including the Petrograd soviet. In a number of areas, these organizations began to function as a dual government to the institutions of the moderate-dominated Provisional Government, many of which were inherited from the czarist state bureaucracy. That is, in the soviets and other bodies, the Bolsheviks challenged the authority of the Provisional Government in the last weeks before the actual Bolshevik seizure of power. In some localities and regions, non-Bolshevik factions also refused to accept the Provisional Government. In addition to becoming a majority faction in some of these local bodies, the Bolsheviks also organized support in the ad hoc conventions and congresses that were meeting in Petrograd in 1917 in order to create a new overall structure for the Russian state.

The Bolsheviks' tightly organized party was an excellent mechanism for coordinating individual member's participation in other bodies, such as the soviets. The soviets became the organs through which the small, partially clandestine party contacted the public. In other words, democratically organized bodies (the soviets) were first infiltrated and then coordinated by a much more closed and centrally run organization—the party of the Bolsheviks. (The Bolsheviks didn't officially become known as the Communist party until March 1918.) Along with this double organization came a double decision-making structure. On the one hand, the party made internal decisions in terms of its own goals and strategies. On the other hand, it participated in the decision-making of the soviets, through the activity of persons who were members of both the party and the soviets. Note how this double organization also appeared in the American Revolution. For example, the revolutionary faction captured the Continental Congress and turned it into a vehicle of revolution against England.

3. Another crucial aspect of Bolshevik organization was their ability to gain support within the armed forces and to establish the Red Guard as a strong paramilitary force. In other words, they effectively built armed support for insurrection and the years of civil war that followed it. Their leading military organizer, Leon Trotsky, has described the beginnings of their control over the means of violence.

The first task of every insurrection is to bring the troops over to its side. The chief means of accomplishing this are the general strike, mass processions, street encounters, battles at the barricades. The unique thing about the October revolution, a thing never before observed in so complete a form, was that, thanks to a happy combination of circumstances, the proletarian vanguard had won over the garrison of the capital before the moment of open insurrection. It had not only won them over, but had fortified this conquest through the organization of the Garrison Conference. It is impossible to understand the mechanics of the October revolution without fully realizing that the most important task of the insurrection, and the one most difficult to calculate in advance, was fully accomplished in Petrograd before the beginning of the armed struggle.

This does not mean, however, that insurrection had become superfluous. The overwhelming majority of the garrison was, it is true, on the side of the workers. But a minority was against the workers, against the revolution, against the Bolsheviks. This small minority consisted of the best trained elements in the army: the officers, the junkers, the shock battalions, and perhaps the Cossacks. It was impossible to win these elements politically; they had to be vanquished. The past part of the task of the revolution, that which has gone into history under the name of the October insurrection, was therefore purely military in character. At this final stage rifles, bayonets, machine guns, and perhaps cannon, were to decide. The party of the Bolsheviks led the way on this road.

What were the military forces of the approaching conflict? Boris Sokolov, who directed the military work of the Social Revolutionary party, says that in the period preceding the overturn "in the regiments all the party organizations except those of the Bolsheviks had disintegrated, and conditions were not at all favorable to the organization of new ones. The mood of the soldiers was tending definitely toward the Bolsheviks. But their Bolshevism was passive and they lacked any tendency whatever toward active armed movements.". . . The commanding staffs were against the Bolsheviks. The political backbone of the troops was composed of Bolsheviks. The latter, however, not only did not know how to command, but in the majority of cases hardly knew how to handle a gun. The soldier crowd was not homogeneous. The active fighting elements were, as always, a minority. The majority of the soldiers sympathized with the Bolsheviks, voted for them, elected them, but also expected them to decide things. The elements hostile to the Bolsheviks in the troops were too insignificant to venture upon any initiative whatever. The political condition of the garrison was thus exceptionally favorable for an insurrection. But its fighting weight was not large —that was clear from the beginning.

However, it was not necessary to dismiss the garrison entirely from the military count. A thousand soldiers ready to fight on the side of the revolution were scattered here and there among the more passive mass, and for that very reason more or less drew it after them. Certain individual units, more happily constituted, had preserved their discipline and fighting capacity. Strong revolutionary nuclei were to be found even in the disintegrating regiments. In the Sixth Reserve Battalion, consisting of about 10,000 men, out of five companies, the first invariably distinguished itself, being known as Bolshevik almost from the beginning of the revolution and rising to the heights in the October days. The typical regiments of the garrison did not really exist as regiments; their administrative mechanism had broken down; they were incapable of prolonged military effort; but they were nevertheless a horde of armed men a majority of whom had been under fire. All the units were united by a single sentiment: Overthrow Kerensky as soon as possible, disperse, and go home and institute a new land system. Thus that completely demoralized garrison was to rally once more in the October days, and rattle its weapons suggestively, before completely going to pieces.

What force did the Petersburg workers offer from a military point of view? This raises the question of the Red Guard. It is time to speak of this in greater detail, for the Red Guard is soon to come out on the great arena of history.

Deriving its tradition from 1905, the Workers' Guard was reborn with the February revolution and subsequently shared the vicissitudes of its fate. Kornilov, while Commander of the Petrograd military district, asserted that during the days of the overthrow of the monarchy 30,000 revolvers and 40,000 rifles disappeared from the military stores. Over and above that, a considerable quantity of weapons came into the possession of the people during the disarming of the police and by the hands of friendly regiments. Nobody responded to the demand to restore the weapons. A revolution teaches you to value a rifle. The organized workers, however, had received only a small part of this blessing.

During the first four months the workers were not in any way confronted with the question of insurrection. The democratic régime of the dual power gave the Bolsheviks an opportunity to win a majority in the soviets. Armed companies of workers formed a constituent part of the militia. This was, however, more form than substance. A rifle in the hands of a worker involves a totally different historic principle than the same rifle in the hands of a student.

The possession of rifles by the workers alarmed the possessing classes from the very beginning, since it shifted the correlation of forces sharply to the advantage of the factory. In Petrograd, where the state apparatus supported by the Central Executive Committee was at first an indubitable power, the Worker's Militia was not much of a menace. In the provincial industrial regions, however, a reinforcement of the Workers' Guard would involve a complete change of all relations, not only within the given plant but all around it. Armed workers would remove managers and engineers, and even arrest them. Upon resolutions adopted by a factory meeting the Red Guard would not infrequently receive pay out of the factory exchequer. In the Urals, with their rich tradition of guerrilla fighting in 1905, companies of the Red Guard led by the old veterans established law and order. Armed workers almost unnoticeably dissolved the old government and replaced it with soviet institutions. Sabotage on the part of the property owners and administrators shifted to the workers the task of protecting the plants—the machines, stores, reserves of coal and raw materials. Roles were here interchanged: the worker would tightly grip his rifle in defense of the factory in which he saw the source of his power. In this way elements of a worker's dictatorship were inaugurated in the factories and districts some time before the proletariat as a whole seized the state power.

Reflecting as always the fright of the property owners, the Compromisers tried with all their might to oppose the arming of the Petrograd workers or reduce it to a minimum. According to Minichev, all the arms in the possession of the Narva district consisted of "fifteen or twenty rifles and a few revolvers." At that time robberies and deeds of violence were increasing in the capital. Alarming rumors were spreading everywhere heralding new disturbances. On the eve of the July demonstration it was generally expected that the district would be set fire to. The workers were hunting for weapons, knocking at all doors and sometimes breaking them in.

The Putilov men brought back a trophy from the demonstration of July 3rd: a machine gun with five cases of cartridgebelt. "We were happy as children," said Minichev. Certain individual factories were somewhat better armed. According to Lichkov, the workers in his factory had 80 rifles and 20 big revolvers. Riches indeed! Through the Red Guard headquarters they got two machine guns. They put one in the dining room, one in the attic. . . .

The July Days introduced a sudden change in the situation of the Red Guard. The disarming of the workers was now carried out quite openly—not by admonition but by force. However, what the workers gave up as weapons was mostly old rubbish. All the very valuable guns were carefully concealed. Rifles were distributed among the most reliable members of the party. Machine guns smeared with tallow were buried in the ground. Detachments of the Guard closed up shop and went underground, closely adhering to the Bolsheviks.

The business of arming the workers was originally placed in the hands of the factory and district committees of the party. It was only after the recovery from the July Days that the Military Organization of the Bolsheviks, which had formerly worked only in the garrison and at the front, took up the organization of the Red Guard, providing the workers with military instructors and in some cases with weapons. The prospect of armed insurrection put forward by the party gradually prepared the advanced workers for a new conception of the function of the Red Army. It was no longer a militia of the factories and workers' districts, but the cadres of a future army of insurrection.

During August, fires in the shops and factories multiplied. Every new crisis is preceded by a convulsion of the collective mind, sending forth waves of alarm. The factory and shop committees developed an intense labor of defending the plants from attacks of this kind. Concealed rifles came out into the open. The Kornilov insurrection conclusively legalized the Red Guard. About 25,000 workers were enrolled in companies and armed—by no means fully, to be sure —with rifles, and in part with machine guns. Workers from the Schlüsselberg powder factory delivered on the Neva a bargeful of hand grenades and explosives —against Kornilov! The compromisist Central Executive Committee refused this gift of the Greeks! The Red Guards of the Vyborg side distributed the gift by night throughout the district.

"Drill in the art of handling a rifle," says the worker Skorinko, "formerly carried on in flats and tenements, was now brought out into the light and air, into the parks, the boulevards." "The shops were turned into camps," says another worker, Rakitov. . . . "The worker would stand at his bench with knapsack on his back and rifle beside him." Very soon all those working in the bomb factory except the old Social Revolutionaries and Mensheviks were enrolled in the Guard. After the whistle all would draw up in the court for drill. "Side by side with a bearded worker you would see a boy apprentice and both of them attentively listening to the instructor. . . ." Thus while the old tzarist was disintegrating, the foundation of a future Red Army was being laid in the factories.

As soon as the Kornilov danger passed, the Compromisers tried to slow up on the fulfillment of their promises. To the 30,000 Putilov men, for instance, only 500 rifles were given out. Soon the giving out of weapons stopped altogether. The danger now was not from the right, but the left; protection must be sought not among the proletarians but the junkers.

An absence of immediate practical aims combined with the lack of weapons caused an ebbing of workers from the Red Guard, but this only for a short interval. The foundation cadres had been laid down solidly in every plant; firm bonds had been established between the different companies. These cadres now knew from experience that they had serious reserves which could be brought to their feet in case of danger.

The going over of the Soviet to the Bolsheviks again radically changed the position of the Red Guard. From being persecuted or tolerated, it now became an official instrument of the Soviet already reaching for the power. The workers now often found by themselves a way to weapons, asking only the sanction of the Soviet. From the end of September on, and more especially from the 10th of October, the preparation of an insurrection was openly placed on the order of the day. For a month before the revolution in scores of shops and factories of Petrograd an intense military activity was in progress—chiefly rifle practice. By the middle of October the interest in weapons had risen to a new height. In certain factories almost every last man was enrolled in a company.

The workers were more and more impatiently demanding weapons from the Soviet, but the weapons were infinitely fewer than the hands stretched out for them. "I came to Smolny every day," relates the engineer, Kozmin, "and observed how both before and after the sitting of the Soviet, workers and sailors would come up to Trotsky, offering and demanding weapons for the arming of the workers, making reports as to how and where these weapons were distributed, and putting the question: 'But when does business begin?' The impatience was very great. . . ."

Formally the Red Guard remained non-party. But the nearer the final day came, the more prominent were the Bolsheviks. They constituted the nucleus of every company; they controlled the commanding staff and the communications with other plants and districts. The non-party workers and Left Social Revolutionaries followed the lead of the Bolsheviks.

The basic military unit was the ten; four tens was a squad, three squads, a company; three companies, a battalion. With its commanding staff and special units, a battalion numbered over 500 men. The battalions of a district constituted a division. Big factories like the Putilov had their own divisions. Special technical commands—sappers, bicyclers, telegraphers, machine-gunners and artillery men —were recruited in the corresponding factories, and attached to the riflemen— or else acted independently according to the nature of the given task. The entire commanding staff was elective. There was no risk in this: all were volunteers here and knew each other well.

The working women created Red Cross divisions. At the shops manufacturing surgical supplies for the army, lectures were announced on the care of the wounded. "Already in almost all the factories," writes Tatiana Graff, "the working women were regularly on duty as nurses with the necessary first-aid supplies." The organization was extremely poor in money and technical equipment. By degrees, however, the factory committees sent material for hospital bases and ambulances. During the hours of the revolution these weak nuclei swiftly developed. An imposing technical equipment was suddenly found at their disposal. On the 24th the Vyborg district soviet issued the following order: "Immediately requisition all automobiles. . . . Take an inventory of all first-aid supplies, and have nurses on duty in all clinics."

The history of the Red Guard is to a considerable extent the history of the dual power. With its inner contradictions and conflicts, the dual power helped the workers to create a considerable armed force even before the insurrection. To cast up the general total of the workers' detachments throughout the country at the moment of insurrection is hardly possible, at least at the present moment. In any case, tens and tens of thousands of armed workers constituted the cadres of the insurrection. The reserves were almost inexhaustible.

The organization of the Red Guard remained, of course, extremely far from complete. Everything was done in haste, in the rough, and not always skillfully. The Red Guard men were in the majority little trained; the communications were badly organized; the supply system was lame; the sanitary corps lagged behind. But the Red Guard, recruited from the most self-sacrificing workers, was burning to carry the job through this time to the end. And that was the decisive thing. The difference between the workers' divisions and the peasant regiments were determined not only by the social ingredients of the two—many of those clumsy soldiers after returning to their villages and dividing the land- lords' land will fight desperately against the White Guards, first in guerrilla bands and afterwards in the Red Army. Beside the social difference there existed another more immediate one: Whereas the garrison represented a compulsory assemblage of old soldiers defending themselves against war, the divisions of the Red Guard were newly constructed by individual selection on a new basis and with new aims.

The Military Revolutionary Committee had at its disposal a third kind of armed force: the sailors of the Baltic Fleet. In their social ingredients they were far closer to the workers than the infantry are. There are a good many Petrograd workers among them. The political level of the sailors is incomparably higher than that of the soldiers. In distinction from the none too belligerent reserves who have forgotten all about rifles, these sailors have never stopped actual service.

For active operations it was possible to count firmly upon the armed Bolsheviks, upon the divisions of the Red Guard, upon the advanced group of the sailors, and upon the better preserved regiments. The different elements of this collective army supplemented each other. The numerous garrisons lacked the will to fight. The sailor detachments lacked numbers. The Red Guard lacked skill. The workers together with the sailors contributed energy, daring and enthusiasm. The regiments of the garrison constituted a rather inert reserve, imposing in its numbers and overwhelming in its mass.

In contact as they were from day to day with workers, soldiers and sailors, the Bolsheviks were aware of the deep qualitative difference between the constit- uent parts of this army they were to lead into battle. The very plan of the insurrection was based to a considerable degree upon a calculation of these differences.

The possessing classes constituted the social force of the other camp. This means that they were its military weakness. These solid people of capital, the press, the pulpit—where and when have they ever fought? They are accustomed to find out by telegraph or telephone the results of the battles which settle their fate. The younger generation, the sons, the students? They were almost all hostile to the October revolution. But a majority of them too stood aside. They stood with their fathers awaiting the outcome of the battle. A number of them after- ward joined the officers and junkers—already largely recruited from among the students. The property holders had no popular masses with them. The workers, soldiers, peasants had turned against them. The collapse of the compromise parties meant that the possessing classes were left without an army.

(Trotsky, 1957:181–191)

The Lessons of Revolution

I would like to pull together the preceding two sections on revolutionary organizations and point out some similarities (as well as the more obvious differences). The similarities we find mark out to some extent a theory of revolutionary organization. But we must keep in mind that these generaliza- tions do not necessarily apply to future revolutionary changes.

Differences

1. Obviously, the two societies—America and Russia—were completely different. One was a dispersed settlement of small farmers and a few urban merchants and laborers. The other was composed of a vast mass of poor peasants and a small modern sector of urban workers and industrialists. In both societies, commercial agriculture and industrial capitalism were just beginning; but to be "just beginning" had different consequences for capitalist institutions and national development in 1776 than it did in 1917. "Just beginning" in the first decades of the twentieth century meant that Russia was a backward country, relative to western Europe and North America. State institutions were also quite different in the two societies. In America, the British government was weak because of poor communication and transportation. In Russia, the state itself was fairly strong, at least in the sense of having a large bureaucracy, but it was overcentralized and had no "second line of defense," that is, it had no functioning party system, no supportive press, and so on.

2. The goals of the revolutionary organizations were quite different. The American revolutionaries primarily sought independence, and they were ready to develop representative institutions in the process of attaining independence. The Russians sought state power in order to transform the society.

3. In America, partly because they faced relatively little repression from the British, the revolutionaries organized fairly openly and maintained a loose structure. Nor was there a multiplicity of revolutionary factions in conflict with each other. In Russia, on the other hand, the Bolsheviks were tightly organized, and they considered not only czarist supporters and the Provisional Government as their enemies but also other left-wing groups.

It would seem that there is hardly any point in discussing similarities, given these overwhelming differences in goals, in structure, and in the social conditions of the two cases. Nevertheless, the number of similarities is fairly large and particularly important from the viewpoint of organizational structure and tactics.

Similarities

1. Both revolutionary organizations developed an effective and reliable military arm. Military buildup preceded the formal seizure of power (symbolized by the American Declaration of Independence and by the capture of the Winter Palace, the seat of the Russian Provisional Government). In both cases, the military arm included units composed of armed civilians—militias in America, Red Guards in Russia. These units had largely or wholly developed out of an armed populace and had no history of loyalty to the "old regime."

The need for loyal armed units is an important lesson for revolutionaries to learn from this characteristic of two successful revolutions.

The fall of the Allende government in Chile demonstrates the consequences of failing to learn this lesson. Reliance on the loyalty of the presocialist Chilean army proved disastrous and, for a variety of reasons, armed units of workers had not been encouraged. A revolutionary organization without a reliable military and paramilitary arm is probably not viable. It will succumb either immediately when the actual crisis of state power occurs or later when it tries to institute revolutionary change. While revolutionary change could conceivably *begin* at the ballot box, it is likely to end in the graveyard if it has no armed support. This is so because a revolution necessarily threatens a substantial number of relatively powerful groups—if it doesn't, it isn't very revolutionary—who will not hesitate to use force to reverse the revolution. Furthermore, revolutions since the end of the eighteenth century have generally been complicated by foreign intervention, usually against the revolutionary governments. Armed force is necessary against these interventions even if there is no armed counterrevolution within the society. A revolution must consider the prospect of a civil war, involving possibly some kind of outside intervention.

The technological sophistication of the weapons in the hands of antirevolutionary elites and their foreign supporters has now become a major problem for revolutionaries. A relative equality of weaponry between the revolutionary militias and the antirevolutionary forces prevailed in the American Revolution and, to some extent, in the Russian Revolution. Today the technology of the antirevolutionary forces presents problems, although not unsolvable ones.

2. Another similarity is that both revolutionary groups patiently built up a structure with local roots. They created a kind of dual government that competed with the legitimate government. As the government in power blundered and made worse the life situation of a majority of the population, the organs of the revolutionary government took its place. The revolutionary bodies stole the government's legitimacy, established new routines, changed patterns of decision-making, and meted out a new set of rewards and punishments. In the American Revolution, these local vehicles of revolution were at first the Sons of Liberty and the Committees of Correspondence and, subsequently, the Committees of Safety; in Russia, they were the soviets and the local party units.

3. In addition to developing a revolutionary structure as I have just described, the revolutionary faction or party can take over bodies that are not initially committed to revolution. The reader is reminded of how the revolutionary faction won out in the Continental Congress; similarly, the Bolsheviks took over a number of the soviets. This action transformed these initially contested bodies into organizational vehicles of the revolutionary faction.

4. A society-wide coordinating organization is necessary. We saw how the revolutionaries in America, previously linked by the Committees of Corre-

spondence, took over the Continental Congress and made it serve the purpose of society-wide coordination. In Russia, the coordination mechanism was built into the revolutionary party itself when it developed the centralized structure advocated by Lenin.

5. Revolutionaries cannot force the pace of revolution. The widespread favorable sentiment that makes possible local action and an armed popular organization cannot be created where people's life experiences are such that revolution is not yet a reasonable alternative. Note how in both America and Russia the nucleus of a revolutionary movement existed but had to wait through a quiet period before its actions could be more than short-lived disturbances.

In both countries, the life experiences of the people changed for both immediate and fundamental reasons. The immediate reasons were the stupidities and mistakes of those in power—for instance, the tea fiasco and the Intolerable Acts in the colonies and the mishandling of participation in World War I in Russia. The fundamental reasons were the changing social and economic conditions of the society, conditions that we shall examine in the next part. Once the social conditions, and with them the life experiences, had changed, revolution became one of several reasonable alternatives. Once revolution was a possible alternative, the revolutionary movement closed off the other alternatives and made revolution the only possible path.

The Multinational Corporation

The final set of organizations that I would like to single out as having had marked effects on the lives of many people are the modern multinational corporations.

Corporations in general have shaped the economy—and hence the lives —of the western capitalist nations. They have also shaped the economies and societies of the rest of the world, sometimes directly, by benefiting from colonial rule, and also indirectly, by buying materials and selling products. Companies like Firestone and United Fruit Company have dominated the economic development of some countries for years; Firestone's rubber plantations in Liberia and United Fruit's banana plantations in Guatemala have distorted the economies and political systems of these countries. Singer Sewing Machines and International Harvester have sold their products abroad for decades. In more recent years, they have been joined in overseas markets by a number of other large companies.

A special form of these corporations that operate overseas as well as within the United States is the multinational corporation. There are approximately two hundred multinationals with annual sales or income over $100 million. Of these two hundred, about 75 percent are primarily affiliated with the United States. Some analysts note that the search for markets for American products has been a key goal of our foreign policy since the 1890s (Williams, 1972). Exporting the "American way of life" has meant exporting not only values and a form of government but also the desire for American goods— jeans, soft drinks, sewing machines, snowmobiles, motorcycles and automobiles, radios and television sets, baby foods and snack foods, comic books and watches.

Multinational corporations go beyond both the exploitation of raw materials and the establishment of markets. They are corporations that have set up foreign subsidiaries. In other words, they have established satellite companies in other countries. According to formal definition, a multinational corporation has foreign subsidiaries that account for at least 10 to 20 percent of its total assets, sales, or labor force. Note that this is a rather flexible definition. Some people might add as a defining characteristic that multinationals operate in at least six foreign countries in addition to their home country (Horowitz, 1974:32).

Three-quarters of U.S. direct investment abroad is accounted for by about two hundred multinational companies; all of these are among the five hundred largest U.S. industrial corporations (Fortune, 1973a:59). In other words, a relatively small number of corporations account for a great deal of wealth and power. They have profit margins and a rate of growth that is above the average of exclusively national firms.

What advantages do multinational corporations have?

For one thing, they can use national and international monetary systems to their advantage. Specifically, this statement means the following: (a) Profits can be left in subsidiaries that operate in a country with a lower tax rate than that of the United States. U.S. taxes don't have to be paid on the profits of the foreign subsidiaries until these profits are repatriated—"brought home." (b) As the value of the dollar has shrunk in recent years, the practice of leaving profits in foreign subsidiaries in the local currency has had the additional benefit that these foreign-currency profits can be converted into dollars at the highest possible exchange rate. (c) If a temporarily hostile power freezes the profits of a foreign affiliate, the parent company can still bring the profits back to the U.S. by raising prices on shipments to the foreign subsidiary. Thus the money comes home in the form of higher payments on shipments even as the profits appear to be frozen. (d) Multinationals can borrow in countries where interest rates are low and use the money in countries where interest rates are high. (e) Investment abroad gets around U.S. antitrust laws. According to Fortune (1973a), these are some of the advantages in monetary management that the multinationals can gain from their organization, although not all multinations are structured to do so.

Another set of advantages that multinationals have over one-nation firms concerns relationships with governments, consumers, and worker organizations. The money management advantages listed above are really only one consequence of the multinationals' ability to pick and choose from a variety of different environments and thus to be able to find the most favorable environment for a given activity.

Example: "They can take advantage of the protectionist system of closed markets in the U.S. [markets closed by tariffs to foreign firms but not to U.S.-based multinationals] while pursuing an antiprotectionist approach for trading abroad. They can thereby derive the payoffs of having the American workers as customers at high prices, while employing overseas workers at low wages" (Horowitz, 1974:32).

Example: Research and development as well as actual production can be carried out in secondary (or peripheral) countries at lower cost.

Example: The establishment of subsidiaries may satisfy some nationalist governments that would not allow old-style raw material exploitation and market development in their countries. Sometimes such subsidiaries have names that dissociate them from the American company; in any case, they employ the local population for managerial and research jobs as well as for manual and clerical labor.

What are some of the consequences of this style of organization? Very broadly and abstractly, the multinationals help create new patterns of consumer behavior, new patterns of behavior between workers and employers, and new patterns of relationships between states and economic enterprises. Let us look at these consequences in more detail.

1. The fact that multinationals affect consumer behavior is not very surprising. It is an effect that is not unique to multinationals, being more an extension of older forms of imperialism in which large firms sought markets abroad. It is important in that it helps standardize taste throughout the world. National (not to mention regional and ethnic) traditions in food, clothing, and entertainment are disappearing; language itself is transformed. Canadian Eskimos buy Japanese motorcycles, young Frenchmen eat hamburgers, Russian cities are clamoring for their own Pepsi bottling plant. Along with the creation of consumer preferences, multinationals create uniformities in weights and measurements, auditing systems, codes for air travel and telephone systems, banking regulations, and so on. These uniformities and interchangeabilities are set by what one writer calls *organizational fiat,* that is, by organizations' insisting on habits and routines, rather than through the action of states (Horowitz, 1974:42).

2. Multinationals have introduced three major changes in the relationships between classes, the major groups involved in production in each society:

First, they have accelerated the emergence of an *international* class of owners and top managers. The men (and a tiny number of women) who manage the foreign operations of the multinationals are drawn from both the local country of the subsidiaries and the home base of the multinational. Their education is cosmopolitan. They have spent their adult lives, and in some cases their childhood as well, in more than one country. They are accustomed to travel and to a casually elegant life-style. Their loyalties are often more to their companies, which are international in scope, than to a particular national government.

Second, paralleling the emergence of an international class of top executives is the objective development of a class of workers with international interests. Workers in different countries are no longer simply linked by some abstract shared trait like "being a worker" but are often the employees of the same company. Although firms are organized on a multinational basis, unions have been much slower to cross national boundaries. Subjectively, and in terms of worker organization, workers have not fully kept pace with the organization of multinationals.

Third, the multinationals have been one of the major stimulants to the growth of a native middle class in many countries. As I've already indicated, multinationals have generally employed indigenous people at all levels of the organization. For example in Germany, only 20 of Opel's 61,000 employees are Americans; only 50 Americans work for Union Carbide in Europe, out of 17,000 employees in forty production plants and twenty-six affiliated companies (Fortune, 1973b:68–69). Especially in developing countries (obviously less so in Europe, which has had a middle class of long standing), the multinationals are a major employer of middle-class technical workers (engineers, computer workers, accountants, managers and supervisors, clerical staffs, and so on). Many of these employees probably do not think of themselves as part of an international work force, but rather as a new national middle class. They feel that their interests and those of their country are tied into the kind of capitalist development represented by the multinationals. The expulsion or withdrawal of multinationals from their economy would at least temporarily leave these groups in a precarious financial position. Similarly, indigenous entrepreneurs may develop a dependence on multinationals by becoming suppliers or local distributors for them. Managers, professionals, and entrepreneurs associated with foreign capital are usually called the *comprador* class. In a developing country, the middle classes generally, but especially those associated with multinationals, may identify strongly with political forces that promise stability and a maintenance of the status quo. Such persons oppose Socialist parties. A case report on Chilean affiliates of Dow Chemical, for instance, indicates the hostility of middle-level managers and engineers there to the Allende government (Meyer, 1974:145).

3. The multinationals have affected the course of international politics and the role of the nation-state. My discussion of their money management suggests the extent to which multinationals can derive the maximum benefit from nation-states, using them to create favorable climates for investments. For instance, a U.S.-based multinational might persuade the U.S. government to resort to troop deployment or covert operations that insure host-state hospitality to corporations and the downfall of governments that oppose them. At the same time, they can use their multinationalism to circumvent unfavorable tax, investment, or labor policies of the nation-states. By transcending

nation-states in their scope of operations, multinationals can create favorable environments for themselves. At the same time, multinationals help to cement the current detente between the major powers. They assert the primacy of economic advantage over ideological consideration (which is, of course, an ideological position in its own right, but in veiled form). The multinational corporations indicate the existence of a system of political decision-making that includes the nation-states but is larger than they are and, unlike them, is not even in theory accountable to the general public.

Conclusion

We have looked at four types of large organizations. Each has had a massive effect on the lives of millions of people. They have had an effect on governments, on the distribution of wealth, on the routines of everyday life, and ultimately on the values and well-being of people.

We can fully understand the rise and impact of these organizations only in terms of larger society-wide and worldwide trends, which we will examine in Part Three.

References

Commager, Henry Steele, and R. B. Morris (eds.)
   1958   The Spirit of Seventy-Six. Volume 1. Indianapolis: Bobbs-Merrill.

Fortune.
   1973a   "How the multinationals play the money game." Fortune 88(August):59–62+.
   1973b   "Enterprising ambassadors of American business." Fortune 88(August):66–73.

Garner, Larry.
   1974   "Marxism and idealism in the political thought of Antonio Gramsci." Ph.D. dissertation. New York: Columbia University.

Horowitz, Irving Louis.
   1974   "Capitalism, communism, and multinationalism." Society 11(January):32–36+.

Lenin, V. I.
   1967   What Is To Be Done? New York: International Publishers.

Meyer, Herbert E.
   1974   "Dow picks up the pieces in Chile." Fortune 89(April):140–152.

Reed, John.
   1967   Ten Days that Shook the World. New York: International Publishers.

Trevelyan, G. M.
   1942   English Social History. London: Longmans, Green.

Trotsky, Leon.
   1957   The Russian Revolution. Volume 3, The Triumph of the Soviets. Translation by Max Eastman. Ann Arbor: University of Michigan Press.

Williams, W. A.
   1972   The Tragedy of American Diplomacy. New York: Dell.

Chapter 9

Methods of Observing Change in Organizations

In this chapter, I would like to discuss methodologies that are appropriate to studying organizations. Studying change in organizations presents special methodological problems that are not encountered when studying change in individual behavior and attitudes.

THE TIME SPAN OF ORGANIZATIONAL CHANGE presents problems to the researcher. Important changes in organizations may take decades or even centuries to accomplish. Bursts of obvious accelerated change may be followed by periods of apparent quiet. Changes that were initiated during the bursts of reform may require many years of gradual transformation before they are fully realized. During such quiet periods these reforms may also be channeled into forms that were unintended by their activist originators. For example, studies confined to the bursts of demonstrations and political activity on campuses in the late 1960s would have missed the way in which these patterns played themselves out in subsequent years. The problem of the time span of organizational change becomes even more acute when the organizations have a very long history and a very long-term perspective on history, like the Roman Catholic church or the great nation-states. The actual gradual playing out of the potential for change that appears during a crisis is also a problem in studying individuals, of course, but less so than it is in studying organizations. Academic colleagues or contracting agencies pressure the researcher for fast findings and conclusions; yet the time span of change in organizations can be a matter of years, decades, or even intervals that exceed any one lifetime.

This problem in studying change in an organization is compounded by the ability of organizations to shield themselves from the researcher. Many organizations are committed to partial or complete secrecy for a variety of reasons. To keep out observers, organizations develop specialized departments and procedures, including deceptive public relations departments, guards, secret files, and the cold shoulder. Factions or departments within a larger organization may also try to maintain secrecy and invulnerability.

Another problem in studying organizations is the need to develop ways of understanding structure. Our conceptual frameworks, and especially our methodologies, are not as fully developed for carrying out research on structures as they are for studying individuals. An organization is a more abstract entity than a person. We all understand where a person's boundaries are and which organisms are persons and which are not. Boundary and pigeonholing problems are much more acute with organizations. When we are surveying or observing individuals, our data come from precisely the same source as the object of our study—the individual herself. When we are studying an organization, however, our data are of necessity often generated by various individuals, for instance, the person who has been interviewed or the one who has made entries into the records; therefore, we see the organization through the eyes of these individuals. We develop a composite picture of the organization made up of the bits and pieces gleaned from each individual. We are thus precisely in the situation of the seven blind men studying the elephant: one feels the legs and declares the elephant to be like a tree, another touches the trunk and says it is like a snake, a third grabs the ear and announces it to be like a sail, a fourth seizes the tail and compares it to a rope, and so on. In other words, methods such as questionnaire analysis and interviewing, which are based on individual responses, will produce only a composite picture of the organization. To really see the relationships between people, the interactional glue that holds the structure together, we will probably also need to use observation.

Research Design

What you want to know about organizational change depends on your larger purpose. You may want to develop some general ideas about how organizations change; you may want to find out more about how organizations change their environments or members, in other words, what effects they have on people; or you may want to explore what tactics can be used to change organizations. These different goals involve different research strategies. Information that is needed to develop tactics for starting organizational change yourself will probably also contribute to a general theory of organizational change and vice versa. Given limited amounts of time, money, and energy, however, you may not be able or interested in doing research to meet both goals at once.

Formulating Questions

You can usually begin your research with a series of questions. Unless you have a very large sample of organizations, you probably won't want to carry out statistical tests of formal hypotheses anyway, so there is little virtue (and a good deal of the vice of pseudoscientific mumbo jumbo) in stating formal hypotheses. Furthermore, formulating relatively simple straightforward questions will make the results of your research easier for others to understand.

One set of questions you can ask concerns *effects* of organizational behavior. Organizations change peoples' lives. Organizations have effects on their members and on people in their environment. They alter the routines of everyday life. You can collect and analyze data concerning such effects. Examples of this kind of research include:

— Studies of occupational health and safety hazards, in which the researcher shows how workers are affected by unsafe working conditions. A general description of such hazards could be supplemented by a comparative analysis of different industries or factories, comparing, for example, unionized and nonunionized workers, white and minority-group workers, and so on.

— Studies of the effects of medical practice and hospital organization on the clients of the health care system.

— Studies of the effects of planning agencies and private developers on the quality of city life.

Studies of the effects of organizational behavior are a relatively easy way to study organizations and change and are useful if you want to initiate change. Such studies can be carried out without having to penetrate too far into an organization that wants to shield itself from the researcher because much of your data can come from individual people in the organization's environment rather than from the organization as an entity. You will probably still want to see organizational records on individual clients or members, but at least some of your data can be obtained by interviewing individuals affected by the organization. It may be hard to track down an adequate sample of such people, however, especially if the organization does not reveal the information.

A second set of questions about organizations and change has to do with *structure.* The researcher looks at patterns of relationships to see what kinds of changes take place in these patterns. A structural study will probably also include some analysis of the organization's resources. The researcher will want to know how the distribution of power and resources shifted in the organization. Structural studies can also be concerned with effects. One might ask how organizational behavior affected the structure of its environment (instead of asking how it affected individual life experiences). Also, different kinds of effects may be caused by different kinds of structure; for example, the school children of one city may do better on standardized tests than those of another city because the school bureaucracy in the first city is differently arranged. When we are studying structure and structural effects, we are looking less at people's experiences, at their everyday lives and feelings, and more at the patterns of their relationships.

Structural data can be obtained from several different sources. Members of the organization may be able to provide insights through interviews, but sometimes they may be reluctant to do so or actually not have a clear idea of informal patterns. Organizational records are also a good source of information on the formal structure, but contain little except clues about the informal structure.

A third set of questions you could ask about an organization concerns its internal *processes,* specifically, the sequences of interactions and behavior that are involved in it. Rather than looking at fairly static patterns of power, control over resources, hierarchies of command, and so on (as we do in a structural study), in a process study we look at how individuals act in these structures and how they maintain and re-create these structures by their actions. Structure is captured in the organizational chart of an organization; informal as well as formal structure can be charted by indicating positions and people and by using lines to represent relationships of power, authority, friendship, and so on between these people or positions. Process analysis is less like a chart and more like a movie or play. We want to see it happen. Process studies are inherently studies of change, usually over relatively short time spans. For this reason, process almost always has to be observed directly or reconstructed from transcripts or reports of meetings. Structure is easier to summarize than is process (unless it is a very large structure, as in the case of organizational linkages in an entire metropolis). To adequately present process, you may want to use a tape recorder or videotape. Even so, you have to select from this continuous record those items that answer your questions.

These questions about the effects, structure, and process of organizations can be related to each other. Often the effects of the organization on individuals are related to structural features of the organizations or to characteristics of processes that take place within the organizations. An organization may also develop a certain type of structure or set of procedures because it is designed to have a certain type of effect. But in formulating these statements, we should not lose sight of the larger context—of the environment of the whole society, with *its* structure and values, in which the organizations are embedded.

Selecting the Sample

There are different ways of selecting the number and kind of organizations to study. In the case-study method, the researcher selects one organization and carefully examines how it changes and how it affects its environment.

A good case study describes change in one organization. We cannot be sure that other organizations change in the same way. However, the case study provides at least one good example of change, and it provides clues to what we may expect in other organizations. A case study may have only limited *analytic* scope because there is little with which to compare the description of the single case. We learn relatively little about which *types* of factors can account for organizational change and under what *range* of conditions such change takes place. These limitations of the case study can be mitigated by comparing the case-study material with reports on other organizations, thereby in effect transforming the case study into a comparative analysis without extending the required amount of fieldwork.

Comparative studies of organizations are often more directly analytical than are case studies; they identify differences and similarities between organizations and seek to explain them. There are a great many one-shot comparative studies that are essentially static comparisons of two or more organizations, in which differences are viewed in terms of current goals, structure, or environmental conditions. It is easier to carry out and present comparative studies of static differences than it is comparative studies of *change* in organizations.

The kind of study I want to emphasize here, however, is comparative and *historical,* in the sense that different paths of development are traced. The different organizational histories may either be part of the explanation for why the organizations are different at the time of the study or be part of what needs to be explained. The study can be even further complicated when the compared organizations are located in different societies (or different environments). Finally, the comparative study of organizations can be expanded to the point where sophisticated statistical techniques can be applied. Instead of comparing only two organizations, a very large number can be included in the study. Then it is possible to break them down into many subclasses and to identify many possible factors that account for their differences.

Getting the Data

I have already discussed at some length how the invisible—and not so invisible—shields that surround organizations make data collection difficult. A useful way to begin is by using published sources and organizational records that are accessible to the public. According to one researcher, *the information is always there.* The organizations you want to study need the information for their own purposes. They collect it—although not always very well—and store it (North American Congress on Latin America, 1970).

In the case of most government agencies, these records are public, and you are entitled to see them. There are two exceptions to this general rule that government records are easily accessible: "classified" documents (generally relating to military matters and diplomatic negotiations) are not available to unauthorized persons, and there is always the possibility that crucial documents that are not officially classified as secret have been hidden or destroyed. By and large, however, you are more likely to run into three other obstacles: getting the run-around from bureaucrats; not being able to understand the notation, code numbers, or technical language of the documents; and finding that useful material is buried in massive amounts of documents that you have to sort through. The first two obstacles can only be overcome by polite persistence. As a citizen you are entitled not only to see the documents but also to receive an explanation about how to read them. The third obstacle can be lessened by talking to someone who has seen the records and can help you get started, and by learning to use index volumes and other classifactory material.

The records of private organizations are harder to obtain. Government agencies (and all of their public records!) are a good place to start research on corporations. In particular, the Federal Securities and Exchange Commission supervises all corporations that have public stock and bond offerings. The SEC file libraries (in Washington, New York, Chicago, and San Francisco) contain records on these corporations that include a prospectus on each corporation (a statement detailing its history, financial condition, law firm, directors and officers and their stockholdings, etc.) and a proxy statement listing salaries and holdings of corporate directors who are up for election. Some private firms are regulated, that is, under the supervision of federal or state regulatory agencies. The broadcasting, power, and airline industries nationally and race tracks and insurance companies (in Illinois, for example) are examples of regulated enterprises. The regulatory agencies therefore have public information on such firms. Furthermore, the government has conducted studies of a number of different types of corporations. The Patman report—*Commercial Banks and Their Trust Activities: Emerging Influence on the American Economy* (Banking and Currency Committee, House of Representatives, 1968)—is a particularly important study of this kind. Court records are also a useful possible government source about corporate behavior. There are also, of course, many private directories and registries.

At some point you may have to penetrate the organization itself. To understand informal structure and the flow of events, as well as to see private records, you will have to be ready to get inside the organization. Some questions cannot be answered by simply searching public records and published sources. Some of the sources listed in the reference section and in the bibliography at the end of the book contain many useful suggestions for how to enter an organization and carry out observations within it.

In addition to collecting data on the day-to-day functioning of an organization, you may be fortunate enough to see an organizational accident. An organizational accident is a major blunder or collapse in the structure, routines, or effects of an organization. When a termite hill is knocked down, you can see the structure of the tunnels, the scurrying of castes of termites that normally do not leave the hill, and the behavior of termites when faced with an emergency. Similarly, organizational accidents reveal both the hidden normal workings of the organization and its response to emergencies. Sometimes organizational accidents are deliberately caused by other organizations. Watergate would not have become an organizational accident of national scope if it had not been for the action and persistence of the *Washington Post* and the other media, and eventually of Congress itself. Other accidents, like the Santa Barbara oil spill, are initially accidents in a stricter sense of the word; but they too lead to an exposure of organizational behavior to the larger public (Molotch, 1969).

In your own work, you probably will not be fortunate enough to be able to observe such large-scale breakdowns. But you may be able to observe smaller foul-ups within an organization in which official "lines" or facades are disrupted long enough for you to see how parts of the organization actually work.

References

Banking and Currency Committee, House of Representatives.
  1968   Commercial Banks and Their Trust Activities: Emerging Influence on the American Economy. Staff report for Subcommittee on Domestic Finance, 90th Congress, 2d session (July 8). Two volumes. Washington, D.C.: U.S. Government Printing Office.

Molotch, Harvey.
  1969   "Santa Barbara: Oil in the velvet playground." Ramparts 8(November): 43–51.

North American Congress on Latin America.
  1970   Research Methodology Guide. New York: NACLA.

Part Three

LARGE-SCALE
CHANGE

"The materialist method disciplines the historian, compelling him to take his departure from the weighty facts of the social structure. For us the fundamental forces of the historic process are classes; political parties rest upon them; ideas and slogans emerge as the small change of objective interests. The whole course of the investigation proceeds from the objective to the subjective, from the social to the individual, from the fundamental to the incidental. This sets a rigid limit to the personal whims of the author."—Leon Trotsky, *History of the Russian Revolution.*

IN THIS PART, I shall finally turn to the underlying causes of many of the changes I have discussed in the preceding two parts. There I looked at changes that individuals could see, experience, and participate in within their lifetime. But again and again we saw how these changes had causes as well as consequences that went far beyond the places or times that one person could experience.

We saw how individuals were often caught up in changes that they had no part in originating. We saw how even very large and powerful organizations could affect the routines of everyday life but were unable to force or hold back the pace of certain kinds of changes. They could "seize the time" but not create the right conditions. In other words, to understand social change we shall have to go beyond the environments of individual experience and look at how entire societies change over long periods of time. Some writers refer to these kinds of processes as macro social change; macro is from a Greek word meaning "large," so macro social changes are changes that involve whole societies.

In the next pages, I shall be concerned with three types of change.

First, I shall consider changes in systems of production. All human societies have to include activities to provide for the material existence of their members—people have to be fed, sheltered, and clothed. Human beings continually act on each other and on the environment in the process of arranging for their physical survival. In some societies, these activities are very few and simple. But in many societies, especially modern industrial ones, the range of productive activities is large and complicated, and the way people organize themselves in groups to carry out these activities is also complicated. Productive activities, and the social relationships associated with them, have undergone definite cumulative changes over the course of human existence.

Second, I am going to examine long-term changes in political behavior. People have had changing definitions of what is public and what is private life. They have arranged themselves in different patterns of equality and subordination. They have developed a special form of political activity called the state, a specialized coercive organization for administering the affairs of a society. And they have invented ways of attacking the state.

Third, I shall look at long-term changes in ideology, in systems of beliefs and values.

My main focus in the following chapters is going to be an examination of how all these forms of human action have changed in the course of human existence. They have not changed in a random or a cyclical fashion but cumulatively, with a definite direction. There has been an evolution in social organization from simple, egalitarian hunting and gathering societies to complicated, large, inegalitarian modern industrial societies. When I say *evolution,* I do not mean a biological evolution. Since the appearance of *Homo sapiens* several millenia ago, there has been no modification of the fundamental genetic character of human beings. A person living in a modern society is not, as an individual, more evolved, more intelligent, more articulate or in any way superior to an individual living in a simple hunting or farming society. Nor does evolution mean progress in happiness or the quality of life; on the contrary, life in simple societies may be happier and more satisfying for individuals. The evolution of social organization just means that technology, the process of production, and the patterning of human behavior have become larger scale and more complicated. Some of my discussion will be concerned with evolution in this sense.

In the course of social evolution, many different types of societies have appeared. Change processes have not been identical in all societies. For example, the transition from an egalitarian society to a society with classes and a state was not identical in Egypt and China. Or to take another example, industrialization proceeded at different times and in different ways in England, Germany, Russia, and Japan. So a second focus of this discussion will be the way in which large-scale evolutionary processes have unfolded in different types of societies.

Finally, I shall examine in greater detail the most recent stages of the general evolutionary process. In the last few centuries, the diverse societies of the world have been welded into a capitalist world-system in which social change is qualitatively different from change in the past. We have already looked at various facets of this emerging world-system—European expansion and conquest (the conquest of Mexico, the African slave trade, the mercantile companies, and the modern multinational corporations), industrialization, the growth of various forms of modern states and political movements, and the transformation of traditional workers into a modern labor force. In this part, I shall pull all this material together and present a summary of trends in the world-system.

Chapter 10

Changes in the Mode of

Production In this chapter, I shall define *mode of production* and discuss how productive activities are fundamental to all societies. I shall present the concept of classes, the distinct groups that are involved in production. I shall discuss how modes of production and their associated classes have evolved in the course of human history. I shall identify the major classes in the modern United States. In order to examine the way productive systems change and to show how the nature of technological change is itself constrained by class structure, I shall conclude with a set of case studies of technological change.

IN THIS SECTION, the terms *substructure, mode of production, forces of production, relations of production,* and *classes* are defined. They are fundamental concepts for the understanding of a whole society and types of societies.

Definitions

Let us begin by looking at those aspects of human society that we shall henceforth refer to as the *substructure.* In our view of change, these aspects of human behavior are the most fundamental. They have to do with meeting the needs of human beings as physical organisms—with the need for food, shelter, and other necessities of subsistence. For several million years, these were the main concerns of everyday human life. For billions of people right now, meeting these needs is virtually the only concern of everyday life.

In the everyday life of many readers of this book, the central importance of production is veiled in a variety of ways. We have little to do with the production of food or shelter. Little of our time has to be allocated to these activities. Our own activities may be only distantly related to fundamental biological needs. A teacher or an accountant or a piano player appears to have little contact with the organization of production. But this view is erroneous for several reasons. First, we obviously depend for physical survival on productive activities, even if we do not see them or engage in them. Second, the nature of our society is such that production activities are hidden away at the core of the economic system, surrounded by layers of activities and types of workers who are only distantly connected to them. This practice of obscuring the activities of production is an important characteristic of modern capitalist societies.

Mode of Production

Let me define a few more terms. A society can be said to have a *mode of production*. It is the way in which the goods and services of the society are produced. It necessarily involves some production of goods essential to sustaining human life. Food and shelter must be provided. They must be provided in amounts sufficient to meet the needs not only of working adults but also of infants and children who cannot contribute to production. A group or a society that cannot accomplish this goal will die out, although isolated members may survive long enough to join other groups. In addition to basic subsistence needs, other kinds of goods and services are produced. In almost all societies people make weapons, toys, games, ornaments, and religious objects; they decorate or modify the basic subsistence tools to make them attractive.

In many societies, basic subsistence activities are wrapped in many layers of related activities. For example, in our society, the distribution of food involves shipping of produce, construction of supermarkets, packaging, advertising, manufacturing shopping carts and cash registers, accounting procedures and inventorying, and so on. Some of these activities seem to be definitely necessary in a large society where most people do not produce food and live some distance from farms. Shipping, canning and freezing, the construction of distribution centers—all these activities seem necessary. Other activities, such as advertising and fancy packaging, seem to be irrational additions to the basic process of food production. Although they are not part of food production itself, these "irrational" activities are important aspects of the way in which production is organized in our society.

Let's word these considerations in a slightly different way. By mode of production we mean all those activities that human beings enter into in order to sustain themselves. These activities include skills and tools as well as the actions themselves, and they include the reciprocal impact of the actions on the natural environment and of the natural environment on human actions.

Not *all* human activity is part of the mode of production. Games, religious services, lovemaking, elections—these are all examples of human activity, but they are not generally part of that system of action that we call the mode of production. But the boundaries are hard to draw. The generally rational life-sustaining productive activities are often interwoven with or expanded by fundamentally irrelevant kinds of activities. For instance, most hunting societies have rituals and magical beliefs that shape hunting activity. Sometimes these apparently irrational accretions to productive activity have rational consequences; for example, taboos on the type or amount of game that can be bagged may prevent a tribe from depleting its environment.

In our society there are also nonrational activities and practices associated with production, many of which are "ultimately" less sensible than many of the rituals or taboos of simpler societies. But many of these practices may have a short-run rationality in a profit-oriented society. Tailfins on automobiles and brand-naming are examples of such additions to basic productive activities. In some societies, as we shall see, the mode of production is hard to differentiate in terms of time, space, or social roles from other human activities. There are no factories, no time clocks, no "nine-to-five," no special titles or job categories. Yet the observer and, in most cases, the participants can identify those actions that produce and process the material resources of the group.

Forces of Production

As we look at how goods and services are produced, we may come to see that there is a core area of behavior that is directly involved in production and a set of human relationships that revolve around this core area. For example, in our society people use power looms to weave cloth. A certain amount of know-how and concentration are necessary to set up and monitor the looms and to repair them when they break down. Cooperation is needed to handle the finished product and to ensure its distribution to people who will cut and sew it and, ultimately, to people who will wear it. It is more efficient to run and monitor machinery if a number of machines are located together. This total set of arrangements and actions is an example of what has come to be called the *forces of production.* The forces of production include the tools and other equipment, the know-how, the patterning of behavior, and the actual work effort necessary for production.

Relations of Production

Let's take another look at the textile factory. We would observe the following: The workers who monitor the power looms and handle the finished product cannot take the cloth home with them and sell or barter it or give it away as they see fit. They cannot do this as individuals nor as a group. We would further notice that they do not own the tools. The company many wink at their using some occasionally for their own purposes, but in general the workers cannot dispose of them. We would also notice that on payday the workers are given money. However, the amount of money they receive is not equal to the amount of money that is left after all expenses—the costs of materials, the power and water bills, depreciation of the physical plant, and so on—have been paid. Some of this money is given to the owners, who have not participated in making the cloth. Some of the money is given to supervisory workers who also do not make the cloth but rather direct the work of those who do. These considerations of ownership of the finished product, ownership of the tools, distribution of money, and supervision of workers are not directly part of the production of the cloth. Rather, they are social relationships—patterns of behavior between people—that are connected to production but not an integral part of it. When considered for a whole society, these relationships are called the *relations of production.*

Characterizing a Whole Society

The system of behavior and tools that make up the forces of production —know-how, equipment, and actual work effort and organization—and the relations of production—the patterning of ownership and supervision of the productive process—is called the *mode of production* of the society. Note that although our example of the textile factory was confined to the production of only one item, the terms *forces of production, relations of production,* and *mode of production* refer to a whole society. Thus, for example, American society is industrialized and capitalistic. In terms of the forces of production, most production is carried out with technically sophisticated machinery in mass quantities. Hence we can speak of America as an industrialized society in terms of the forces of production. Productive enterprises are privately owned; that is, they are owned by private individuals or groups of individuals, not by the public at large or by the workers who make the finished goods or supply the services. Owners hire workers in a labor market. Owners of productive enterprises do not own workers as slaves or control their labor as serfs. These types of social patterns can be summarized by saying that relations of production in the U.S.A. are capitalistic.

These statements do not mean that everything is produced in large factories by people who are hired workers. Of course there exist small communal workshops in which handicrafts are made and in which income is shared among all the craftspeople. But these workshops are not characteristic of the society. They are small, few in number, and do not account for a large volume of the society's goods and services. Their legal standing is much less firmly guaranteed than that of enterprises privately owned in the usual manner. Both the small workshop and public institutions (like municipal service systems) are economically and legally marginal.

Similarly, in societies that we might refer to as state socialist (such as Russia or Poland), some peasants may have private plots whose produce they can sell in a market. However, the economically and legally dominant form in state-socialist countries is the state enterprise, in which state or party officials and, to a limited extent, the workers themselves make decisions and hire and supervise workers. In Catalonia, Spain, during the revolution of 1936, some small shopowners were permitted to stay in business: Most, however, were expropriated, and the relations of production were the relationships between and among the workers themselves.

Assigning a specific mode of production to each society is a somewhat abstract way of looking at the concept. In reality, there are all sorts of transitional modes of production. Often a society cannot be neatly pigeonholed as having this or that mode of production. In the long run, however, the concept provides a certain amount of intellectual clarity.

Class

Once we've defined relations of production, defining *class* is relatively easy. *Classes are the groups of people that are distinguished by different positions in the mode of production.* They are the groups that are connected by the relations of production. For example, in the United States, owners of productive enterprises are one class. Production workers are another class. Other groups, such as supervisory personnel, government workers, owners of very small "mom-and-pop" enterprises, and so on, are not as clearly class groups. In medieval society, serfs and landholders were the two major classes. In the antebellum South, plantation owners, slaves, and non-slave-owning whites were three clearly identifiable classes. In very simple farming and hunting and gathering societies, there are no classes; all people of the same sex are equal in their access to resources and participation in production. A classless equality in control over enterprises and decision-making about resources and incomes prevailed in Catalonia during the revolution, despite differences in skills and wages.

Class, as I have defined it, exists above all as an *objective* category. It does not depend on people's opinions and feelings. If a factory worker earning $10,000 a year believes he is middle-class because he has a bungalow in the suburbs and sends his children to college, we do not have to accept this self-perception as being a reflection of a correct view of American class structure. Self-perception, that is, a person's subjective interpretation, may be very useful in predicting how he or she will behave in the near future—for example, in predicting voting behavior or attitudes toward busing. But the subjective interpretations of the actors in a situation are not the same as a correct understanding of the structure of the situation. *To be able to use the concept of class to explain and understand long-term social change, we must use it to refer to structural positions in society and not to subjective classifications, self-identifications, opinions, and so on.*

Relationships

All of this preceding discussion has been rather abstract. I shall flesh it out shortly with a description of changes in the mode of production. First, I would like to pose two analytical questions:

1. What is the relationship between the forces of production and the relations of production? To what extent does a particular level of development of the forces of production constrain or necessitate a particular pattern of the relations of production? Marx once said, "The hand-mill gives you society with the feudal lord; the steam-mill, society with the industrial capitalist." In other words, to what extent does productive capacity limit or force a certain set of relationships between producers and other people in the society? It is quite clear, for example, that a society with a hunting and gathering way of acquiring food in a harsh environment could not support a group of people who did not contribute to food production. Among Bushmen and Eskimos, all ablebodied adults must put some effort into obtaining food.

Note that we are talking not only about productive tools or skills but also about the interaction between the techniques and the environment. For instance, the Indians of the northern Pacific Coast were also hunters and gatherers who fished and collected berries, using techniques that were in many respects less ingenious than those of the Eskimos. However, the rain forest and the ocean were such lush environments that even with simple fishing and berry-collecting techniques the Indians were able to develop societies with considerable inequalities, including chieftainships, wealth differences, and slavery. Few of these people were either completely freed from food production or completely cut off from access to the resources of the sea and the forest, but class distinctions were certainly beginning to appear at the time of the first contact with whites.

As I will point out when I present the historical data, the development of the forces of production seems to limit the type of possible relations of production but not in a simple one-to-one way. Some match ups are clearly impossible because technology and environment are too unproductive; as in the case of the Bushman and the Eskimo, their environments and technologies cannot support adults who do not work at collecting food. In other situations, more options are available. Moreover, different societies with roughly similar productive capacity seem to have taken different routes in their development of the relations of production.

We cannot predict the match for any given single case. But for the totality of cases of a given form of the forces of production, a particular pattern of relations of production will be the numerically preponderant form. For instance, while inegalitarian hunting and gathering societies exist (like that of the northern Pacific Coast Indians), most hunting and gathering societies have little inequality. The exceptions can sometimes be explained by special circumstances, as in the instance where the richness of the environment was an important factor. In other cases, the exceptions are the results of transitions in the relations of production. As Braverman (1974:19) remarks:

> It means that the same productive forces that are characteristic of the *close of one epoch* of social relations are also characteristic of the *opening of the succeeding epoch;* indeed, how could it be otherwise, since social and political revolutions, although they may come about in the last analysis because of the gradual evolution of the productive forces, do not on their morrow provide society with a brand new technology.

For example, in some industrialized present-day socialist countries, private ownership and production for profit in a market no longer exist, but technology and even work organization are still similar to that of capitalist countries. In yet other cases, we may not yet have enough information to account for anomalies in the fit between the relations of production and the forces of production.

2. What is the relationship between the mode of production and other features of the society, such as its value system and its political life? To what extent are the latter types of institutions (the superstructure) constrained by the mode of production (the substructure)? What kinds of matches between substructure and superstructure are likely? Possible? Impossible? The superstructure is constrained by the mode of production but not determined by it. For instance, capitalism is associated with political democracy in countries such as the United States, Sweden, and England, but it was associated with fascism in Nazi Germany. The task is to identify the constraints or "outer limits" of the possible and to account for variations in the fit between substructure and superstructure.

These abstract considerations will become much clearer when I discuss them in terms of real societies and real modes of production. The questions makes sense only when examined in terms of specific historical changes.

A Materialist View of World History

The unfolding of history provides evidence for a perspective that argues that the mode of production accounts for the broad outline of change.[1] At any one time, the attitudes, values, customs, political institutions, and characteristic

---

[1]The material in this section relies heavily on *Culture, Man and Nature* by Marvin Harris (1971), especially chapters 5, 9, 10, 11, 16, and 17.

personalities of the age seem to be important factors in shaping events. In intervals of decades or even centuries, the overall pattern of change cannot be clearly seen. But once we take the long view, the importance of the mode of production in determining general outcomes (although not particular details) becomes more visible.

Food Collection

Human progress began in the Lower Paleolithic period—the first phase of the Old Stone Age. Until about 500,000 years ago, ape people roamed the warmer grassland areas of the world. We can imagine life in a band of ape people. Most of the day was spent foraging for food. They ate primarily seeds, roots, and small game. They used crudely made pebble tools, wooden spears, and clubs. There was little or no differentiation in the food-collecting work of males and females. Nor did they extensively share their food with each other, beyond feeding the helpless young. Occasionally, however, they cooperated in catching somewhat larger animals, such as antelopes and monkeys, and in fending off large predators.

In personal appearance, these creatures were about five feet tall, small toothed, bipedal most of the time, and less hairy than apes. Their personalities were shaped by two important biological developments: the capacity for language, for a use of symbols that far exceeded that of other primates; and the sexual receptivity of the female during the entire menstrual cycle instead of only during an estrus period ("heat") at ovulation. These two biological developments contributed to humans' relative freedom from an instinctual basis of behavior. The capacity for language meant that communication, planning, and abstraction could begin to take place. The ape people could coordinate their activities with each other, discuss events or objects that were not physically present, and explain to others better ways of arranging their lives. The bands that included substantial numbers of ape people with language ability survived more easily than did the relatively taciturn bands. (In this discussion, I have not presented the debate about exactly which varieties of ape men produced particular types of tools).

By about 500,000 B.C., a new form of human being had emerged— *Pithecanthropus erectus*. These people had larger brains and always stood upright. Their capacity for language was much greater. They made new kinds of tools—hand axes—that became increasingly sophisticated during the next several hundred thousand years, and an increasing number of flake tools, which were produced as by-products of making the axes. The ape people's individualistic foraging for small game and vegetable foods was replaced by big-game hunting for elephants, horses, wild cattle, and so on.

This decisive change in the mode of production (properly speaking, food *collection* rather than production) had important social consequences. It produced the "original sin" in human inequality, namely, the sexual division of labor. Previously males and females had carried out the same kind of leisurely browsing for collectable food. Ape women were not markedly hampered in these activities by pregnancy or nursing children. Big-game hunting, however, usually necessitated fast treks for long periods far away from camp. Women with children generally could not effectively participate in these chases. They remained near the campsite, where they continued to collect vegetable foods and small animals.

In regions where hunting did not always involve long marches in pursuit of fast-moving game, women participated in hunting. For example, among the Copper Eskimo, who hunt seal by waiting at the seals' breathing holes, women become seal hunters. Because of high infant mortality and the practice of female infanticide, family size is small in this group, so women spend relatively less of their adult life caring for children than do women in other societies. Generally, however, the organization of big-game hunting is incompatible with child care.

Big-game hunting not only initiated sexual division of labor, but it also required more complicated coordination of activities, both among the hunters and between the hunters and those who stayed behind at the campsite. Part of this coordination was the sharing of the kill. No longer did people individualistically consume what they collected, fulfilling needs for protein, carbohydrates, and other essential foodstuffs by their isolated activity. Now there had to be an interchange between hunters and foragers, with each making a distinct and vital contribution. Also people had to come to grips with the fact of unequal participation in the kill. One man might consistently aim better or be bolder in running up to the dying animal to administer the coup de grace, or be a better tracker, or see better. Yet whatever his outstanding accomplishment might be, the kill also depended on the backup efforts of the whole group of hunters. The band also had to contend with the occasional wastrel who contributed little or nothing. The growing ability to speak made possible coordination, the analysis of how to share, praise for the contributors and censure for the lazy and inept, and the planning of the hunt.

Between 100,000 and 50,000 B.C., this hunting culture was fully developed among a biologically new form of prehistoric human, the Neanderthaloids. These in turn gave way gradually to fully modern *Homo sapiens*. The Neanderthaloids were probably not a dead-end branch of our family tree that was lopped off through extermination by the modern form; rather, local variation and extensive interbreeding made for a gradual genetic changeover. The period of the Neanderthaloids is known as the Middle Paleolithic and is characterized by a larger proportion of flake tools and a greater variety of tools, including borers, wood shavers, burins, and scrapers as well as better hand axes and flakes. The dead were buried with supplies of meat and tools.

From this point on, the pace of change became very fast. The development of new productive techniques, interacting with the capacity for language, provided a momentum for cumulative change. Each improvement in tool production and food collection freed more time and energy for further elaboration of these activities. Each improvement was explained and passed on to the rest of the group and to succeeding generations. A takeoff point was reached: social evolution was no longer bound by the slow processes of genetic variation and biological selection among diverse bands. Humans were beginning to free themselves from the constraints of nature; they were starting to shape their own lives. Each band of people had a larger realm of human control than ever before. A child was born into a world filled with artifacts made by human beings and a way of life created by preceding generations. Humans had become the most powerful predator. With weapons and fire at their disposal, they no longer had to fear other animals. Their tools, their campsites, and their cemeteries formed a powerful ring of human extensions into nature. *Homo sapiens* began to have a sense of control over at least some parts of nature.

By the Upper Paleolithic period—45,000 B.C. to 14,000 B.C.—this sense of control was extended both in fact and fancy. It was extended in fact in the sense that this was a very rich cultural period. As evidence of the wealth of their material culture we need but list the variety of manufactured objects: blades, knives, scrapers, awls, arrow straighteners, single-blade knives, beads, bracelets, pins, daggers, laurel leaf spear points, eyed needles, harpoons, spear-throwers, and bows and arrows. These long-lasting stone and bone tools attest to an even larger number of perishable goods of skin, wood, reeds, and so on. Men hunted mammoth, horse, reindeer, bison, and other large herd animals. Women not only collected vegetable food but engaged in the complicated manufacture of fur clothing, shelter, utensils, carrying cases, ornaments, and so on. The world of the average person was filled with the evidence of human production: meat drying on racks, clothing, tents, jewelry, tools, household goods, and so on.

In fantasy and imagination, human beings in the Upper Paleolithic period became intensely aware of their increasing transformation of and control over nature. Through ritual and ritual art, they both asserted their power over nature and indicated their fear of losing this power. They covered cave walls with paintings and engravings of animals and with carved statues of pregnant women. Having separated themselves from the natural world by their productive capacity, and understanding that they were interfering with nature and altering it, they begged the spirits of nature to permit these encroachments.

The Upper Paleolithic was followed by a short period in Europe and Asia known as the Mesolithic (14,000 B.C. to 11,000 B.C.). Forests of birch and pine succeeded grasslands; the great herds of mammoths, woolly rhinoceros, and horses gave way to elk, deer, and wild cattle that lived in the forest. To some extent the Mesolithic was a "dark age," a period during which the art (and presumably the ritual underlying the art) of the Paleolithic period was abandoned. But this judgment reflects the error of confusing the shifting developments of human religion and art with the relatively straight-line development of productive capacity. Productive techniques did not degenerate. The mode of production had to shift from grasslands hunting to fishing and forest living. Vegetable foods and seafood became more important in the diet. Boats and fish-catching devices were perfected. Woodworking became a major activity. Dogs joined men. When tracking game animals in the dark forests, hunters found that a dog's sense of smell was superior to man's grassland-nurtured sense of sight. Sleds and skis were invented. Human ability to survive the rather swift transition from grasslands to forests and to maintain, if not actually advance, the level of production attests to the extent to which human society had a force of its own, a freedom from nature that was built into tool use and social structure.

In the history of humanity, the end of the Mesolithic period marked the end of the exclusive existence of *food-collecting* modes of production. In food-collecting societies, human beings have no effect on the stock of animals and plants except to deplete it. They do not intervene in the reproduction of plants and animals. Their control over their food supply is therefore rather limited. As we have seen, there was not one, single food-collecting (or hunting and gathering) mode of production but many, distinguished by the environments they acted upon (for example, forest or grassland, arctic tundra or coastal rain forest, and so on), the richness of the tool kit, and the extent of cooperation between people.

While the forces of production—the know-how, tools, and work patterns —were rather diverse and unevenly developed, the corresponding relations of production almost universally had an important element in common—there were no classes. Division of labor was simple and based almost exclusively on gender and age. All people in the group had equal access to natural resources, although they may have owned their own tools and these may have varied in quality from individual to individual. The kills in big-game hunting were shared, generally regardless of the ability or contribution of the individual hunters. Foraging areas as well as herds of game were not owned by individuals, and often not by groups either. Within each age group and sex, individuals with more experience or savvy may have directed the efforts of others, but they did not have permanent or unquestionable authority over them. There were no able-bodied people who were exempt from food production. Nor were there full-time specialists in supervising others or coordinating work efforts. Lazy or incapable people may have been subjected to informal pressures, but they were not deprived of food, access to resources, or tools. People in a group knew each other personally.

After the Mesolithic period, new modes of production appeared. Some groups continued to live by hunting and gathering, however. To a large extent, these groups remained in geographically marginal areas or were pushed into them by other groups. They lived (and continue to live) in Arctic tundras (the Eskimos), in deserts (the Bushmen of the Kalahari, the Indians of the Great Basin area of Nevada and Utah), in tropical forests (the Pygmies of the Ituri Forest in Zaire, the Negrito of Southeast Asia, as well as some Amazonian groups), in northern forests with a very short growing season (the Northern Athapascans), and in the inhospitable climate of the extreme tip of South America (the Ona, Yaghan, and Alacaluf). All together these groups now represent only a small fraction of humanity. Because of the harshness of the environments in which most of them live, it is hard to generalize from their way of life to that of the Paleolithic peoples who had similar technologies but applied them to much richer environments.

Food Production

In the years between 11,000 and 5,000 B.C., a new invention transformed human productive activities and made possible new forms of social structure. I am referring to the development of agriculture and livestock-raising. Humans began to control the reproduction and growth patterns of plants and animals. Thus they moved from various forms of food-collecting to food-producing.

This invention was made in at least four places: in the Near East between 11,000 and 10,000 B.C., in Mexico and Peru between 9,000 and 7,000 B.C., and, more or less at the same time, in West Africa and Southeast Asia. We know most about the invention of agriculture in the Near East. Throughout the area that is now eastern Turkey, Syria, Iraq, and Israel, people had settled into fairly large preagricultural villages. They subsisted on wild grasses similar to present-day wheat and barley as well as on other vegetable foods and small game. The wild wheat and barley grew in great abundance, and the people invented sickles; cleaning, grinding and roasting equipment; and storage facilities.

Eventually someone—perhaps a woman, since women are usually the ones in charge of collecting plant foods—discovered that plants sprang up on garbage heaps where seeds had been accidentally scattered. Thus began the deliberate planting of seeds. Over the next few generations, trial-and-error experimentation produced new breeds of improved grain. While less able to propagate by self-seeding, these new varieties, once they were planted by humans, produced higher yields and provided more predictable food sources than the wild grains. At about the same time, Neolithic men turned to capturing the wild sheep and goats that they had previously hunted and started breeding them for docility, milk yield, and other desirable features. By 9,000 B.C., wheat and barley, goats and sheep were all domesticated together in the Near East.

Agriculture was independently invented in the New World. In Mexico and Peru, a rather different set of crops was domesticated: maize as well as other grains, beans, manioc, potatoes, sweet potatoes, squash, avocados, tomatoes, pineapples, chili peppers, and cacao. Maize was the most important of these crops in Mexico. As in the case of Near Eastern grain cultivation, maize production seems to have been preceded by harvesting of wild maize. Eventually domesticated maize became capable of reproduction only with human assistance, since the ripe kernels do not fall off by themselves. There were relatively few animals suitable for domestication in the New World, and livestock-raising was much less developed there than in the Near East. Hunting remained an important activity and source of protein.

From each of the four centers, the knowledge of food production rapidly diffused to most of the rest of the world. The domesticated plants and animals had to be modified or replaced by local varieties as the invention spread into diverse environments. For example, the damp forest climate of Europe necessitated changes in many of the grains, less domestication of animals, and eventually decisive attacks on the environment itself, such as burning the forests and draining the marshes. From the Near East, food production spread to Greece (8,000 B.C.); to the lands bordering the North Sea, including England (6,000 B.C.); to the Indus Valley of northern India (6,000 B.C.); and to northern China (4,000 B.C.). From Southeast Asia, the cultivation of rice, peas, beans, tropical roots, the water buffalo, chickens, and pigs spread to China, making that region the recipient of two different streams of food production. In the New World, food production spread from highland Mexico northward to the lands of the Pueblo Indians and eventually as far as the northern woodlands, and into the lowland regions of the Gulf of Mexico and the Pacific Coasts, into Central America and the islands of the Caribbean. From Peru, it spread into the Amazon basin and southward toward Patagonia. In Africa, food production spread from the west into the Congo basin, then south and east, where it met the diffusionary stream from the Near East via Egypt. Within a few thousand years almost the whole world was transformed.

The first impact of the spread of food production was to increase population size and density and to make life easier and more predictable. Control over the reproduction of plants and animals gave human beings greater control over nature and greater independence from the environment. One can imagine that the first reaction was a sigh of relief that endless wandering in search of game was over (although a few older men may have grumbled at the sissified way of life of the younger generation). More children survived to adulthood, and older people and sick people had an easier time. Famines were not unknown but became rarer. Some of these advantages had already been enjoyed by peoples living as hunters and gatherers in very fertile environments, such as the fishing tribes of the Pacific Northwest (in historic times) or the grain gatherers of the prehistoric Near East. But the invention of food production meant that population density and a settled way of life could spread to less naturally abundant regions.

The Rise of Class Societies

The invention of agriculture and livestock-raising was followed in many areas by changes in the organization of the production and distribution of goods. It was followed by changes in the *relations* of production. Specifically, class societies replaced more egalitarian forms.

To explain this process, we need to begin by looking at how production and distribution are organized in classless societies such as the hunting and gathering societies we discussed earlier or simple agricultural societies. In these societies, individuals or small groups hunt game and gather or harvest grain, fruits, and vegetables. The food is distributed to kinspeople and neighbors at the end of the day or at the end of the hunt. Everyone in the camp receives food each day. Everyone sooner or later makes a contribution. Free-loading is discouraged but is not impossible. In general, the prevailing principle is "from each according to his ability, to each according to his need." Each person has access to land and raw materials and to tools and technical skills. Individuals in informal cooperation with each other decide on work time and work schedules, on the place, pace, and form of production, and on the distribution of the products of their work. (As always, there are exceptions to these statements; for example, among the Yir-Yoront, an Australian hunting and gathering group, the old men "owned" the stone axes and other people in the group had to ask their permission. In general, however, such restrictions were more ritual formalities than real control.) *General reciprocity—informal sharing—and egalitarian cooperation in work characterize small, technologically simple societies.*

In these societies people were socialized to be generous without drawing attention to generosity as a virtue. People who showed off their ability to collect and distribute food were met with disapproval. Competition and bragging as well as public displays of gift-giving were discouraged. Socialization as well as self-interest in the face of the harshness of nature contribute to egalitarianism. Everyone sooner or later depends on everyone else. These groups have a shrewd understanding that the man who repeatedly draws attention to his superior abilities and productive capacities threatens the band's cooperativeness and spirit of equality. "Gifts make slaves, like whips make dogs," say the Eskimo (Harris, 1971:246).

As food output rose in the Neolithic period, many settlements remained organized on the principles of general reciprocity and equality of all producers (of the same sex). The larger output meant better, more secure lives and more leisure time. Leisure, like work and food, was casually and usually equitably shared.

But some settlements found new ways of using their larger food supply. They found that they had enough food to support full-time specialists in some form of crafts activity. These specialists were freed from food production but they produced other goods and services. For example, some people might become blacksmiths, weavers, potters, boat makers, tanners, and so on. Their products were exchanged for food on a daily basis or at regular market times. Meanwhile other people who were less involved in crafts work perhaps lost these skills. Such a society was still egalitarian in access to resources and subsistence needs; skills and tool use were differentiated, however. Such a society might be said to have specialization without classes.

In yet other settlements a new way of distributing food arose. Instead of informally sharing food with each other with little or no accounting, people began to hang on to what they produced long enough to make invidious comparisons. The man who produced a great deal could not keep his wealth; he was expected to distribute it, just as he had under the rules of general reciprocity. Now, however, attention focused on his achievement, and he gained a reputation as a "big man." He gave away his own surplus output and sometimes collected and then distributed everyone else's. Everyone ended up with his original share of goods, but one man gained fame by collecting and redistributing these goods, often at a feast or special occasion.

Many societies include such ranking systems in which some people have more prestige than others based on their distribution of goods. For example, the peoples of New Guinea developed these customs. The distributors are admired and may come to play an important role in village affairs. However, they cannot bar other people from access to resources. They do not control the pace or place of other people's work. They have to work like everyone else. They have no way of maintaining their ability to control the flow of goods in the community if their luck or circumstances change. Not only is this pattern of "egalitarian redistribution" the dominant one in many simple agricultural societies, it also appears in vestigial form in our own society. In a gang or other peer group, a youth with more money than his fellows is expected to be generous, to "treat" the others, to provide money for parties, the jukebox, liquor and marijuana, and so on. He loses friends and prestige if he is "cheap" and tries to save his money for long-term or individualistic goals.

In some Neolithic communities, these "big men" began to consolidate their control over resources. Instead of redistributing wealth to its original producers and even giving away their own goods to demonstrate their generosity, they began to skim off a share of the collected goods for themselves. This holding back of a portion of the wealth that a chief or big man handled very rapidly produced a new kind of inequality in the community. The chief no longer had to work. He might participate in the production process only in order to bless the fields and give speeches. Not only was he recognized as a leader, but his whole kinship group may also have had special privileges, had to do less work, and got more than a fair share of goods.

Finally, the leading group (for at this point ranking often involves a kin group rather than an individual) gained hold not only of a lion's share of products (both food and handicrafts) but also of productive resources—land, tools, seeds and other people's labor. At this point the society may be said to be stratified—to have a class system. "A stratified society is one in which members of the same sex and equivalent age status do not have equal access to the basic resources that sustain life" (Fried, 1967:186).

One more factor is necessary to stabilize a class system. That factor is the use of some of the collected products to sustain a group of specialists in maintaining the flow of goods. In other words, without these specialists the person or group who collects the products has little power to make the rest of the community keep turning the produce over to him. He has to resort to moral suasion, threats of magic, appeals to custom, and promises of favors to keep the goods coming in.

In the Trobriand Islands off the coast of New Guinea, for example, the chief has sixty wives, and the kin group of each wife is expected to provide a gift of yams at harvest time. Most of the yams are redistributed to their contributors, but the chief holds back some to pay canoe builders and magicians and to free himself from having to work. He has no organization to enforce the yam contributions, however. He has no tax collectors or policemen to ensure that the yams will be brought to his house. If they are not, the chief can appeal to Trobriand values to try to persuade his in-laws to provide the yams. He can threaten them with magical spells, and he can hire more and better magicians than his in-laws can. But if the latter do not want to bring the yams, and are reasonably confident of their own magic, they cannot be forced to support the chief.

In a state-level society, the group that controls the basic resources can force others to act accordingly. They can prevent other people from using the tools and other resources for production. For example, where land is privately owned, a police force can be called in to drive squatters off the land. Those in control can force other people to provide them with the output of productive activity; a tax-collection system exists, and police stand by to force producers to "share" their crops, to pay land rents, or to turn over a finished object to the owner of the workshop. *A state-level society is one in which some people are specialized to defend the interests of the class that controls access to basic resources.* This apparatus of specialists includes ideologues, whose job it is to convince people that the social order is good; coercers, who use physical force to ensure the maintenance of the stratified order; and administrators (and their clerical staffs), who coordinate the activities of the ideologues, coercers, and the producing masses of people. All the people in the state apparatus are paid out of the goods that are produced and collected.

For obvious reasons, most stratified societies have a state apparatus. A stratified society without such an apparatus is fragile; there is little that the controlling class can do if everyone else seizes the resources.

The nature of class society is revealed when one looks at its development and sees how it functioned early in its history. Nowadays, the picture of oppression, exploitation, and coercion is hard to recognize, at least in the capitalist democracies of Western Europe and North America. It is hard to see capitalist owners as rapacious expropriators; the cop on the corner who finds lost children and chases muggers is hardly recognizable as the guardian of ruling-class interests. But, as we shall see shortly, the skeleton of class societies is always the same: a producing class, a controlling or ruling class, and a state apparatus that maintains the class order.

In modern societies, this core structure is hard to recognize because of (*a*) the availability of consumer goods, (*b*) the relatively wide range of choices in the labor market and in the market in goods and services, (*c*) the many welfare activities of the state, (*d*) the mechanization of work and the high productivity of labor backed up by machinery, (*e*) the relatively high ratio of state and quasi-state workers to production workers, (*f*) the tremendous differentiation and specialization of work, and (*g*) the prevailing ideology. But in its early forms the core structure was much easier to recognize. A small ruling class of king and nobles used tax gatherers, overseers, priests, and soldiers to force peasants to turn over to them their products in the form of labor service, taxes to the state, produce to the landowners, and tithes to the temples. Because of the low productivity of agriculture and the lack of machinery, most people had to work on the land. A few were artisans; very few were scribes, priests, or other workers in the state apparatus.

By about 5,000 B.C. in the Near East, 3,500 to 2,500 B.C. in the New World and in China, the transition from egalitarian classless societies to stratified states was complete. The following kinds of processes took place. Neolithic societies with improved food-production techniques had several options for what to do with their surplus food: (1) they could use it to provide themselves with more leisure time; (2) they could use it to support specialists in various kinds of crafts production; (3) they could use it to support more people; and (4) they could use it to support people who initially acted as redistributors but shortly thereafter acted as expropriators, as a ruling class backed up by a state apparatus.

The dominance of the fourth of these options is *not* a product of "human nature"—of fundamental human greed and aggressiveness. Rather, all the different options were experimented with by different Neolithic settlements. But the communities that developed stratification and statelike institutions won out over the communities that opted for more leisure or for egalitarian specialization. The stratified statelike communities had advantages over their neighbors. They had available trained specialists in violence, that is, soldiers and police. They developed state organizations that forced people to build irrigation systems and to produce more food. Their food output thus increased and their populations grew larger, causing pressure against available land resources. More people, more soldiers, and more centralized coordination gave these communities an advantage in wars of territorial expansion against their neighbors. Eventually, the small egalitarian groups and the transitional settlements were conquered by the statelike communities.

In the next couple of thousand years, small kingdoms and city states dotted the Near East. They usually had a central city, which was the seat of the ruler and his court, the home of the nobility, and the site of the temple and the priesthood. Surrounding the city were smaller settlements and their fields, many of which were absorbed into the state by conquest. Food and other goods were delivered to those in power in the central city in a variety of ways: through rents (in the form of food and services) to the ruling class; in the form of labor services on land owned outright by the ruling class; through taxes; through payments to the temple; through slavery imposed on the conquered nonstratified groups and weaker city-states, which provided a source of labor.

The rise of these stratified city-states and the accompanying cultural changes, such as the development of temple cults, writing, and a priesthood and the construction of a variety of public works, and so on, has somewhat euphemistically been called "the urban revolution." But the key feature of this period was not urbanization per se (the increase in the size and density of settlements), but *the rise of stratified states. What changed were the relations of production, the ways in which people behaved toward each other in the process of producing and distributing the basic resources and goods of the society.*

Precapitalist Class Societies

Precapitalist types of class societies shared the following characteristics:
1. A mode of production based on a fairly productive form of agriculture, often supported by large public works such as irrigation systems, and frequently using plow agriculture
2. The existence of stratification—a class system—including a small ruling class of kings and land controllers, a large class of producers, and a rather small apparatus of functionaries who collected the produced goods and maintained social order
3. The absence of industrialization and capitalist investment
4. The presence of a state apparatus
5. A value system marked by a "high" literate cultural tradition shared by the ruling class and upper levels of the apparatus and distinct from the nonliterate folk traditions of the slave or peasant class; and a temple-cult type of religion that preached order, justified existing inequalities, and drew people into religious festivals and temples to entertain and mystify them at periodic intervals
6. A state apparatus that not only maintained internal order but undertook expeditions of territorial expansion against other states as well as "barbarians" (that is, less rigidly stratified people)

These kinds of societies developed in the Near East, in China, in Mexico and Peru, in India, in Europe, in Southeast Asia, in Japan, in Africa, and in a number of more marginal areas. My main concern will be with the sequence of such states in the Near East and Europe. It was the line of development in these two areas that culminated in feudalism, which in turn brought forth capitalism and industrialization, which in turn transformed the entire world within the last two centuries.

The Near East and Southern Europe: The Mediterranean World.

In the first few millenia of stratified society, these city-states developed in Mesopotamia and in Egypt. The ruling classes were essentially the upper levels of a royal hierarchy and a priestly hierarchy. Their control over basic resources took the form of taxation rather than land ownership. In other words, a largely free peasantry, who ran their private lives and community affairs much as they had in the Neolithic period, had to deliver produce to the court and temple located in the central city. In addition, there were a number of craftsmen and slaves.

Similar city-state patterns appeared in Greece and Italy at a somewhat later date. Later there were also empires: Egypt, Assyria, Persia, and later the Hellenistic and Roman empires. In many respects, the empires of early antiquity were merely city-states swollen to large sizes by conquest. But their expansion depended on improved administration, record-keeping, communication, transportation, and military technology. They also had to devise ways of controlling an ethnically diverse population. Large public works such as irrigation systems began to be very important. Slaves accounted for more of the work force in the empires than in the city-states. The free peasants of the city-states were partially expropriated (in Egypt, for example) and their land became the private property of the nobles of the court and the temples. Forced labor for the state *(corvée)* and rents were added to taxation and temple payments as a way of extracting produce and labor power from producers. The following advice, preserved on an Egyptian papyrus, gives a glimpse of the life of the workers:

> I have considered hard manual labor—give thy heart to letters. I have also observed the man who is freed from manual labor, assuredly there is nothing more valuable than letters. . . . I have seen the metal worker at his toil before a blazing furnace. His fingers are like the hide of the crocodile, he stinks more than the eggs of fish. . . . The weaver sitting in a closed-up hut has a lot that is worse than that of a woman. His thighs are drawn up close to his breast and he cannot breathe freely. If for a single day he fails to produce his full amount of woven stuff, he is beaten. . . . Only by bribing the watchmen at the doors with his bread-cakes can he get a glimpse of the sunlight. . . . I tell thee that the trade of the fisherman is the worst of all trades; he can't really make a living at it, and he is in constant danger of attack by crocodiles. Verily there is no occupation that is satisfactory except that of the scribe, which is the best of all. The man who knows the art of scribe is the superior through that fact alone, and that cannot be said of any other of the occupations that I have described to you. . . . No man says to the scribe, "Plow the field for this person." (Quoted in Bernal, 1971:130; revised by the author.)

The European city-states and small kingdoms underwent similar processes of diversification and expansion. Under Philip of Macedon, the Macedonians (a people living directly to the north of Greece) conquered the Greek city-states. They rapidly adopted Greek culture. Under Philip's son, Alexander, a basically Greek army conquered the entire area of the eastern Mediterranean—Greece, Asia Minor (now Turkey), the Near East, Egypt, Persia, and even parts of northern India. While the state created by Alexander collapsed rapidly after his death into a number of successor states, Greek culture became the high culture of most of these new states. The ruling classes as well as substantial numbers of the rest of the population adopted Greek customs in language, art styles, clothing, religion, recreation, and general world outlook. This Hellenistic world of the eastern Mediterranean was absorbed into the Roman Empire. The Romans also conquered other peoples, many of them "barbarians" with much simpler preliterate societies in terms of population density, degree of urbanization, complexity of the class system, strength of the state, and so on.

During the period of the Greek city-states, the Hellenistic Age, and the Roman Empire, cultural innovation flourished. Among the city-states there was considerable experimentation with political institutions, ranging from Athenian participatory democracy (at least for free male citizens) to Spartan militarism, with its constant preparedness, its barracks life, and its sharp differentiation between the soldier-citizens and the food-producing "helots" (a subjugated stratum of workers). In the Roman Empire, there was less experimentation with possible political forms and more concentration on administering an empire. A stratum of officials—tax collectors—existed to extract grain and other crops from the provinces and send them to Rome. A class of nobles owned the large estates, which were worked by both slaves and peasants. During the course of the empire, the peasants became increasingly serflike— bound to the estate but not owned as individuals, as were the slaves.

All the states of Greco-Roman antiquity included large numbers of slaves. Family structure was patriarchal; women were often secluded (except among slaves, courtesans, and the poor) and were dependent on their husbands. Religious observances were designed to equate the favor of the gods with the power of the state: gods and goddesses became the patrons of cities and kingdoms and were even identified with particular rulers. The gods of conquered peoples were absorbed into the existing Greek or Greco-Roman pantheon, although within it they tended to appeal more to the urban lower classes (who in Rome, for example, worshipped Isis, the Egyptian goddess) or to particular occupational groups (such as the Roman soldiers who worshipped the Near Eastern sun-god, Mithras, the divine child who assumed the form of a bull). Food production became reasonably efficient, based on the Near Eastern irrigation systems and plow agriculture.

These city-states and empires preceded feudalism in the Near East and Europe. They are not neatly lined up in a pattern of unilineal development.

Within the general framework of stratification, state-level institutions, agricultural production, some urbanization, and the flowering of an elite culture, many different forms appeared. The strength of their state apparatus (and their military institutions), the productivity of their particular technology operating on their particular environment, their geographical location, and various still unknown factors determined whether the society "rose" or "fell," whether it expanded or was conquered by its rivals.

For the members of the ruling classes, the particular fortunes of the society made a great difference—often a life and death difference. Many lost their lives in the wars between states or were enslaved. Even if the conquered ruling classes remained puppet princes within an empire, they had to change their religion, their language, and their life-style when their state was absorbed into a larger one. For the peasant and artisan working classes, these changes were generally less traumatic, as long as they were not enslaved. A new tax collector took away their grain, a new god was added to their pantheon; for many, these changes made little difference. It was the "barbarians"—the peoples such as the Celts, the Germans, and the Jews—who struggled most fiercely against foreign rule and tried to protect their freer, more egalitarian way of life.

Beyond the Mediterranean World. Outside of the Mediterranean world there were also many agricultural state-level societies. In Polynesia, in the southeastern United States (among the Natchez Indians, for example), in some areas of Africa, in parts of Meso-America, and among the "barbarian" Germanic and Celtic tribes of Europe, institutions of stratification and the state were just emerging. In some cases these developments were independent (like the institution of divine kingship in Hawaii); in some cases they came about through diffusion from more complex neighboring societies (as among the Nubian kingdoms of Africa, adjacent to Egypt); and in some cases they resulted from a combination of both independent development and diffusion. The list of peoples with stratification systems and some state-level institutions also includes a variety of expansionist nomadic or seminomadic pastoralists such as the Asiatic Hyksos who invaded Egypt; the Huns (and later Mongols) at the northern borders of China; the Jews before the establishment of the kingdom and the building of the temple; the Indo-European invaders of India; the desert tribes of North Africa; the Bantu pastoral kingdoms of East Africa; and so on.

City-state societies like those of Mesopotamia or classical Greece also emerged elsewhere. In West Africa, for example, the Yoruba (among other groups) organized themselves politically into city-states. In the Mayan areas of Guatemala and Yucatán, city-states were the major form of the state. At the time of the Spanish conquest, the Aztecs were on the verge of transforming a city-state society into the core of an empire. During early phases of Chinese history, small warring states emerged. All these societies were organized around a court or a temple city, which often was also a market center, while the majority of the population remained agricultural. (*Agricultural* does not always mean rural; among the Yoruba, for instance, most people lived in cities of from 10,000 to 20,000 population but continued to be farmers.)

Empires as well as city-states and stratified pastoralists also rose and fell outside of the Near East and Europe: in West Africa (Songhay and Mali), in South America (among the Incas), in India and Southeast Asia, and, above all, in China. The most powerful of these empires were hydraulic states (Egypt, for example,) in which the state controlled an extensive system of irrigation. This was also true of China at various times in its history and of the Inca empire. In these hydraulic states, the state constructed gigantic public works involving complex systems of irrigation canals, aqueducts, dams, and terraces. With water-control systems, an arid land could support a fairly dense population. At the same time, this irrigation-based mode of production gave the state great power. The state was responsible for building the projects, which required extensive recruitment and supervision of laborers. The hydraulic system also required regional coordination to ensure efficient and equitable use of the water. It allowed the rulers to "turn the 'rain' on and off as if from a central spigot" (Harris, 1971:403). In these hydraulic states, the upper levels of the state apparatus—the officials—were as much a part of the ruling class as were the large landowning nobles.

On the whole, most of these class societies lacked a dynamic mode of production. Change in technology and social relationships was not built into their class system. The systems tended to expand geographically, especially in a search for more land or for a new source of slaves, a major form of labor. In the course of expansion, they clashed with a variety of other states and barbarian peoples. It is this pattern of expansion and conquest rather than technology and changing internal social organization that is a major factor in the rise and fall of many of these states.

Feudalism

In A.D. 476, the Roman Empire "fell"; specifically, the state institutions of the western half of the empire collapsed. The capital city was sacked by barbarian tribes. Roman troops and officials could no longer administer the western provinces of the empire. The high culture of the Roman upper classes —their art and way of life—largely disappeared. While the state apparatus and high culture collapsed, other aspects of life continued. Many characteristics of the stratification system survived the fall of Rome. Latin continued to be spoken, although in gradually altered forms that were heavily influenced by the languages of the Germanic tribes (Franks, Goths, Vandals, and others). Christianity continued to be the religion of those areas that had formerly been part of the western half of the empire. Above all, much of the agricultural technology developed in the west was maintained. Thus, the blend of Roman and Germanic institutions, the collapse of the Roman state, the transformation and large-scale loss of Roman high culture, and the collapse of urban society in the west—these factors combined to produce the type of society that we call feudal.

Meanwhile, in what had been the eastern half of the Roman Empire and in the regions beyond its eastern margins, the large traditional civilizations continued to develop: Byzantium, Persia, the Islamic world and, later, the Turkish empire. But let us look at the development of feudal society in more detail, since it presents a very important example of social change.

As noted above, feudal society emerged from the contact of Roman and Germanic cultures. Block (1964:443) sums up these origins and their consequences:

> European feudalism should therefore be seen as the outcome of the violent dissolution of older societies. It would in fact be unintelligible without the great upheaval of the Germanic invasions, which by forcibly uniting two societies originally at very different stages of development, disrupted both of them and brought to the surface a great many modes of thought and social practices of an extremely primitive character. . . . The feudal system meant the rigorous economic subjection of a host of humble folk to a few powerful men. Having received from earlier ages the Roman villa (which in some respects anticipated the manor) and the German village chiefdom, it extended and consolidated these methods whereby men exploited men; and combining inextricably the right to the revenues from the land with the right to exercise authority, it fashioned from all this the true manor of medieval times. And this it did partly for the benefit of an oligarchy of priests and monks whose task it was to propitiate Heaven, but chiefly for the benefit of an oligarchy of warriors.

By the fourth century, the economy of the western Roman Empire was already collapsing into a more localistic economy based on the subsistence needs of estates. Pay in kind or in land became relatively more important than pay in money. With these economic shifts came less commerce and crafts production. The western half of the empire had never been as urbanized as the eastern half, and during this period became even more rural. Rome was not an industrial center but rather a parasitic growth of state officials, military men, and a large, impoverished, underemployed population fed on a grain dole from the provinces. Thus the collapse of Roman state institutions had relatively little impact on the local features of the economy.

Tenant farmers of free birth *(coloni)* gradually slid into the status of serf as they lost the right to move, to dispose of the land they worked, and to bear arms. Meanwhile, the number of slaves diminished; those remaining were "emancipated" into serfdom, which was a more profitable institution for the owner of the estate. From the point of view of the farmer-serf, the transition from late Roman society to early feudal society was quite gradual, being perceived as a loss of freedom, a decline in contact with towns, and a shift in culture, all taking place in the localistic economy of the manor. Even for the ruling classes, the transition from the Roman Empire to the Romano-barbarian successor states of Goths, Franks, Lombards, and so on was fairly easy. Many of the Roman or romanized landlords in the west continued to control their estates. The barbarian chieftains did not decimate them but rather intermixed with them and copied their economic institutions.

The economic substructure of the early Middle Ages was thus in large part a Roman one; the agricultural technology was based on Roman practices, and the relationships between the landlord of the estate and the peasantry were like those of the last century and a half of Roman rule. Technologically, the Dark Ages were not particularly retrograde. Some craft techniques were lost, but agricultural technology did not deteriorate. As a matter of fact, plowing was actually improved and swamps were drained. Political institutions beyond the lord-serf relationship, however, were strongly influenced by Germanic customs of chieftainship and loyalty to war leaders.

In some ways, the early feudal period was a plateau or resting place, not a setback. Preceding forms of social organization, particularly state institutions, had collapsed. The higher forms of culture—art, literature, science, and so on—seemed to be lost. But underneath this collapsed superstructure, the foundations remained sturdy. Techniques of food production remained effective. They sustained people physically while a new start in social forms— political institutions, culture, and so on—was begun. The period's apparent primitivism and localism in terms of the state and the high culture actually permitted more experimentation with new forms than had the highly developed and centralized institutions of the great empires.

What kind of society appeared after this transition? A noted historian presents the following portrait of medieval life in about the year A.D. 1,000:

> A man's condition was now determined by his relation to the land, which was owned by a minority of lay and ecclesiastical proprietors, below whom a multitude of tenants were distributed within the framework of the great estates. To possess land was at the same time to possess freedom and power; thus the landowner was also a lord. To be deprived of it, was to be reduced to serfdom. . . . It is of no importance that here and there among the rural population a few individuals happened to preserve their land and consequently their individual liberty. As a general rule serfdom was the normal condition of the agricultural masses, that is to say, of all the masses (Pirenne, 1937:12).

Here, then, are some key features of feudal society:
1. It was predominantly an agricultural society.

2. Its most important relationship between groups of people was that between landowners and serfs, who were bound to the land. While serfs were not owned as individuals (like slaves), they could not leave the noble's land and had to make available to him a substantial share of their produce and labor.

3. The noble or lord "always lived on the labor of other men" (Bloch, 1964:288), generally through control of land but also through tolls, market fees, fines, and the produce of workshops.

4. The manors or estates were the focal points of society. Little urban life existed until fairly late in the medieval period. Subsistence needs were met by local production.

5. Production was organized primarily for consumption, not for profit. The noble supported an entourage of knights, men-at-arms, and various retainers, and generosity was considered a virtue.

6. Neither land nor labor were commodities, as they are now. They could not be sold. Land was bestowed on vassals by lords who controlled large territories or was inherited. Labor was provided by serfs who had no choice between masters.

7. Violence in all forms from war to brigandage was endemic in the society and was practiced by all classes. It was related to the concentration of power in the local estates, which meant that there was no large centralized state to monopolize force. Fighting was also the major source of income, other than landed property, of the knight. For the lesser knights who did not own land, it was the sole source of income. Fighting brought plunder and prisoners to be held for ransom. Feudal culture glorified violence.

8. By the later Middle Ages, differences in rank within the class of nobles became more hereditary and more codified in a growing body of law. Prior to the legalization of relationships between groups and individuals, there had developed many ties of dependency and obedience both between nobles and serfs and between various levels of nobles. Overall these ties, which were not kinship ties, formed a hierarchical structure. "In feudal society, the characteristic human bond was the subordinate's link with a nearby chief. From one level to another, the ties thus formed—like so many chains branching out indefinitely—joined the smallest to the greatest" (Bloch, 1964:444). The ties of obedience and protection, on the one hand, were based on the superior force of the overlord; but, on the other hand, they also foreshadowed the capitalist notion of *contract,* an agreement protected by law and binding people to each other for a limited period of service, outside of kinship ties.

9. Despite the high degree of local autonomy and the absence of a strong state, much of Europe was unified by a common culture composed of various strands: a literate Catholic culture carried by a small number of the class of clergymen; an upper-class culture of chivalry, which put a veneer of glamor, religious symbolism, knightly honor, and notions of romantic love (possibly of Oriental origin) over what was basically a situation of little more than

localistic banditry; and a folk culture with roots in the pre-Christian past. We shall see later how the relationships characteristic of feudalism paved the way for the social relationships of capitalism. Since I shall devote a whole chapter to industrialism and capitalism and their effects, I shall not consider in great detail the transition from feudalism to capitalism here.

Capitalism

The period between 1500 and 1800 was a period of transition from feudalism to industrial capitalism. In a later chapter, we shall explore this transition in more detail. Here it suffices to make two major points.

First, industrialization is a major transformation, as revolutionary as the shift from food-collecting to food-producing. Industrialization provides an enormously expanded volume of goods. It is manifested in agriculture by mechanization, which makes it possible to feed a very large population using the labor of only a very small number of people. Industrialization means an altogether new relationship toward nature. The average person comes to live in an environment that is almost completely filled with "human extensions," an environment in which very little of nature is visible. Industrial processes are insulated from inclement weather and seasonal change. Control and planning can now cover years. Under food-collecting systems, control and planning were confined to a few days at best; under nonindustrialized food production, to a season or so.

Second, the transition in technology from a feudal to an industrial mode of production took place as capitalism emerged as the corresponding form of the relations of production. The new technologies did not "cause" capitalism; neither did capitalism "cause" industrialization. The two developed together out of the feudal mode of production. Capitalism may be defined as a way of organizing human behavior in which the following characteristics exist:

1. Productive property (the means of production—land, machinery, and so on) is owned privately. Ownership is unequally distributed in the society. The products are also privately owned. The main goal of the productive process is understood to be to earn a profit for the owners of the productive property rather than to provide goods and services.
2. Those persons who do not own the means of production exist by selling their own labor as a commodity in a labor market. They thereby provide the labor necessary for production. Unlike slaves or serfs, they are free to use their leisure time—the time they have not sold—more or less as they wish. On the job, they are restricted in the following ways: they lack control over their work time and work schedules, over the technology of production, and over the products of their labor.
3. A surplus is extracted from the labor force through the following mechanism: labor is paid in wages a sum less than the market value

of the objects it produces in the labor process. Some of the difference goes into overhead, including supervisory workers' pay. Some of it goes into profits. This unequal exchange of wages for labor power is veiled. Most people believe they are exchanging a fair day's work for a fair day's pay in a market situation in which labor power is sold like any other commodity. In slavery and serfdom, the dominant classes exploit the labor force in a direct and highly visible way. In capitalism, the extraction of a surplus—exploitation—is veiled by the commodity form of labor.

These are fundamental defining features of capitalism. Different types of capitalism (which have appeared at different time periods) are distinguishable from each other by the way in which the privately owned productive enterprises are related to the state and by the values and beliefs of the period.

Capitalism is a class society. It shares with other class societies, such as the ancient city-states and empires and feudal Europe, a fundamental inequality in access to resources and the control of a surplus produced by labor. Specifically, the two major classes are (1) the owners of the means of production, the bourgeoisie, and (2) the much larger group of people who sell their labor power, the proletariat. But capitalism differs from the other class societies in its overriding emphasis on investment for profit and the existence of a free market in labor. Finally, it differs from preceding class societies in its historical linkage to industrialization. The harnessing of industrial technology to the search for profit has produced a very rapid pace of change in the last two hundred years or so; new techniques and products are constantly being developed. At the same time, industrialization is in many ways fettered by its association with capitalism; nonprofitable directions for innovations are not explored.

The present state of the world in all of its details—the impoverishment of two-thirds of humanity, the population explosion, the impending ecological crises, the potential for affluence and leisure—can only be understood as an outcome of the way in which industrialization and capitalism have spread from Europe and have become a worldwide system.

Quantification of the Mode of Production: Efficiency

The mode of production can also be defined in a rigorously quantitative fashion. Wealth of all kinds, including agricultural products, is made by applying energy and labor time to materials. Thus we can describe the forces of production in terms of the amount of human and nonhuman energy that has to be expended to obtain the products. This would be a very concise way of characterizing the forces of production; however, it would leave out many aspects that cannot be quantified, such as the type of tools and type of product involved. It also omits the behavior that we have called the relations of production, that is, the different ways in which groups are involved in production. As we shall see, human history is the story of higher and higher inputs of nonhuman energy into production accompanied by an actual loss of leisure and freedom.

So far, most research has focused on the quantification of the characteristics of food production. At the heart of every mode of production is a food-producing subsystem that has to provide a certain number of calories per day to every person in the society. Failure to provide a minimum level of calories means malnutrition and, in the long run, death for some or all of the society's members and a drastic alteration of the culture. Production of a surplus quantity of food means that the society has a larger number of options for the use of its members' time and energy. It also opens the way for some groups to gain control of this surplus, to free themselves from the need to work, and to force others to continue to live at subsistence level while producing the surplus.

The efficiency of a food-production system is measured in calories of food energy expended to obtain a calorie of food energy. As more and more tools and nonhuman energy are introduced into food production, the ratio of calories obtained to calories expended increases.

> One of the most important results of the increased efficiency of food production is the enlargement of both the absolute and relative size of the non-food-producing segments. Among the Bushmen, 100 percent of the adult population participates directly in the food production process. Among contemporary underdeveloped nations, 35 percent to 40 percent of the adult population does not contribute directly to the food production process; while in the United States, 95 percent of the adult population is exempt from basic food production tasks.
>
> The majority of non-food-producers have never been withdrawn entirely from productive activities. That is, most non-food-producers expend their energy in non-food-producing specialties associated with manufacture, trade, personal services, communication, management, and administration. While a small percentage of non-food-producers constitute a "leisure class," the overwhelming bulk of the non-food-producing group work harder and longer than any Bushman would ever dream of doing.
>
> The study of primitive economic systems lends no support whatever to the widespread belief that "civilization" is associated with a general increment in "leisure time." On the contrary, except for a very small percentage of the very rich and the very poor, higher productivity is associated with increasing amounts of work time per individual. Indeed, the main trends in cultural evolution can only be understood in relation to the fact that increased agricultural efficiency is "adaptive"

principally because people are now able to work longer and harder than ever before, both in food-producing and non-food-producing activities.

The culmination of this trend has been reached under industrial systems where the average wage worker puts in some 2,000 hours of work per year (not including travel to and from office or factory). True, there has been a decline from the nineteenth century when the average was probably well over 3,500 hours per year (not including unemployed adult males). But nineteenth-century wages and hours were associated with unprecedented suffering and social ferment and they must be regarded as temporary phenomena.

At the moment, there is very little indication either in socialist or capitalist countries that work time is about to be cut back to the Bushman level. The basic reason for this and for the general upward trend in productivity and specialization is that human populations are organized into territorial groups that have not been able to develop reliable systems of mutual security. Undoubtedly many societies have attempted to utilize increments in technoenvironmental efficiency not to increase E [the total amount of food energy produced], but to cut back on work input while holding E constant. Such experiments are doomed to failure, however, as long as there is no guarantee that all other groups will utilize technoenvironmental increments in the same manner. Any group that increases E, increases its power with respect to those groups that hold E constant. This power is manifested in denser, larger, more specialized, and better coordinated populations that have either wiped out or assimilated the low-energy groups. In this fashion, high-energy societies have inevitably replaced low-energy societies, and band and tribal organizations in all but the most remote and inaccessible regions of the globe have now become extinct (Harris, 1971:217–218).

Measurements of the quantity and efficiency of the production of food or other wealth do not by themselves give us much insight into the social relationships of production. However, the nature of the social relationships can also be summarized quantitatively, at least for the capitalist system of production. For instance, we might look at the ratio between the surplus value produced by laborers (designated by s) and the value that is returned to them in wages (usually designated by v, variable capital). This ratio can be defined as the rate of exploitation (s'):

$$s' = \frac{s}{v}$$

Obviously, precisely quantifying these terms for an industry or for a particular epoch of the capitalist system as a whole is difficult. Also, we must remember that all these terms are only shorthand ways of summarizing social relationships that involve continued struggles between real groups of human beings fighting over wages, hours, the speedup of assembly lines, piecework rates, and so on. The quantification of some of these relationships, their summation in terms of equations, should not blind us to the realities of these struggles (Applebaum, 1976).

Role of the Mode of Production in Social Change

Having provided both a quick overview of the evolution of class societies and a rigorous empirical basis for the concepts of mode of production and surplus, we are now ready to summarize the importance of these concepts for the understanding of social change. Over short time periods, change is made by individuals and organizations. But the long sweep of history involves changes in the organization of whole societies. The economic substructure places limits on the kinds of changes that are possible. Low-energy societies cannot sustain large amounts of stratification and the accompanying state institutions. *Thus the mode of production sets the conditions under which shorter-term changes can take place.*

A second way in which the mode of production shapes change is through the replication of the relations of production in other institutions so that the character of these relations pervades the entire society. For example, the owner-worker and buyer-seller relationships that characterize capitalist production also appear in leisure, in the pursuit of knowledge, in politics, and so on: the candidate is "sold" to the public and "packaged" for the media; knowledge is sold in universities by people who are paid salaries for this effort; music and sports are organized for profit and consumed by largely passive spectators. In this way the ruling classes of a society—the groups that control basic resources—directly influence institutions. Nonproductive institutions also reflect, although more indirectly, the relationships between the ruling class and other groups. Under these circumstances, some kinds of change are difficult to carry out. Such changes meet with a great deal of opposition, either because they directly challenge ruling-class interests or because they fall outside the general frame of reference of the society (for instance, giving away quality goods and services if everyone else sells them). Thus the mode of production—specifically, the relations of production—not only sets physical limits in terms of energy production within which change must take place but also generates a political and ideological framework that sets limits on changes that are possible.

Determining the Fit

How does this fit between the mode of production and the ideological and political superstructure come about? Some of the features of the superstructure are directly planned by the economically dominant class. For instance, in the United States, the Federal Reserve system and the federal regulatory agencies are the product of the conscious need of capitalists for a more stable and predictable economy. Other political and ideological institutions are linked to the mode of production by the shared beliefs of the people involved. For example, the media tend to defend American capitalism not only because of direct control (corporate sponsors may cancel advertising accounts) but also because media elites share the values of corporation executives. Finally, the form of superstructural institutions is also a product of the class struggle. The institutions reflect compromises forced on the economically dominant class. For example, some features of American school systems reflect capital's need for a disciplined, trained, presorted labor force; but other aspects of the school system reflect working-class struggles for literacy. Similarly, modern American labor unions have helped to tame and regulate the labor force in the interests of capital, but they are also the products of struggle for better pay and working conditions. As long as one class dominates the society and controls its economy, it will tend to "win" in the superstructure, to impose its interests and world view on superstructural institutions; but often it does not win until a long struggle has forced it to make some compromises.

Within the limits set by the physical capacity of production, there is a potential range of alternative political and ideological institutions. One or another of these alternatives is realized, depending on the intensity and timing of class struggles. At some points during the transformation of the mode of production, the range of possible alternatives is relatively greater than at other points. These periods represent turning points in history or, if you prefer a slightly different analogy, places where the fast-moving river of history slows down and branches into a number of channels.

Through which channel most of the water flows—which set of political and ideological institutions is actually realized—depends on political action to some degree. For example, industrialization and capitalism were closely associated from the start. But by the latter half of the nineteenth century, industrialization began to be connected not only with competitive market capitalism (characteristic of England and of early nineteenth-century America) but also with state-regulated capitalism in Germany. By the middle of the twentieth century, the industrial system of production was associated with a variety of class relationships and superstructures.

In the countries of Western Europe and North America, advanced industrial production was associated with capitalist class relationships. In many of these capitalist countries, the superstructure has been a formally democratic one, with freedom of the press, civil liberties, and regular elections to governing bodies. In Western Europe, this capitalist superstructure has even been able to accommodate itself to large working-class-based Socialist parties and extensive welfare measures. In the United States, left-wing parties don't exist and the government has not been forced to give priority to the general welfare. In industrial countries like Nazi Germany and Fascist Italy, industrialization and capitalist class relationships were associated with a superstructure of a powerful single-party state and extensive physical and ideological repression. So an industrial capitalist substructure can be associated with a variety of superstructural forms, depending on the specific history of the country and the political organization of its classes.

Industrialization and Socialism

Industrialization is not necessarily connected with capitalism although it started in a capitalist system. In Eastern Europe, industrialization is now associated with a variety of noncapitalist ways of organizing the productive system. These are forms of state socialism. The countries vary in the way in which power is balanced between the state bureaucracies, the Communist party, and the worker self-management organizations.

Clearly, *in the short run,* there are a number of reasonable institutional arrangements to accompany an industrial base. (However, primitive egalitarian, slave, and feudal societies have not historically been associated with industrialization.) Perhaps *in the long run,* the full development of industrial technology requires a system other than capitalism.

Direction of Change

Specific political and ideological institutions grow out of the struggles and organization of class groups as capitalism itself changes and runs into crises. This idea that more alternatives open up during periods of crisis than during periods of stability, and that organization and political struggles become relatively more decisive during times of crisis is elaborated in the following selection:

> Once a social order is firmly established and its "law of motion" is in full operation, power naturally gravitates into the hands of those who understand the system's requirements and are willing and able to act as its agents and beneficiaries. In these circumstances, there is little that individuals or groups can do to change the course of history: for the time being a strictly deterministic doctrine seems to be fully vindicated. But when the inherent contradictions of the system have had time to mature and the objective conditions for a revolutionary transformation have come into existence, then the situation changes radically. The system's law of motion breaks down wholly or in part, class struggles grow in

intensity, and crises multiply. Under these circumstances the range of possibilities widens, and groups (especially, in our time, disciplined political parties) and great leaders come into their own as actors on the stage of history. Determinism recedes into the background, and voluntarism seems to take over (Huberman & Sweezy, 1968:125).

The main movement in the mode of production is not, however, a cyclical one, as some of the preceding observations may appear to suggest. The main direction of substructural change has been cumulative and evolutionary. It has not been unilineal. Alternatives and experiments have repeatedly appeared. But the overall direction of change has been toward more energy production, larger populations, more technology, larger territorial units encompassed in a single economic system, and more differentiation and specialization.

In the present context it must suffice merely to point out that, apart from the invention of language, there had been no more spectacular event in human history than the development of compulsory systems of production and exchange. These systems oblige men to increase their work input not merely by promising them prestige, but by threatening them with socially imposed material sanctions (as distinct from those naturally imposed) leading ultimately to physical annihilation. Such systems conform to local and regional conditions and are highly variable in detail. But everywhere, the common irreducible element is the existence of a class of people who have the power to compel others to do their bidding. The expression of this power in the realm of production and exchange results in the economic subordination of the labor force and the partial or total loss of control over all phases of production and exchange. Specifically the labor force loses control over:

1. Access to land and raw materials
2. The technology of production
3. Disposition of work time and work schedules
4. Place and mode of production activity
5. Disposition of the products of labor

Forms of production and exchange that depend upon the coercive effects of power can be understood only within the framework of a combined political and economic analysis. All of the concepts appropriate to the analysis of contemporary economic systems, such as wages, rent, interest, property, and capital, have a political dimension to them (Harris, 1971:253).

Classes in the United States

Having defined class (as position in a system of control over resources) and discussed different types of class systems, I shall now focus on classes in the United States.

At some very abstract level, one might argue that the class system is based on two categories: those who own the means of production and buy the labor power of others, and those who sell their labor power and do productive work. The former are usually referred to as capitalists (or, the bourgeoisie), the latter as proletarians. Although the relationship between these two groups is the key relationship in the system, there are also a number of other strata and class fractions whose actions have some effect on the relationship between the bourgeoisie and the proletariat. For instance, in American society at least four distinct groups could be identified:

1. Capitalists associated with large firms make up the first group. These firms include the basic industries (steel, rubber, oil, automobiles, chemicals, pharmaceuticals, coal, paper, agribusiness, food processors, and so on), the large financial institutions (banks, insurance companies, and so on), and some smaller firms. Top executives as well as actual controlling shareholders can be included in this class. This class is not a small conspiracy of "seventeen families" or a social clique. It includes a substantial number of people—perhaps as many as several hundred thousand (Domhoff, 1974:3). Its power does not lie in its income (although this class does have a disproportionate share of America's income) but in its control over institutions, specifically firms that produce and distribute the goods and services essential to the survival of the country's population, and the firms that distribute the capital needed to run the producing firms. Control over these institutions gives this class direct and indirect power in the state and in the production of beliefs and values in ways that I shall discuss later.

This class is not completely monolithic but is split into class fractions along various lines. For instance, one can make a distinction between monopoly capital associated with the very large firms that dominate an industry and medium capital associated with smaller firms in more competitive sectors. Although all of this class depends on the continued existence of the capitalist system as a whole and acts to support it, on some specific short-run issues, class fractions may have differing interests.

2. The second major class includes persons holding professional and managerial positions. Most people in this group depend on the sale of their labor power to make a living, although a number of them are partially free from this constraint. Their work is aimed at maintaining the social order, at making existing organizations viable and productive, and at creating an appropriate ideology. Specifically, this group includes middle-level managers, lawyers, teachers at all levels, media workers, and government workers with decision-making powers. This stratum of workers shares a number of charac-

teristics: (a) As I have already noted, most subsist by selling their labor power. (b) Many have received fairly specialized training, the main content of which is an interpretation of human behavior and the methods for modifying or coping with it. In other words, this group of workers processes people (and ideas) rather than physical objects. Related to this managerial-ideological group in general conditions of life, but differing from it in terms of the content of the work, are scientific and technical workers. While they do not process human behavior, they often work in the same organizations as the managerial-ideological workers and share their life-style.

As a whole, this class is descended—figuratively speaking—from the scribes, priests, and state officials in the early class societies. But unlike these forebears, contemporary managers and professionals are extremely numerous and diversified. Their function of support for the class system is buried in modern society. The mechanisms of class rule that are blatant in traditional empires are much more complex, ideologically veiled, and diversified in modern societies.

Some writers have referred to this stratum as a "new middle class" or "the technostructure"; others see it as part of the petite bourgeoisie. Some writers have probably overrated the ability of this stratum to make fundamental decisions for the society independently. Of course, government officials and intellectuals do not have to get every decision of theirs okayed by corporations; but the general ideological climate, their own socialization, the prevailing system of material rewards, and the goals of the organizations for which they work—all *tend* to limit the kind of decisions they make. Moreover, these decisions do not generally attack the fundamental institutions: private ownership of the means of production; sale of labor power, land, goods, and ideas as commodities; and profit-making.

3. A third group in capitalist societies is the traditional petite bourgeoisie, the owners of small enterprises. They are not numerically significant (less than 10 percent), but their existence has ideological consequences. First of all, they tend to identify themselves as "the little man," opposed to big business, big labor, and big government (Trow, 1958:270–281). This opposition realistically reflects the way in which this stratum has lost out to large firms. Competitive smaller enterprises still exist in some fields—restaurants, gas stations, clothing stores, repair shops, some farming, and so on—and employ about one-third of the labor force (O'Connor, 1973:13–15). The owners of these enterprises, particularly of the small, financially insecure ones, claim to oppose the monopolistic private sector as well as labor and the state (which they see as intervening in behalf of labor and monopoly capital). In fact, they tend to support the same political organizations that the bourgeoisie does. When hard pressed, they form a support base of right-wing, Fascist, and counterrevolutionary movements. Thus the petite bourgeoisie was a major source of electoral backing for Hitler. In France in 1968, they supported DeGaulle against the worker-student disruptions. In Chile, the strike of the independent truckers

(who owned their own vehicles and were small businessmen rather than wage-paid truckers) was a precipitating cause of Allende's downfall. The petite bourgeoisie experiences individualistic, isolated, competitive work more than any other sector of the society.

4. The fourth major group in American society is the working class. In the following reading, Braverman (1974:377–380) identifies the working class in a capitalist society.

Labor and capital are the opposite poles of capitalist society. This polarity begins in each enterprise and is realized on a national and even international scale as a giant duality of classes which dominates the social structure. And yet this polarity is incorporated in a necessary identity between the two. Whatever its form, whether as money or commodities or means of production, *capital is labor:* it is labor that has been performed in the past, the objectified product of preceding phases of the cycle of production which becomes capital only through appropriation by the capitalist and its use in the accumulation of more capital. At the same time, as living labor which is purchased by the capitalist to set the production process into motion, *labor is capital.* That portion of money capital which is set aside for the payment of labor, the portion which in each cycle is converted into living labor power, is the portion of capital which stands for and corresponds to the working population, and upon which the latter subsists.

Before it is anything else, therefore, the working class is the animate part of capital, the part which will set in motion the process that yields to the total capital its increment of surplus value. As such, the working class is first of all raw material for exploitation.

This working class lives a social and political existence of its own, outside the direct grip of capital. It protests and submits, rebels or is integrated into bourgeois society, sees itself as a class or loses sight of its own existence, in accordance with the forces that act upon it and the moods, conjunctures, and conflicts of social and political life. But since, in its permanent existence, it is the living part of capital, its occupational structure, modes of work, and distribution through the industries of society are determined by the ongoing processes of the accumulation of capital. It is seized, released, flung into various parts of the social machinery and expelled by others, not in accord with its own will or self-activity, but in accord with the movement of capital.

From this is derived the formal definition of the working class as that class which, possessing nothing but its power to labor, sells that power to capital in return for its subsistence. As we shall see, this, like all definitions, is limited by its static quality. But in itself it is perfectly correct and forms the only adequate starting point for any attempt to visualize the working class in modern society.

We may gain a rough first approximation of the working class in this century by considering at the outset the mass occupational categories which embrace, with a few anomalies and exceptions, the unmistakably working-class population. These, as classified by the U.S. bureaus of the census and labor statistics, are the craftsmen, clerical workers, operatives, sales workers, service workers, and nonfarm laborers. We exclude from these groups foremen, who are usually classified in the craftsman's category; from among the sales workers, we exclude the salesmen, agents, and brokers of advertising, insurance, real estate, and stocks and bonds, as well as manufacturers' representatives and salesmen in wholesale trade, the latter being generally higher-paid and privileged sales workers, thus leaving in this category chiefly salespersons in retail trade. In these six categories, so modified, we find the overwhelming bulk of the nonagricultural working class, whose growth and changes of composition can be seen in the following table.

Table 1

Structure of the Working Class

	Workers (in millions) 1900–1970							
	1900	1910	1920	1930	1940	1950	1960	1970
Operatives and laborers	7.3	9.9	11.5	13.0	14.4	15.5	16.4	18.1
Craftsmen	2.9	4.0	5.0	5.7	5.6	7.3	8.0	9.5
Clerical workers	.9	2.0	3.4	4.3	5.0	7.1	9.6	14.3
Service and sales workers	3.6	4.9	4.9	7.3	8.8	8.7	10.6	13.4
Total workers	14.7	20.8	24.8	30.3	33.8	38.6	44.6	55.3
Total "active" or "experienced labor force"	29.0	37.3	42.2	48.7	51.7	57.9	64.5	80.0
	Workers (as percent of total "labor force")							
Percentage	50.7	55.8	58.8	62.2	65.4	66.7	69.1	69.1

At this point the author discusses some difficulties in the use of these occupational categories, such as the fact that some persons who are classified as managers or are included in the professional and technical grouping should actually be reclassified into the working-class occupational categories, while a few persons who are included in the working-class categories may in fact function as managers. The data also neglect the chronically unemployed who are no longer looking for work and reflect the undercounting of inner-city populations in the census. Braverman (1974:381) concludes:

These considerations, rough though they may be, tend toward the conclusion that the nonagricultural working-class portion of the "experienced civilian labor force" has grown since the start of the century from half to well over two-thirds, perhaps as high as three-quarters of the total at the present time.

Braverman's definition of the working class seems quite consonant with my conception. It specifically excludes from the proletariat the petite bourgeoisie and the bourgeoisie, as well as much of the somewhat more ambiguous salaried managerial and professional class. It may be useful to distinguish within the working class the unionized, better paid workers, who generally work in the monopoly sector, from the less well-paid, largely nonunionized workers, who generally work in smaller competitive industries.

5. At the bottom of the class system stand those persons who are unemployed for long periods of time, are irregularly employed, or are employed only on a part-time basis at low wages. This underclass includes not only those who live below the absurdly low official poverty line but also a substantial number of people above it. In times of high employment and prosperity, this class may shrink a bit. It provides a "reserve army of labor," a pool of people whose existence depresses the wages of employed workers.

Each of these classes includes not only those who are active in the economy and those who have dropped out but also the dependents of these people. At this point our conception of class structure could be diagrammed to look something like Figure 5. Note how the diagram indicates a "fuzziness" or overlap between these categories. There are a number of places in the system where drawing lines is hard. For example:

— At what level of the corporate structure are executives no longer part of the economically dominant class but part of the managerial stratum?

— What indicator can be used to distinguish the petite bourgeoisie from the dominant class? (The mom-and-pop grocery store or hot dog stand obviously does not confer a dominant-class position on its owners; but what about medium-sized businesses?)

— Which technical and supervisory workers are working class and which are part of the managerial-ideological class?

— How poor is poor? In other words, where is the line between the working class and the poor?

During good times—the boom of the 1960s, for instance—more people move up into the next class level. For example, during the sixties poor people found steady working-class jobs. Owners of medium-sized businesses did well and developed local or regional political power. Managers and technical experts enjoyed a period of power and prosperity. Within the working class, workers from the less well-paid competitive sector were able to find better jobs in high-paying oligopolistic industries. Intergenerational upward mobility was

Figure 5

Class Structure in the United States

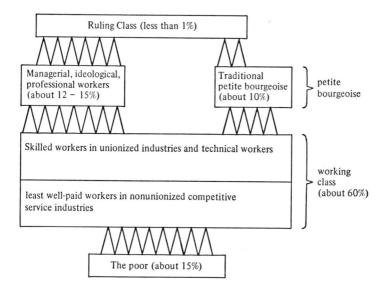

also possible across some of these class lines. In hard times, people sink into lower class levels.

Another way of looking at this system is to argue that once a dominant class has been identified, everyone else should be placed on a *continuum* (a smooth range instead of a series of distinct categories). At the top of the continuum are the corporate owners, the top executives, and the high government officials; at the bottom are the very poor. This image of a continuum rather than discrete pigeonholes corresponds to some extent to the distribution of income (and prestige) in the society and perhaps to our personal experience of inequality. But it tends to obscure the contribution that distinct groups make (or are forced to make) to keep society going. In other words, it is analytically unsatisfactory since it describes the distribution of certain *consequences* of class (e.g., it describes the distribution of income) without doing much to clarify patterns of control over resources and labor. Such descriptive pictures of inequality in modern capitalist society are even less satisfactory when prestige is the dimension of ranking. A prestige-based categorization of the society tells us something about the society's ideology but very little about actual control of resources, including labor power.

Case Studies of Technological Change

In the preceding four sections of this chapter, I have taken an extremely *macro* approach, emphasizing changes in production and class structure that take place over centuries or even longer. Some understanding of micro processes of technological change may also be useful because, in some sense, a large number of these micro processes add up to new forces of production, especially when the technological innovations occur in clusters, with one leading to a number of others.

We have already briefly discussed the vitally important innovation of the domestication of grains. Here I would like to discuss four innovations of our own time. The first is the automobile, selected because of its effect on the American economy and American life-style. The second is the computer, the effect of which has been less personal but possibly equally far reaching. The third is the introduction of snowmobiles into the Arctic, which, while not in itself of widespread importance, presents an exceptionally clear picture of how technology affects social structure. The fourth is the electronic media—radio and television. Each one illustrates the way a class society shapes and constrains technological innovation.

The Automobile: American Dream/American Nightmare

Car sales fluctuate unpredictably, oil prices skyrocket, expressways destroy neighborhoods, auto workers rebel against their working conditions, roadways are turned into noxious traffic jams: America's love affair with the automobile is turning into the bitterness of an ill-fated marriage on the rocks. The love affair began in Henry Ford's Detroit-area plant, where a large capital investment in machinery and a minute subdivision of work into small tasks geared to the pace of the assembly line ushered in a boom period of mass production (Rothschild, 1974). Three technologies joined together—the invention of the gasoline-powered, internal-combustion engine; the technology of metal working with mechanized equipment; and the social technology of reorganizing work to make it more "efficient," that is, to make human activity a repetitive, subdivided, interchangeable part of production. The disadvantage of mass production was the degradation of human beings as producers. Its advantage was the uplifting of human beings as consumers since, as a result of mass production, a vast flood of new products became cheap and easily accessible.

In 1910, there was 1 automobile for every 44 American households; in 1930, there was 1 automobile for every 1.3 American households (Rothschild, 1974:32). The profits of the automobile manufacturers soared while the price of cars actually fell. Americans began to shape their cities and their life-styles around the automobile. Rural areas were linked to cities by highways. Mass transit, which had generally been excellent in American cities, began to be underfunded by investors and public agencies. During the Great Depression, the automobile market slumped; and in World War II, auto plants were devoted to war production. Meanwhile, in the 1930s, Alfred Sloan of General Motors had introduced some new inventions in marketing—installment selling, trade-ins, and the used-car market; the yearly style change; and variety marketing (different equipment at different prices added to the standard car). Sloan remarked that "the primary object of the corporation was to make money, not just to make motor cars" (Rothschild, 1974:38).

This policy paid off in the late forties and early fifties, the second honeymoon of America's automotive romance. By the early 1950's there was 1 automobile for every 3.75 Americans, and more automobiles than households. The appeal of the automobile was twofold. The irrational appeal—carefully fostered by advertising—emphasized power, speed, and glamour. Phallic tailfins (for example, on the Cadillacs of the late 1950s), chrome strips, whitewall tires, radios, convertibles (hardtop and otherwise), banks of lights—all promised adventure and sex appeal. Advertisers debated whether the automobile was a mistress or an extension of the male body. But underlying the irrational appeals was a hard fact: automobiles had become real necessities in cities that were increasingly being built to accommodate an auto-driving public. In some areas, mass transit systems fell into the hands of the automotive interests who deliberately neglected them. This was the case with the Los Angeles trolley lines, which were destroyed in the 1940s by a consortium of General Motors, Standard Oil of California, Phillips Petroleum, and Firestone. In other cities, no public transportation was provided for the suburbs at all. Eighty-two percent of American workers drive to their jobs; 56 percent drive alone (Rothschild, 1974:249).

By the 1970s, the euphoria of car ownership was wearing off. The necessity of owning an automobile in America has overwhelmed the pleasure of driving one because of congestion, pollution, and the rising cost of new automobiles, fuel, and repairs. The automobile market is nearly saturated, with about one-third of American households having two cars (Rothschild, 1974:44). Since the 1950s (and in many respects, since the 1920s), the automobile has characterized and dominated American culture. Americans were conceived in automobiles; and, at least in southern California, weddings and funerals were performed at drive-in chapels. Automobiles also kill Americans, as many as fifty thousand annually in recent years. The culture of the suburbs and of the entire newer urban areas of Florida and the Southwest is organized around the automobile. Expressways link residential areas with shopping centers and drive-in movies, banks, cleaners, chapels, restaurants, and virtually every other kind of service. Children have become dependent on their parents for transportation and, as a result, adults tend to organize and intrude upon the lives of middle-class children. Automobiles encourage urban sprawl and low-density housing development. Industries and commercial establishments have moved out of the central city into industrial parks and shopping centers that have grown up along the major highways and expressways.

The centrality of the automobile in American society is more than a quaint folkway. It reflects basic inequalities in American life and decision-making. The common man's automotive love affair is, in part, an arranged marriage, agreed upon by the automobile manufacturers, the oil companies, and government agencies. I have already mentioned the neglect of mass transit. Along with this neglect went the expenditure of enormous sums of taxpayers' money for roadbuilding, especially the federally funded interstate highway system. Parking lot operators, car dealers, automobile manufacturers, suburban real estate developers, and the oil companies have formed powerful lobbies to persuade government at all levels to channel public resources into support for the automobile as the dominant means of transportation.

Meanwhile, some groups have been shut out of the automobile culture because they cannot drive or afford a car. The elderly, the inner-city poor, and many women are reduced to second-class status in a culture organized around automobiles. The poor and the elderly have been stranded in parts of the city that are losing jobs and services to the suburbs. At the same time, the areas that have been destroyed in order to build expressways to carry middle-aged, middle-class commuters rapidly from city centers to suburban bedroom communities have been mainly inner-city neighborhoods. Urban renewal often has also meant the destruction of these poorer neighborhoods to create car-oriented facilities, such as sports stadiums and "civic centers," for the benefit of suburbanites. Decision-making about automobiles illustrates the inequities inherent in market processes (which favor the rich and penalize the poor) as well as the direct connivance of the state and the corporations.

In more social-psychological terms, the centrality of the automobile in American life is related to the privatism of the American nuclear family. The automobile helps to disperse people into single-family dwellings. It helps to insulate people from each other during the routines of everyday life. Unlike urban mass transit or even price-segregated interurban transit, automobiles cut people off from those who are different from them in class or ethnicity. Thus automobiles help to make the poor invisible to the middle class.

Today the market is saturated, and driving a car is more of a nuisance and a necessity than a pleasure. Meanwhile, the technology of automobile production has become obsolete. It has remained rooted in the metal-working industry, in assembly-line organization, and in scientifically managed degradation of labor that characterized industry of the late nineteenth and early twentieth centuries. It lacks the economic growth of the continuous-process chemical and petroleum industries. Unlike these, the auto industry can be automated only at prohibitive cost because it is overcommitted to a particular type of mechanized factory. Human labor remains cheaper than automation. At the same time, ideological as well as economic inflexibility chains management to a system of monotonous, subdivided work imposed on laborers through rigid discipline. Even relatively high pay cannot compensate the workers for the monotony, noise, and other stress of the job, for the mindless discipline by supervisors who are forced into competition with each other, and for compulsory overtime. Wildcat strikes, refusal to work, absenteeism and turnover, and other signs of the loss of management control over workers beset the industry. Profits have fallen decisively in the American auto industry.

The rise and decline of industries is an important feature of industrial capitalism. Any economic system committed to technological innovation is going to have industries that grow rapidly as they innovate, and then decline. Industries decline for several reasons, but primarily because their markets become saturated and they are overcommitted to a physical plant that has become obsolete compared with those of the other industries. The danger in the decline of the auto industry is not that its profitability is declining—that would be a problem only to its stockholders—but that it is so central to the American economy both in terms of production and in terms of the organization of everyday life, especially residential and commercial patterns. Lagging sales and resultant layoffs in the auto industry affect employment in the steel, rubber, petroleum, and construction industries, among others.

In England, the decline of the textile and railway industries in the early twentieth century had deleterious consequences for the English economy as a whole. These economic problems, in turn, made it difficult for England to reverse the mistakes and overcommitments brought about by these industries in the first place, especially the poor housing, pollution, and general welfare problems of the industrial cities. It remains to be seen whether the United States can reverse the uneven development caused by the dominance of the auto industry.

The Computer

The development and effects of computer technology illustrate a number of general characteristics of technology. I shall use material about the history and present impact of computers to illustrate some general principles.

Principle 1: The development of an idea cannot outstrip the development of necessary techniques, materials, and social organization. Computers can be defined as machines that solve problems by accepting data, performing operations on the data including both arithmetic and logic operations, and providing the results of these operations (Dorf, 1972:2). Unlike calculating machines, computers do not require human intervention at each step of the operations but can perform them according to a set of instructions, called a program.

In the early nineteenth century, an Englishman named Charles Babbage invented a computerlike device that he called the "Analytical Engine." It was composed of several smaller devices: the "mill," or arithmetic unit; the receiver, or input unit; the printer, or output unit; a device to transfer information from one unit to another; and a place to store the information. The information was to be fed in on cards and was of two types: instructions and data. Punched cards had already been successfully used to direct the weaving of intricate patterns on Jacquard looms in France. But Babbage's machine could not be built. Without the availability of electrical (let alone electronic) technology, the machine would have required extremely intricate mechanical works calling for machining beyond the tolerances of early nineteenth-century technology. Therefore, the Analytical Engine existed only as a blueprint. The programming for it—the writing of the instructions—was carried out by Ada Lovelace, Lord Byron's daughter. More than one hundred years later, the development of electrical engineering and electronics made possible the construction of machines whose design was very much like that developed by Babbage.

Principle 2: Technology develops within existing institutions and is shaped by them. The machine that is generally recognized as the first computer was the Mark I, completed in 1944 by its inventor, Howard Aiken, an instructor in applied mathematics at Harvard University. In association with three engineers of the International Business Machine Corporation, Aiken worked five years to construct the Mark I. This early cooperation in computer science between universities and private companies came about to some extent in response to wartime pressures to process numerical data. Some principles of computer technology also grew out of the need to control guns and radar during World War II, specifically analog devices called servomechanisms, which translated motion into signals and could be incorporated into gunsights. After the war, developments in the radio and telephone industries provided electronic inventions that were also incorporated into computer technology. In other words, war needs and corporate profit-making provided systems of incentives for technological inventions.

During the fifties and sixties, computer technology was strongly influenced by the structure of the computer industry, which for a number of years was described by the phrase "IBM and the Seven Dwarfs" (Burroughs, RCA, Sperry-Rand, General Electric, Honeywell, Univac, and National Cash Register). While the seven dwarfs shifted, merged, and dropped out, IBM maintained its hold on about 70 percent of the sales in the computer field. IBM's strength lay less in the sophistication of its equipment than in the power of its marketing and the appeal of its service bureau, which provided services to customers. IBM dominated computer use abroad. The company also gained a hold on the sales of peripherals—devices attached to a computer to accomplish specific ends, especially in the input and output of data.

One consequence of IBM's dominance was the widespread use of FORTRAN, a programming language developed by IBM. In the United States, FORTRAN to a large extent replaced ALGOL, a more scientifically-oriented language used in Europe and the Soviet Union. In other words, oligopolistic market dominance can lead to technical decisions (such as the adoption of a programming language) that are not necessarily most efficient and that reduce communication and interchangeability between different societies.

Another, perhaps more positive consequence of the development of computers in the American economy has been the rapid growth of peripherals and languages that make the computer very accessible to people with little technical expertise. Typewriter keyboards and televisionlike display terminals make getting data into and out of the computer easier. Languages such as BASIC or COBOL, which are very close to either natural English or specific occupational jargon, help to demystify computer technology. Some of the developments came about through the search for new markets for computers among people and organizations who wanted machinery that was easily used by persons with relatively little training. In the Soviet Union and China, computers were built to process scientific data, and for a long time little effort was put into user-oriented peripherals and languages.

Principle 3: In monopoly capitalism, important decisions about technology are made by the large corporations, partially but not completely influenced by the state. An example of this type of decision-making can be seen in the settlement of a pair of antitrust suits brought against IBM, one by a rival corporation, Control Data, and one by the Justice Department. Control Data's suit was settled out of court. According to the deal that was worked out, Control Data was to be able to purchase IBM's service bureau for a trifling price; in return, Control Data would destroy its extensive files on IBM, putting the files out of reach of a Justice Department subpoena.

A case of this type suggests the difficulties that trust-busting reforms can run into. Meanwhile there have been a number of court decisions—especially the one declaring that computer programs cannot be patented—that shape the industry and award more or less power to different types of companies. For instance, the patent decision tends to benefit larger companies which can thus freely use software (programs) specially devised by the smaller companies that specialize in software. Another type of dispute is developing between AT&T and a number of other companies in which the latter (including IBM) are going to challenge AT&T's monopoly over telecommunications (the transmitters, cables, receiving devices, and so on used to carry data and instructions from one computer to another or from a computer to its remote terminals).

The following set of principles has more to do with effects than antecedents of computer technology.

Principle 4: In the context of a class society, technological advances tend to impoverish work. We have already seen how the Industrial Revolution enhanced humanity's ability to produce goods and services and lightened the physical strain of labor. However, the political and social circumstances of early capitalism led to millions of people being forced to spend long hours at tedious, unsafe, and dehumanizing factory work. The introduction of computer technology—what some writers have called the "second industrial revolution"—has had similar consequences for white-collar work. Potentially the machinery could free people from filing, bookkeeping, mailing, and other routine parts of clerical work. In fact, it has made white-collar jobs more like blue-collar jobs. The work is often monotonous. The machinery is noisy. The tasks are broken into small components, and each worker has to repeat the subdivided task. Some skilled blue-collar jobs, such as typesetting, which were formerly held by highly paid unionized workers, have been converted to unskilled white-collar jobs, often held on a part-time basis by underpaid women who work in their homes, a situation not unlike the cottage industry of eighteenth-century England.

Principle 5: The political uses of new technology impose new ideas about the rights of individuals and help shift power into already powerful organizations. Under early capitalism it was possible to conceive of a private realm, hidden from the government and only indirectly controlled by the market, in which individual and family life could exist. (A number of nineteenth-century stories—*Wuthering Heights, Dr. Jekyll and Mr. Hyde,* Poe's fantasies—are set in this often bizarre private world.) Since then central governments have attempted to expand their knowledge of and influence over personal lives. These efforts are not *caused* by better techniques for collecting, storing, and retrieving information on people, but the new techniques do make the goal of a society without privacy more attainable. Businesses, such as credit bureaus and banks, as well as government agencies want data on individuals and organizations.

Once data banks are established, they are extremely difficult to open up or dismantle. Data files can easily be transferred to another organization. Many of the disclosure laws that now exist or are being proposed put the burden of obtaining information on the individual. It is the individual who must initiate getting her records from an agency or credit bureau in order to see if they contain damaging information. The demand for disclosure is supported by law but, in fact, may take time and money to enforce. Few people have the resources to do so. People who are hard pressed for credit, for a job, or for clearing themselves of charges are precisely the people who have least resources to enforce disclosure and yet are most harmed by the data in their records. Thus data banks not only pose problems of individual privacy, they also pose problems of the distribution of power. In the sense that data banks are tools for concentrating power in certain government agencies and private organizations, they represent political issues. Such organizations gain power at the expense of poorer citizens who have few resources to challenge them (Westin, 1968).

Computers are also tools for changing the distribution of power within organizations as well as between organizations and unorganized individuals. Within organizations, power seems to flow into the hands of technical experts and central decision-makers when computer technology is introduced. Members of the lower levels of the organization, particularly those members "out in the field" (whether at the precinct level of the city power structure or the front lines in a war) are used to funnel information to the central decision-makers. On the one hand, they lose their ability to make decentralized local decisions; on the other hand, their work gains in importance because the central elite depends on their information.

The disastrous consequences of introducing this combination of technology and social organization into the military was illustrated by incidents in the war in Vietnam, where lower echelon officers and noncoms lied to protect their own interests. Their lies—for example, the absurd "body counts"—became the basis for decision-making in Saigon and Washington. It was the social organization of the military, not the data-processing techniques, that caused the lying; but the techniques raised the lies to the status of numerical facts used in policy-making.

Computer workers refer to this phenomenon as GIGO—"garbage in, garbage out." Poor information is not improved by technologically advanced data-processing. The same phenomenon can be seen in some American cities or counties which use data banks. The data banks provide officials with detailed material on neighborhoods, institutions, and individuals; but the data is not always accurate. The possession of data distances officials from the citizens to whom they should be responsible. Detroit's pioneer data bank, for example, has not made the city more livable nor prevented the riot of 1967.

Principle 6: Under present social conditions, the introduction of technology reduces responsibility for the consequences of one's action; technology can substitute for socialization as a support for dehumanizing behavior. Military technology provides an excellent illustration. As weaponry became increasingly sophisticated, it permitted the wielder to be more and more detached from the consequences of his actions. Men in rifle companies in World War II seemed reluctant to fire their weapons; only 15 to 25 percent did so, even when attacked. A weapon that involved the cooperation of several individuals to fire was discharged more frequently than were rifles. The individual's reluctance and confusion were overcome by technology and division of labor (Marshall, 1947).

The introduction of bombing allowed soldiers to kill and maim large numbers of people, including civilians, without having to see the effects. In the past, soldiers were often recruited from brutalized, violence-ridden subcultures; their training was also oriented to bringing out feelings of violence and anger. Modern warfare no longer calls for this kind of psychological and cultural baggage for its soldiers. The most important trait now is the suppression of imagination. During the war in Indochina, bomber crews made runs over North Vietnam by day and in the evening returned to their bases—often to their wives and children—in Guam and Thailand. They could relax, take a hot bath, have a drink, play golf, and tuck their children into bed on the same day that they had dropped napalm, bombs, and antipersonnel pellet bombs on other people. Evidence from social-psychological experimentation indicates that many more people are willing to hurt another human being if they are physically distant from the victim than if they have to see, hear, or touch him (Milgram, 1974).

Computer technology is being adapted to guide remotely controlled aircraft. At little risk to their own lives, without disruption of their personal routines, and with no experience of the effeets of their behavior, technicians at distant bases can direct these drone aircraft and short-range missiles. Thus warfare can be carried out by small numbers of technical specialists, trained to suppress their emotions and imagination rather than to engage in brutal face-to-face combat. Both they and the rest of the nation can continue to enjoy their private lives. This portrait only borders on fantasy; the technology for it is almost completely developed, and the bombing of Laos and North Vietnam from bases in Thailand prefigures warfare that is completely remotely controlled.

Principle 7: New technology (and science) provides images for conceptualizing human nature. In the eighteenth century, the perfection of mechanical devices—clockwork, for example, provided images of human nature that were compatible with the contemporary ideology that human beings are perfectible and understandable. Enlightenment philosophers were ready to tinker with society, which they pictured as precise and beautiful machinery, humanly created, and not as part of an immutable divine order. In the late nineteenth century, the Darwinian theory of evolution captured the ideological imagination. Human society was depicted as a state of nature, a struggle for survival. Only the "fittest" survived, that is, made money and rose from poverty. Fitness was equated with the ruthless abandonment of personal ties, family, and ethnic group in the pursuit of wealth. The biological model of struggle for survival was used to explain and justify unethical business practices, corruption, exploitation of workers, and the grinding poverty of the mass of people, particularly recent immigrants.

The computer and related information-processing methods have helped to provide modern ideologues with a new set of images. Society is in a delicate state of equilibrium; it is a "system" (a vaguely biological analogy) in which all the parts hang together. Continual feedback from each of its parts to its central coordinating mechanisms provides information on how society is doing and helps keep it in equilibrium. With the rise of a strong state and monopolistic corporations, society came to be seen not as a struggle for survival, but more as an organism, a nervous system, or its electronic counterpart, a computer system. Society was depicted as a communications network, an entity of interdependent elements, each carrying out a specialized function, all responding to the "brain" at the center—monopoly capitalism and the executive branch of government. There was a unity in it, and the purpose of each part contributed to the whole. It was, in short, a system held together by specialization and information flow. This conception of society as a cybernetic (guided and coordinated) system was very different from the struggle-for-survival conception, just as modern monopoly capitalism is very different from early competitive capitalism.

Meanwhile computers served another ideological purpose. They could be blamed for what were, in fact, power grabs, illegal practices, and mistakes by organizations. Grossly incorrect telephone bills or terminated magazine subscriptions could be blamed "on the computer." So could the decision to route an expressway through a working-class residental neighborhood. Mistakes or potentially unpopular deliberate decisions are thus mystified by reference to quantitative data and "the computer."

Principle 8: In a class society, the full liberating potential of new technology is unlikely to be realized. For example, computers and related devices could be used to eliminate the drudgery of clerical work and to control industrial processes that are monotonous or unsafe for human beings to carry out. In our society, such an introduction of computers would be incompatible with wage labor, the labor market, and production for a market. Picture a fully automated society: the processes by which firms make profits would break down. They could no longer hire workers, pay them a wage to make goods, and then sell them the goods at a profit. Everything would be made by machinery, and there would no longer be wage earners to buy the products. The present form of relations between employer and employee would cease to exist.

Even a more moderate extension of automation is unlikely for similar reasons. In many industries, it is presently cheaper to pay workers than to introduce machinery. Further automation would not only be costly but, if widespread, might produce higher levels of unemployment. Larger numbers of unemployed people means a shrinking market for goods and a decline in sales and profits. Widespread unemployment would also cause unrest and increasing pressure on the state to provide jobs or welfare. Insofar as capitalism depends on the sale of labor power, on the use of labor power in the production of goods, and on the sale of these goods to wage earners, a capitalistic society cannot fully replace human labor by machinery.

A systematic transfer of dangerous or monotonous work from humans to computers and robots would probably destroy the capitalist mode of production. The *technology* is essentially ready, but it is fettered by a social organization—relations of productions—that prevent its implementation.

Snowmobiles in the Arctic

In the 1960s, small snowmobiles replaced reindeer sleds in northern Europe and dogsleds in North America. (Pelto & Muller-Willie, 1972). Among Eskimos, the innovators who bought the snowmobiles tended to be wage earners (e.g., government employees) and prowhite in their attitudes.

More traditional full-time hunters were less likely to buy them. Snowmobiles made travel less difficult and much faster. Even a full-time wage earner could find time to hunt if he had a snowmobile. The increased speed enabled the men to get to their traps before other predators, such as wolves, could eat the kill. Snowmobiles relieved the loneliness and isolation people felt when working remote trap lines or living in small, isolated settlements. A man could live in a regional center of several hundreds or even thousands of people and still reach hunting grounds in a few hours. Leisure activities have become more westernized and better attended since the introduction of the snowmobile. Movies, dances, shopping, and so on have been facilitated by greater mobility and less-isolated living patterns.

The impact of snowmobiles on stratification is complex. In some regions they have clearly increased the "social differentiation between the haves and the have-nots" (Pelto & Muller-Willie, 1972:194). For example, in some areas of Lapland "the mechanization of herding is forcing all except the wealthiest owners out of the reindeer business" (Pelto & Muller-Willie, 1972:194). Reindeer roundups take place more frequently; those Lapps who have no snowmobile (or telephone) cannot get to many of the roundups anymore. In Lapland, snowmobiles seem to be increasing stratification and creating a class system of differentiated access to the basic resources, a situation that had not existed previously. There had been wealth differences in the past, but each Lapp once had enough reindeer to meet his family's needs.

Among the Eskimo, the effects are more varied. In some locations (Aklavik in the MacKenzie Delta, Pond Inlet on Baffin Island), purchase of a snowmobile not only reflects the difference between acculturated wage workers and "bush people" but also increases the gap between rich and poor (Pelto & Muller-Willie, 1972:195). There is a sense that two distinct classes are emerging. The wage-earning snowmobile owners do not share their new resource and are seen as stingy and mean by the poorer, more traditional families. In other areas, this differentiation between owners and nonowners is (as yet?) more a matter of taste and life-style than of sharply unequal access to a vital resource. However, as K. E. Francis (cited in Pelto & Muller-Willie, 1972:196) warns:

> A certain minimum cash income is essential to hunting and fishing, which is the major occupation of the villagers of Arctic Alaska. Because of increasing mechanization of an effective hunting system, the minimum cash income is continually rising. Unless wage opportunities increase accordingly, there is reason to suspect that the gap will grow between the properly equipped and the ineffective hunter.

The situation is exacerbated by the fact that snowmobiles make possible extermination of whole species of game animals that could not have been wiped out by hunters without mechanized equipment.

The Electronic Media

Different societies have characteristic media of communication. Primitive classless societies usually rely on speech as the major means of communication. Writing developed as an important medium in the early urbanized class societies. Unlike speech, writing was not mastered by all members of a society. In the city-states and empires as well as in feudal society, literacy was confined to a small elite stratum. With the invention of movable type in the middle of the fifteenth century in Europe, literacy became far more widespread. The written word ceased to be a way of mystifying the masses of the population and became a way of making historical and religious books accessible to them. The new technology of printing was reflected in the ideology of Protestantism, in which each person was encouraged to read the Bible himself, without depending on the clergy. Some people have argued that printing and literacy have created new world concepts and personality types—analytical, "linear" in their emphasis on cause-and-effect-reasoning, rational, antimythological.

We can ask similar questions about how the technology of communication supports or threatens the current prevailing ideology. What are the effects of radio and television on the societies in which they are major media? This question has not yet been adequately answered. The point of this example is to make you think about some possible types of answers. Below are listed some effects that have been suggested. Note that some of them appear to contradict each other.

1. The electronic media are undermining literacy. The effect of this change is to make people more passive. They are not able to produce the messages themselves. Since it it harder to make and circulate videotapes than written or even printed messages, people tend to become receivers rather than initiators of opinion.

2. Electronic media encourage the staging of spectacular but meaningless pseudoevents akin to Roman circuses. The print medium lends itself to analysis, to presentation of arguments about causes and effects, to careful documentation; electronic media do not. The same list of figures or involved logical argument that one can follow in print is intolerable or incomprehensible on radio and T.V. Radio seems to encourage harangues in which the voice is used to build up an emotional frenzy apart from any reasoned argument. Television seems to lend itself to sensationalistic momentary displays. For example, if a beach has been polluted by oil spills from offshore drilling, television tends to report this event by showing officials visiting the beach. This is a pseudoevent. It displays the officials. It does not inform the viewer of the crucial facts about the *long-term* effects of oil spills (which cannot be captured at that time but could be described in print); nor does it inform the viewer of the structure of the oil industry and its irresponsible use of power because this fact is not very visual (Molotch, 1969).

Many of the news events that appear to "happen" in our society are really staged for T.V. They are fleeting and of little importance in themsleves. The important events that have long-term consequences have little visual appeal.

3. The electronic media (especially T.V.) harden the viewer to violence. Violence is made entertaining and unreal. Children and even adults cannot distinguish between the exploits of fantasy heroes and the deaths of human beings.

4. Television makes human beings more aware of their common humanity and the interdependence of societies and groups. One reason for the widespread opposition to the war in Vietnam was that everyone could see the realities of war on a daily basis, was repelled by it, and did not want to participate in it.

Note how Effect 3 largely contradicts Effect 4. It is possible that both are true but pertain to different groups in the society.

5. The electronic media and motion pictures are "opiates." They help people to escape reality. The viewing experience tends to be not only passive but also isolating. Instead of talking to each other, people absorb the media either in total isolation or in isolated nuclear families. Thus the media interfere with the ability to act politically.

6. The media are an important part of the ideological apparatus. Radio has potential for the repeated hammering home of a simplistic emotional political message. Television, on the other hand, has a more diffuse effect. Its ideological strength lies in its ability to present shimmering, shifting fantasies and to hook up soundtracks to visual images. Our critical facilities are distracted because of the short time each set of images is shown and because the sound can be separated from the picture. Television is excellent for selling goods and manipulating moods. The moods tend not to be the highly emotional moods aroused by radio but shifting, passive, fanciful, and dreamy moods.

References

Appelbaum, Rich.
   1976   "Marx's theory of the falling rate of profit: Towards a dialectical analysis of structural social change." Santa Barbara, September (Unpublished).

Bernal, J. D.
   1971   Science in History. Volume 1, The Emergence of Science. Cambridge, Mass.: MIT Press.

Bloch, Marc.
   1964   Feudal Society. Volume 2. Translation by L. A. Manyon. Chicago: University of Chicago Press.

Braverman, Harry.
   1974   Labor and Monopoly Capital: The Degradation of Work in the Twentieth Century. New York: Monthly Review Press.

Domhoff, G. William.
   1974   "State and ruling class in corporate America." Insurgent Sociologist 4 (Spring): 3–16.

Dorf, Richard.
1972   Introduction to Computers and Computer Science. San Francisco: Boyd Fraser.

Fried, Morton H.
1967   The Evolution of Political Society. New York: Random House.

Harris, Marvin.
1968   The Rise of Anthropological Theory. New York: Thomas Crowell.
1971   Culture, Man and Nature. New York: Thomas Crowell.

Huberman, Leo, and Paul M. Sweezy.
1968   Introduction to Socialism. New York: Monthly Review Press.

Marshall, S. L. A.
1947   Men Against Fire: The Problem of Battle Command in Future War. New York: Morrow.

Milgram, Stanley.
1974   Obedience to Authority: An Experimental View. New York: Harper and Row.

Molotch, Harvey.
1969   "Santa Barbara: Oil in the velvet playground." Ramparts 8 (November): 43–51.

O'Connor, James.
1973   The Fiscal Crisis of the State. New York: St. Martin's Press.

Pelto, Pertti J., and L. Muller-Willie.
1972   "Snowmobiles." In H. Russell Bernard and Pertti J. Pelto (eds.), Technology and Cultural Change. New York: Macmillan.

Pirenne, Henri.
1937   Economic and Social History of Medieval Europe. Translation by I. E. Clegg. New York: Harcourt, Brace & World.

Rothschild, Emma.
1974   Paradise Lost: The Decline of the Auto-Industrial Age. New York: Random House-Vintage Books.

Trow, Martin A.
1958   "Small businessmen, political tolerance, and support for McCarthy." American Journal of Sociology 64:270–281.

Westin, Alan F.
1968   Information Systems and Political Decision-Making. Cambridge, Mass.: Harvard University Program on Technology and Society.

Chapter

11

Changes
in the
Superstructure

In this chapter, I shall define the superstructure—those activities that accompany, reflect, and help to maintain the class system and productive activities of a given type of society. I shall examine the two major components of the superstructure. One is political activity, the exercise of power, which in class societies involves a state, a specialized coercive institution. The second component is ideological activity, the production of beliefs and values. I shall then present some examples of changes in the superstructure: changes in the special system of beliefs called science; changes in the political system, especially that violent seizure of state power called revolution. I shall present an analytic summary of a number of revolutions, identifying the classes involved, the organizations that carried out the seizure of the state apparatus, and the consequences of the revolution for class structure and superstructure. The chapter concludes with a definition of two important concepts for the analysis of how superstructures are associated with substructures—hegemony and contradictions.

IN THIS CHAPTER I shall address myself to changes in the superstructure. The superstructure consists of the relationships, groups, institutional arrangements, and beliefs that form around the relations of production. A society's form of production shapes its way of life, and it is this "way of life" that is referred to as the superstructure. The way of life of an agricultural society is quite distinct from that of a hunting and gathering society, and both are quite different from that of an industrial society. Agricultural societies in turn have different forms: on the one hand, there are societies that use simple farming techniques and have egalitarian access to resources; and, on the other hand, there are societies that use intensive methods such as plowing or wet rice-growing and have stratification. These forms in turn can be categorized into subforms that vary in environmental conditions, food-production technology, and the details of the class system. From this substructural foundation grow customs, beliefs, characteristic patterns of interpersonal relations, and various institutional arrangements.

The fact is, therefore, that definite individuals who are productively active in a definite way enter into these definite social and political relations. Empirical observation must in each separate instance bring out empirically, and without any mystification and speculation, the connection of the social and political structure with production. The social structure and the State are continually evolving out of the life-process of definite individuals, but of individuals, not as they may appear in their own or other people's imagination, but as they really are; i.e. as they are effective, produce materially, and are active under definite material limits, presuppositions and conditions independent of their will.

... We set out from real, active men, and on the basis of their real life-process we demonstrate the development of the ideological reflexes and echoes of this life-process. The phantoms formed in the human brain are also, necessarily, sublimates of their material life-process, which is empirically verifiable and bound to material premises. Morality, religion, metaphysics, all the rest of ideology and their corresponding forms of consciousness, thus no longer retain the semblance of independence. They have no history, no development; but men, developing their material production and their material intercourse, alter, along with this their real existence, their thinking and the products of their thinking. Life is not determined by consciousness, but consciousness by life (Marx & Engels, 1947:13, 14–15).

In the next few pages I shall discuss two especially important parts of the superstructure—the political system and the belief system. I shall concentrate on these two aspects of the superstructure for two reasons: first, I have discussed other parts of the superstructure in earlier parts of the book where I looked at change in interpersonal relations, personality structure, and a variety of organizations. Thus the reader can reread those sections with the understanding in mind that they concern the superstructure. Second, I would like to address myself to politics and belief systems because these are two parts of the superstructure that give coherence to the whole society. Along with the economic substructure, beliefs and political institutions unify a society. Finally, in stratified societies, beliefs and political institutions not only reflect the class system but also protect it.

Political Systems

In this section, I shall discuss how a political system accompanies a mode of production. I shall define the term *state* and discuss how class power and state power are related.

Concepts and Definitions

Lasswell has defined politics as the issue of *who* gets *what, when,* and *how.* He states that "the study of politics is the study of influence and the influential. . . . The influential are those who get the most of what there is to get. Available values may be classified as *deference, income, safety.* Those who get the most are *elite;* the rest are *mass"* (Lasswell, 1958:13). In other words, this definition suggests that the political system is the set of arrangements for distributing and exercising power that I defined as the ability to realize one's will, regardless of resistance. (*One,* of course, can refer to groups as well as individuals.) Power is the ability to obtain rewards and avoid punishments. But power is more than that, and thus more sweeping than Lasswell's definition. Power is also the ability to impose rewards and punishments on others.

If politics is the set of arrangements for distributing and exercising power, then we can find *political* issues everywhere. Some people believe that the word *politics* refers only to election campaigns or to power exercised by or on the government. But our broader definition allows us to look at situations in which there are neither elections nor government. By our definition, the tension between men and women, the authority of adults over children, the conflict between workers and supervisors, the helplessness of a defendant before a judge, the disagreements between students and teachers are all political. Each relationship involves different amounts of power, different amounts of access to rewards, different amounts of ability to shape a system of rewards and punishments and, ultimately, different amounts of ability to realize one's will regardless of resistance. Hence each situation is in some sense political.

Politics and the issue of differential power is thus an endemic feature of all human societies and, for that matter, of all human relationships. To say that the issue of power differences is latent in all human relationships is not quite the same as saying that it is part of a genetic heritage of human behavior. Even the well-documented dominance hierarchies of apes and monkeys are not manifestations of purely instinctual or genetic impulses like "aggression" or a "dominance drive." Even these hierarchies are not simply biological givens but vary with environmental conditions. For example, a certain species of baboon has a rigidly hierarchical band organization with a powerful old male monopolizing females and ruling the band under conditions of scarcity. In a more abundant environment, the same species has looser band organization with free sexual access.

In human beings, the development of the forebrain, the capacity for language, the cycle-free sexual receptivity of the female are all biological changes that have freed humans from biology or "nature." The exercise of power in human relationships is therefore a very complicated matter, depending more on objective social conditions, features of the immediate situation, and cultural baggage than on any instinctual base. The reader should also keep in mind that during the millenia in which ape people turned into human beings, habits of competition, dominance hierarchies, and individualistic foraging for food turned into habits of cooperation and sharing in game-hunting. In other words, to note the ubiquity of politics and power is not the same as asserting that politics and power have a biological basis.

At this point, the reader may rightly feel that our definition of politics is too general, that it includes too many different kinds of relations, and that we need to distinguish the realm of personal power relationships from the realm of public or collective politics.

Let me begin by noting that in very simple societies—classless, unranked, egalitarian societies—this distinction really does not exist. Power resides in three types of characteristics: (1) personal characteristics, such as intelligence, articulateness, and experience, which make some people better choices for leaders than others and correspond to the conventional wisdom about some people being "natural leaders"; (2) situation-specific knowledge or skills, such as hunting expertise, which tend to make leadership in these societies fairly limited in scope, since the skills are tied to specific activities, and in some sense rather "rational," since the leaders maintain power only as long as they "deliver the goods"; (3) position in a kinship network, which includes both general age and sex categories ("old man") and specific kin roles ("mother's brother"), and in which power resides in the roles rather than in personal characteristics and abilities.

To some extent, these bases of power are at cross-purposes with each other. A "natural leader" or skilled individual who happens to be born into the wrong sex or kin-role slot will not be able to develop her full potential. As long as the group is very small, informal personal characteristics may overcome the formal restraints. As the introduction of agriculture made possible larger communities (say of several hundred people instead of twenty to fifty), the location of power in formal kinship roles became more important. Meanwhile, the "big men" and redistributors also gained deference, if not other types of rewards.

The existence of settlements with permanent buildings may also have contributed to the development of political institutions. Private areas could be permanently separated physically and visibly from public ones as villagers built houses and public structures. The men's house or the public square could become the site of public decision-making. At some time between the invention of food production and the rise of state-level class societies, political activities —the exercise of power and decision-making—began to be differentiated from other activities. Politics, in the sense of collective decision-making, was still generally participated in by adult males, but now it was more confined in time and space, situated in meetings or council sessions in special areas. Private politics—the exercise of power in personal relations of all kinds—continued as well but as a separate activity.

With class societies, the exercise of power involved still fewer people who were full-time specialists in political roles. Their entry into these roles often had little to do with their personal characteristics. They could enter roles of power if they were born into the right kin group or stratum or if they received specialized training. Their activities were confined in time and space to special buildings and were removed from the eyes of the masses of the society. This group of full-time specialists in exercising power are the members of the state apparatus.

The state apparatus developed shortly after the rise of classes, of groups that control basic resources. This development of political institutions is closely tied to the development of the mode of production. The existence of a surplus of food (and other goods) has two effects:

1. It makes possible the appropriation of this surplus and of the means of producing it by a particular class.
2. It makes possible the physical maintenance of those groups that become specialized in extracting the surplus from the producers.

The state apparatus cannot exist if there is no surplus to sustain it. And, so long as no surplus exists, no class can seek to control it.

In the earliest class societies, there is very clear evidence that staffs of soldiers, tax collectors, administrators, and overseers were required to collect the surplus. In the city-states of the Near East, such as the growing kingdom of Egypt, for example, the state was the mechanism by which one class (the elite of the pharaoh, his court, the nobles, and so on) exploited another class (the peasant and slave producers). For our own society this view seems perhaps excessively cynical and oversimplified. Class exploitation is veiled by the complexities of modern society and by the reasonably high standard of living. Let us therefore turn to two issues: (1) What is meant by exploitation—can this word be explained by the use of a more precise and less emotional phrase? (2) What, specifically, are the mechanisms involved in the relationship between classes?

Let me restate the definition of the state:

It is the task of maintaining general social order that stands at the heart of the development of the state. And at the heart of the problem of maintaining general order is the need to defend the central order of stratification—the differentiation of categories of population in terms of access to basic resources. Undoubtedly, as already indicated, one means of doing this is to indoctrinate all members of society with the belief that the social order is right or good or simply inevitable. But there has never been a state which survived on this basis alone. Every state known to history has had a physical apparatus for removing or otherwise dealing with those who failed to get the message (Fried, 1967:230–231).

Let me list the component parts and assumptions of this definition:

1. Stratification—a class system—is a system of differentiated access to basic resources, both to the products and to the means of producing them.

2. Such a system must face two tasks from the point of view of the class that controls resources: one is the day-to-day concrete physical control over resources by the ruling class, and the other is the maintenance of order. To the extent that order can be generally maintained, the first task of resource control and surplus extraction is made much easier. Maintaining general order eases the concrete task of managing property, controlling the supply of raw materials and tools, supervising the labor force, and extracting a surplus. In rather simple class societies, and especially when a class system is newly imposed on a conquered group, these two tasks are not yet very clearly differentiated; the same soldiers and armed tax collectors or overseers maintain order and seize produce.

3. In every class society, maintaining order has two subtasks associated with it: encouraging belief in the social order, or the ideological task; and using force to suppress efforts to upset the social order, or the repressive or coercive task. All existing class societies include some institutional arrangements for applying physical force to persons who disrupt the order of the society. Some theorists even equate the state with that set of organizations that monopolize the legitimate exercise of armed violence in a society. (There are a number of problems in this definition; one is that it neglects the class basis of state institutions, and another is that it raises the question of what is meant by *legitimate.*) In any case, states maintain police forces and standing armies as well as systems of criminal law. In other words, there are specialized armed personnel and specialized institutions to keep order. This order involves the use of force both against individual disrupters of order (such as thieves or madmen) and against groups of disrupters. Usually this apparatus of repression is fairly centralized. However, in some types of societies—feudal societies, for example—it is dispersed and under local control; each manor had its squad of men-at-arms, like King Lear's "hundred knights and squires." Even in modern countries, there are often local police forces.

But order cannot be maintained by repression alone. Continuation of the status quo of the stratification system depends on some kind of ideological consensus, at least in the long run. The apparatus for creating and maintaining ideological unity is more complicated than the repressive apparatus, and we shall return to a longer discussion of it shortly.

So far, then, we have defined political institutions as any arrangements of behavior involving the exercise of power. In primitive egalitarian societies, these institutions are more or less integrated into the round of all individuals' daily lives, so that there is little differentiation of political behavior from other activities in terms of time, place, or specialization of personnel. In ranked societies, power becomes increasingly attached to slots in the kinship system, to certain kin groups, to "big men," and to special times and places. As yet, however, this power does not mean differential access to resources. In class societies, such differential access does exist. In class societies, power is exercised by full-time specialists in order to maintain the stratification system. Power is still exercised by other people in diverse situations (e.g., by parents over children). However, in addition to all the private or local exercises of power, there is an overriding set of institutions that is specialized to exercise power and that largely monopolizes armed violence—the state.

Three analytic questions arise in conjuction with this definition of the state:

1. What is the relationship between class power and state power?
2. Why do people work in the state apparatus—what's in it for them?
3. What is the relationship between the ideological apparatus and the repressive apparatus?

Class Power and State Power

The first question—the relationship between class power and state power —is by far the most difficult to answer. Class power and state power are linked. Historically, the state appears when it is needed to protect the newly developed stratification system. Its task is to maintain the stratified order, that is, to safeguard the existing relations of production. Class power is thus chronologically prior to state power; it is the core or heart of the society, protected by the armor of state power. Class power requires state power if class power is to be viable; however, they are not the same thing. This argument can be developed more concretely by specifying some misleading ways of looking at the relationship between the ruling class and the state apparatus.

Two Mistaken Views: Conspiracy and Corruption.   The first misleading formulation of this relationship is the conspiracy model of class-state relationships. In this model, the state is "really" a sham. The society is "really" run by a small clique of the very rich, who know each other personally; conspire together in little closed, secret meetings; make all major decisions; and generally constitute a secret government. Conspiracy models are usually held by people who lack better information about how the state works. Such models are very oversimplified and leave out important aspects of the workings of the state. They leave out the role of ideology, of social-welfare functions of the state, of interest groups and power struggles, and of factions within the ruling class. Conspiracy models show a lack of understanding of decision-making processes and put too much emphasis on personal loyalties and family ties. Often they involve a very paranoid way of interpreting the world. An example of a conspiratorial model of the relation between class power and state power is the assertion that the country is secretly run by a clique of Rockefellers, Morgans, Fords, and Duponts; or the even more farfetched fantasy that the Rockefellers and Rothschilds not only run Western capitalist societies but are plotting to make them Communist. Conspiratorial models appeal to people who see that there is indeed a relationship between class power and state power but lack the information and the conceptual skills to see this relationship as something other than secret planning by an all-powerful familial or ethnic clique.

A second commonly held but erroneous model of the relation of class power to state power is the corruption model. In this view, the state is reasonably independent from the dominant economic class, but every once in a while there are moral and legal lapses in this independence. Influence-peddling, nepotism, conflict-of-interest cases, tax evasion, illegal destruction of records, special favors and gifts, and excessive lobbying are examples of these sorts of links between the class system and the state. The argument that corruption is a major link between class power and state power is the approach taken by "muckrakers," journalists who devote themselves to exposing illegal or clearly unethical relations between those who control resources and those who run the state.

The emphasis on corruption in politics has been strong in the media recently and to some extent has obscured more important issues. For example, Richard Nixon was finally held accountable and forced to resign because of his corruption—his illegal behavior—and not because he ordered the bombing of Hanoi and Haiphong. Nelson Rockefeller was questioned by Congress about his gift-giving habits; official bodies did not, however, hold him accountable for the shootings at Attica or for the punitive welfare statutes and drug laws that he supported as governor of New York. Nor was he grilled about the involvement of Chase Manhattan in the repressive system of South African racism. A few years ago, the Eisenhower administration was criticized when presidential advisor Sherman Adams accepted a vicuna coat as a gift but was much less criticized for giving tideland oil rights—a national resource—to the states and thus to private developers.

In other words, the muckraking or corruption model focuses too much on illegal behavior and neglects the normal routine relationship between class power and state power. Unlike conspiracy models, corruption models are true, but they are limited in scope and miss the central features of the linkages between class power and state power.

Let's now turn to three better ways of looking at the linkage. The first we might call the overlap-in-personnel view; the second, the organizational view; and the third, the total-structural view.

Overlap of Personnel.   The *personnel-overlap* view holds that the linkages between the economically dominant class and the state lie in particular position holders (Domhoff, 1970). These position holders are sometimes members of the dominant class who hold appointive or elective jobs in the state. For example, Nelson Rockefeller, Averell Harriman, McGeorge Bundy, the Kennedys, Charles Percy, Henry Cabot Lodge, and so on are all representatives of corporate wealth. Or, position holders may be men who have executive positions in large corporations who then attain positions in the state—Robert McNamara is a very good example. Although not a member of the dominant class himself in the strict sense of the word, McNamara's association with Ford Motor Company suggests connections to this class. Sometimes the overlap is in the other direction. People with experience in the state later become involved in the corporate sector as executives or even as members of board of directors—a frequent career line for retired generals and admirals. Finally, dominant-class individuals are also prominent in the political parties, as party policy-makers and donors.

The overlap-of-personnel approach rests on the assumption that when members of a class (e.g., Rockefeller) or persons directly responsible to this class (e.g., McNamara) hold state positions, they will make decisions in the interests of the class. The personnel-overlap approach accounts for many decisions of the state in capitalist society, but personnel overlap (and personal ties) is not the only linkage between class and state. In fact, it is not the most important linkage, either. The state can very well protect the stratification system even if not a single member of the economically dominant class is a member of or personally acquainted with the state apparatus. Interlocks are important for understanding specific organizational behavior, but they are not necessarily a feature of the structure of power in the society as a whole.

Organizational Links.   The *organizational* view asserts that the important linkage between the state and the dominant class is not constituted by specific individuals, be they elected officials, appointed officials, campaign donors, or party officials. Rather, the linkage is the existence of organizations and processes that form ties between the state and the corporations. These organizations are above all the regulatory agencies (such as the Federal Trade Commission, the Federal Communications Commission, the Federal Aviation Agency, the Securities and Exchange Commission, and so on) and the advisory committees (such as the Council on Foreign Relations and the Committee on Economic Development).

The *regulatory agencies* are primarily agencies of the executive branch of the federal government that are designed to stabilize the behavior of the corporations. Arising during the Progressive era of the early twentieth century and the period of the New Deal, they were designed to save capitalism by "rationalizing" it, that is, by using state power to make economic behavior more predictable and more subject to planning. They helped to produce monopolies and oligopolies either by driving out the small corporations directly (as they have in the telecommunications and utilities fields) or by introducing regulations that smaller enterprises could not meet (as in the case of the pure food and drug laws). Far from attacking capitalist relations of production, regulatory agencies help to protect these relations in a casing of stability, predictability, and oligopoly. In the process, small, inefficient, or corrupt capitalists have lost their businesses, but the system as a whole has been preserved.

The *advisory committees* are more oriented toward the future than are the regulatory agencies. Their task is to plan policy. In part, they include or are influenced by members of the dominant class itself. They are the setting in which different factions of this class can informally discuss and sometimes settle their differences, where dominant-class members can meet with hired experts from universities and other research institutions such as foundations and think tanks like the Stanford Research Institute (Domhoff, 1974:3). But in part, the advisory committees, like the regulatory agencies, serve and protect the stratification system even when no members of the economically dominant class participate in these bodies. In other words, the sanctions and strategies available to these groups always assume the continuation of the core character-istics of capitalism (private ownership of the means of production, profit maximization, labor power as a commodity) even if secondary characteristics can be changed. The policy-planning of these advisory committees is oriented toward making this stratification system more stable.

Figure 6 suggests some of the linkages between the class system and the state through policy-making bodies.

A third major organizational linkage between the state and the stratifica-tion system is *state spending*. The flow of money from the state to other groups in the society has two functions: it stabilizes the economy (although at the time of this writing, government spending policies do not seem to have dealt with inflation and recession very well); and it ties a variety of groups more closely to the existing social order, setting them to work on nonthreatening projects and keeping them from lashing out in despair. Recipients of government money include large corporations, especially in the defense sector, that are awarded contracts guaranteeing costs plus a fixed margin of profit. Here the effect of government spending is to help these corporations to plan, predict, and insure their profits. Other recipients include local-level private interests (such as hospitals and real-estate developers funded through urban renewal and FHA programs), universities, and the middle class and the poor through a variety of welfare payments. Some of these expenditures are of little direct benefit to the American corporate economically dominant class, but such expenditures maintain order and increase confidence in the legitimacy and viability of the stratification system. Thus they help maintain it (Kolko, 1963).

Another structure in which state power and class power coincide is the *party system*. In capitalist countries with representative government, a number of positions are filled by election and are thus open to competition. One of the purposes of a political party is to run candidates for these offices. A second purpose is to place issues on the national agenda, something that most individ-uals cannot do. In other words, parties are organizations whose purpose is to capture in a nonviolent and procedurally legitimate way the state apparatus for limited amounts of time, or, if not actually to capture the state apparatus,

Figure 6

The Power Elite Policy-making Process

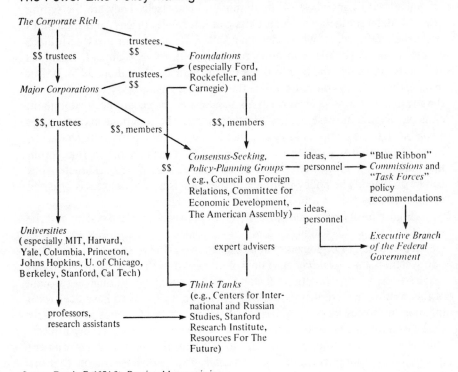

Source: Domhoff (1974:9). Reprinted by permission.

to direct its attention to certain issues. There are several ways in which the party structure can act as a bridge between the economically dominant class and the state apparatus.

First, and most simply, the parties need money—money to run candidates in elections, to maintain a grass-roots structure, to finance publications and public relations, to pay legal counsel, and so on. Those who control resources—very simply, the wealthy—are in a better position than any one else to finance the parties. While they do not necessarily dictate the details of party policy nor run for office themselves (although this has been known to happen), the wealthy—large corporations as well as individuals—can use money to exert influence over the parties and to ensure that some issues or possible candidates are ignored. The financial contributions of the wealthy are perhaps even more crucial in the routine day-to-day organizational practices of the parties than in specific dramatic election campaigns. The day-to-day party activities set the framework of grass-roots groups, volunteer workers, media coverage, and so on within which every candidate must operate in order to have an effective campaign.

Second, the economically dominant class and its allies among managers and professionals are more likely to have the leisure, the contacts, and the training to make them effective in party work. The man who works at a punch press for eight hours a day is not likely to have the leisure and energy to involve himself in party politics.

Third, the party system allows issues that might upset the status quo to be obscured in a number of ways. Election campaigns tend to focus attention on "personalities" (and often on the most trivial and irrelevant features of a candidate's life-style) rather than on issues. The media aid this shift in focus, not because they want to trivialize the campaigns in a sinister, conspiratorial way, but because "personality" and "human interest" stories make better copy than do issues, especially key economic issues. Once the party machinery is in motion and the candidates have been selected, elections help to maintain the existing order by masking inequality in the control of resources by the apparent equality of voting ("one man, one vote"). They also force people to choose the "lesser of two evils."

In summary, then, the party and election systems tend to maintain the status quo not so much because the parties are figureheads for dominant-class interests but because they are organizational filters of routines, procedures, and contacts, through which passes little that directly attacks the relations of production.

Structure and Function.   Our third useful view of the state-class linkage is basically an abstraction from our second view, which dealt with organizational links. In the total-structural view, the state is not only tied to the economically dominant class by particular organizations and institutional arrangements (and by specific interlocks of personnel), it is *defined* to be those institutions that make a particular class system (a particular system of control over re-sources and production) lasting and viable. In this view, interpersonal rela-tions, even interorganizational relations, do not explain how the state supports the ruling class. Rather, such relationships are the effects of the *fundamental function of the state—to protect the class system.*

Understanding the various relationships is useful and demystifies partic-ular state decisions, but this understanding should not keep us from seeing the larger totality. It is the totality of the state, not the particular backgrounds or relationships of its members or the functions of particular organizations, that serves to support the class system, that is, that maintains the existing relations of production, that serves the interests of the ruling class in the broadest possible way. Only by looking at the state in this rather abstract fashion can we understand how the state protects the capitalist order yet is clearly not simply a tool of the ruling class, responsive to its every whim. Thus we can also understand, for example, how it is possible that large Socialist or Labor parties in Western Europe have actually controlled the state apparatus for periods of time and have sustained capitalism during their administrations although not personally related or loyal to the capitalist class.

Perhaps the best procedure for explaining the way in which the state is both entirely committed to protecting the class system and is yet independent of direct ties to the economically dominant class is to suggest an analogy. Suppose the dominant class represents the passengers on a ship. The state apparatus is the crew. Generally, the crew and the passengers are two distinct groups; there is no overlap in individuals. The ship takes the passengers precisely where they want to go, but the crew decides how best to get there. On any reasonably well-administered cruise, the passengers do not scurry about trying to get into the engine room or onto the bridge of the ship, nor do they give advice to the crew. Some passengers will remain completely passive—those in the dominant class who "play polo, ride to hounds" (Domhoff, 1974:4) or make up the jet set. Other passengers may take a lively interest in the voyage, look at maps, and even converse with the crew. The crew is committed to smooth sailing for several reasons. At its upper levels, the crew's officers have a tradition of service to passengers, a love of the sea that is shared with the passengers, a sense of accomplishment at running a tight ship, and a substantial remuneration. At the bottom levels, pay is less, but it is the major incentive because the sailors must make a living. The crew does not openly question its passengers' desire to enjoy the cruise and to arrive at a certain destination.

I do not want to strain this analogy, but it seems to me to be a helpful way of seeing how a state apparatus can serve to support a class system without being continually influenced by the dominant class. The state independently protects the totality of the class system according to a broad understanding of the fundamental aspects of this system (Miliband, 1969, 1973; Poulantzas, 1973, 1975).

The degree of autonomy of the state varies from type of society to type of society. It is particularly great in the example I have just discussed in detail, namely, modern capitalism. In some types of societies,[1] the state and the economically dominant class are very closely fused; in the hydraulic states, the ancient Near Eastern city-states, and the New World city-states and empires, the state apparatus and the dominant class are completely identical. In Peru, for example, the Inca royal house and high nobility were the state as well as the ruling class. Similarly at some points in Egyptian and Chinese history, the

---

[1] I am using the phrase "types of societies" more or less synonymously with the concept of "social formation" in Marxist terminology.

landowning class was very marginal, and both the control of resources and the maintenance of order were vested in a single institution, the state.

Under feudalism, as we have already mentioned, the state was largely dispersed; maintenance of order was in the hands of the class that controlled the land. In other types of societies, the state apparatus is quite distinct from the economically dominant class. For example, in some European societies (such as France during the Second Empire under Louis Bonaparte) and some Third World societies, the state apparatus is largely run by the military officers in the interests of a native oligarchy of landowners and capitalists.

The extreme development of this distinctness between the capitalist class and the state apparatus can be seen in fascist societies, especially Nazi Germany and Fascist Italy. Here the state apparatus becomes enormously powerful and, while maintaining a generally capitalist class system, it begins to involve itself in regulating the relations of production. To return to our ship analogy, it is as though the passengers are extremely passive (and rather intimidated by their crew), and the crew not only runs the ship but also begins to involve itself in the passengers' private financial dealings. The two groups remain distinct—the Nazi party can be distinguished from the German industrialists such as Krupp, I. G. Farben, Thyssen, and so on. The relations of production typical of capitalism prevail throughout the economy. However, the state not only involves itself in regulating these but it also begins to establish a separate sphere of relations of productions, in the slave labor camps and S. S. enterprises. We do not know, of course, whether or not these state productive enterprises based on unfree labor would eventually have swallowed up the capitalist sector.

Capitalism represents a relatively high degree of autonomy between the state apparatus and the class system. There is, however, some variation in this respect between capitalist countries. The important point is that considerable autonomy is possible, that the state protects a particular class system but is not totally subservient to every demand of the economically dominant class of that system, and that the relationships between the dominant class and the state apparatus vary in concrete historical cases.

Constraints on the State Apparatus

Why does the state apparatus preserve the social order, especially in those cases where it is not fused with the dominant class? (The reader is reminded that this is our second analytical question.) Why do people bother to support the existence of a particular system of classes when they are not generally its direct beneficiaries? There are three types of answers to these questions.

First, the state apparatus supports the class status quo because its members have accepted the prevailing ideological status quo. "The ideas of the ruling class are in every epoch the ruling ideas" (Marx & Engels, 1947:39). People learn throughout their childhood and youth that the prevailing class system is reasonable. Once class rule is established, the status quo–maintaining apparatus runs the educational institutions and distributes the appropriate ideology. People generally accept certain notions about the sociey in which they live. In feudal society, many people believed that the division of society into estates (noble, priest, serf) and the exploitation of serfs were divinely sanctioned. In our society, we are taught to believe that a "free" labor market, "free" enterprise, and profit maximization are rational, efficient, and close approximations to "human nature." Many of us believe that human beings are naturally aggressive and competitive, that human material wants are innately unlimited, and that prices follow the laws of demand and supply. Some of these conceptions are not only absurd in view of human history, they are not even good descriptions of the state of affairs in our own society. People who rise to the top of the state apparatus generally have a more sophisticated view of the society than the views dispersed through the mass media to the public at large. Also not only is this view more sophisticated, it is also more strongly held. The system of training for upper-level state positions screens out people who do not believe in what they are doing. This point does not need to be belabored.

Second, the state apparatus maintains the class system because the state's structure makes it good at that task and ill-suited to alternative tasks. This is the sad lesson learned by every radical who gets elected to office. These limitations on the actions of the state correspond closely to the organizational inflexibilities discussed in Part Two. Here is a brief listing of some of them:

1. State activities that threaten the class system are not funded or are underfunded. For example, the Justice Department does not have sufficient information or legal staffs to seriously attack monopolies or oligopolies. IBM and Mobil Oil (not to mention scores of other firms) have more lawyers than the entire Justice Department.
2. People who threaten the class status quo are not rehired or reappointed.
3. The state apparatus cannot legally initiate certain kinds of action that threaten class relations. For example, corporations are protected against forced disclosure of their records by the Fourteenth Amendment, originally introduced to protect emancipated slaves at the time of the Civil War.
4. Each set of organizations introduced during one historical period conditions the behavior of the state apparatus in the following years. For example, Supreme Court decisions have lasting effects. Given the initial intentions of the Constitutional Convention to safeguard capitalist property relations in America, historical development has a

snowballing effect in which each round of accretions to the state apparatus strengthens its initial direction.

5. Organizations' commitment to their own survival works toward continuing to commit the state apparatus to the status quo.

All of these ideological and organizational reasons for the commitment of the state apparatus to the class status quo can be explained by the structural fact with which we began our discussion of the state: the state apparatus is supported out of the same surplus whose appropriation by the dominant class it serves to protect. Put perhaps too simply, the state is dependent on the economy (Bridges, 1974). It is dependent on it in two ways. First, a state that becomes associated with a faltering economy loses legitimacy and may be swept away by a social movement backed by the economically dominant class or the other classes. The Weimar Republic in Germany is a good example of such a fate. The industrial capitalists supported the Nazis because the Weimar government could not cope with the economic crisis. Second, and even more important, the state depends on the economic surplus for its continued existence. "A state that ignores the necessity of assisting the process of capital accumulation risks drying up the source of its own power, the economy's surplus production capacity and the taxes drawn from this surplus (and other forms of capital)" (O'Connor, 1973:6). Third, the economically dominant class can refuse to invest if the state acts against its interests, thereby precipitating an economic crisis that destabilizes the state. Such was the situation of Allende in Chile, when his administration began to support the expropriation of capitalist enterprises and landowners. An "investment strike" of this kind sets limits on the reforms that the state can safely undertake.

Our third analytic question was, What is the relationship between the state and the ideological apparatus? If we take the narrower definition of the state—the coercive and administrative institutions that maintain the class system—then societies differ in the extent to which ideological apparatus is integrated with the coercive state apparatus. In the ancient hydraulic kingdoms, the Meso-American states, and the theocracies of Tibet and southern Asia, the ideological and the coercive apparatus are highly fused, and this overall state apparatus is in turn fused with the economically dominant class to a high degree. The same individuals directly issue orders to both soldiers and priests; temples and monasteries control land and have their own police forces; the rulers of the state identify themselves as priests and as gods. In other societies these spheres of action are considerably more differentiated. In feudalism, for example, ideological activity was carried out by a separate estate, the clergy, as well as by specialized lay personnel such as troubadours, minstrels, jesters and, in the late Middle Ages, university professors.

The turmoil of the transitional period between feudalism and capitalism had as one of its direct causes the issue of whether the state should and could control the churches of the society. The partial separation of church and state, which was better realized in Protestant than in Catholic countries, was one aspect of emerging capitalism's emphasis on a sphere of private "free" relationships. In early capitalism, as the heir to feudal society, ideology and coercion were also fairly separate. The state did not directly control the media, the churches, and a sizable proportion of the school system.

In modern capitalism, the looseness of the relation between the state (in the narrow sense) and the ideological apparatus persists. Much of the ideological apparatus, in the form of the media, is privately owned and is organized exactly like other capitalist production. Some of the ideological apparatus is directly part of the state—the public school system, for example. Some of it is embodied in voluntary associations that form additional lines of defense (to use that metaphor once again) that back up the state apparatus. These multiple lines of defense are typical of Western capitalist societies. In the peculiar form of capitalism that is called fascism, the state has regained control of most of the ideological apparatus.

In conclusion, one might note that, whatever the patterning of these relationships, any viable dominant class will to some extent involve itself in ideological production. "The class has the means of material production at its disposal, has control at the same time over the means of mental production, so that generally speaking, the ideas of those who lack the means of mental production are subject to it" (Marx & Engels, 1939: 9). A dominant class that fails to involve itself in ideological production weakens its own position.

Those Who Take the Meat from the Table
Teach contentment.
Those for whom the taxes are destined
Demand sacrifice.
Those who eat their fill speak to the hungry
Of wonderful times to come.
Those who lead the country into the abyss
Call ruling too difficult
For ordinary men.

Bertolt Brecht, *Selected Poems*

Ideology

In this section, I shall discuss how an ideology—a system of beliefs and values —accompanies a mode of production.

Concepts and Definitions

Every society has beliefs and values. The contents of these beliefs and values reflect the circumstances of the group's life. All persons, in every group, carry around with them knowledge, feelings, and fantasies about the world. Many of these are coded in the form of language. They are learned from socializing agents, both in childhood and later. To a large degree, these beliefs and values reflect the socializing environment and the whole way of life of the group. Each individual has some original views, arising out of the uniqueness of his or her existence, but largely they are learned from others in the course of a group's activities. Sharing knowledge and feelings is one of the ways in which human beings act on the world around them. Thus the production of beliefs, values, knowledge, feelings, and so on is one form of human production. This mental production, like all other human activities, is constrained by the society's mode of production, by the way in which the group maintains it physical existence.

For example, in a hunting and gathering group, knowledge will be concerned with the plants and animals on which the group relies for food, with the seasons, and with the experience of extreme hardship and famine. Feelings will focus on the other members of the little band, on their common struggles, shared pleasures, and conflicts. Fantasies produce a mythology that tries to account for the natural environment, for the fluctuations in food supply, for band structure, and for sickness and accidents. Sometimes mythology creates a world of the distant past or of the future, where food is abundant and people's personal relationships are harmonious. The point is not that all primitive belief systems are exclusively filled with material concerning real or imagined food and kinship patterns. Belief systems also include specifications of ideal conduct for men and women and, in primitive societies, this often includes support for competence and cooperation combined with self-reliance.

In some class-differentiated agricultural societies, the mode of production includes the submission and exploitation of a large number of people. These people are kept at subsistence level while a tiny minority of landowners or state officials live in luxury. Beliefs have to explain this inequality, which is absent among the primitive hunters and gatherers. In different types of class societies, different legitimating ideologies exist to justify inequality. Three of the most common are:

1. The belief in the "limited good"—the peasant's fatalism, apathy, cynicism, resignation, and absolute conviction that the social order can't change for the better
2. The mythology of reincarnation or of heaven and hell, in which submissiveness in the present is rewarded in an afterlife
3. The claim that the present order is created and supported by supernatural forces

One or a combination of these beliefs helps to immobilize the exploited peasantry. The physical force available to the ruling class and the isolation of rural households or villages provide the structural underpinnings of this exploitation; but the beliefs that encourage apathy, resignation, and obedience are important lubricants for class relationships. As long as a majority of peasants are apathetic or superstitious, the individuals who do rebel can be isolated and killed. Compared with hunting and gathering peoples, peasants are often more apathetic, resigned, numbed in affect, and suspicious. This sort of personality structure is particularly common among the most oppressed and exploited, for example, among the Indians of the Andean highlands who were oppressed under the Incas, under colonial rule and in modern society (La-Barre, 1948; Harris, 1971:475–487).

There is, of course, a vast amount of variation among peasant societies, and by no means all of them have belief systems that support apathy and superstitious acceptance of the status quo. Nor do all people in the producing class in any one of these societies accept all of these beliefs. As we saw in our discussion of Afro-American and British working-class cultures, the oppressed classes may develop their own belief systems in opposition to the official ones of the society.

The point is that in class societies two developments take place in belief systems: (1) An official belief system develops that justifies the class system; such a belief system is called an *ideology*. (2) Belief systems are differentiated. Whereas classless hunting and gathering societies had only one shared set of beliefs, class societies maintain several—the ideological belief system and also, generally, an oppositional system as well as a number of specialized ones such as those of certain occupational groups). In other words, the production of a surplus makes possible not only differentiation of classes (and skill specialties and urbanization) but also, indirectly, differentiation of the belief system, corresponding to the differentiated social groups.

The belief systems of complicated societies are further complicated by historical change. Literacy, the keeping of records, and the existence of a formal school system mean that past belief systems can be carried into the present. Not only does each person carry around "baggage"—the beliefs and values learned in childhood and in other previous situations—but the society as a whole carries with it the baggage of earlier belief systems, which often gets in the way of a clear understanding of the present.

For example, many people like to describe the modern American economy as a "free-enterprise" system. This phrase is verbal baggage inherited from the past. It calls up images of freedom, of lack of regulation or other intervention in the economy by the government, and of opportunities for competing small entrepreneurs. Whatever validity these images may once have had (which is questionable anyway), they now obscure our understanding of an economy that is, in fact, dominated by a large sector of monopolistic and oligopolistic industries (in steel, chemicals, rubber, oil, autos, and a number of other vital areas) and is strongly regulated and supported by the federal government. Yet the phrase "free enterprise" continues to make many people feel emotionally committed to capitalism by keeping them from thinking clearly about capitalism's present structure.

Political forms can also be protected or justified by imagery from the past. Political elites in some state socialist countries attack their critics as "betraying the revolution." Thus a long past event is used to veil present inequalities in the distribution of power. Repeatedly in human history ideology has drawn on past events to justify present actions. Often the actors themselves —even revolutionaries—do not understand their present circumstances except in terms of the past (Marx, 1963: 15–17).

Thus any effort to analyze belief systems in a large stratified society is difficult because of the existence of many subbelief systems: the ideology (beliefs justifying the class order); oppositional belief systems; belief systems of different subgroups, such as ethnic minorities, specialized occupations, life-style groups, or social circles and networks (bikers, readers of the *New York Review of Books,* people in psychoanalysis, etc.); and so on. Some of these belief systems are very complete, including specifications for behavior and outlook in every part of a person's life. Others—like those of some occupational groups—cover only some activities or times and places. Each of these belief systems is loaded down with baggage from the past. Sometimes this material has been carried into the present in a more or less continuous tradition; for example, Catholic beliefs have a very long unbroken history. In other cases, the elements from the past are deliberately and self-consciously selected in the present; for example, the "ethnic revivals" or Eastern religion fads are examples of such innovative picking and choosing of parts of old traditions by people who were not socialized in them.

Several approaches can be used to understand the nature of belief systems in a modern society and their contribution to the functioning of the society as a whole. One is to try to identify and *describe* some of the major belief systems. For example, one might look at the ideology per se ("corporate liberalism"); at several oppositional belief systems that would differ in self-consciousness, coherence, and degree of explicit opposition to the prevailing order (Marxism, black and working-class cultures, religious traditions such as Hasidic and Hutterite culture); and at a number of subcultural belief systems of occupations and life-style groups. Such an analysis would be hampered by the fact that modern society not only has a large number of belief systems but most of them are intertwined. Any one person may carry around more than one system; there are many points of overlap between belief systems.

A second approach would be a *structural* approach to beliefs and ideas. In other words, we would look at the institutions, organizations, and groups that produce beliefs. We would see what kinds of people work in these institutions, how the institutions and organizations are structured, how their products are distributed (for example, through the media), and how they are related to the state. A structural study might also include consideration of the relationships that people engage in as they "consume" the produced beliefs; for example, one might observe how a family behaved as it watched a television program.

A structural analysis of ideology and other belief systems also has the advantage of clarifying the linkages between classes, organizations, and the state on the one hand and belief systems on the other. The sources of a particular belief system would be more visible. A structural analysis also permits us to trace the dilution of belief systems as they are propagated further from their sources or chief carrying groups. Thus the structural approach would merge with a process approach, with emphasis on how belief systems are spread or carried.

The reader should note how the issues raised here concerning belief systems overlap and complement the issues raised in Part One, where we saw how individuals absorb changes in belief systems.

Let me very briefly describe our own society in terms of its belief systems and their structural origins.

There is a dominant or prevailing belief system—"prevailing" both because it is so widespread and because it tends to smother or absorb its rivals. This belief system we can call the ideology of the society. It tends to protect the existing class system through ideas, just as the state protects the class system by force and administrative methods.

Part of the ideology is a rather explicit set of statements concerning the economy, the political system, and the role of the individual in each. Currently this explicit part of the ideology might be summarized as follows:

1. The economy should be organized predominantly in the form of private corporations.
2. Ownership of the means of production should be primarily private, but a high level of state involvement in the economy is not only acceptable but desirable.
3. The state should provide a stable climate for long-term profit maximization.
4. It is proper for the state to provide welfare services, education, and related services to stabilize the society and provide a reasonably trained labor force.
5. The nation-state is currently the most reasonable form for organizing human beings politically.
6. Most human beings exist by selling their labor power as a commodity in a labor market. This arrangement for securing the labor of producers is preferable to serfdom or slavery, which are inhuman. Production by independent artisans is no longer feasible, efficient, or realistic. Most people will work only if they have to—if their material well-being depends on it—and will require supervision by trained managers.

7. Representative government is a method for expressing political interests. As a community resident and citizen, one should have political rights to representation, freedom of speech, and so on. These do not apply at the workplace, however.

8. It is possible to maintain political freedom and democracy while maintaining gross inequalities in access to resources.

These are the beliefs that specifically protect the existing relations of production and the existing relation between class power and state power. Some writers have referred to this set of beliefs as "corporate liberalism." But just as important in maintaining stability is a vast number of rather vague related ideas and modes of thought that we might call "mass culture." The striking aspect of modern American ideology is that it is diffuse, absorbent, and vague. There is no single creed to which everyone must adhere. There is no state-supported religion. There are no terrible punishments for dissident opinions, even opinions that contradict any or all of the ideological core outlined above.

Corresponding to this tolerance and vagueness in the dominant belief system is the absence of a centralized structure for producing ideology. Other societies have had a pope or a priesthood, state newspapers, a centrally controlled school system, a ministry of communications or information, a state-controlled intelligentsia (or stratum of intellectuals), an officialdom of classically educated mandarins. Modern capitalist countries, and especially the U.S.A. (but less so Western Europe), lack these centralized structures for mental production. Mental production is not controlled by the state (in the narrow sense of government institutions) or even supervised by it. Therefore much of it is in the form of mass culture, which is produced under the same conditions as other goods and services of the society.

Mass culture, while partly a welfare function of the state, is primarily organized as private and usually as profit-seeking enterprises. The school systems are examples of state functions provided in a very decentralized way. Books, movies, magazines, television and radio programming, advertising, public relations, games and entertainment, architecture and art—all are organized as private profit-seeking enterprises. A variety of nonprofit private concerns, such as churches or universities, take on many of the characteristics of production for a commodity market. Universities publish bulletins to "sell" their services to students and write proposals to "sell" their services to government. In a period of reduced enrollments and federal funds, this salesmanship has been particularly frantic and has in some cases involved replacing liberal arts courses (especially language and history) with prevocational courses that make the university seem more attractive to its potential market. Its graduates are then, in turn, more likely to be able to "sell" themselves (that is, their labor power) in the job market. Electives replace required courses to make the product—the curriculum—more attractive and individually tailored.

Similar processes of adaptation to the marketplace shape the churches. They compete with each other for congregations. They "marginally differentiate" their product from that of competitors by adding small special attractions. Many water down their product to make it appeal more widely; thus, for instance, the Roman Catholic church replaced the use of Latin in the service with the vernacular. Others settle for intense product loyalties on the part of small market segments. Some sectarian churches and cults reflect this strategy.

The cultural market has several drawbacks. First, those ideas that represent the status quo win out. The competition appears to be so great, the range of choices so wide, that any possible opposition to the status quo is hopelessly fragmented. Ideas backed by the economically powerful have a particularly good chance of prevailing because they are supported by the most advertising.

A second related drawback is that, in the "free marketplace of ideas," there are no standards of excellence or even of good sense. Look at the shelves of any major bookstore. Nonsense of the most idiotic kind vies for space with serious books, and nonsense generally wins out. Books on third-rate movie stars, the occult, "gothic romances," and soft-core pornography crowd out works on the economy and the political system. The latter are hard to read; the former are "fun." Like the universities that drop language or history requirements to attract more students, bookstores and other sellers of culture provide "what the public wants." This policy is the cultural equivalent of selling sugary cereal to children.

Third, oppositional cultures are absorbed into mass culture and repackaged to be sold in acceptable form. Mass culture absorbs many of the oppositional cultures, particularly those that have no coherent analysis of the existing social order. The best example of such absorption is the commercialization of the counterculture of the 1960s; its music, clothes, and life-styles were all made available as commodities through the recording industry, the clothing industry, therapeutic institutes, and so on. Marijuana dealing was "professionalized"—that is, more closely linked to organized crime—and hard drugs were introduced into the white middle-class youth market. In the process of converting the counterculture into commodities, the "hip capitalists" dropped the counterculture's specifically oppositional elements—its rejection of bureaucratic organization, the state, the military-industrial complex, the formal educational system, and so on. This was not done deliberately but because these portions of the counterculture had no marketability. The entire process is symbolically captured in the degradation of the peace symbol from the oppositional graffitti used by the antiwar movement throughout the world to a piece of jewelry merchandized in chain stores and hippy boutiques.

The imposition of market considerations on culture—in other words, blandness, success of a cultural commodity measured by sales and supported by advertising, product diversity without strong differences ("marginal differentiation"), and the disappearance of difficult or disturbing ideas—more effectively assures a culture in harmony with the class system than outright state repression would (Marcuse, 1964). This situation is not historically unprecedented. It also appeared in Hindu society, where castes, subcastes, and regional groups had distinct cultures. These in turn were distinct from the "great tradition"—the literate orthodox Hindu culture of the elite. The diversity of subcultures effectively destroyed the unity of the lower castes, absorbed and compartmentalized dissent, and helped make Indian society freer of peasant revolts than most other traditional societies.

In addition, the apparent diversity of the market obscures the increasing concentration of the ownership of the means of mental production. For example, the number of competing newspapers is declining. Only 45 out of 1,500 American cities have newspapers under separate ownership (Parenti, 1968:168). There are only three major television networks. Each of these in turn owns a number of other businesses, often but not always in the sphere of culture and entertainment. The executives of these enterprises do not usually censor the producers directly. Censorship is the exceptional case, not the general rule. However, self-censorship and marketability ensure a mass culture that does not threaten the class structure.

To summarize: In modern capitalist societies, the belief system is characterized by extreme diversity, overlaps of subcultural belief systems, layers of beliefs inherited from different periods of the past, and substantially private ownership of the means of mental production. There is relatively little ideology manufactured by the state. Ideological functions—protection of the class status quo—of the belief system are contained in its very diversity and its indefiniteness.

An Example of Changes in Belief Systems: Science

In the next few pages I shall address myself to an example of a change in belief system, namely, the belief system of science.

The Origins of Science.   Science is a system of ideas and institutions aimed at examining and explaining natural phenomena. All human societies have developed science in the sense of observing, categorizing, and explaining the environment. Science as a set of institutions differentiated from other structures is, however, relatively recent. In primitive and traditional societies, all individuals share in the fund of scientific knowledge in that they are able to name, observe, catalog, and analyze plants and animals and their relationships, the weather, the health of people and livestock, and so on. Primitive systems of classification and explanation are not like our own. In many cases, this rudimentary science is confused by magical and religious practices in which phenomena are explained by reference to unobservable supernatural forces or beings whose existence and behavior depend on faith and fantasy rather than on evidence that can be obtained through the senses by reliable procedures. (*Reliable* means subject to replication by another observer.) Magic is especially important in activities of low certainty and high risk (such as crossing the open ocean in a canoe); these are activities for which primitive peoples lack the knowledge and techniques to control or predict outcomes.

In precapitalist class societies, science is also interlarded with magic and religion. But in class societies, all of these activities often become confined to a small, specialized group of experts, priests, or "wise men." While the class society as a whole may have in its possession more and better information about nature than primitive societies do, this information is controlled by a small group. Thus an overall societal gain in understanding coincides with a net loss in knowledge and control for many people.

In class societies, scientific activity is not restricted to priest-scientists but also exists in the technical know-how of various crafts specialists—masons, metal workers, miners, architects, doctors, and so on. This knowledge tends to be specialized, to involve control and prediction more than general theory, to be relatively free of magical and religious practices, and sometimes to be used in opposition to the knowledge of the priest-scientists.

In the late Middle Ages, these two strands of scientific activity began to merge to produce modern scientific institutions in western Europe. One writer has called the beginnings of this process in the fourteenth and fifteenth centuries "the marriage of the craftsman to the scholar" (Bernal, 1971: 385). Scholars increasingly became "experimental philosophers." The world view and logical methods of the Greeks, transmitted through Islamic culture into medieval Europe, still predominated. During the Renaissance, however, scholars added a renewed interest in observation, in the beauty of the real world, and in the individual human being. The mystical and hierarchial aspects of medieval thought were stripped away from the humanistic core that had been inherited from the Greeks. In this sense, the period of the fourteenth, fifteenth, and sixteenth centuries was a Renaissance, a "rebirth" of interest in human beings, in the real world, in secular pursuits, in observation and action—values that had been important to the free-citizen classes of the Greek city-states. With these interests came higher status for artisans and a unity of crafts techniques, arts, and science. Engineering, architecture, mining and metallurgy, navigation and astronomy, as well as literature and art flourished.

These developments—in particular, the unity of intellectual and crafts production, and the growth of science—did not "just happen." They reflect the growth of a new order within the feudal economy. They were manifestations of the end of feudal agrarianism, the end of the rigid separation of classes ("estates"), and the growth of a new class interested in trade, industry, and empirical understanding. The intellectual accomplishments of the Renaissance and the subsequent two or three centuries did not happen by themselves in the midst of the localistic and castelike order of feudalism. Feudalism first began to collapse as an economic and class order. People established towns as trading centers; serfs fled to these towns, swelled their populations, and helped to create an economy based on trade and crafts productions as well as agriculture.

Once the towns and their burgher and artisan classes were established, the world view of medieval Catholicism began to seem inadequate. It justified a static rural social order when what was emerging was a rapidly changing, urbanized commercial and crafts system with more fluid class lines. The collapse of the Catholic world view took a variety of forms: the development of secularized humanistic Renaissance thought, the growth of a liberal reformed Catholicism (which was associated with Erasmus, and did not fully survive the Counter-Reformation), Protestantism, and nationalism.

These different belief systems each represented an effort to find an ideology suitable for the emerging bourgeoisie. We can think of the bourgeoisie as a growing adolescent and the belief systems as a sequence of clothes: the first outfits the boy selects are still closely tied to his father's tastes; as he grows older and larger, he chooses clothes that more strongly reflect his own individuality. Just so with the beliefs of the emerging bourgeoisie. At first, liberal variants of Catholicism and early Protestantism were the world views through which the aspirations, interests, and experiences of the bourgeoisie were expressed. Only later did secularized elements appear in the bourgeoisie's belief systems; these were eventually to predominate. It was not until the eighteenth century—until the period of the Enlightenment, the bourgeois seizure of the state in France, and the bourgeoisie's rise to dominance in England—that fully secular, political, explicit, and universalistic bourgeois ideologies appeared. These "tryings-on" of different belief systems were not deliberate or planned; rather, the bourgeoisie and other new strata had interests and experiences that did not fit into medieval Catholicism. Beliefs had to be revised to fit the objective conditions of craft workshops, town life, increased trade, greater freedom to choose an occupation (within limits), an emerging money economy, and more centralized states.

Meanwhile, during the period of transition (from the time the bourgeoisie first appeared in the late Middle Ages until it became the dominant or "hegemonic" class in western Europe in the late eighteenth century) belief systems overlapped each other, and pieces of one belief system provided the foundation for others. For example, Protestantism had many elements that could feed into the belief systems of nationalism, science, and early forms of the "spirit of capitalism." Protestantism did not *cause* the emergence of these belief systems, much less the emergence of the capitalist class, but it did provide images, metaphors, and justifications for the belief systems. For example, in the sixteenth and seventeenth centuries, science grew partly in response to practical problems of navigation, shipping, and ballistics and partly because there were strata of secular intellectuals whose interests lay in the world of nature. Nevertheless, the pursuit of science was often justified in religious terms; scientific study was one mode of glorifying God, by contemplating and understanding His works.

Science developed more rapidly in Protestant areas where religious beliefs supported scientific work. However, we must not credit only Protestantism with nurturing science. Wherever urban merchants and craftsmen appeared, science appeared as well. As I have already indicated, this happened also in Catholic northern Italy during the Renaissance. It was not so much Protestantism as opposed to Catholicism that supported science; rather, it was that science and the urban, secular, intellectual and artisan strata that carried it out were systematically repressed in the countries of the Catholic Counter-Reformation (Trevor-Roper, 1968).

One historian of science, J. D. Bernal, summarized this process from a similar perspective:

> The development of towns, trade, and industry that was gaining momentum towards the end of the Middle Ages was to prove incompatible with the economy of feudalism. These changes slowly maturing under the surface of the feudal order finally found expression, and in one place after another inaugurated a new order in economy and science. With better techniques, better modes of transport, and more ample markets, the production of commodities for sale steadily increased. The towns where these markets were found had long played a subsidiary, almost parasitic, role in feudal economy; but by the fifteenth century the burghers or bourgeoisie had grown so strong that they were beginning to transform that economy into one in which money payments and not forced services determined the form of production. The triumph of the bourgeoisie, and of the capitalist system of economy which they evolved, took place only after the most severe political, religious, and intellectual struggles. Naturally the process of transformation was slow and uneven; it had begun already in the thirteenth century in Italy, yet it was not until the mid-seventeenth century that the bourgeoisie had established their rule even in the most progressive countries of Britain and Holland. Another two hundred years were to elapse before the same class had come to control the whole of Europe.
>
> The same period—1450–1690—that saw the development of capitalism as the leading method of production also witnessed that of experiment and calculation as the new method of natural science. The transformation was a complex one; changes in techniques led to science, and science in turn was to lead to new and more rapid changes in technique. This combined technical, economic, and scientific revolution is a unique social phenomenon. Its ultimate importance is even greater than that of the discovery of agriculture, which had made civilization itself possible, because through science it contained in itself the possibilities of indefinite advance (Bernal, 1971: 373).

The abstract problems in which scientists of the sixteenth and seventeenth centuries were interested were suggested by current industrial, economic, and military development. For example, water transport required knowledge of the behavior of bodies floating in or moving through liquids in order to improve ship design; optical instruments, observations, and charts for navigation; and knowledge of the movement of liquids in order to design canals. Mining required knowledge of the movement of air for ventilation devices, the movement of both air and water for pumping equipment, and the effects of friction for the design of cogged wheels and transmission mechanisms used in raising ores. War required knowledge of trajectories and the forces within a firearm.

These practical problems, *in abstracted form,* are precisely the important scientific issues of the sixteenth and seventeenth centuries. For instance, they form the basis for much of Newton's *Principia* and of other works that marked the beginning of modern science. We do not need to posit a crude relationship between the practical problems and their abstracted scientific forms. Newton and other scientists did not choose to work on these topics because the merchants and generals paid them to do so; they picked the problems because they were genuinely scientifically exciting. But the problems were not recognized as interesting intellectual puzzles until they had surfaced into people's consciousness through the circumstances of everyday economic life (Hessen, 1974).

Characteristics of Modern Science.   Science is one of the specialized belief systems of modern societies. Like any belief system, it is carried by groups of people, structured into institutions and specific organizations. Having looked briefly at the origins of this belief system (and its accompanying institutions), we can now turn to its present character and patterns of change.

The belief system of science has two important characteristics:

1. It is carried by groups of specialized, trained people whom we may call the scientific community. The scientific community is organized around and by universities, other kinds of research laboratories, professional associations, and journals. It maintains ties with funding bodies in the government and elsewhere. In other words, science is not a disembodied system of ideas but is created by people involved in groups and in organizations within a particular economy. The general scientific community also has subcommunities, corresponding to specialized areas.

2. The form that scientific belief systems take is the paradigm, or model. Paradigms are clusters of statements about the real world or some part of it that include the following:

— Statements defining or identifying basic concepts (For example, heat is identified with the motion of molecules.)

— Statements relating these concepts to each other, sometimes in a quantified form (For example, heat of a gas is related to volume and pressure in the statements known as Boyle's Law.)

— Statements specifying what types of instruments and methods are best used in pursuing empirical manifestations of the concept (For example, heat is measured by thermometers.)

— Statements identifying satisfactorily solved "puzzles" or problems in the particular scientific field (For example, Boyle's Law again.)
— Statements identifying as yet unsolved puzzles (Why is temperature related to the resistance of materials to electrical currents?)

A scientific community agrees on a paradigm for extended periods of time. Most people in the community work on the puzzles specified by the paradigm. They try to solve these puzzles using the concepts and methods specified by the paradigm. This activity may be called "routine science." Routine science—i.e., science within the bounds of a given paradigm—is also taught to aspiring young scientists through textbooks and courses. Statements identifying satisfactory solutions to puzzles within a paradigm are used as examplars to train the student.

Every once in a while, however, the paradigm breaks down. A "puzzle" (or problem) posed within a paradigm cannot be solved. The paradigm is only an approximate fit to empirical reality; either it does not really correspond to reality very well, or it is not sufficiently wide in scope. For instance, in physics, Newtonian mechanics is excellent for describing and predicting the behavior of bodies within the earth's gravitational field; it is good for most predictions concerning the motion and mutual attraction of objects in the solar system. Sending a rocket to the moon, for example, is quite feasible within the Newtonian paradigm. However, the puzzle of the exact configuration of the orbit of Mercury cannot be accounted for by Newton's theory. This puzzle (and a number of others) can be solved by a different conceptualization of these aspects of nature, the paradigm of Einstein's general theory of relativity. The basic definitional statements of Newton's paradigm concerning gravitational forces between bodies with mass are now replaced by statements that posit that masses influence the geometrical structure of space and time. The Newtonian paradigm is then seen to be only a special case of the theory of relativity, the case in which velocities are small, duration is independent of the system of reference, and space-time is flat rather than curved. In other cases, the superseded paradigm cannot be incorporated as a special case of the new paradigm but simply has to be junked (Kuhn, 1970).

In some fields, there is no single agreed-upon paradigm, and there never has been. The social sciences tend to be in this state. (The absence of consensus on a paradigm does not mean that no paradigm exists that is *in fact* the best approximation to reality; it just means that the community of scientists has not agreed on which one it is.) In other fields, the agreed-upon paradigm has just broken down and has not yet been replaced. For example, in the 1960's in particle physics, the rapid discovery of a large number of subatomic particles produced a period of confusion.

There have been two major approaches to studying change in science: the "externalist" and the "internalist." The externalist approach tries to account for changes in science by relating them to changes in the larger surrounding society. My analysis of the emergence of science is an example of such an externalist approach. The changes in the larger society can be transmitted to scientists in two different ways: through the institutional structure of science, in which some activities may be rewarded and others neglected or discouraged; and through general developments in societal belief systems, in which a particular conception, metaphor, or preoccupation is reflected in scientific beliefs. For example, with the growth of a market system in Western capitalism in which outcomes are determined by the aggregate decisions of individual buyers and sellers, probabilistic models of social and physical processes become more popular in scientific paradigms. No person or organization has forced these models on scientists; rather, people are socialized by their experiences and the current imagery to conceive of natural processes in a new way, consonant with their conception of how society works.

The internalist view of changes in science emphasizes how new scientific paradigms arise out of the collapse and reworking of old ones. The internalist view is subject to a number of criticisms: (1) Often the most important discoveries are made (or new paradigms invented) in a discipline by people who were trained outside the discipline, because they are free from the blinders imposed by training within a single paradigm. Thus even an internalist approach must take into account developments in related fields. For example, the discovery of the double-helical structure of the DNA molecule was spearheaded by Watson who was trained as a biologist rather than as a chemist. (2) The internalist account seems to treat science as different from other human institutions, as a progressive and disinterested search for truth. While later paradigms are usually more accurate and more encompassing depictions of nature, their development is subject to the same institutional and structural constraints as other human belief systems.

Changes in the Political System

We can now look at how societies change. We have already traced change in the mode of production. In this section, I would like to discuss how changes in the superstructure—especially in the political system—accompany substructural changes. Changes in the substructure, the political system, and the ideology do not occur separately from each other. As each of them changes, the totality—the whole configuration of substructure and superstructure—changes. The society as a whole changes. I shall begin this discussion by looking at political-system change.

Types of Political Change

Prior to the appearance of the state, a very common form of political change was factionalism and the creation of new communities. A group that was not satisfied with its share of power in the community or with a specific decision would simply split off from the community and start a new settlement. The society as a whole grew through the growth in the number of new communities. Each new community or segment was much like the old one. Since in prestate societies population was often rather sparse, new settlements could be established in "frontier" regions. The Hopi (an Indian group of the Southwest) are a good example of a society that used splitting off and the establishment of new communities to settle internal political disputes.

Once states appeared, this "looseness" of the political system diminished. To some extent, individuals could still emigrate or flee to frontier areas. Even in modern states, frontier areas exist to which rebellious and adventurous people can move. However, it became harder for groups to pull out of the state and create their own communities. Such pullouts or segmentation would damage the social order both because they diminished the legitimacy of the state and because they diminished the number of producers in the class system. Note, for example, in Exodus, the great ease with which people in tribal Jewish society moved around with their households, sometimes as the result of disputes in a community or family. Contrast this freedom of movement with the pharaoh's reluctance to let the Jews leave the state of Egypt. Tribal Jewish society was on the verge of stratification but as yet without state institutions; Egyptian society was a highly stratified society in which slaves and enslaved ethnic groups were an important labor source. From the point of view of society as a whole, the development of the state meant a unified and at least partially centralized political system. From the point of view of individuals, it meant a considerable depoliticization.

In egalitarian and even ranked societies, most men (and sometimes women) expected to take part in public decision-making during some period of their lives, either throughout adulthood (as in band-level egalitarian hunting and gathering groups and in some agricultural societies) or as a member of a council of elders. In state-level stratified societies, most people cannot assume that they will take part in decision-making because increasing numbers of decisions are transferred from their domain to the ruling class and/or to officials and experts in the state apparatus. However, some class societies do maintain a politicized general public: the free-citizen strata of ancient Athens, and citizens of the revolutionary societies of the period of Enlightenment and the rise of the bourgeoisie (in France and America in the late eighteenth century). However, at the same time these revolutions repoliticized people as citizens—as members of local and national territorial communities—they tended to depoliticize people in the workplace. In capitalist societies, the individual can be a political being at home but is expected to remain largely apolitical at work. To alter this situation of fragmented politicization, one author has proposed a workplace bill of rights.

1. No one shall direct the labor of others unless elected.
2. No one shall be discharged except by a jury of his or her peers, for a good cause, after a public opportunity to confront those critical of his or her work (Lynd, 1974: 22).

What kinds of political change can take place in state societies, given the fact that simple segmentation is usually not possible because of its threat to the control of resources, to the control of a labor force, and to legitimacy?

It is not easy to construct an adequate typology of political change. There have been many efforts to do so, but there are so many different dimensions along which change can take place that no typology is wholly satisfactory.

Change in the Relations of Production.   One dimension is the extent to which the political change is accompanied by change in the relations of production. In some cases, a group seizes the state apparatus and uses this source of power to alter class relationships. For example, during the French Revolution, the lands of nobles and the church were expropriated, and French agriculture was organized into small, privately owned farms. The relation between landowning nobles and tenant farmers was no longer the dominant relation in French agricultural production. Similarly, in the Russian, Chinese, and Cuban revolutions, private owners of land and industry were expropriated. We also discussed how owners were expropriated when the Catalonians established their own anarchist society in Spain in the 1930s. A political change in which the relations of production are altered after the protective armor of the state is torn away is very rare. Such an act is a revolution in the fullest sense of the word.

Change in State Institutions.   Major structural reforms may occur even if the relations of production remain unaffected. The state apparatus can be changed. Party organizations can be started or come to an end. Substantially new policies for connecting the state to the economy can be instituted. For example, new regulatory agencies or monetary and fiscal (taxing and spending) policies can be created. Welfare policies can be instituted. The right to vote can be extended. New regulations for holding office or conducting elections can be enforced. For example, in the 1830's, a British working-class movement, Chartism, demanded universal male suffrage, secret ballots, pay for officeholders, and the abolition of property restrictions for membership in the House of Commons. These changes, when eventually enacted (after the collapse of the movement), made possible greater working-class participation in English politics. A more recent example of structural reform short of change in the relations of production is the Wagner Act, which supported and regularized the process of unionization in the United States. As I pointed out in a previous chapter, this act was one of several ingredients that made possible the union drives of the 1930s.

Change in Ideology.   A third dimension is the amount of ideological change that accompanies the political change. Destruction or seizure of the state apparatus and transformation of the relations of production are almost always accompanied by extensive ideological change. But even very extensive structural change may involve only gradual or relatively slight change in ideology. In the long run, ideology will generally swing into line with the economic and political structure; but in the short run, it may not be greatly altered. For example, in America, the state has come to intervene extensively in the economy through monetary and fiscal policies, government regulations and contracting (a specific form of spending), and so on; yet the phrase "free enterprise" has not yet completely disappeared from the minds, tongues, printed pages, and television screens. In other cases, the *absence* of structural change is obscured by a language and ideology of upheaval. For example, some elites in developing nations claim to be modernizing these societies and introducing socialism when in fact they are not.

Related to the amount of change in ideology is the extent to which the change is *legitimate* in terms of the initial change in ideology. *Legitimacy* is a particular aspect of the ideology of a society. It is the cluster of norms and rules that identify political behavior that is formally correct. (Some behavior, while not posing a threat to the state apparatus unless it reaches massive proportions, nevertheless is not legitimate—for example, bribing a policeman to beat a traffic ticket. However, this type of behavior is of only marginal interest to us.) Legitimacy is often defined by a constitution or laws. Some political change is entirely legitimate; for example, the election of Allende's Socialist administration in Chile was legitimate within the formal rules of Chilean politics. It is rare that legitimate change is so fundamental in its consequences for class relationships.

Having outlined some of the major dimensions of political change, I would like to comment on some major types of change. We must keep in mind that these types are not a typology; they do not form an exhaustive and mutually exclusive list.

Reform

Reform is any change that (1) does *not* involve seizure of the state apparatus, (2) does *not* fundamentally alter the relations of production, but (3) goes beyond routine changes in the incumbents of political offices. This definition seems close to the general usage of the word. Unfortunately the definition obscures some of the differences between types of reforms. For one thing, reforms differ in terms of the social groups that initiate them.

Elite-Initiated Reforms.   Some reforms are initiated by the ruling class itself in order to strengthen its hold on the state apparatus. For example, during the Progressive era in the first decade and a half of the twentieth century, a number of U.S. cities switched from elected-mayor governments to city-manager governments. This reform was introduced ostensibly to make city government more efficient and less corrupt. In fact, it was introduced by local economic elites who felt threatened by the working class (especially working-class immigrants) and wanted to keep them from being able to elect a mayor who would represent their interests. (Of course, the reform was also supported in good faith by middle-class persons who were appalled at the deception and corruption of the machine politics that was being developed by many ethnic politicians.) In cities with strong, well-organized working classes, these proposed reforms were blocked. Where the working class was weaker and less well-organized, in the South and Midwest, city-manager governments are more numerous. In this case, an apparent reform was actually initiated by those in control of the local economy (Hays, 1972).

Some reforms are indeed initiated from below but are addressed only to short-run substantive issues, not to changes in structure. For example, high school students in the 1960s demanded changes in dress codes. These were often granted, sometimes only after very stormy confrontations between students and high school administrators. By themselves, however, such changes do little to alter the function of secondary education, to change the kind of preparation it provides, to attack its compulsoriness, and so on. Even some structural changes, such as the various reforms of university structure that took place during the 1960s in both Europe and America, may be concessions that do not markedly affect the distribution of power in the organization, much less in the society. However, some reforms whet people's appetites for further change and leave them in a structurally stronger position to organize for further change. This type of reform has been called nonreformist reform (Gorz, 1967).

Nonreformist Reforms.   We cannot give a simple formula to distinguish "reformist" reforms from nonreformist reforms. Obviously, elite-initiated reforms are hardly ever nonreformist reforms or if they are, only accidentally and unintentionally so. Nonreformist reforms are usually demands put forth by a strong movement organization. Sometimes the identical reform may have different consequences, depending on the strength and longevity of the movement that initiated it. Packages of reforms put forward by strong movements are less likely to be pulled apart and handled in a piecemeal fashion than are "packages" that lack such backing.

For example, in the late nineteenth-century America, the Populist movement (with a strong base among Midwestern and Southern farmers) demanded regulation of corporations; direct election of senators; initiative, referendum, and recall; low-cost federal loans for farmers; and public ownership of railroads, telephones, and telegraphs. As a package, this set of reforms represented a strong attack on the form of modern capitalism that was then emerging.

However, weakness in the Populist movement prevented it from backing all these reforms independently. Instead, some (but not all) of them were picked up by the Democrats and by the Progressive movement. Insofar as these reforms were implemented, they were implemented in a piecemeal fashion. The constituency that wanted these reforms was partially satisfied by the implementation of some of them and failed to press for the more radical ones, the public ownership ones. In any case, as the reforms were not implemented immediately and as a package, other issues rose to importance (the Spanish-American war, for instance), and the backers of the reforms lost their momentum. In other words, lack of strong movement support sometimes leads to piecemeal reform in which the original intentions of the reformers are lost; and, as piecemeal reforms are instituted, the movement's followers may be sufficiently satisfied to weaken their support for the movement.

Finally, reforms that produce structural as well as substantive changes tend to be more nonreformist (although the structural reform of universities indicates that many structural reforms can also be co-opted). In summary, nonreformist reforms have the following qualities:

1. They affect the nature of class relations, even though they fall short of fundamentally altering them. According to Italian Marxist Lelio Basso, who is quoted in the November, 1974, issue of the *New American Movement:*

> Anticapitalist structural reforms . . . are those reforms that "modify the process of accumulation to the disadvantage of profits and modify the organization of power in favor of the workers." Such reforms, writes Basso, render "the equilibrium of capitalism more and more precarious by forcing it to cohabit with social relations and a network of institutions which are expression of principles of organization incompatible with its system."
>
> In order for public ownership to "modify the process of accumulation to the disadvantage of profits," the capitalist owners of the targeted industry or enterprise must be paid as little as possible for their holdings (outright expropriation is preferable), and the industry or firm's price structure must be such that big corporations are forced to pay considerably more than smaller consumers for a given volume of goods or services.

2. They include structural changes as well as short-run substantive changes.
3. They are initiated by or help to build strong movement organizations.
4. They are won by the use of power rather than by supplication of elites.
5. They are part of a large package of reforms that is instituted in its entirety rather than in piecemeal fashion.
6. They whet the appetite for further and even more fundamental change.

Examples of Nonreformist Reforms.   I believe that in the history of capitalist societies there have been at least two such "packages" of nonreformist reform. One is the extension of the right to participate in representative government to propertyless people—to the urban industrial working class—that took place in the capitalist countries of North America and Western Europe. It was accomplished earliest and most peacefully in the United States, where it was essentially well under way by the "Jacksonian revolution" of 1828. After that point, the economically powerful, while they may still in fact have indirectly or directly controlled the government, were no longer legally empowered to do so. Universal male suffrage (in the North), secret ballot elections, regular elections at times and places accessible to working people—all ensure mass participation in at least some aspects of decision-making. A second round of extension of participation came in the U.S. during the first decades of the twentieth century. These reforms included the extension of suffrage to women; introduction of initiative, referendum, and recall; and the direct election of senators.

These types of reforms started later and were accomplished at different times in Western Europe. They add up to the assertion of the right of all adults to participate in representative government, regardless of whether they control property. The critic may be inclined to argue that these are only legal rights and that in fact, those who control productive resources also control the state. The critic may further assert that these "rights" blind the public to the fact that they cannot effectively exercise them in a society with such great inequalities in the control of resources. These criticisms are valid. The point, however, is not that these rights are sufficient, but that they are necessary, structurally and ideologically, to the attainment of mass participation in political decision-making. People now believe they have the right to be citizens. Furthermore, in the European countries where these rights were more stringently resisted by propertied classes than they were in the U.S., the fight to acquire them was an important project of the working-class movements. Thus the reforms not only had some effects on the structure of the whole society, but they also helped to build organizations that could alter that structure further.

A second important package of reforms was the hard-won right to unionize. Like citizen rights, unionization rights were attained only over a long period of time in often violent struggles. In the U.S., these rights were not supported by the state until the Wagner Act of 1935. Unionization meant a major change in capitalist relations of production. Workers no longer had to face their employers (or, more likely, employing corporations) as isolated individuals. Again, a rather cynical critic might point out that union leaders have often negotiated away the demands of the rank and file at the bargaining table, that most unions have regularized and streamlined the relationship between owners and producers rather than challenge it. The critic would be right. However, the right to organize, like the right to vote, is a necessary but not sufficient condition for social change in capitalist society.[2] Unions provide a structural framework for pressing for further reforms such as control over the production process. In Western Europe, unions actually form an important network of organizations that support left-of-center political parties.

It is possible that the reforms demanded by the environmentalist and consumer movements will also produce fundamental changes, short of actual revolution, in modern capitalism. They are already having a major effect on the use of capital: due to environmental and occupational health and safety statutes, somewhere between $10 and $20 billion of the $65 billion available to American corporations for investment in 1973 had to be spent in these areas (Booth, 1974). This shift indicates the ability of these movements to change the economic priorities of the society by bringing pressure on the state for regulation. Occupational health and safety provides an especially potent package of reforms. Health and safety demands clearly state that the well-being of the workers shall take precedence over profit. These demands potentially bring together unions and the more generally middle-class support base of the environmentalist movement. They have already produced legislation—the Occupational Safety and Health Act of 1971—which, while not adequately enforced, brings legitimacy and state support to worker demands.

The civil rights movement of the early 1960s is another good example of reform. As with other major reforms, a package of changes—rather than an isolated one—was demanded: desegregation of public facilities, a faster pace of school desegregation, affirmative-action hiring practices, the abolition of poll taxes, an end to the harassment of black voters, and more federal funding for programs directly benefiting blacks. The desegregation of public facilities such as lunch counters, restrooms, drinking fountains, waiting rooms, movie theaters, hotels, bowling alleys, and so on proceeded more rapidly than the other reforms. Note how these are the issues least connected to the organization of the economy, to the function of the school as a route from blue-collar to white-collar jobs, to the competition for a relatively scarce supply of attractive jobs, and so on. The reforms aimed at the "class" issues (school integration, community control of schools, and more jobs) occurred most slowly and were least well supported and enforced. The reforms aimed at participation in the state—an end to poll taxes, increased voter registration, jury participation, and so on—have proceeded at a medium pace.

Civil rights reforms were initiated from below, by a strong movement that had widespread grass-roots support. The movement spread rapidly and maintained a high level of rank-and-file participation and militancy. The movement was successful in increasing political participation and opening up public

[2]I am aware of the argument of groups like the Sojourner Truth collective in Chicago that unions are entirely bankrupt and cannot be revived as a progressive political force. I am impressed, but not convinced, by these arguments.

facilities. Success meant both state support for these reforms (the Civil Rights Act of 1964) and actual changes at the community level.

At this point, however, the movement's focus shifted geographically northward, substantively to economic issues, and structurally to ghetto organization and fewer white participants. These shifts, although absolutely necessary for the attainment of equal economic status by blacks, made it difficult for the movement itself to survive. The movement's new set of reforms struck much closer at the class core of American society. They threatened the status of white property owners and the security of white workers, who depended on urban blacks as a cushion against unemployment (during hard times, blacks would be laid off first) and as automatic occupants of the least desirable jobs —hospital work, foundry work, spray painting and other jobs involving fumes or noxious liquids, domestic labor, and so on. The movement lost its appeal to the media, its ability to use moral suasion and nonviolence as effective tactics, and its white middle-class support base.

By the late sixties and early seventies black civil rights movements were making much slower progress than they had in the early sixties, as they struggled on issues that were much closer to the central core of society. Major gains have probably come on two fronts: an increase in college enrollments, providing a slow, highly filtered influx of blacks into professional, paraprofessional, and white-collar jobs; and the election of blacks to public office, opening the possibility of increased access to government jobs and funds. The changes in ideology ("blacks are equal as citizens and human beings"), public behavior, and political institutions attained by the civil rights movements are associated with the attainment of more fundamental changes in class position.

Power-Limiting Reforms.   Another way of thinking about reforms—the hard-won reforms that are more than handouts from an elite—is that they set limits on the power of the ruling classes or the ruling state elites. They define a perimeter within which this power is constrained and must be shared. Reforms also force us to revise our view of the state.

While from a very abstract perspective the state is indeed that set of institutions that protects the class order, in actual historical instances, subordinate classes have restricted the power of the state to carry out this function. For example, subordinate classes have forced the state to protect the class order by instituting welfare programs rather than repression. They have even forced the state repeatedly to act against the interests of the economically dominant class. The state apparatus is a major part of the spoils of class conflict. In the routine nonrevolutionary forms of this conflict, parts of the apparatus may be captured by the subordinate classes. This capture seems especially possible in advanced capitalist countries in which the economically dominant class is only very indirectly involved in day-to-day operation of the state, in which representative institutions make the state relatively open to a variety of classes and strata, and in which the sheer size of the state and the society make it impossible to keep the entire apparatus under tight class control (Dreier, 1975).

Direct Action. There are numerous tactics of reform. We shall confine ourselves to those that typically appear in industrial countries. One is direct action. Direct action—demonstrations, sit-ins, boycotts, and so on—sometimes produce the reform by putting intolerable pressure on an elite and by raising the costs of resistance so high that the elite gives in. For example, the sit-down strikes of the 1930s, by halting production and seizing the company's valuable equipment, forced the company to recognize the union. Workers and consumers are especially advantaged in this use of direct action because, if they are well organized, they can disrupt the profit-making of a company, of a sector of the economy, or even of the whole economy.

Sometimes direct action is not used as a force in itself but rather as a device to focus the attention of the media and the public at large on an issue. This tactic makes sense only when the media *and* the public both care enough about the issue to be concerned by it *and* when the particular elite in question is relatively weak and susceptible to pressure from more powerful groups. The civil rights movements presents a good example of this tactic. Freedom rides and lunch counter sit-ins drew widespread sympathetic responses from both media and public. Most Northern whites, although they might have benefited from black *economic* disadvantages, felt that blacks were entitled to the same use of public facilities as all other citizens and human beings. The local groups who wanted to maintain the segregation of public facilities were quite weak compared with those opposed to it. Once direct action attracted the media and put the issue on the national agenda, the segregationists had few resources (except local police force) to use in defending their stand.

Lobbying. Another tactic of reform is lobbying and similar "insider" pressure. The advantage of this tactic is that it produces results fairly rapidly, especially specific legislation. The disadvantage is that no broad reform movement is built and proposed reforms are sometimes instituted in a piecemeal fashion. Some environmental reforms have been achieved by lobbying, by creating legal-action pressure groups, and by developing financial contributors and mailing-list constituencies.

Some reforms may involve several of these tactics. Thus the Joe McCarthy "reforms"—the purge during the 1950s of Communists from positions in the state and ideological institutions (Hollywood, universities, etc.)—were effected through such a combination. Media attention was focused, insider pressures (especially on politicians who felt uneasy about their constituency and who were afraid of being thought "soft on communism") were applied, and a following was built up. However, this following consisted mainly of names on a mailing list; it was not a real movement organization with an internal structure.

Electoral Action.   Another major tactic of reform movements is electoral effort. Sometimes it is directed at referenda on substantive issues. For example, during the war in Indochina, some groups worked to get antiwar resolutions on the ballot. This tactic is easier in some states—California, for instance—than others, for historical reasons. More frequently, reform movements try to run reform candidates. To do this they have to first capture local party committees. In these instances, reform movements become wings of the major parties. When this happens proposed reforms are implemented only in a piecemeal fashion, pulled from their original context, and incorporated into an otherwise conventional party platform.

Note that in our use of the term *reform,* we have emphasized how a reform depends on and often changes the distribution of power in a society as well as in an organization. In practice, many reforms involve the state; but since political power is never entirely monopolized by the state, reform can also involve nonstate institutions.

Revolution

Revolutions are a second major type of change in political institutions. We will define a revolution as a change in the distribution of power that (1) involves seizure, transformation, and/or destruction of the state apparatus, and (2) fundamentally alters the relations of production. These two defining characteristics imply that revolutions also are accompanied by ideological change.

We have already commented on the fact that seizure of the state apparatus combined with alteration of class relations also produces a new ideology. The revolutionary class asserts that its interests and values are universal interests and values, valid for everyone in the society and perhaps even valid for all human beings at all times. This assertion is made by the organizations that represents the class and by its spokesmen in the ideological apparatus. The assertion is usually made in good faith; revolutionaries genuinely believe their own ideology. Thus, for instance, in the French Revolution, the rights that the bourgeoisie demanded included the end of a hereditary aristocracy, the weakening and expropriation of the Catholic church, the dismantling of the monarchy, the right to sell and buy land and labor power as commodities, the opening of careers to talent and enterprise, and freedom to participate in political institutions.

To a considerable extent these were rights that strengthened the power of the emerging capitalist class in France. But the list of rights that the bourgeoisie supported was *not* just a cynically formulated, thinly veiled set of economic interests. On the contrary, many of these rights appealed to all nonaristocratic strata in France. Most of the rights were not specifically economic. Their effect was to ensure a better climate for capitalist class rule in France, but this was not a specially planned effect. The groups that asserted these rights genuinely saw them as "the Rights of Man," as progressive steps away from feudalism, religious oppression, and royal absolutism.

Only when a class (through its organizations) can rally support from *all or most* nonruling classes and strata in a society can it develop enough support to hang onto the state apparatus against the opposition of the former ruling class. Only when it mobilizes such widespread support can the revolutionary class effectively use the state apparatus to initiate structural change. In other words, in a revolution there is both a revolutionary class and an ideological consensus that draws in other classes and strata.

I have already discussed another important feature of revolutions, namely, the role of a revolutionary organization that coordinates violence, ideology, day-to-day administrative decisions, and overall policies. This organization represents the revolutionary class and its allied strata as well. The members of a revolutionary organization do not all necessarily come from the revolutionary class, however.

Using the two-part definition above, we can point to only relatively few examples of revolutions: probably the revolution that took place in England during the second half of the seventeenth century, the American Revolution (albeit a marginal case); the French Revolution; perhaps the American Civil War; the Russian, Chinese, and Cuban revolutions; perhaps the Mexican revolution of 1910 and the Communist seizures of power in Yugoslavia and Albania at the end of World War II; and the Vietnamese revolution. These are the hard core of revolutions in which both of our defining criteria are fulfilled. Yet even a number of these are questionable; a really strict application of the second criterion—change in the relations of production—might well reduce the number even further.

Revolutions are related to a number of other phenomena: wars of national liberation, elite revolutions, electoral victories of radical parties, coups d'état, and counterrevolutions. None of these meets both criteria, however.

Wars of Liberation.   Wars of national liberation are revolts against colonial powers or against puppet rulers who are subservient to an imperial power. There have been several waves of such revolts in world history: in the empires of antiquity (for example, the Jewish wars against Rome, which resulted in the mass deportation of Jews from the Near East into other parts of the empire); the revolts by national groups in southern and eastern Europe in the nineteenth century against the large empires of Austro-Hungary, Russia, and Turkey; and the revolts against European colonial rule in Asia and Africa after World War II.

When successful, most of these wars of liberation involved extensive shifts in political power, in control of the state apparatus. Their impact on the relations of production was less unequivocal. Sometimes they simply transferred ownership of land or industries from foreign owners to a native class that acted as representatives of the foreign interests. In other cases, the former colonial power was in fact excluded from direct or indirect use of the new countries' resources, but the new native ownership class maintained similar control. In other cases, programs of land reform, new forms of ownership of industries, and so on were at least attempted or actually carried out. In other words, wars of national liberation (and here we are discussing primarily those that took place after World War II) fall along a continuum from revolution, on the one hand, to replacement of foreign personnel by indigenous personnel in the state apparatus and private enterprise, on the other hand.

Elite Revolutions.   In the broadest sense, elite revolutions are transformations of the state and the relations of production that are initiated and carried out by part of the state apparatus itself. In other words, under certain special historical conditions, groups arise within the organization of the state that use the state apparatus to change rather than to protect the existing order. Historically, these cases generally seem to involve nationalist bureaucrats or military men who find that they can build a strong society vis-à-vis foreign imperial powers only by changing the whole structure of society. They capture the remainder of the state apparatus, usually by limited armed conflict, and use the state to raise capital for industrialization (Trimberger, 1972: 191).

The best documented examples of elite revolutions are the Meiji Restoration (1868) in Japan and the Ataturk revolution (1919–1923) in Turkey. Nasser's revolution in Egypt and the Peruvian military coup of 1968 also share some features of elite revolutions. In Japan and Turkey, the revolutionaries' program of economic change was based on developing a stratum of rich peasants which could "extract an increasing surplus from the peasant masses" to provide capital for industrialization and a stratum of urban entrepreneurs and officials who would back a "mixed public-private plan for industrialization" (Trimberger, 1972: 206).

If we do not insist on this particular plan of economic development as a defining characteristic of elite revolutions, we might be able to apply the term to a larger variety of historical cases. For instance, Stalin's rise to power and his extermination of the rich peasants (kulaks), collectivization of Russian agriculture, and industrialization have many of the characteristics of an elite revolution. The pattern of takeover of the whole state apparatus by one wing of it, elite control of decision-making, and transformation of the economy in order to attain national strength and industrialization—all of these Stalinist policies are familiar features of elite revolutions. However, Stalinist modernization did not depend on the encouragement of a class of rich peasants but on the destruction of this class in order to seize the surplus agricultural product needed to support industrialization.

Counterrevolution.   Another type of change in the political system that is related to but distinct from revolution is counterrevolution. Some writers use the word *counterrevolutionary* to refer to any movement or elite action that is opposed to revolution, as we have defined it. But when such a movement or elite uses the state apparatus to destroy a revolutionary movement, we may refer to this behavior as counterrevolutionary in a narrower sense.

Counterrevolutions differ in character depending on which groups are in control of the state apparatus. If groups opposing revolutionary change in class relations are in power, then counterrevolution really takes the form of defending the status quo; such, for example, is the situation at present in Brazil. But quite frequently, counterrevolution involves recapturing the state apparatus from reformers who have won it through elections and are using it to modify existing class relations. This recapture is often violent and nonlegitimate. The military coups in Chile, Brazil, Bolivia, and Greece are fairly recent examples of such counterrevolutionary action. Franco's revolt in Spain and the subsequent Spanish Civil War of the late 1930s is another example. The "White Russian" offensive against the Bolsheviks after the Russian Revolution is an example of an unsuccessful counterrevolution. Finally, Italian fascism and German nazism are especially interesting examples of counterrevolutionary movements.

The mechanisms of rule in all these cases of counterrevolution are fairly similar but are most extensively developed in fascism and nazism. Property owners, both large and small, feel threatened by efforts of either moderately socialistic or left-liberal governments to curtail their class power, and by strong militant left-wing movements. Weakness or crisis in the economy may add to the sense of being threatened and may also spread confusion to professional and lower-level white-collar strata. The counterrevolutionary forces promise protection against the Left and assert that they can restore order and even prosperity. They gain sufficient support, primarily among the bourgeoisie, the petite bourgeoisie, and some white-collar employees, to be able to capture the state apparatus, sometimes through elections, sometimes through political or paramilitary pressure on weak politicians, and sometimes by gaining support in the army in order to stage a coup.

Once in power, the counterrevolutionaries use this combination of public support, political and paramilitary pressure, and control of the police and armed forces to develop an extremely strong state apparatus. The status quo of property relations— class relations—is preserved but at the cost of sustaining a large and overbearing state apparatus. The state apparatus (or the counterrevolutionary party or movement that controls it) uses violence against any possible opposition. It regulates the economy, preserves private property and profit-seeking, destroys the independence of unions, and sets priorities in production. The resulting economy is capitalistic but it certainly is not a free-market capitalist economy. The state takes an active role in shaping personal relationships, in generating ideology, and in running the society. For example, it destroys opposition parties, makes voluntary associations (such as youth groups) part of the state (or party) structure, takes over or tightly censors the media, and penetrates local decision-making groups.

Ideologically, the counterrevolutionary government seeks to give a revolutionary aura to its essentially conservative protection of the class order. Its appeals are repeatedly to "the common man" or the "little man"—basically the hard-pressed family farmer, small entrepreneur, or white-collar worker rather than the industrial proletariat. The state also tries to breathe new life into the economy, sometimes by going to war and encouraging expansion of the military sector, sometimes by initiating state-run ventures, such as the S.S. industries in Nazi Germany. Fascism has been variously analyzed as a terminal stage of capitalism and as a type of society in which a strong state dominates a weakened private economic sector. It is perhaps most useful to sidestep the question of whether it is a "terminal" form of capitalism and emphasize instead how capitalist profits and relations of production are preserved but only at the cost of state regulation of most other aspects of the society.

Coup d'état.   A much less interesting form of nonrevolutionary phenomena that involves seizure of the state apparatus is the coup d'état. A coup is a seizure of the upper levels of the state apparatus that involves only a replacement of incumbents by a new elite. The class allegiance of the state, the state's policies, the behavior of its functionaries, its ideology, and the structure of the society remain unaltered. In some societies coups are a rather routine way of changing elites.

Examples of Revolutions

In the following pages, I shall very briefly summarize some characteristics of major revolutions. For each one, I shall try to identify its class base, the organization or organizations that carried out seizure of the state apparatus, the way in which the class relationships were altered, the way in which the state apparatus was restructured, and the way in which the ideology was changed. These summaries are *not* meant to be descriptions of the events of these revolutions. The reader should turn to a standard history text, a good encyclopedia, or one of the works listed in the bibliography (e.g., Moore, 1966; Wolf, 1969) to obtain a descriptive summary.

The English Revolution or "Civil War."   The first revolution I shall discuss began with the English Civil War of 1642–1651 and culminated in the bloodless Glorious Revolution of 1688–1689. This period saw the end not only of absolute monarchy in England but also of the last vestiges of feudalism.

Class base.   At the core of the transformation of English society in the second half of the seventeenth century were commercial strata, especially those groups who sought a free hand in establishing profit-making commercial agriculture and sheep-raising. In England during this period, the line between landlords who turned to commercial enterprises and capitalists is virtually impossible to draw. The Civil War swept away the last remaining barriers to the enclosure system. Thereafter, the landed upper classes freely expropriated peasant communities and drove peasants from the land, thus freeing the land for commercial rather than subsistence uses. For a variety of reasons, urban commercial interests tended to join these landholders in opposition to the crown and the Anglican church.

The organizational vehicle.   Parliament and the Puritan army were the vehicles of revolution.

Changes in class relationships.   I have already commented on the fact that the major change was the dominance of a capitalist organization of production over subsistence production forms. This switch occurred most dramatically in the countryside. The victims were peasants who lost their common lands and their own plots and became landless laborers. At the same time, commercial agriculture provided the food, the wool, and the capital that would eventually be needed for industrialization. What changed was not so much the incumbents of ruling-class positions (landlords dominated English society both before and after the Civil War); but rather the terms of their dominance (from feudal lord to enterpreneur), the nature of the productive process that they controlled (from subsistence to commercial agriculture), the kinds of relationships they had with the peasants (from landlord to capitalist employer), the purposes of landownership (for profit rather than direct consumption), and the nature of peasant life (from subsistence farming to labor as a landless worker or tenant or to existence on poor relief—in other words, from bad to worse).

Changes in the state.   The power of the crown was greatly diminished. After the Glorious Revolution of 1688, "England settled down in the eighteenth century to government by Parliament" (Moore, 1966: 21). The absolutist monarchy, its court, and its rather weak bureaucracy, along with some vestiges of democratic local government, were replaced by Parliament "as a committee of landlords" and of urban commercial interests.

Changes in ideology.   Much of the language of this dispute was religious: the *Puritan* army and Parliament opposed the *Anglican* crown. But the English Revolution marked the final end of violent religious conflict in most of Europe. The emphasis on changing political and economic forms repeatedly breaks through the Old Testament imagery of the Puritan army and parliaments.

The American Revolution.   The second revolution I shall discuss took place in England's American colonies between 1776 and 1781.

Class base.   The American Revolution's class base was primarily among the small entrepreneurs and propertied and tenant farmers who constituted a large proportion of the population. The revolution had some support from property-less urban white laborers, from some large landed proprietors, and from some urban merchants. It was opposed by factions of landed proprietors, merchants, and slaves. Insofar as the revolution directed much of its opposition toward classes outside of the colonies—the British mercantile interests and the West Indian planters—it drew some support from almost all colonial strata.

Organizational vehicles.   The Sons of Liberty, the Committees of Correspondence, the Continental Congress (most importantly), the Committees of Public Safety, and the Continental army comprised the vehicles of revolution.

Changes in class relations.   Some writers question whether the American Revolution was in fact a revolution because it produced no dramatic change in class relations within the colonies. During the war, Loyalists' estates were confiscated, and the land was distributed to the tenants. In general, small landholders and small entrepreneurs probably benefited from the defeat of British mercantile interests but not nearly as much as they had hoped to. The unrest among veterans and small holders in the years between the war and the framing of the Constitution attests to considerable disappointment.

Political changes.   The American Revolution was much more a transformation of political institutions than of class structure. It unified the colonies and separated them from the British crown. The nationalist and antiroyalist thrust of these changes were precursors of the demands of revolutionaries throughout Europe in the early nineteenth century. Thus, while a somewhat geographically isolated case, the American Revolution was a preview of bourgeois support of limited representative government, nationalism, and national economic development. The American War of Independence was one of a series of revolutions to curtail and abolish monarchical power and to open political institutions to elected representatives.

Ideological change.   The ideology of national independence, decision-making through representative government, and citizenship were all explicitly presented in the writings of the revolution. Emphasis was on the right of the citizens of a state to participate in its decision-making procedures. The state was to be demystified—stripped of religious and other traditional trappings. In the American Revolution, unlike later revolutions, there was little effort to use the political system—the state apparatus—to alter class relations. However, men like Jefferson were aware that their vision of mass participation in government was possible only in a society of relative economic equality.

For Jefferson, this equality could be realized only in a nation of farmers and small entrepreneurs. But the Industrial Revolution, the increasing power and concentration of capital in the hands of a financial and manufacturing class, and the increase in the number of landless urban laborers—all these made Jefferson's dream of a small-holder republic fade almost at the moment of its realization. Lacking the ability and perhaps also the desire to use the state to impose a particular class structure on the society, the left wing of the American Revolution lived to witness the ease with which the institution of representative government turned away from its earlier economic base of small entrepreneurs and farmers to embrace the rise of modern large-scale capitalism.

The French Revolution. The next revolution I shall discuss took place in France between 1789–1794. It grew out of a deep discontent with the Old Régime and was fired by the sentiments and accomplishments of the American Revolution.

Class base. The French Revolution is a good example of a revolution based on a number of classes temporarily and uneasily working in more or less the same direction. We can distinguish the targets clearly—the royal court and the landed aristocracy. Also easy to discern were the various revolutionary groups —the rich peasants, the landless peasants, the urban poor (the *sans-culottes*, a stratum of artisans and workers not yet transformed into an industrial proletariat), the bourgeoisie proper, and a more radical wing of the bourgeoisie composed of smaller property owners and intellectuals.

The French Revolution was in many respects a number of different revolutions with distinct class bases. Some of these revolutions were successful while others failed. Specifically, the power of the king and the court were abolished. The landed aristocracy was destroyed by the combined forces of the richer and poorer peasants and did not become a force in the commercialization of agriculture (as the landed gentry had in England). The bourgeoisie gained control of the state apparatus; however, for a period of time they lost it to their radical left wing, which was more ready to support the revolutions of the propertyless rural and urban poor. These latter groups were never in control of the state apparatus either in Paris or the countryside, but they did force the parties that controlled the state to requisition food, compel its sale at controlled prices, and to institute the Reign of Terror. The means available to the propertyless groups were primarily riots and direct seizures of property.

Organizational vehicles. For the bourgeoisie, the major occupational vehicle was the Gironde, a party that included moderate revolutionaries as well as representatives of commercial and shipping interests. For the radical bourgeoisie and its allies, the vehicle was the Jacobin faction and the Committee of Public Safety (the Jacobin organization that managed the Terror, created the army to repel the expropriated nobles and their allies, defeated the counter-revolution, and attempted to requisition and distribute food). The poor were not organized into distinct lasting society-wide parties. As is generally the case, there is not a perfect fit between classes and parties.

Changes in class structure. The bourgeoisie consolidated its already established economic power by gaining control of the state. The wealthy peasants became the dominant force in the countryside. They blocked the radical revolution of the Jacobin left and of the urban and rural poor and kept their hold on the development of commercial agriculture in France into the twentieth century. The urban and rural poor did not succeed in maintaining the redistribution of wealth for which they fought.

Changes in the political system. The French Revolution wiped away the complex of monarchy and aristocracy. In its place it established the prototype of the modern state and the beginnings of the relation between state power and bourgeois class power that we have discussed. The revolution established citizenship and equality before the law. At the same time, the revolutionary state maintained the centralized form that had characterized the French state before the revolution. In some respects, the state's power increased, and it developed new functions and prerogatives, such as universal conscription.

Changes in ideology. With the French Revolution, the rights of citizenship, equality before law, and private property (especially the ability to buy and sell land as a commodity rather than to control it as a feudal right) were linked together ideologically as well as in the actions of the state. Social institutions were declared to be the result of human actions, not of divine or traditional forces; thus political behavior was demystified. As part of this process, church and state were separated. The world view of a sizable segment of the revolutionaries came to be formulated in the universally appealing term, *the rights of man.*

The American Civil War. The next revolution I shall discuss took place between 1860 and 1865. The American Civil War has been called the "last bourgeois revolution" in the sense that it is the last conflict in which the bourgeoisie used state power to destroy a precapitalist ruling class. Specifically, the federal government destroyed the Southern slave-owning class.

Class base. The class base of this conflict was the coalition of Northern small landholders and entrepreneurs, who felt threatened by the possible westward expansion of slavery, and Northern industrialists who were eager to open up the South to Northern capital. Like all major revolutions, the Civil War depended on class coalitions. And like all major revolutions, it had an ideology

—the revulsion that Northerners felt for the institution of slavery. I must emphasize that this was not "mere ideology," that is, cynical lip service to a set of ideals that cover up economic self-interest. On the contrary, the beliefs were held in good faith and were part of a whole way of life, a *system* that included the mode of production, political institutions, and a vision of human behavior.

The South represented a distinct system. As in capitalism, the Southern system produced for a market that brought profit to the class that controlled its resources. Cotton-growing was commercial and not subsistence agriculture, and it actually depended on the capitalist industrial production of the British textile industry. But, unlike capitalism, the Southern system was based on unfree labor. The ruling class of Southern planters controlled not only land and tools but also the bodies of the producers rather than only their labor power for a limited number of hours. Regardless of whether the Southern economy was moving toward industrialization, the nature of the relationship between producers and the ruling class made it distinct from capitalism. Tied to this difference was a difference in ideology, in values and beliefs.

Organizational vehicles.   The carriers of this "last bourgeois revolution" were the Radical Republicans acting through the federal government and the Union army. Also important as the generator of Northern ideology was the abolitionist movement.

Changes in class structure.   The Civil War destroyed the Southern system. It turned the slaves into a class of free laborers. The Radical Republicans' dream of confiscating estates and distributing them to former slaves was not realized, so the emancipated slaves became landless laborers and sharecroppers, bound to the plantation South by debts, terrorism (after Reconstruction), and limited alternative economic opportunities. The ruling class of slaveholders lost much but not all of its power; Northern steel and railroad interests became important forces in the Southern economy.

The South continued to exist as a distinct region, more agrarian than the North, still partially dominated by a planter elite, and weighed down with its ideology of defeat and racial hierarchy. However, it was no longer a distinct *system,* with a mode of production and, particularly, a set of class relationships that were qualitatively different from those of Northern capitalism. Nor did the South have its own state apparatus as it did in the period of the Confederacy. But some people argue that the reluctance of Northern property owners to confiscate land and give it to the former slaves who had worked on it prevented a real revolution that would have turned blacks into small landholders. In other words, given a choice between protecting property rights of landowners and creating a new group of small property owners, the Northern authorities opted for the former.

Political change.   The efforts of the Southern ruling class to have its own state —the Confederacy—were decisively defeated. The destruction of the state armor that protected the Southern system of class relations—slavery—led to the collapse of slavery itself. Reconstruction was in many respects a battle for local political institutions. Insofar as Radical Republicans lost on both land reform and the continued presence of Union troops, this struggle marked the defeat of Southern blacks. They were kept from access to political institutions by terror and later by legislation and custom.

Changes in ideology.   The South maintained separate folkways and laws in the area of race relations. Its culture was distinct but lacked centralized state support. It was converted from an ideology into a subculture within a larger system. In terms of American society as a whole, the federal government reaffirmed a free-labor market and supported the emerging capitalist/industrial way of life.

The Mexican Revolution.   The next revolution I shall discuss took place in Mexico between 1910 and 1920. For thirty-four years (1876–1910), President Porfirio Díaz controlled Mexico with absolute authority. During his long administration, Indian and communal lands came into the possession of the large landowners, economic concessions were granted to foreign companies, the working classes were exploited, and participation in government was limited to a favored few. The overthrow of Diaz initiated an era of revolution.

Class base.   The class base of the Mexican Revolution was very diverse. It included the peasantry, especially in the northern state of Chihuahua and in the south-central state of Morelos, but also middle-class liberals and radicals. In the rural areas, revolutionaries included not only Indian communities and laborers on haciendas, but also small landholders and provincial officials. A still small industrial work force in the textile mills, mines, and railroads also was involved. As in other major revolutions, the class base was in fact a broad coalition, initially united against the dictatorial central government and the large landowners.

Organizational vehicles.   Among the intellectuals, liberal clubs were organized to combat peonage and brutality on the haciendas and to establish free elections. More radical socialist and anarchist groups also formed an initial political nucleus. Later, power was concentrated in the revolutionary armies commanded by Zapata (in Morelos) and by Pancho Villa (in the north). Among the liberals who first supported reform but later opposed Zapata and Villa, power was concentrated in the constitutionalist army. Unlike other twentieth-century revolutions, the Mexican Revolution had no central revolutionary party or even "any one group organized around a central program" (Wolf, 1969: 27).

Changes in class structure. The Mexican Revolution produced only partial changes in class structure. Some land reform and labor legislation did result. Where Indian communities had seized back land that landowners had taken from them (as in Morelos), they were able to keep it. Other peasant communities also regained their land. Peonage was abolished. "But there was no general redistribution of land" (Wolf, 1969: 44). Nor did the small group of industrial workers seize the companies, despite the socialist and anarchist language of the revolution's ideologues. Foreign capital was neither thoroughly nor permanently driven from the country. What changes did take place in rural class relations were drawn out over many years. The liberal aim of creating a free labor force (embodied in the abolition of peonage) to some extent conflicted with the anarcho-socialist goal of supporting communal landownership instead of private commercial agriculture. These issues were not resolved during the revolutionary period, and they continue to be sources of conflict into the present.

Political changes. The overall result was a constitutional government with a strong central executive:

> Final victory rewarded an elite [the middle-class constitutionalists] which had created a viable army, demonstrated bureaucratic competence, and consolidated its control over the vital export sector of the economy. This elite also proved flexible enough to initiate agrarian and labor reforms demanded by the revolutionary generals within a larger policy of national economic progress, congruent with the interests of an expanding middle class of entrepreneurs and professionals. The result has been the formation of a strong central executive which fosters capitalist development, but is in a position to balance the claims of peasants and industrial workers against those of entrepreneurs and middle-class groups (Wolf, 1969:47–48).

Wolf (1969:46) also points out:

> The government party has become as much an instrument of control as an instrument of representation. Within it interest groups—organized into formal associations of agrarians, workers, entrepreneurs, military, bureaucrats, and professionals—are linked to territorial groups, based on the several federated Mexican states. This linkage makes for a powerful executive, able to play off interest groups against territorial units and interest groups against each other. The final product bears a strong resemblance to the corporate state structure of fascist Italy or Spain, albeit with the rhetoric of social justice and socialism.

Ideological changes.   Paralleling the overlap and conflict of the liberal and radical revolutions, one finds a mixture of liberal ideology (citizenship, free labor, etc.) and anarchist and socialist ideology. Lacking a large industrial working class, the Mexican radicals tended to emphasize anarchist imagery of peasant communes rather than socialist visions. All of these ideologies, combined with nationalism, have produced an un-unified ideological base for the postrevolutionary society. As in France, where the radical revolution also eventually lost out to the liberal revolution, Mexico has a strong national revolutionary tradition and a great uncertainty as to what that tradition means.

The Russian Revolution.   In many respects, the Russian Revolution really consisted of three subrevolutions in which the society moved from a condition of backward capitalism with an absolutist monarchy to a condition of industrially developed state socialism. The long process of transformation began in February 1917 and was not fully consolidated until the 1930s.

Class base.   The three subrevolutions that made up the Russian Revolution were: (1) a liberal revolution in February 1917, in which parties with a middle-class base and strong support from all other sectors of the society swept away an inept czar and diminished the power of the landed aristocracy; (2) a socialist revolution in October 1917, in which one of several parties representing the interests primarily of industrial workers and secondarily of peasants seized power; and (3) in 1929–1930, a much delayed movement against rich peasants, in which the state undertook to destroy their power, force the collectivization of Russian agriculture, and extract a larger agricultural surplus in order to provide a basis for industrialization.

Organizational vehicles.   For the February revolution, an organizational vehicle is scarcely identifiable, although several parties had spent the preceding years organizing among workers, peasants and soldiers. The government fell to the spontaneous action of workers, soldiers, and peasants. In the next few months, however, the Provisional Government was guided by an uneasy collection of parties, many of them with middle-class support. In the October revolution, the Bolsheviks emerged as the dominant party. The Stalinist collectivization of agriculture in 1929 was largely the work of the Communist party and the state apparatus. In the Russian Revolution, power was more effectively wielded by a radical antibourgeois party than by the organizations primarily representing middle-class moderates. In this respect, the Russian Revolution was decisively different from preceding revolutions.

Changes in class structure.   The first phase of the revolution, the fall of the czarist government, made possible (although not legitimate) the expropriation of large estates. Power shifted de facto into the hands of soviets (councils) of peasants, soldiers, and workers. The Bolshevik revolution merely gave formal recognition to this land seizure. For a while after the October revolution, the peasant revolt in the countryside and the revolution of workers and soldiers under Bolshevik leadership were synchronized and compatible. In the winter of 1917–1918, anti-Bolshevik forces launched a counterattack. As the civil war intensified in the following years, the Bolsheviks had to raise food and men for the Red army. They began a program of food requisitioning and conscription, and started the struggle for agricultural surplus by separating the "poor peasants" and "middle peasants" from the kulaks (rich peasants). The reliable core of the army was proletarian rather than peasant. The years between the civil war and collectivization were years of uneasy truce in the countryside. In 1929, the kulaks were defeated and many of them were killed in what amounted to a war in the countryside; collectivization was enforced. The peasantry was largely transformed from a mixed group of small entrepreneurs and landless laborers into workers in national enterprises.

Meanwhile, after the Bolshevik revolution, the aristocracy, the wealthy bourgeoisie, and some parts of the intelligentsia (the managerial and ideological middle classes) disappeared through death or flight. A new intelligentsia began to develop, much of it of proletarian or even peasant background. The industrial labor force greatly increased, especially after 1929. The end result is a society with the following social structure: (1) a higher percentage (than in the West) of agricultural workers, who are the least-advantaged people in terms of income, access to education, urban amenities, and so on; (2) a substantial industrial work force; and (3) a large intelligentsia, who perform professional, ideological, and managerial tasks, and whose upper levels make the major decisions about the use of resources and the goals of the system of production. The power of this third group is built into organizations, above all the Communist party and the state bureaucracies, including those bureaucracies in charge of productive enterprises.

Political changes. Russian society has traditionally had a strong state apparatus and large centralized bureaucracies. These features appeared in the postrevolutionary as well as czarist regimes. The exigencies of civil war, collectivization, and World War II led to an expanded state apparatus. The state failed to wither away as some Socialists had hoped it would after the consolidation of the revolution and the decisive victory of the proletariat. A variety of institutions that may be necessary in the early stages of socialism—concentration of power in the upper levels of the Party, unequal wage scales, strong centralization of decision-making, and limitations on cultural expression—have continued to persist for a very long time.

Ideological change. Party ideologues legitimated the new order in terms of the exigencies of war, the hostility of the encircling capitalist nations, and the need for rapid development. With the failure of revolutionary movements in western Europe in the 1920s and the war against Nazi Germany, strongly nationalist ideology was coupled to socialist ideology.

Revolution in China.   The next revolution I shall discuss took place in a country that had just emerged from two thousand years of dynastic rule, a floundering republic fragmented by competing warlords and foreign economic interests. Two forces were to contend for the new China: the old revolutionary Nationalist party (Kuomintang) of Sun Yat-sen, which turned conservative under his successor, Chiang Kai-shek, and the Chinese Communist party of Mao Tse-tung.

Class base.   The Chinese revolution was won primarily in the countryside, where increasingly large areas of land were wrested away from the landlords, warlords, nationalist groups (especially the Kuomintang under Chiang Kai-shek), and the Japanese invaders. Not until the late 1920s and the 1930s, when Kuomintang forced the Communists out of the cities and away from their hoped-for working-class base, did the Communists begin to focus on the peasants, above all the poorer peasants who were first organized against the landlords and later against the rich peasants as well.

Organizational vehicles.   In the earlier years of efforts to modernize Chinese society, the Chinese Communist party (CCP) had worked with the Nationalist party (KMT). After the rupture of this alliance following a KMT massacre of CCP members in Shanghai in 1927, the CCP became the revolutionary organization, along with its military arm, the Red army. Communist party membership fluctuated, reaching more than one million by the end of World War II. In the beginning, many Party members came from rich peasant backgrounds and were trained as intellectuals; many were from industrial working-class backgrounds. Later, however, Party membership included many more children of poor peasants.

Changes in class structure.   Following the Communist victory, the major change in class structure was the destruction of the landlord class, the reduction of rich and middle peasants to ordinary commune membership, and the uplifting of poor peasants to commune membership. In other words, in the countryside, private land ownership was abolished, and the peasantry was organized into large communities (communes of up to ninety thousand members) with communal control of the land, subject to state and Party decision-making. The same type of socialized control of factories replaced private ownership, including foreign ownership in China's growing industrial sector. The large number of tiny entrepreneurs (street vendors, beggars, prostitutes, and so on) characteristic of the economy of underdeveloped countries was absorbed into large-scale urban and rural production.

At the micro level, this reorganization of production in China permits considerable local decision-making by communes and work teams—that is, considerable amounts of worker control. At the macro level, the reorganization of production allows peasants to have a much higher standard of living than before while producing a larger surplus for use in national economic development.

Political change.   The fragmented, faction-ridden pre-Communist government was replaced by a strong central state with a nonhereditary elite and considerable openness to mobility through the Party hierarchy. Some decisions are made locally. Even upper-level decision-making strongly depends on information and public opinion issued from below. The army remains a strong integrating force that participates in building public works, gives its members a sense of China as a whole beyond the confines of their communes, and keeps order where conflicts cannot be contained in the existing framework of discussion and criticism.

Ideological changes.   The increased standard of living and the vast material improvement over pre-communist China undoubtedly make people accept the new order.

Micro-level institutions—for example, arbitration of disputes, criticism and self-criticism, and discussion based on the writings of Mao—serve to build support for the new society. The symbolic importance of Mao's writings as a guide to conduct are important, as are political dramas and operas. Large public works, such as dams or hillside terraces, not only increase production but also give a sense of common purpose. Although the new ideology attacks much of traditional Chinese culture, some of the new ways of holding the society together seem to be drawn from Chinese culture as well as from Western Marxist thought.

The Cuban Revolution.   The next revolution I shall discuss took place in Cuba between 1956 and 1960. A Spanish colony for over four hundred years, Cuba came under U.S. influence following the Spanish-American War. Cuba's prerevolutionary economy was dominated by sugar, its politics by graft and corruption.

Class base.   The class base of the Cuban revolution was primarily a rural proletariat of sugar workers. These workers were not tenant or small-holding farmers, nor were they traditional peons. On the contrary, they had many of the characteristics of an industrial proletariat, but they were especially disadvantaged by seasonal unemployment. The Cuban bourgeoisie was dependent on American business. The sugar industry (as well as tourism and real estate) was dominated by American capital. In addition, there were large numbers of professionals and government officials and an insecure stratum of "servants, waiters, entertainers, and procurers" (Wolf, 1969:261).

Organizational vehicle.   The rebel army of Fidel Castro developed separately from the existing Cuban Communist party. Castro's guerillas, who numbered about two thousand, included many revolutionary intellectuals—students, doctors, lawyers, and some unemployed. Establishing themselves among a subsistence peasantry in the mountains along the southeastern coast, Castro and his supporters were able to win the revolution without first mobilizing the large mass of sugar workers.

Changes in class structure.   The dependence on American capital was broken but not without some dependence on loans and technical aid from the Soviet Union. Sugar continued to be a major crop, but efforts were made to diversify into other crops, livestock, and light industry. Agricultural enterprises were organized as collectives and state farms. In an economy in which most rural workers were proletarian, this transformation was much less violent than in the countries where the peasant population had hopes of becoming and/or remaining small landholders.

Professionals and the petite bourgeoisie left the country. The nearness of the United States made repression or political conversion of these groups less attractive than permitting them to leave, a policy in effect until 1970. Efforts were made to rapidly open the educational system to the children of the urban and rural poor and to train doctors and teachers. Older people were taught to read and write.

To some degree, a money economy was replaced by distribution of goods on the basis of need, work contribution, and political participation. But the changeover to a moneyless economy has not been complete. The issue of incentives remains. Recently steps were taken to institute piecework and monetary incentives, in addition to social pressure, as an incentive to work. And, as in some other Socialist states, a "black market" of illegal petty entrepreneurial activities exists as a way of distributing scarce goods.

The Party and politically active persons have also tried to change family structure and sex roles and to diminish the macho ideology of male supremacy. These efforts have met with considerable success.

Political changes.   Decision-making is carried out much as in China; however, since Cuba is a smaller society, the magnitude of the problem of direction is much less. As in other countries with state socialism, the Communist party is the effective political elite, but the state is relatively unbureaucratized and is responsive to local opinion. Important issues are discussed in mass political organizations, and experiments with local elections have begun.

Ideological changes.   As a country that was already quite modern, with most of the population in contact with Western urban culture and media, Cuba has had less of a problem with ideological direction than have countries with large backward peasant masses. Castro serves as an important integrating symbol.

In some respects, Cuba presented an ideal laboratory for revolution: the area and population were relatively small; dissidents could emigrate easily; the population was largely uninterested in gaining land for privately owned subsistence farms; and, by socialization and national culture, the people were lively, active, and volatile. Revolution could therefore transform the society with relatively little violence and repression. On the other hand, proximity to the United States and a substantially one-crop economy presented military and economic problems.

Revolution in Vietnam.   The last revolution to be discussed in this section took place in Vietnam, a country with a long history of foreign domination— first by the Chinese, then by the French, the Japanese (briefly, during World War II), and finally the Americans. Equally significant is the Vietnamese tradition of native resistance, for decades if need be. The revolution that ended on April 30, 1975 with the fall of Saigon and the evacuation of remaining American personnel began on the night of February 9–10, 1930 as an unsuccessful military uprising against French colonial rule.

Class base.   Tenant farmers provided the class base of the Vietnamese revolution. Tenancy and landlessness had markedly increased during French colonial rule. As in other revolutions, the revolutionary organization was in the beginning composed largely of alienated intellectuals of professional and petit bourgeois backgrounds.

Organizational vehicles.   The Communists and the Nationalist Vietnamese party provided early leadership, but they were severely repressed following the unsuccessful uprising in the early 1930s. The Viet Minh, a coalition of anti-French and anti-Japanese forces centered around a Communist core, renewed the struggle in the 1940s. With the ouster of the French in 1954, Vietnam was divided in two: North Vietnam and South Vietnam. In the North, the Communists controlled the state apparatus. In the South, after 1960, the National Liberation Front (NLF) became successor to the Viet Minh. The Viet Minh and the NLF in turn created networks in the villages that acted as courts, redistributed land, carried out political education, and maintained paramilitary activities.

Changes in class structure.   Between 1945 and 1953, the Viet Minh began the process of land reform in the areas it held. This land reform transformed tenants into small holders. The areas where the Viet Minh instituted land reform later provided more support for the NLF than did areas where tenancy had been uninterrupted (Wolf, 1969: 202–203).

   In the North, the landlords and rich peasants lost their land and power under conditions of local class conflict organized by the Communist party, much as in China. This first wave of change in rural class structure was very violent. In a second wave, after 1958, the peasantry was reorganized into collectives. By 1960, about 76 percent of the land in North Vietnam was collectivized (Wolf, 1969: 192). This second wave of change was much more relaxed and peaceful than the initial classification of the population into land-lords, rich peasants, middle peasants, and poor peasants and the expropriation of the wealthier categories. Even with collectivization, some inequalities in access to land and individually owned plots and livestock persisted.

In the South, this process is just beginning.

Political change.   In the North, the Communist party controls the state ap-paratus, and political institutions have many similarities to those of China, subject to differences in size and the strains of war. Political institutions provide for extensive information and opinion flow upwards, the politicization of village life, and the creation of many organizations to conduct political discussion, criticism and self-criticism, and so on.

In the South before its final victory the NLF carried out similar "orga-nization-building," providing cohesive and reasonably responsive political leadership in a society otherwise beset by corruption, warring sects, local strongmen, and a morally and politically bankrupt puppet regime.

Ideological change.   There has been a decisive shift from Buddhist, Animist, and Catholic belief systems to revolutionary Marxist ideology.

In our discussion of revolutions, we have emphasized the class base of revolution and de-emphasized nationalist sentiment. Nationalism can, how-ever, be a major expression for the interests of a group and, as such, is closely tied to class revolutions.

Conclusions

There are three ways of looking at these major revolutions: in terms of history; in terms of class structure and the relations of production, that is, whether bourgeois or postbourgeois; and, finally, in terms of shared character-istics.

The Historical Perspective.   First, revolutions can be viewed as unique his-torical phenomena. Each one is to some degree quite different from the others for two reasons: (1) They took place in different countries, with distinct histo-ries, social structures, and ways of life. (2) They took place at different times, in different historical settings. Later revolutions were influenced by the out-come of the earlier ones as well as by contemporary events.

The Bourgeois-Postbourgeois Perspective.   Second, revolutions can be split into two major groups, the bourgeois revolutions (through the American Civil War) and "postbourgeois" ones.

In the bourgeois revolutions, the state apparatus was seized and used to institute capitalist relations of production, sweeping away the remnants of earlier forms. For example, in England, the peasants' traditional rights to land were swept away, opening to large landowners the possibility of unregulated pursuit of commercial farming and livestock-raising. In France, the revolution broke the hold of the aristocracy and the court on the state, opening the way for commercial agriculture on small peasant holdings, and increasing the political power of the industrial and financial bourgeoisie. The American Civil War destroyed a class system based on slaves as the major source of labor in commercial farming.

Note how *each* of these bourgeois revolutions instituted the following kinds of behavior:

— The treatment of both land and labor power as commodities, as something to be bought and sold in a market
— The right to private property in land, with the understanding that it was to be used to make a profit
— Freedom of the labor force to hire itself out rather than to be bound by slavery or tradition to provide work for a feudal lord or a slave owner
—The use of the state to enforce these institutions

Each of these bourgeois revolutions attained these institutional arrangements differently, however, based on differently allied classes and social movements and with different consequences for the society. In England, the landowners transformed *themselves* into a bourgeoisie, which was agricultural rather than industrial and commercial, at the expense of the peasants, who were turned into landless laborers. In France, the rich peasants entered into a coalition with urban capitalists and became the stratum of commercial farmers, protected by a state essentially responsive to the urban capitalists. In the United States, the Northern bourgeoisie destroyed the slave-owning class's power over a state apparatus and asserted the right of the laborer to freely sell his labor power; however, the slaveholders had already been profit-seeking commercial farmers. There are both similarities and unique elements in the bourgeois revolutions.

The postbourgeois revolutions sought to establish new forms of class structure in which capitalist relations of production are superseded, the power of capitalists over the state is broken, and capitalists disappear as a class (if not necessarily as individual human beings). Generally, these revolutions are aimed at establishing some form of socialism, that is, (1) de jure ownership of all enterprises by the people as a whole (sometimes with de facto control resting in the state apparatus and/or a particular organization, the Communist party); (2) the disappearance of profit as a goal or criterion of production and its replacement by the needs and wants of the entire population (in some of the resulting economies, the efficiency of an enterprise is still a factor in its viability; and while profits no longer are a source of wealth, considerable disparities in wage-and-salary income exist); and (3) modification of the labor market by the state and local political institutions.

In fact, each of the bourgeois revolutions contained nonbourgeois movements and demands. In the English revolution, the radical sectarian wing of Diggers, Levellers and Ranters hoped to realize a society of great equality, with property distributed either to communities or to small landholders. Identifying these demands as "Socialist" or "Communist" is somewhat anachronistic; they are as much *traditional* opposition to large landowner and merchant capitalism as they are a preview of later attacks on private property. The imagery is largely religious, often an ecstatic millenarianism.

In the French Revolution, we have already seen how there was a strong and explicitly antibourgeois radical revolution within the larger revolution, how this radical revolution was based on classes of poor peasants and artisans, and how it took the form of rioting, expropriation, and demands for state control of the economy on behalf of the poor. The ideology and imagery of the radical groups in the French Revolution were far more secularized and explicitly political than those of the radicals in seventeenth-century England. We also saw how these demands—for example, Robespierre's assertion that "everything which is necessary to maintain life must be common good and only the surplus can be recognized as private property"—were adopted by the state for only a very short period during the revolution and were soon lost in favor of bourgeois conceptions of the economy and social structure.

In the American Civil War, radical ideas surfaced even less and only in very ambiguous forms. The Radical Republicans pressed for the expropriation of the plantation owners (a violation of property rights) only to establish former slaves as a class of petit bourgeois farmers, not to negate private property in principle. Even this moderate violation of property rights was not acceptable or enforced.

In the postbourgeois revolutions, the situation is reversed. The attack on capitalist class relationships has been the *central* thrust of the revolutions, but of necessity included some attacks on precapitalist social arrangements. In all the countries in which socialist revolutions have taken place, the mode of production was largely agricultural, landlords were an extremely powerful class, and the society was generally "backward"—that is, not a modern industrial capitalist nation at all. Most were dominated by an oligarchy of landowners who were in the process of transforming themselves from traditional landlords into commercial landlords; some even had aspirations to become industrial capitalists. In addition, the industry and commerce of the countries, such as they were, were heavily dominated by foreign capital. Thus the revolutionary groups in these societies had three tasks that were not entirely compatible:

1. To oust foreign capital
2. To use the peasantry to destroy the traditional aspects of landlord rule and thus make the agricultural sector productive enough to sustain

industrial development, that is, to carry out the task previously undertaken elsewhere by bourgeois revolutions

3. Simultaneously to carry out some kind of industrialization without an industrial bourgeoisie or capitalist property institutions

In other words, the postbourgeois revolutions were faced with the problem of also having to carry out the productive task that elsewhere was accomplished by the bourgeois revolutions, namely, to free the agricultural sector from traditional constraints and increase its productivity to provide a base for economic development. The strains of accomplishing this acceleration of development (or this leaping over the stage of capitalism) tended to produce a number of outcomes. One was a society that was not fully socialist and had failed to achieve the first and third tasks (such as Mexico and many countries in Africa, Asia, and Latin America.) Such societies tend to still be economically dominated by the industrialized countries and to have substantial private sectors. Another outcome was a society that had accomplished all three tasks but only at the cost of building up a repressive and bureaucratized state. An example of this outcome is the Soviet Union, with its brutal treatment of the peasantry to achieve an agricultural surplus, its continued lagging behind the West in agricultural productivity, and its large state apparatus. Cuba, China, and Vietnam have been able to cope with their threefold task—national liberation from foreign control, increased agricultural production, and development of a modern partially industrialized socialist economy—somewhat better than the Soviet Union has, having learned from the U.S.S.R.'s mistakes and, to some extent, directly benefited from Soviet aid.

In other words, bourgeois revolutions "already" contained antibourgeois currents of thought and action, while postbourgeois revolutions "still" had to deal with the same tasks of economic development and destruction of traditions that bourgeois revolutions had to accomplish.

The Features-in-Common Perspective.   A third perspective on these revolutions sees them neither as unique historical cases, nor as outstanding examples of a general trend from traditional precapitalist forms through capitalism to socialist society, but as all sharing certain features:

1. All of them, by definition, involved transformations of class structure.

2. All of them, by definition, involved the seizure of the state apparatus by an organization that represented a class or a coalition of classes. By *represented* I mean that the organization not only articulated class interests in a narrow economic sense but also had a vision of an altered society, of a totally new type of existence.

3. All the revolutions involved ideological change, specifically, some view of a new way of life in which the outlook of a particular class could be transformed into universal values. Thus, for example, the capitalist institutions of private property, profit-making, and the hiring of a "free" landless and

toolless labor force could all be encompassed in a world view of freedom, individual pursuit of life, liberty, happiness, and property; freedom from state control; an open class system in place of rigid hereditary castes; emphasis on ownership of wordly goods instead of emphasis on religious salvation; secularism; and so on. It cannot be emphasized enough how these ideas were not cynically manufactured to justify the capitalist relations of production but rather developed along with these relations and were accepted by persons who were uninterested in immediate economic benefits from the system.

4. All the major revolutions were really "packages" or clusters of smaller revolutions that reflected the interests of different classes. Some of these smaller revolutions were more fully realized than others.

5. Revolutions (in the sense in which I use the word) tended to appear only after people had developed a secular concept of society as a collection of institutions that are created by human beings and are, at least within limits, subject to change by human beings. Specifically, this involved some sense that class relationships are not immutable, that change can and should occur, and that the state exists as a possible vehicle of such change. These conceptions developed as the feudal order collapsed, in the turmoil of the transitional period. They reflected the growing strength of the bourgeoisie, its opposition to the fixity of the feudal order, and its interest in economic and technological change as well as in political change. Postbourgeois revolutionaries have inherited the concepts of progress, secularism, and the consciousness of human beings as makers of their own destiny (within the limits set by historical circumstances).

6. The revolutions used violence to acquire control of the state apparatus.

7. Each of the revolutions was a struggle over how agriculture was to be modernized, what classes and political organizations were to control that process, and what was to be done with the resulting surplus—in other words, who was to get hold of it and how was it to be used.

8. Each revolution was a decisive moment of change during a longer series of upheavals. In a narrow sense the revolution was *preceded* by disturbances and abortive revolutions. The actual revolutionary seizure of power was *followed* by violence and local shifts in power as part of the transformation of the class structure.

9. The existing ruling classes were subjected to circumstances that broke their ability to rule: economic crises, the defection of their ideologues, and eventually loss of control over the armed forces. Their inability to weather economic crises and to command the loyalty of ideologues and soldiers in turn reflected strains in the society as a whole that weakened the hold of its ruling class. In the next section, I shall address myself to the question of what types of strains have this effect.

Hegemony and Contradictions

In this section, I shall explore two concepts—hegemony and contradictions—that provide insights into how societies as a whole collapse. The concept of hegemony draws attention to how ruling classes lose the consent of the ruled. The concept of contradictions draws attention to how strains in social structure can produce this loss of consent of control regardless of individuals' or even classes' understanding of the process.[3]

Characteristics of a Hegemonic Class

Why do ruling classes lose their grip? Why do they become unable to maintain a hold on the society? Why do they lose the loyalty of ideologues and specialists in coercion? Why are other groups in the society able to mobilize effectively against them? (In a way, I raised these questions at the end of the preceding section when I suggested that revolutions occurred only after ruling-class power had already weakened substantially.) On the other hand, when does a revolutionary class succeed in becoming a ruling class, in imposing its ideology, as well as its political and economic interests, on other classes? Such a form of rule has been called hegemony. A class that rules with the consent of the governed, that rules not by force alone but through organizations and practices that penetrate the whole society has been called a hegemonic class.

A hegemonic class has the following characteristics:

1. A hegemonic class *commands the loyalty of intellectuals.* It accomplishes this in two ways: by creating its own "organic" intellectuals and by winning over the traditional intellectuals.

Organic intellectuals are so called because they *grow out* of the organizations and institutions that serve the ruling class. In modern capitalist societies, these organic intellectuals include professors in the giant universities and media workers. As long as they do not step over certain boundaries, these organic intellectuals are free to criticize the social order. As a matter of fact, they are particularly valuable insofar as their conception of the social order transcends the narrow economic interests of the ruling class. Organic intellectuals also gain credibility if they come from non-ruling-class backgrounds and have no personal ties with the ruling class. It is their job to convince the masses that the social order makes sense. Most people in "the masses" care little or nothing about these conceptions; however, as more people in a modern society are at least partially educated, have some leisure time, and work as managers or professionals, ideological considerations have become more important than they are in societies where most people are peasants.

---

[3]In this section, I shall draw heavily on the works of Althusser (1970), Gramsci (1971), and Garner (1974).

Traditional intellectuals are "leftovers" from past types of societies. For example, in nineteenth-century European Catholic countries, the clergy were traditional intellectuals who came to support the capitalist state. They had been the organic intellectuals of feudalism—the people whose function it was to support the social order of feudalism. In the nineteenth century, they served the capitalist order instead by running schools, providing charity for the poor, and performing symbolic tasks such as blessing the troops.

Why does a hegemonic ruling class care about the loyalty of traditional intellectuals? Traditional intellectuals may help to assure "the loyalty of declining or marginal social groups for whom they provide intellectual leadership" (Garner, 1974:143). For example, Garner points out that in Italy, "rural intellectuals like lawyers, priests, schoolteachers, notaries and doctors are associated with the peasantry and the rural petty-bourgeoisie"; they assure the loyalty of these groups to the modern capitalist society that is emerging in Italy. Furthermore, traditional intellectuals who are loyal to the ruling class provide "an air of impartiality" to those institutions in which they work. For example, no one is surprised to find advertising copywriters (an organic intellectual of capitalism) praising capitalism. Everyone knows that copywriters support the interests of the capitalist class. But universities (which are heavily staffed by traditional intellectuals, especially in the liberal arts division) have claimed to be value free, concerned only with rational discourse, and in general to be detached from the class structure. This air of impartiality masks the fact that universities provide consultants to corporations and the state and train people for various positions in the capitalist system. Without traditional intellectuals—like professors of the humanities—a university could not keep up a front of impartiality and concern with only universal values.

2. A hegemonic ruling class *has a strong coherent conception of its own role.* For example, it may believe that the social order over which it presides is divinely ordained or natural. A ruling class that lacks this self-conception will have trouble attracting the support of intellectuals and will more frequently have to fall back on the use of violence to support its narrow economic interests. It may have to resort to violent organizations—such as the military or a Fascist party—to protect itself. These patterns are evident in the behavior of the nonhegemonic bourgeoisie of Italy under Mussolini and in some Latin American countries, which needed a fascist party and a fascist state to preserve it against the Left.

3. A hegemonic ruling class *maintains multiple organizational "lines of defense,"* such as political parties and voluntary associations (in a modern society). In one-party societies (like Nazi Germany), these organizational lines of defense provide unity and cohesion in the society because they are all organized by the single party or state. In bourgeois democracies, on the other hand, the strength of these lines of defense lies particularly in the fact that they are not organized by the state or a party, that many of them are organized from the bottom up, that membership is voluntary, and that they are not overtly

political. When a large proportion of the people in a society belong to a wide variety of competing associations or groups, the society tends to be more stable. (For example, the existence of working-class conservatives in England helps prevent that society from splitting into a working-class Left and a bourgeois/petit bourgeois/managerial-professional Right.)

Note that in the definition of hegemony that I present I emphasize not only the ideological aspects of hegemony—the "hearts and minds" of the people—but also the *practices,* the behavior or organizations, that establish class rule. Administrative routines and the way in which constraints on action are built into institutions are as important a part of hegemony as ideology.

Hegemony and Class Power

We might distinguish several situations of class power:

1. A class can be the oppressed class in a social system. The serfs in feudalism or the slaves in ancient Greece and Rome are examples of oppressed classes.
2. A class can be one of several contenders for power in a social system. The bourgeoisie in sixteenth- and seventeenth-century Europe, who were struggling against both the feudal nobility and the masses of the urban and rural poor, are an example of a class competing for power.
3. A class can control the state apparatus but rule mainly by force. The bourgeoisie in Chile and in other countries with right-wing military dictatorships exemplifies such a class.
4. A class can be hegemonic, that is, not only control the state and dominate the mode of production but also be supported by many institutions, voluntary organizations, and the "hearts and minds" of the people. The bourgeoisie in the United States and other advanced capitalist societies have generally enjoyed hegemony in the first half of the twenteith century.

Historically, there have been relatively few cases of long-term viable hegemony. The middle period of medieval feudalism—the years between 1000 and 1300—are perhaps a possible example. In ancient history, such hegemonic periods were probably somewhat longer because of the slow pace of technological change. With the rise of the bourgeoisie and the turmoil of industrial development, hegemony became harder to establish and maintain. The nineteenth century might be seen as a period when the European bourgeoisie established hegemonic control over the whole world: it was the century when the white man proudly carried his burden, when the sun never set on the British Empire, when the bourgeois way of life was believed to represent the pinnacle of human biological and cultural evolution. But capitalism contained within it such dynamic forces of technology and imperial expansion that it rapidly paved the way for its own transformation. Compared with the cultural and political continuity of the ancient empires and hydraulic states, the "triumph of the bourgeoisie" seems unstable.

Breakdowns of Hegemony: Contradictions

When does hegemony break down? There is no single cause for the collapse of a society and its hegemonic class. Rome did not fall in a day. A social order develops strains. Some of these strains can be overcome: adjustments are made or "just happen" that resolve the problem. Other strains indicate fundamental weaknesses in the social structure; over time they tend to get worse. These strains are often referred to as *contradictions* of the society. Many of these contradictions arise because of the different rates at which different types of institutions change. For example, technology and the productive system as a whole tend to change more rapidly than the political and ideological superstructure, which changes slowly and contains a large cargo of cultural "baggage" carried over from the past. This sort of strain has sometimes been referred to as "cultural lag."

Even more importantly, there are strains in the class system. The producers use a technology and develop behavior patterns that are incompatible with the way the ruling class and its managers expect them to produce. For example, modern workers have to cooperate in producing goods but are forced to compete with one another for scarce jobs.

A third reason why a hegemonic class may collapse is that the social system may be at odds with its natural environment; the society destroys the environment or damages it in some way. You may remember that the rise of class societies was associated with increased control over nature through agriculture, livestock-raising, irrigation systems, and so on. These ways of altering the ecosystem can have a variety of effects on the human society in that ecosystem. In other words, the productive capacity of a type of society outstrips the ability of social institutions to absorb and manage it. Sometimes damage to the ecosystem can be so severe that production and distribution of goods and services cannot take place in the manner to which the mass of people has become accustomed. Then social institutions, already strained by the existing productive system, may break down further.

Finally, the class society tends to build up opposition at its boundaries among hostile conquered people. Class societies are often expansionist societies. The conquered people or marginal groups at the boundaries are forced into special kinds of subordinate class positions, and the class society comes to depend on the exploitation of these marginal people. But marginal people are not likely to be favorably impressed by the society's ideology. Unlike the producing classes of long-standing subordination, the conquered or marginal people are ethnically distinct and do not share the cultural baggage of the society. Their geographical location also makes them less vulnerable to physical force. Eventually they may take to armed action against the society, thus precipitating the wars that cause the final crisis of the social order. The Germanic tribes in an uneasy relation of vassalage to the Romans are an excellent example of such a volatile, rebellious, and ultimately uncontrollable subordinate group at the cultural and geographical margins of a society. In the capitalist world system, the more exploited working class of the under-developed countries may come to play a similar role as the class whose struggles destroy the existing system.

In the following reading, Andre Gorz gives an example of a contradiction in capitalism.

The contradiction between the character and level of the training required by the development of the productive forces and the character and level of the training required, from the management's point of view, to perpetuate hierarchic relations in the factory and, more generally, the existing relations of production in society.

. . . Industry expects the universities to produce swarms of skilled workers, who can be put directly to work in production, applied research and management. However, the monopolies are perfectly well-aware of the danger for the existing order of a general upgrading of educational standards. For, once a certain level of culture has been reached, highly skilled workers feel the vital need for professional, intellectual and existential independence as much as workers in old-fashioned industry feel or felt the gnawing need for material satisfaction.

It is for this reason that the monopolies, although they are constantly clamouring for education "more in touch with real life," attempt to cut back the quality of higher education and the number of students enjoying it. For example, the chairman of Kodak-Pathé recently remarked: "It is a bad thing to be in a country where there is a surplus of highly skilled personnel, since, should a crisis arise, young people who have spent a long time in studying but without being able to get a suitable post at the end, are not merely a pointblank loss, from the point of view of wasted investment, but also a threat to the established order." The most extraordinary thing in this particular line of management argument is not only the expressed wish to restrict the number of "highly skilled personnel" to the number of "suitable posts . . . should a crisis arise," but also the utilitarian concept of culture (which is a "pointblank loss" if it does not lead to a "suitable post") and the cultural malthusianism motivated by fright at the thought that too much and too widespread culture might imperil "the established order" or, as we might choose to put it, the capitalist relations of production and the hierarchic relations of the firm.

In fine, the problem for big management is to harmonize two contradictory necessities: the necessity of developing human capabilities, imposed by modern processes of production and the—political—necessity of ensuring that this kind of development of capabilities does not bring in its wake any augmentation of the independence of the individual, provoking him to challenge the present division of social labour and distribution of power. . . .

The general trend of this revolt, rather reminiscent of others in Italy (architectural students, for instance) or in France (at the Sorbonne or the IDES), is that, once a certain level of education has been reached, it becomes out of the question to try and limit the need for independence: it is impossible to teach knowledge and ignorance in the same breath, without those taught finally grasping how they are being stunted; it is impossible to contain the independence inherent in cognitive praxis within tight limits, even by early specialization. In fine, it is impossible, in the long run, to bottle up independence. Monopoly capital dreams of a particular kind of specialized technician, recognizable by the coexistence in one and the same person of zest for his job and indifference about its purpose, professional enterprise and social submission, power and responsibility over technical questions and impotence and irresponsibility over questions of economic and social management. It is the task of the workers' movement to ensure that this dream really does prove a delusion, to bring the contradictions involved into the daylight and to counter the repressive and mystifying ideology of organization capitalism with the possibility, through struggle on every level, of a total alternative and a reconquest of man.

Andre Gorz (1972:487,489)

The hegemony of a class collapses when several of these contradictions generate problems at more or less the same time. These conjunctions of causes are especially serious when they coincide with the troughs of economic cycles that beset any productive system that is beyond the subsistence level, particularly capitalism, which has frequent and severe economic troughs. Not all the types of causes have to be present at the same time. Unfortunately, their conjunction can best be understood by historical hindsight. Predicting the conjunction of problems and economic troughs is much more difficult.

Hegemonic collapses tend to be preceded by symptomatic events. One such event is the defection of intellectuals from the ruling class. The fact that intellectuals no longer support the ruling class is not in itself enough to cause the collapse; such defection is certainly not a sufficient cause. However, it robs the ruling class of one of its means of control over the society as a whole. For instance, the Protestant Reformation was a period during which the feudal nobility in northern and western Europe lost its intellectuals. During the Enlightenment, the intellectuals of France deserted the king, his court, and the remains of the feudal aristocracy. Various other strata that hover between the ruling class and the mass of producers may also defect. For example, in nineteenth-century France, the bourgeoisie occasionally lost its grip on the petite bourgeoisie, who were an important element in the National Guard and hence crucial for maintaining order against the rebellious proletariat. In 1848, this group temporarily defected to the side of the proletariat.

A second symptom of hegemonic collapse is fiscal failure: the state can no longer find the money to run its operations. In other words, sometimes the ruling classes are so hard pressed by general material circumstances that they can no longer support the state apparatus. Sometimes the constriction of funds is caused by the producers, who refuse to turn over a surplus. (This latter situation can spark a vicious—from the point of view of the ruling class—cycle in which producers refuse to turn over the surplus, which in turn makes it impossible to run the apparatus to collect the surplus, and so on.) Thus, a fiscal crisis of the state preceded the fall of the monarchy at the time of the French Revolution.

A third symptom of hegemonic collapse is the inability of the society to supply routine goods and services to the masses of the population. In the case of the Russian Revolution, the czarist government and private enterprise could no longer meet the daily needs of the Petrograd workers.

A fourth symptom—and also a cause—of collapse is the lack of control by the ruling group or the state over the means of violence. The Cossacks ordered to restore order in Petrograd in February 1917 refused to disperse the crowds. French regiments supported rather than prevented the crowd's seizure of the Bastille during the French Revolution.

By the time a ruling class has lost the ability to supply needed services and to control the means of violence, it has lost its hegemony and is fighting for survival. Sometimes a revolutionary class will have developed hegemonic aspirations of its own and be ready to step into the breach of power and ideology left by the collapsing ruling class. Such was clearly the case with the French bourgeoisie in the French Revolution. But often there is a long hiatus —a "time of troubles"—between the hegemony of one class and that of the next. In the meantime, there exist classes with economic interests but with no conception of their role that can weld all the strata together into a unified society. We will explore this sort of transition in the next chapter.

Even if a revolutionary class with a hegemonic *self*-conception is ready to seize power, it may have initial difficulty in establishing hegemony (as opposed to mere rule by force) for a while—even for decades or generations. Thus a revolution is only a crucial moment—the seizure of state power—in a much longer chain of events, involving, *first*, the piling up of contradictions; *second*, the collapse of ruling-class hegemony; *third*, the inability of the ruling class to operate the state, ensure routines of production and distribution, and command the army or police; *fourth*, the act of revolution itself, whereby a revolutionary group, representing a class, attains power over the state apparatus; and *fifth*, the use of the state apparatus and ideologues to establish a new hegemony.

References

Althusser, Louis.
1970   "Contradiction and overdetermination," in For Marx. New York: Vintage Books.

Bernal, J. D.
1971   Science in History. Volume 2, The Scientific and Industrial Revolution. Cambridge, Mass.: MIT Press.

Booth, Paul.
1974   "Inflation." Lecture given at Roosevelt University, Chicago, November 10.

Brecht, Bertolt.
1974   Selected Poems of Bertolt Brecht. Translation by H. R. Hays. New York: Harcourt Brace Jovanovich.

Bridges, A.
1974   "Nicos Poulantzas and the Marxist theory of the state." Politics and Society 4 (No. 2): 161–190.

Domhoff, G. William.
1970   The Higher Circles: The Governing Class in America. New York: Random House.
1974   "State and ruling class in corporate America." The Insurgent Sociologist 4 (Spring): 3–16.

Dreier, Peter.
1975   "Power structure and power struggles." The Insurgent Sociologist 5 (Spring): 233–244.

Fried, Morton.
1967   The Evolution of Political Society. New York: Random House.

Garner, Larry.
1974   "Marxism and idealism in the political thought of Antonio Gramsci." Ph.D. dissertation. New York: Columbia University.

Gorz, Andre.
1967   Strategy for Labor. Boston: Beacon Press.
1972   "Domestic contradictions of advanced capitalism." Pp. 478–491 in Richard C. Edwards, Michael Reich, and Thomas E. Weisskopf (eds.), The Capitalist System. Englewood Cliffs, N.J.: Prentice-Hall.

Gramsci, Antonio.
1971   Selections from the Prison Notebooks. Translation by Quintin Hoare and Geoffrey N. Smith. New York: International Publishers.

Harris, Marvin.
1971   Culture, Man and Nature. New York: Thomas Crowell.

Hays, Samuel P.
1972   "The politics of reform in municipal government," in Barton J. Bernstein and Allen J. Matusow (eds.), Twentieth-Century America. Second edition. New York: Harcourt Brace Jovanovich.

Hessen, Boris.
1974   "Sources of Newton's Principia," in Willis H. Truitt and T. W. Solomons (eds.), Science, Technology and Freedom. Boston: Houghton Mifflin.

Kolko, Gabriel.
1963   The Triumph of Conservatism. New York: Free Press.

Kuhn, Thomas S.
1970   The Structure of Scientific Revolutions. Second edition. Chicago: University of Chicago Press.

LaBarre, Weston.
1948   Aymara Indians of the Lake Titicaca Plateau, Bolivia. Millwood, N.Y.: Kraus Reprint.

Lasswell, Harold.
1958   Politics: Who Gets What, When, and How. Cleveland: World Publishing.

Lynd, Staughton.
1974   No Supervision Without Representation. Working Papers for a New Society 2 (No. 2): 16–22.

Marcuse, Herbert.
1964   One Dimensional Man. Boston: Beacon Press.

Marx, Karl.
1961   Capital. Volume 1, Process of Capitalist Production. Translated by Samuel Moore and Edward Aveling. Edited by Frederich Engels. London: Lawrence and Wishart.
1963   The Eighteenth Brumaire of Louis Bonaparte. New York: International Publishing Company.

Marx, Karl, and Frederick Engels.
1947   German Ideology. New York: International Publishing Company.

Miliband, Ralph.
1969   The State in Capitalist Society. New York: Basic Books.
1973   "Reply to Nicos Poulantzas," in Robin Blackburn (ed.), Ideology in Social Science. New York: Random House.

Moore, Barrington, Jr.
1966   Social Origins of Dictatorship and Democracy. Boston: Beacon Press.

O'Connor, James.
1973   The Fiscal Crisis of the State. New York: St. Martin's Press.

Parenti, Michael.
1974   Democracy for the Few. New York: St. Martin's Press.

Poulantzas, Nicos.
1973   "The problem of the capitalist state," in Robin Blackburn (ed.), Ideology in Social Science. New York: Random House.
1975   Political Power and Social Classes. Translation by Timothy O'Hagan. Atlantic Highlands, N.J.: Humanities Press.

Trevor-Roper, Hugh R.
1968   "Religion, the Reformation, and social change," in The Crisis of the Seventeenth Century. New York: Harper & Row.

Trimberger, E. K.
1972   "A theory of elite revolution." Studies in Comparative International Development 7 (Fall): 191–207.

Wolf, Eric R.
1969   Peasant Wars of the Twentieth Century. New York: Harper & Row.

Chapter 12

Growth of the Capitalist World Economy and Its Consequences

In this chapter, I shall examine the rise and effects of capitalism and industrialism. This will not be just a case study of change; it will be an analysis of the changes that have irreversibly and totally transformed our lives. My analysis has six parts. The first examines the antecedents of capitalism/industrialism; the following five examine components and effects.

The discovery of gold and silver in America, the extirpation, enslavement, and entombment in mines of the aboriginal population, the beginning of the conquest and looting of the East Indies, the turning of Africa into a warren for the commercial hunting of black-skins, signalised the rosy dawn of the era of capitalist production. These idyllic proceedings are the chief momenta of primitive accumulation.

Karl Marx, *Capital*

ANY ANALYSIS OF SOCIAL CHANGE must take into account the fact that since the sixteenth century, and especially since the nineteenth century, local and previously unrelated processes of change have been swept up in a worldwide transformation of society. This transformation began in Europe in the sixteenth century. Its first phase included the voyages of discovery and conquest, the rise of commercial agriculture, the appearance of the modern state, the ascendancy of the bourgeoisie, the spread of Protestantism, and the growth of science.

317

These changes set the stage for the Industrial Revolution in the late eighteenth century, the takeoff into industrial capitalism as a new mode of production, and imperialist expansion in the search for markets and raw materials. Every person in the world today is affected by this transformation. No one lives outside of the world system: the Amazonian Indian gunned down by lumbermen and the Soviet official buying U.S. wheat are as much a part of it as the executive of a multinational corporation. The "case study" of industrial capitalism is a study of all humanity. We can never go back to a preindustrial or precapitalist world. We can only go forward into a society that necessarily develops from the present world system.

The Rise of Capitalism as a Mode of Production

In this section, I shall discuss some of the major features and important trends of the period between the fourteenth century and the late eighteenth century. These centuries are crucial to an understanding of the origins of capitalism and the Industrial Revolution. Capitalism did not suddenly spring full grown from feudalism; on the contrary, there were many transitional forms, including some that failed, between feudalism and capitalism. Early capitalism involved three new kinds of activity—commercial agriculture, reorganized crafts production, and expansion into the rest of the world. Each of these activities involved a rising class—the bourgeoisie— and new ways of exploiting a labor force. Associated with these changes were changes in political institutions and ideology. I shall describe the rise of states and the ideologies of statism, Protestantism, and science. I shall conclude the section by indicating how the bourgeoisie found a new political and ideological independence and strength toward the end of this period of transition.

In the next few pages, I shall discuss the breakdown of feudalism and the rise of transitional societies and institutions.[1]

The Breakdown of Feudalism

In the fourteenth century, feudalism faltered and began to collapse. Its collapse seems to have been caused by the conjunction of two factors: (1) deteriorating natural conditions, specifically, a colder climate and an epidemic of bubonic plague, and (2) a crisis in production and distribution, in which the secular (or long-term) contradictions of the feudal mode of production finally "came home to roost." According to Wallerstein (1974:37), "There was no more to be squeezed out" of the peasants by the ruling class.

Let us look at the second factor in slightly more detail. The years from 1100 to 1300 had been years of expansion. Population had multiplied, forests

---

[1]This section is based on Wallerstein (1974).

and swamps were pushed back, and, above all, technology had advanced. Plowing methods were improved, and the invention of the horse collar had increased agricultural productivity—but not enough to support the increased population. The expenditures of feudal landlords also increased, partly because of the growth of this class and partly because of the increased scale of the wars in which they involved themselves.

We have already remarked that violence and war were characteristic features of feudalism. Between 1100 and 1350, the scale of war and violence increased because of increased population pressure on scarce land resources and because of the large undertakings of the Crusades and the Hundred Years War between England and France, which began in the middle of the fourteenth century. At first the Crusades helped to stimulate the economy by bringing plunder and new living standards to Europe. Ultimately, however, the wars meant that the landed ruling class had to squeeze more out of the peasants, both directly in feudal dues to pay for the lord's men-at-arms and weapons, and indirectly in taxes to increase the military power of the states. Thus, the peasantry was caught between its own expanding population and the lord's increasing demands for the peasants' surplus agricultural product. The technology of agriculture could not change fast enough to meet these increased demands. By themselves, these difficulties might not have caused the collapse of feudalism, but might merely have caused its cyclical contraction with a drop in population, products, and living standards. Perhaps feudalism could have eventually pulled out of this trough. However, the environmental factors made the flaws of feudalism fatal.

The two-fold crisis had grim consequences for human beings. A third of the population of Europe died of the plague. Cities and villages stood empty. Corpses were piled high, and the survivors were too weak or dispirited to dispose of them. Meanwhile, the increasingly severe winters led to the end of cereal-growing in Iceland and of grape-growing in England, and to the abandonment of Scandinavian settlements in Greenland. Forest and wasteland reclaimed areas of human settlement in central Europe (Wallerstein, 1974:34).

War, although endemic in feudalism, now began to have even more devastating consequences. Larger areas and more people were involved. With the introduction of first the long bow and then cannon and handguns, the armored knight on horseback became obsolete. Warfare also meant higher taxes, thus adding to the squeeze on a countryside already suffering from depopulation and low productivity. The lords perceived this crisis as a liquidity crisis; that is, they could no longer obtain enough of a surplus product from their landholdings to support their life-style and their warfare. From the point of view of the producers, this crisis was felt as unbearable pressure from the lords for taxes and feudal dues, and they responded with a series of peasant revolts in northern Italy, Flanders, Denmark, Majorca, France, and Germany.

Thus we see how the contradictions built into feudalism finally ripped it asunder. Constant violence, an agriculture of low productivity, and an exploitation of the peasantry that resulted in no investment or innovation—

all were inherent in feudal society and ultimately led to the collapse of that society. The exploiting landlord as well as the exploited peasant was helpless to prevent the collapse.

War, famine, plague, depopulation, the impoverishment of the country-side, and revolts made the fourteenth century an exceptionally gloomy and violent period. *The collapse of the economy and the strained relations between producers and the ruling class were mirrored in the ideological superstructure.* Catholic beliefs and the institutions of the Roman Catholic church began to show strains: mendicant orders carried images of death and renunciation to the suffering masses; strange heretical movements accompanied the peasant revolts; rival popes competed at Rome and Avignon; outcries of violence, pessimism, and preoccupation with death permeates the literature and art of the period. Doubtless, the entire Middle Ages, after the collapse of the Roman state, had been a period of constant and casual violence. But toward the end of the epoch, the sense of violence and death became more self-conscious. Huizinga (1954:36) quotes the French poet Eustache Deschamps:

> Why are the times so dark
> That people no longer recognize each other as friends,
> And governments go from bad to worse,
> As we can see?
> The past was much better.
> Who reigns? Affliction and frustration.
> There is no justice or law now.
> I don't know where I belong. . . .
> Now the world is cowardly, decayed, and weak,
> Old, greedy, and confused of speech.
> I see only fools. . . .
> Surely the end is coming. . . .
> All goes badly. [Translation mine.]

A leading social historian comments on the late Middle Ages:

> Now, in the Middle Ages, Christian faith had so strongly implanted in all minds the ideal of renunciation as the base of all personal and social perfection, that there was scarcely any room left for entering upon [the] path of material and political progress. The idea of a purposed and continual reform and improvement of society did not exist. Institutions in general are considered as good or as bad as they can be; having been ordained by God, they are intrinsically good, only the sins of men pervert them. What therefore is in need of remedy is the individual soul (Huizinga, 1954:37–38).

During the relative stability of the earlier Middle Ages, this world view was a powerful support for the existing social relationships. Once the economy and the social relationships fell into disarray, this ideology handicapped people in conceiving of ways out of the ruin of their society. Their reactions tended to be ones of individual despair. Over and over again people were reminded of their impending death and putrefaction. Sometimes the theme of death was treated in a tender and touching way, as in the verse about the dying little girl who says to her mother, "Take good care of my doll, my knuckle bones and my fine dress"; or in the folk story of "the dead child who came back to beg its mother to weep no more, that its shroud might dry" (Huizinga, 1954:150).

More often the imagery was horrifying, emphasizing suffering and decay. The living person was reminded that "when going to bed at night, he should consider how, just as he now lies down himself, soon strange hands will lay his body in the grave" (Huizinga, 1954:138). The response was the negation of the world and of any action to change it. Declared Master Eckhart, the Dominican mystic: "All creatures are mere nothing; I do not say they are little or aught: they are nothing. That which has no entity, is not. All creatures have no being, for their being depends on the presence of God" (Huizinga, 1954:224). Or, as Deschamps laments, "If the times remain so, I shall become a hermit, for I see nothing but grief and torment" (Huizinga, 1954:36).

Emergence of Transitional Social Structures

In European society, this state of affairs did not last long. However, the societies that emerged from the crisis of the fourteenth century were very different from the ones that had been plunged into it. In some other types of society, crises tended to be cycles within an overall stable state. China, for example, went through repeated periods of depopulation, famine, Tartar invasions, banditry, and peasant revolt, but the power of the state and of the mandarin bureaucracy was such that they preserved the fundamental social structure and mode of production through the crises. In China, the crises were the troughs of cycles of economic expansion and contraction rather than the end of a society.

In European feudalism, the states were too weak and fragmented to protect the relations of production during a major crisis. The political institutions and the ideological institutions were not sufficiently unified. The pope and the secular rulers were often in conflict. When a crisis occurred, the clergy could not be counted upon to give unswerving support to the princes or the landed nobility. The superstructure of feudalism—the political and ideological institutions—were weak, fragmented, heterogeneous, and in conflict with each other. The system as a whole did not weather the crisis of the fourteenth century. Therein, perhaps, lay the dynamism of European civilization. A more cohesive, unified, all-encompassing system might have survived the crisis and failed to bring forth new forms.

The way out of the crisis in Europe thus did not lie in going back to the stable society of the past. The "solutions" that developed involved three fundamental changes in the mode of production. One was the expansion of a commercial and crafts economy in the cities. This type of activity had certainly existed before the crisis, but it now became more important and less locally oriented. The second was the transformation of agriculture. Agricultural techniques and goals changed and with them the rural relations of production. Emphasis was placed on producing cash crops for a market. Some of these crops were food crops, others were raw materials (especially wool) for the urban crafts economy. Patterns of subsistence farming, peasant rights, and community ties that stood in the way of commercial agriculture were ruthlessly destroyed. The third transformation of production was the expansion of the European economy into the rest of the world, which became the target of plunder and trade. Remote areas of the world were drawn into the European economy as a source of raw materials for manufacture; as a source of labor —slaves and other coerced labor—for commercial agriculture in tropical crops; and as a source of gold and silver that at least temporarily solved Europe's liquidity crisis.

These transformations were accompanied by two political forms: city-states in northern Italy, the Netherlands, the Rhine valley, and southern and northern Germany, which were the sites of commercial, banking, and manufacturing activity; and larger states throughout Europe, in which power became more concentrated in the hands of a prince and a bureaucracy. Accompanying changes in belief systems included the Protestant Reformation, nationalism, and scientific inquiry.

These changes in production, in the arrangement of political life, and in beliefs were carried out by groups of human beings who at first were seldom aware of what the large consequences of their actions might be. Groups of people drove peasants off the land, decided to use new technologies in agriculture and crafts, organized voyages of conquest, supported kings against feudal barons, conducted scientific experiments, and died for their Protestant faith. *The key group that was involved in these activities has been called the bourgeoisie. It was a new class, a group that stood for a new way of organizing production and all the behavior directly or indirectly associated with production.*

One can ask what the origins of this new class were. In fact, they were probably very heterogeneous. Some bourgeois were feudal landlords who "wised up" and changed their economic and social behavior in accordance with the altered conditions of life. They forced some peasants off the land, appropriated the common land of the peasant community, and used this new resource of land to grow cash crops. They struggled to gain royal charters for mercantile trading companies. This pattern, in which the landed nobility became a large component of the bourgeoisie, certainly appeared in England and, in lesser degree, elsewhere.

Some of the bourgeoisie who engaged in commercial farming were of lowlier origin—in England, for instance, yeoman farmers and others of peasant origin. Still other components of the bourgeoisie were wealthy urban merchants. Although they had enjoyed this status for several centuries already, many of these merchants ultimately traced their ancestry to poor peasants and serfs of the tenth century (more or less) who had been crowded off the land during a period of population expansion (Pirenne, 1952).

Finally, some of the bourgeoisie included former serfs who had only recently fled to the cities and acquired some wealth and standing as artisans or entrepreneurs. The "mix" of the bourgeoisie in terms of their social origins varied from region to region within western Europe. Their behavior, however, was everywhere fairly similar: they opposed the traditional powers of the feudal barons; they sought to replace the peasant community with tenants and "free" wage laborers; they opposed the leveling revolts of the poor; they sought profit from production and used their profits to expand their enterprises; they favored individual or family ownership of productive enterprises; and they acted to expand production and apply new technologies.

We now turn to a slightly closer examination of the behavior of this class and its outcomes.

New Productive Activities: Manufacture and Commercial Agriculture

Production was changed from late feudal to early capitalist patterns less by the introduction of technological inventions (although doubtlessly these were inportant) than by the introduction of inventions for organizing labor and distributing products. Let me try to list some of these inventions:

1. "Wage labor and money rents became the means of labor control" (Wallerstein, 1974:116), at least in the core areas of the transition from feudalism to capitalism, namely, England, France, the Netherlands, and parts of Germany. Wage labor and money rents replaced feudal dues (in produce or labor) as the major way of extracting value from the labor force. Serfs were freed from their bond to the land. They became either tenant farmers, wage laborers (many of them seasonally employed and often falling into vagabondage) or, in a few fortunate cases, entrepreneurial property-owning farmers.

2. The enclosure system and the peasants' loss of common lands provided land for wool—"sheep ate men". This displacement of people by livestock simultaneously provided a labor force and a raw material.

3. In areas peripheral to the European core, various other forms of labor control appeared—slavery, coerced cash-crop labor (which differed from serfdom in its orientation to a market instead of subsistence), sharecropping, and debt peonage. Slavery, of course, was of major importance in the Americas. Coerced cash-crop labor appeared both in eastern Europe and the Americas. Sharecropping was a major form in southern France and Italy, where it helped the bourgeoisie evade the problems of monetary fluctuation that occur in tenancy, (where the tenant pays money rent). Debt peonage, in which the entrepreneur pays the producer in advance and thus prevents the producer from finding more favorable terms in the open market, was used by German merchants in the Norwegian fish and fur trade and in eastern Europe (Wallerstein, 1974:121–122).

4. Inventions in business transactions, such as deposit banking, broker-age, and branch offices, enabled the commercial bourgeoisie to obtain more capital.

5. The concept of profit and investment came to dominate not only crafts and commerce but also agriculture: most surplus agricultural products were sold in a market, and the profits were not spent but were at least partially invested by the bourgeoisie to expand production.

Along with these inventions in the technology of human relations went inventions in the technology of production per se, some of which dated back several centuries but were now more effectively used than they had been in subsistence agriculture: windmills, horse collars, pumping devices, Jethro Tull's mechanical seeder, and so on.

The development of commerical agriculture tended to be very traumatic for the work force and involved definite decisions on the part of the landlords. The growth of the urban economy was less traumatic and discontinuous. At the end of the feudal period, the town economy was organized into guilds, associations of artisans in the same craft. The guilds and workshops were headed by masters, essentially entrepreneurs who owned the raw materials and tools and collected the profits. In fact, the number of masters was small, and most apprentices could look forward only to being journeymen—paid work-men—rather than masters (Pirenne, 1937:184).

When production was for international commerce and not for local sale, the position of the workmen was particularly disadvantageous. They were dependent on a series of middlemen who sold the product in distant markets, and the workmen were subject to extreme misery when there was a shortage of raw materials. Paid workmen were hired by the week, and many wandered from town to town. This early form of industrial proletariat was to be found in the textile industry, especially in Italy and the Netherlands. The "proto-proletariat" differed from a modern proletariat in the simpler technology it used and in the absence of large factorylike workshops (Pirenne, 1937:185). Throughout the fourteenth and fifteenth centuries, workmen repeatedly partic-ipated in revolts against the masters and the wealthy city officials.

As modern capitalism emerged from feudalism, the following develop-ments took place in the urban economies:

1. The nationally and internationally marketed products became more important than the local crafts; thus more people entered the proletar-ianized work conditions of production for the larger markets.

2. The local guild masters were displaced by entrepreneurs (some of them former masters) with larger amounts of capital and a larger scope of operations. The guilds began to lose their local monopolies, and their products had to compete, usually unsuccessfully, with goods made in specialized regions and imported into the local economies.

3. For a brief period in the late Middle Ages, the wealthier classes in the towns staked their political future on city-states. These small states

proved not to be viable, partly because they were not strong enough to back international commerce and partly because they were unable to deal with the revolts of the poor. Thus, the bourgeois city-states of the late Middle Ages represent an experiment in matching political forms to class structures. Artistically, they were brilliant successes; much of the great architecture and painting of the late Middle Ages and the Renaissance comes from the Italian and northern European city-states and urban republics. As political units, they soon gave way to new forms, which we will discuss shortly.

4. Despite their repeated revolts, the workers and poor people of the towns failed to establish control over either town politics or the work process.

Voyages of Discovery and Conquest: Origins of a World Economy

We now turn to the third of three major ways of changing the feudal mode of production to the capitalist one: the expansion of the European economy into the rest of the world. This expansion has unified a diversity of societies into a single world system. It began in the late fourteenth century in Portugal, which initiated voyages of plunder and trade along the African coast, into the Indian ocean, and eventually to the China Sea. Portugal launched this expansion for a number of reasons, mostly having to do with the country's geographical position at the far western tip of the continent. On the one hand, Portugal's location made voyages to Africa relatively easy and an obvious choice for explorers. On the other hand, its location made wars of conquest within Europe (like those pursued by more centrally located European states and feudal principalities) difficult.

Internal causes also played a part. The Portuguese commerical bourgeoisie was already relatively powerful, while the feudal lords were weak. As a correlate of this class structure, the Portuguese state was relatively stable. Portuguese expansion into Africa was a prototype for later European imperialism: its bourgeoisie profited from new markets, new raw materials, and new —that is, coerced—labor forces; its nobility had an outlet for heroic military exploits; its urban protoproletariat and rural poor were less likely to revolt because they found jobs in the imperialist ventures and were able to oppress peoples even more wretched than themselves.

Following the Portuguese lead, the Spanish rapidly conquered large parts of the Americas. A little later, the Dutch and English started their economic expansion. Unlike the Spanish, the Dutch and English first tried trading rather than direct conquest, although the latter eventually also happened. (I discussed this pattern in the section on the great trading companies.) France also participated in the expansion. By the end of the sixteenth century,

Europeans had "discovered" much of the world (although not the interiors of the continents) and had drawn it into the European economy.

West Africa furnished gold and slaves. East Africa and Indonesia provided spices. Pepper was of special importance because it was used for preserving meat and therefore altered the diet and food distribution system of Europe. From China and Japan came metals, silk, and luxury goods. Most important of all, the Americas provided food (grain, cattle and hides, sugar, and various tropical products) and precious metals. While the Asian trade supplied primarily luxury goods (with the possible exception of pepper), the Americas and Africa were forced to contribute the vital ingredients of a world economy: gold and silver, food, and labor power.

The massive amounts of American gold and silver in some ways were detrimental to the European economy. They first poured into Spain, a society that was ill-equipped to absorb such wealth. It had a weak bourgeoisie because trading activities had been carried out by Moors and Jews, not Christian Spaniards. The Spanish upper classes were the nobles who had driven the Moors and Jews from Spain. The inflow of New World bullion exacerbated the upper classes' proclivity to rely on military feats and the squeezing of unfree labor as a source of wealth. Wealth was consumed or loaned rather than invested in production. Having seized the American gold and silver, the nobility saw no reason to develop new productive activities either in commercial agriculture or in craft manufactures. They maintained a strongly feudal organization of agriculture, and wealth that was not simply squandered on luxuries and high living was loaned to individuals instead of invested in agriculture, trade, or manufactures.

Already wiser Spaniards recognized this foolish waste of capital resources and lamented that Spain was a poor country *because* she had so much gold and silver. The decline of Spain began at the very moment of her greatness, with the capture of the gold and silver of the Indians. The nature of this wealth made it easy for the Spanish upper classes to avoid the task of building up Spanish commerce, manufacturing, and commercial agriculture. Their misuse of the bullion was one of the *causes* of Spain's decline to backwardness and underdevelopment. Their misuse of the bullion was a *result* of their rise to power as a crusading feudal warrior stratum, recapturing their country from the more cultured and economically developed Moors, for their experiences in this *reconquista* made them ideologically and structurally tied to a antibourgeois feudal system.

Meanwhile Spanish bullion flowed into the European economy and was one of the causes of a general long-term inflation that lasted into the first decades of the seventeenth century.

By the end of the sixteenth century, the most successful states were in northwestern Europe: England, the Netherlands, and France. Their bourgeoisie controlled a large portion of world trade. The bourgeoisie of these countries were involved in trade, in manufacturing, and in commercial agriculture. The labor force of these areas was controlled through cash payments and was largely free.

A second tier of countries, the semiperipheral areas, had lost their autonomy to the core states. These areas chiefly provided commodities for daily use (especially food) and for manufactures to the core areas. Their labor force was mainly organized as sharecroppers and landless laborers on large estates. Southern Italy, parts of eastern Europe, and the Iberian peninsula fell into this category. The semiperipheral areas had a weak bourgeoisie (insofar as they had any at all) that depended more on expediting the affairs of the core-area bourgeoisie than on their own ventures.

A third area was the periphery. It too provided food and raw materials to the core area. However, in the periphery, the labor force was often coerced —slaves, forced laborers, debt peons, and so on.

Finally, during the transitional period before nineteenth-century capitalist imperialism, there were still external areas, areas that were not economically dependent on the core states. These areas—China, Japan, Russia, the interior of Africa, the Ottoman Empire—had a class structure and culture that were separate from the core states. These external areas were related to the core states through trade, but this trade involved a relatively small percentage of their total output. In contrast, the peripheral areas had been either directly conquered by the core states or involved in trade that completely tied their economy to that of the core states.

World history after 1600 can be interpreted as a struggle by nation-states to stay out of the category of peripheral state. Inevitably, increasing numbers of areas were forced into this relation of dependency either through direct conquest or by externally imposed "backwardness"—i.e., domination of their economy by the stronger economies of the core areas. A few peripherals made it into the ranks of core states; Germany is the best example. Some regions with potential as core states fell back into the semiperipheral categories—Spain, Portugal, and Italy (especially southern Italy). Many external areas were forced to become part of the periphery: India and Indonesia rather early, and China and Africa much later, during the nineteenth century.

By the middle of the transitional period (1400–1800), in the late sixteenth century, the world was more or less organized as follows: England and the Netherlands were the core states, soon to be joined by France. On the semiperiphery were Germany and parts of eastern Europe, as well as Portugal, Spain, and Italy; these last three states had almost made it as core states but were now losing out. On the periphery were the Americas, parts of the African coast, the Philippines, parts of Indonesia, and parts of eastern Europe. External areas included China, Japan, the Ottoman Empire, the interior of Africa and—but not for long—parts of southern Asia.

In this division of the world in terms of geography and economic power, we can see the beginnings of modern imperialism. Although the word *imperialism* is related to the word *empire,* in fact, the dominant regions of the world

after 1600 were not always empires. Some of the core states exercised powéı
over other regions without militarily conquering them. For our purposes, it is
useful to distinguish colonialism (as in Spain's military conquest of Mexico)
from imperialism in a broader sense. Imperialism in the broader sense has been
defined as the situation in which "an advanced industrial nation plays, or tries
to play, a controlling and one-sided role in the development of a weaker
economy" (Williams, 1972:55). In the sixteenth century, the core states were not
yet industrial, but the definition is to a large extent applicable anyway. We will
soon see how their position in the world economy enabled the nations of
northwestern Europe to *become* industrial.

The geographical and economic division of the world was also accompanied by a particular class structure and division of labor. It can be summarized as follows:

> The world-economy at this time had various kinds of workers:
> There were slaves who worked on sugar plantations and in easy kinds
> of mining operations which involved skimming off the surface. There
> were "serfs" who worked on large domains where grain was cultivated
> and wood harvested. There were "tenant" farmers on various kinds of
> cash-crop operations (including grain), and wage laborers in some agri-
> cultural production. This accounted for 90–95 percent of the population
> in the European world-economy. There was a new class of "yeoman"
> farmers. In addition, there was a small layer of intermediate personnel
> —supervisors of laborers, independent artisans, a few skilled workmen
> —and a thin layer of ruling classes, occupied in overseeing large land
> operations, operating major institutions of the social order, and to some
> extent pursuing their own leisure. This last group included both the
> existing nobility and the patrician bourgeoisie (as well as, of course, the
> Christian clergy and the state bureaucracy).
>
> A moment's thought will reveal that these occupational categories
> were not randomly distributed either geographically or ethnically within
> the burgeoning world-economy. After some false starts, the picture rap-
> idly evolved of a slave class of African origins located in the Western
> Hemisphere, a "serf" class divided into two segments: a major one in
> eastern Europe and a smaller one of American Indians in the Western
> Hemisphere. The peasants of western and southern Europe were for the
> most part "tenants". The wage-workers were almost all west Europeans.
> The yeoman farmers were drawn largely even more narrowly, principally
> from northwest Europe. The intermediate classes were pan-European in
> origin (plus mestizos and mulattoes) and distributed geographically
> throughout the arena. The ruling classes were also pan-European, but I
> believe one can demonstrate disproportionately from western Europe.
>
> Why different modes of organizing labor—slavery, "feudalism,"
> wage labor, self-employment—at the same point in time within the

world-economy? Because each mode of labor control is best suited for particular types of production. And why were these modes concentrated in different zones of the world-economy—slavery and "feudalism" in the periphery, wage labor and self-employment in the core, and as we shall see sharecropping in the semiperiphery? Because the modes of labor control greatly affect the political system (in particular the strength of the state apparatus) and the possibilities for an indigenous bourgeoisie to thrive. The world-economy was based precisely on the assumption that there were in fact these three zones and that they did in fact have different modes of labor control. Were this not so, it would not have been possible to assure the kind of flow of the surplus which enabled the capitalist system to come into existence (Wallerstein, 1974:86–87).

So far we have looked at changes in class structure and the mode of production. We have encountered a new class, the bourgeoisie, and three new ways of organizing production: (1) the development of craft manufacture for an international market, (2) commercial agriculture, and (3) expansion into peripheral areas in which production—chiefly commercial agriculture—is based on coerced labor. We are now ready to discuss changes in political institutions and beliefs that accompanied these developments.

Changes in the Superstructure

The change in the mode of production and the rise of a new class were accompanied by changes in political institutions and value systems.

The Absolutist State

The major political development of the transitional period was the rise of the absolutist state. During this period, the loose, decentralized political system of feudalism was dropped. Power passed from the grip of feudal lords to a royal court, a central government. City-states were a way station on the road to centralized states. As we have seen, however, the city-states were unable to back large-scale international commerce and conquest and were unable to handle the revolts of the poor. The form that developed and survived was a larger unit, with a centralized state apparatus. In the sixteenth and seventeenth centuries (and also in the eighteenth century in most places except England), these states were absolute monarchies in which—in theory—all power was in the hands of the king and the bureaucracy directly accountable to the king. Representative institutions like parliaments were weak or nonexistent. In fact, the king's power was constrained by the power of the remaining feudal aristrocracy, the large commercial landowners, the commercial bourgeoisie, the powerful banking interests, even the restlessness of the poor. However, in the absolute monarchies, there were few routine, public, openly accepted channels through which these groups could exercise power.[2]

Some of these absolute monarchies took the form of empires in which a single royal house controlled far-flung territories that included diverse ethnic groups. The Habsburg domains are an example of such an empire. Until 1556, the Habsburgs controlled parts of central Europe, Spain, the Netherlands, and the Spanish colonies in the New World. Even after the splits and revolts of the late sixteenth century, the remaining empire still was extremely large and diverse.

Why did these states emerge as the political forms associated with the new mode of production? As we have already seen, other political forms failed to survive. Specifically, the city-states of the Netherlands and northern Italy (with the exception of Venice) fell under the control of the Habsburg dynasty. Second, the bourgeoisie deliberately supported a monarchy as their ally against the feudal aristocracy. Later on—during the French Revolution—the bourgeoisie turned against the monarchy. In the earlier years of their ascendence, however, they were not yet strong enough to forge new political institutions. Therefore, they formed a coalition with one of the feudal princes to help him become an absolute monarch who would protect their interests. This protection meant preserving law and order against the restless urban and rural poor, providing force for carrying out enclosures (although we have seen how, in England, the commercial farming interests turned on the king for not doing this vigorously enough), granting monopolistic charters for trading ventures, and maintaining facilities, such as ports and navies, that furthered the pursuit of international trade.

We must remember that during this period antagonism between the feudal aristocracy and the bourgeoisie was not open or constant. The crown acted as a mediator between the two, royal absolutism being in many ways the institution that represented a compromise between the two groups. Furthermore, during this period neither group was fully conscious of its identity: the bourgeoisie often wanted to become landowners, while the feudal lords were increasingly turning to commercial agriculture. In other words, the bourgeoisie and the feudal aristocracy were not openly antagonistic groups during the fifteenth, sixteenth, and the seventeenth centuries; rather, they blended into each other. The absolutist state was the political form corresponding to the

---

[2]To some extent, I am simplifying the important and complicated argument of whether, during the period of transition, the absolutist state was the last political superstructure of a dying feudalism, the first political superstructure of a newborn capitalism, or some sort of transitional hybrid. I am aware that the situation can be interpreted in a number of different ways that I cannot fully explore here.

changes in class structure—to the declining power of the feudal lords and the growing economic power of the bourgeoisie.

The absolute monarchies used a number of strategies to strengthen the central state apparatus. One was to build up a state bureaucracy. By borrowing from the great banking houses and other rich bourgeois and by taxation, the king raised enough money to hire full-time administrative specialists. This staff in turn helped the king to impose taxes more effectively.

The king also used his money to buy an army. The period of transition from feudalism to capitalism was the heyday of the mercenary army. The uprooted poor throughout Europe, especially those from its marginal regions (Switzerland, Scotland, Wales, Corsica, Sardinia, and so on), found a way out of vagabondage, banditry, and the idiocy of rural life by joining the mercenary armies. The armies were generally assembled by military entrepreneurs who made profits by contracting with the monarchs to provide military manpower. In other words, military establishments were created by capitalist enterprise. Since nationalist feeling was still rather weak, neither soldiers nor military entrepreneurs were troubled by the frequent changes of sides to obtain the best hiring and contracting terms and the finest plunder.

The monarch used the bureaucracy and the army not only to fight foreign wars but also to impose order and uniformity within his realm. Banditry, revolts of the poor, uprisings by the remnants of the feudal nobility and by displaced peasants, and religious conflicts had to be suppressed. By the seventeenth century, places of confinement—workhouses, hospitals, asylums for the insane, prisons, and so on—were established to force industry and sobriety on the unruly, the vagabonds, the madmen, the beggars, and all those who violated the "monarchical and bourgeois order" that was being organized by the state (Foucault, 1965:40). Generally speaking, the king, the bureaucracy, the army, and the places of confinement were not very adept at dealing with these problems. Compared with modern states (socialist, fascist, or parliamentary-capitalist), the states of the transition period were chaotic, weak in the powers of taxation, lacking the loyalty of their subjects, and unable to monopolize violence effectively. They were powerful and absolutist only when compared with the feudal state, in which violence and decision-making had been almost entirely in the hands of local nobles. The modern state is more representative and more attuned to popular demands and public opinion, but it is also much more able to maintain stability and monopolize violence.

The sixteenth and seventeenth centuries represent the age of great monarchs and courts: Henry VIII and Elizabeth I of England; Ivan the Terrible; Gustavus Adolphus of Sweden and his mannish daughter, Christina; the Habsburgs; Louis XIV—"The Sun King"—and the scheming Cardinal Richelieu; Ferdinand II of the Holy Roman Empire and his generalissimo, Wallenstein, the sinister military entrepreneur of the Thirty Years War. The pomp, glitter, and cruelty of our fantasies about kings and princes date from this age.

New Ideologies

Three new kinds of ideologies accompanied this transition period: statism,
religion, and scientific inquiry.

Statism.   "Statism is the claim for increased power in the hands of the state machinery" (Wallerstein, 1974:147). Much of this claim was fought out in struggles over religion. For example, kings repeatedly tried to force their religion on their subjects: the principle of *cuius regio eius religio* ("the ruler shall determine the religion") produced relative religious homogeneity within each state. But this principle of ideological unification could also work against the empires and for smaller, more "naturally" homogenous states. The revolt of the northern Netherlands against the Spanish crown in the last decades of the sixteenth century was largely conceptualized as a revolt by Protestants against their Spanish Catholic rulers. "In fact"—that is, in the reconstruction of history by modern historians—the objective outcome of this revolt was the establishment of a genuinely bourgeois state in the Dutch republic, a state that was in many ways the forerunner of the bourgeois states of the nineteenth century. But the participants in the revolt tended to see it in religious terms rather than in terms of classes and national political institutions.

The ideology of statism focuses more on the king and court than on the nation as a whole, insofar as it was secularized at all. Statism is not yet clearly combined with nationalism. Typical of the political writings of this period is the work of Hobbes, who tried to justify state power as protection against a state of nature in which lives would be brutish and short.

Machiavelli was another major ideologue of statism who used secular language. His *The Prince* was intended to be a handbook of useful advice for the rulers of the northern Italian states who were trying to grow stronger vis-à-vis their subjects, their neighbors, and their large imperial enemies (Machiavelli, 1952). Most of this book is addressed to statism, to increasing the powers of the prince and not those of the people as a whole. But Machiavelli was among the first to suggest that the strength of a state may be increased not only by military and administrative practices but also by the nationalism of its people.

Protestantism.   The second major ideological development of the period was the Protestant Reformation, which began in 1517 (two years before Cortes' conquest of Mexico). A modern historian, Sir Lewis Namier, has commented that "religion is a sixteenth-century word for nationalism" (quoted in Wallerstein, 1974:207). Indeed, both Protestantism and nationalism reflected the new structure of society that was emerging in Europe.

In the early sixteenth century, the bourgeoisie tired of a church that seemed corrupt. The Roman Catholic church seemed to justify the rule of the feudal lord and the stability of the peasant community against the interests of the bourgeoisie. The beliefs that the Protestant theologians formulated seemed more compatible with the aspirations of bourgeoisie: the solitariness of the individual before God (paralleling the solitariness of the wage laborer before his employer, once the laborer is uprooted from the peasant community); the concept of a calling, the individual choice of a vocation that is not merely inherited from one's father (paralleling the antagonism of the bourgeoisie to inheritance of status and the protectionist policies of the local guilds); the importance of lay life and the breaking down of the priest's role as intermediary (an attack not only on the concept of the priesthood but also on the vast wealth and power of the Catholic church).

Many of these elements were already present in Catholicism. Reforms were underway in Catholic beliefs that might ultimately have made Catholicism as compatible with bourgeois enterprise as Protestantism was. But once the schism occurred, the reformist elements were purged from Catholic doctrine (Trevor-Roper, 1968). Protestantism became the religion of the states with a strong bourgeoisie in commerce and/or agriculture. Catholicism remained the religion of areas where the bourgeoisie could not assert their power adequately against either the feudal aristocracy or the court itself.

In the areas where the Church's mobilization against Protestantism, against secular humanism, and against reforms within Catholicism was strongest, the bourgeoisie were often driven into exile and fled into Protestant countries. Bourgeois enterprise was destroyed. Thus the Counter-Reformation (the mobilization against Protestantism) was one of the factors that turned Spain, Portugal, Italy, and some of eastern Europe into a semiperiphery, an agricultural area with a weak bourgeoisie. Bourgeois institutions could not survive in a society in which the state and the Catholic church cooperated in the Inquisition, in maintaining huge clerical and state bureaucracies, and in attacking bourgeois cities and enclaves. (Here the argument is somewhat circular: where the bourgeoisie was weak in the first place, it could not force the state to become Protestant and thus fell victim to the Counter-Reformation, which in turn further weakened the bourgeoisie as a class.) In this context, the German principalities, France, and Belgium fall between the clearly Protestant bourgeois-dominated states of England and Holland and the Counter-Reformation areas of Italy, Spain, Poland, and Hungary.[3]

In short, Protestantism was *one* ideological option that the bourgeoisie had at its disposal. *Protestantism was not a necessary precondition of bourgeois development but a convenient conceptual framework for expressing and universalizing the world view of the bourgeoisie during a historical period when religion was extremely important to most people.*

---

[3]Once launched, Protestantism also developed a radical wing that appealed to the protoproletariat in northern Europe. The major Protestant denominations, however, did not stand for the rights of the poor as is clear from Luther's condemnation of the German peasant revolts.

Science. A third new ideology was science. I have already discussed this development at some length in Chapter 11, where I indicated how science reflected the bourgeois interests in progress, in the natural world, and in the possibility of deliberate transformation of nature by human effort, as well as provided solutions to more immediate practical problems in navigation, ballistics, and other applied areas.

It is no accident that these three ideologies developed together. Each represented some effort by the bourgeoisie to universalize its own world view.

Toward Bourgeois Hegemony

An economic crisis caused trade and production to stagnate and population to decline throughout the first decades of the seventeenth century. By 1648, the end of the Thirty Years War, the transitional period of European history entered a distinct phase. Three important developments occurred that set the stage for the Industrial Revolution. One was the end of religion as a central ideological concern. The Thirty Years War was the last major war in Europe in which people were motivated by religious enmity and conceptualized their conflict primarily as religious.

Second, after the Thirty Years War, the states began to raise national armies instead of hiring mercenaries. Prussia took the lead and tried to build up an army by conscription, although in practice most men evaded the draft. Other countries pressed (physically coerced) poorer men into service or hired volunteers. In each case, however, it was primarily the subjects of the state who were included. In other words, national loyalties replaced religious ties. Once the state had committed itself to building these loyalties, it could not hire foreigners to fight its wars. Nationalism was yet in its infancy and was not to be clearly expressed as an ideology until the eighteenth century, but it was already present.

Third, after the Thirty Years War, the bourgeoisie in the core states became disenchanted with absolutist monarchy. The king had been useful as an ally against the most reactionary of the feudal aristocrats, rebellious peasants, and urban mobs. The crown had provided support for commercial ventures. But by the late seventeenth century, the large court and state bureaucracies appeared parasitical to the rest of society. Furthermore, as we have already seen in the section on the English revolution, the crown had some commitments to traditional groups (such as peasant communities) that displeased the bourgeoisie. After all, the monarch was ultimately a special kind of feudal prince. The absolutist state still protected the declining feudal form of society.

This disenchantment with the crown took various forms. In Holland, the bourgeoisie had already taken the lead in creating a state without a large court and bureaucracy. In England, the process was begun in the Civil War (1642–1651) and continued gradually after that. In France, the desire of the bourgeoisie for a more appropriate kind of state built up more and more pressure until the dam of royal power finally burst in the French Revolution. In the semiperipheral and peripheral areas, the bourgeoisie was too weak to force the creation of political institutions that met their wishes.

Ideologically, bourgeois disenchantment with absolutist monarchy and its attendant bureaucracy was expressed in works like Adam Smith's *The Wealth of Nations* and the writings of John Locke in England, where bourgeois ideologues proposed a capitalist economy with a limited government. In France, where the antagonism between groups was greater and less civilly expressed, the works of the Enlightenment philosophers attacked royal power, the surviving privileges of feudalism, and the Counter-Reformation church. After the Thirty Years War, the aspirations of the bourgeoisie could finally be clearly expressed. They were no longer dependent on the king as a power broker between them and the feudal aristocracy. They no longer used the language of religion to envision a society freed from the power of the feudal lords. The imagery of their ideologues become increasingly secular. Bourgeois rights were no longer identified with Protestant doctrine or a stronger central state but with the Rights of Man, representative government, and (especially in England and America) less governmental intervention in the economy.

These changes in the political and ideological superstructure were associated with a decisive change in production: the Industrial Revolution.

Capitalism after 1800

In the following sections, I am going to describe briefly how capitalism and its accompanying trends developed after 1800. From 1800 to 1917, capitalism was the dominant form of social organization on the entire globe. It was challenged from without only by communities of peoples living in precapitalist societies, and these it consistently defeated—in the Opium War, the Sepoy Mutiny, the Zulu wars, the battles against the Pathans, the pacification of the Barbary Coast pirates, the extermination of the American Indians, and many other similar encounters. From within, capitalism was challenged by working-class movements; but in the short-run, the bourgeoisie was able to defeat these movements.

Only after 1917 and the Bolshevik revolution was a whole nation-state organized to present a continuing challenge to capitalist social organization. After World War II, examples of socialism multiplied in China, Cuba, Vietnam, and Eastern Europe and offered a diversity of paths to socialism.

What forms did capitalism take after 1800? Until about 1870, the system was most completely established in England, where it was mostly competitive and relatively unregulated by the government. In other areas of Europe, capitalism more gradually displaced other kinds of social organization, especially the last remnants of feudalism. After 1870, in Europe and North America, capitalism was the only form of social organization. Areas that were colonized or economically dominated by Europeans were also integrated into a capitalist system, but on unfavorable terms, as suppliers of raw material and cheap labor.

After 1870, capitalism became more monopolistic. In the industrializing countries, very large firms emerged in key areas of production such as steel, chemicals, railroads, oil, and electricity. Finance capital also became more concentrated. The great names of modern capitalism—Rockefeller, Dupont, I.G. Farben, Carnegie, Mellon, Morgan, Rothschild—date from this period. Monopoly capitalism—the situation in which a few giant firms dominate an industry—was clearly linked to technological advances.

Monopoly capital was linked not only to new technologies but also to new ways of organizing the superstructure. The state took a more active part in supporting and stabilizing the capitalist economy. The state was no longer only a "nightwatchman," guaranteeing the sanctity of private productive property but otherwise exercising only a small role in the economy (as in early nineteenth-century England), but to an increasing extent was using its resources to support private industry. Public lands in the United States were made available to the railroad companies. Taxpayers' money was used in state institutes and universities to train personnel and carry out basic research for the private sector. National armies conquered continents and died in the trenches to expand or defend the interests of the nation's firms.

In other words, the growth and transformation of capitalism as a mode of production was accompanied by changes in technologies and production processes (industrialization), by changes in the superstructure (political modernization), and by changes in the conditions of everyday life (changes in residence patterns and the family, and proletarianization). In the next sections, I shall discuss these accompanying changes as they took place both in the core capitalist states and in the more peripheral areas.

Industrialization

In this section, I shall define industrialization, explain the beginnings of the Industrial Revolution, describe the organization of work in the last two centuries, describe how industrialization spread to many countries, and discuss more recent technological and social developments.

We live in an industrial society. Most of our production depends on energy sources that do not rely on human or animal muscle but rely instead on the use of fossil fuels (coal, oil, natural gas), hydroelectric sources, and (in the last few years) nuclear fuels. These energy sources are used to run the machinery that performs the operations involved in extracting raw materials (agriculture, mining, forestry, and fishing), processing raw materials (manufacturing), and transporting finished goods. Additional machinery performs some tasks of controlling the machines used in manufacturing and in performing routine clerical work or data-processing. In the United States, about 40 percent of the labor force is employed in activities directly related to the processing of raw materials. Another 6 percent are employed in agriculture. The remainder of the population depends on agricultural and industrial production (within the United States and abroad) for its jobs and the goods it uses even if it is not directly involved in such production.

Industrialization is the form that the "forces of production" take under both modern capitalism and in many state socialist societies. The industrialized countries are the economically dominant countries in the modern world. How, then, did industrialization begin?

The Industrial Revolution

The changes in energy sources and the organization of productive activities that we call the Industrial Revolution came about in England in the last decades of the eighteenth century. These changes involved mechanization—the use of power equipment (based on burning coal to obtain steam)—first in the textile industry, then in other industries. These changes also involved reorganization of human labor—the factory system. Finally, these changes meant the institutionalization of change. Change in productive activities thereafter was the *typical* situation, not the isolated exception; constant technological innovation became the norm.

Why did the Industrial Revolution—mechanization, factories, and a takeoff into constantly increased production and improved technology—take place in England? Hobsbawm (1969) identified six outstanding reasons:

1. Commercial farming was already strong and provided a basis for industrialization in three ways: *(a)* It was sufficiently productive to feed a substantial nonagricultural population (i.e., the industrial labor force and its dependents); new agricultural techniques had been introduced that increased productivity; and food was fairly effectively marketed. *(b)* The enclosure system and the destruction of peasant communities "freed" people to become an industrial labor force. *(c)* The profits of commercial farming and sheep-raising provided capital that the land-owning bourgeoisie could use to invest in industrial ventures.

2. The class structure was suitable for industrialization. A class that was interested in profit and investment already existed. Land was privately owned, providing a model for private ownership of industry. The government, influenced by the bourgeoisie, had committed itself to economic development as government policy.

3. The state as part of its policy of supporting economic development (i.e., suitable conditions for profit-making by the bourgeoisie in production

rather than only in trade and finance) provided social overhead capital by backing shipping, port facilities, waterways, and roads.

4. England had substantial amounts of coal and iron.

5. England had an industry that could serve as the takeoff point into industrialization—the cotton industry. Cotton cloth manufacture lent itself well to technological innovations such as spinning jennies and power looms. The product was cheap enough to sell in a mass market, unlike luxury goods, which could only be produced for a small market. The supply of raw materials could be expanded much more easily than in the wool industry because cotton depended on the slave labor of blacks in the American South. The supply of cotton could constantly be extended, first, by increasing the number of slave workers and later by the geographical spread of cotton-growing. (The extension of cotton-growing was made possible by the invention of the cotton gin in the 1790s, which made short-fibered inland cotton profitable.)

6. England had available an empire of both colonies and areas (like Latin America) that were economically subordinate to her. The empire provided a market for the manufactured textiles. In colonies like India, the British could impose "deindustrialization" policies that discouraged native crafts and forced the population to buy English manufactured goods.

The reader should take note of two important features of this outline of preconditions. One is that some of these characteristics were also present in other European societies, but only in England did they all exist together. For example, the Dutch also had a class that could have conducted industrialization and a state that would have backed that class, but Holland lacked the natural resources and the land area for commercial agriculture. Second, the reader should note that idustrialization was achieved at the cost of vast human misery and exploitation. Its profits were reaped by the English bourgeoisie; its costs were borne by the displaced English peasants, by the new industrial proletariat, by slaves in American cotton fields, and by the peoples in England's colonies.

The Factory: New Relations of Production and Work Organization

In part, capitalist relations of production had been established before the Industrial Revolution. In England and the other core states, the following institutions were already present before the Industrial Revolution: private property was used to make profits that were invested; land and labor were commodities; labor power was sold to employers; and the state had committed itself to economic development. What altered in the Industrial Revolution was the nature of the work itself; also, the characteristics of capitalist relations of production became more decisive and clear. Specifically, the "putting-out" system, in which the laborer contracted to make a product using his own tools in his own workplace, disappeared. Virtually all labor was performed by wage laborers who worked at times, in places, and with tools that were controlled by the employer. Factories were established; power machinery was installed; production *had* to take place in this setting.

The process of shifting production into factories was rather gradual.

> As late as the 1830s, cotton was the only British industry in which the factory or "mill" predominated; at first (1780–1815) mainly in spinning, carding, and a few ancillary operations, after 1815 increasingly also in weaving. The "factories" with which the new Factory Acts dealt were, until the 1860s, assumed to be exclusively textile factories and predominantly cotton mills. Factory production in other textile branches was slow to develop before the 1840s and in other manufactures was negligible (Hobsbawm, 1962:56).

However, the process of locating work in factories (and eventually, also office buildings) began in the Industrial Revolution. With it came the time clock and closer supervision. I have already discussed the human consequences of the factory system in Part One.

The first decades of the twentieth century saw a second qualitative leap toward closer supervision. On the one hand, workers successfully struggled for a shorter working day—first ten hours and eventually eight hours. Better machinery allowed productivity—output per man-hour—to rise and compensated for the shorter workday. On the other hand, employers believed that proper application of scientific principles to work organization could make workers more disciplined and more productive. Factories swarmed with "scientific managers" and "time-and-motion" men who measured every movement the workers made and tried to force on the worker more efficient motions and use of time. Jobs were subdivided into minute tasks. In other words, efforts were made to supervise workers even more closely and to remove all self-determination and initiative from manual labor.

Workers, of course, resented the "scientific managers" and ignored their schemes. When time-and-motion men came by to observe their work, the workers moved languidly with many excess motions so that the time-and-motion men would advise eliminating movements that the workers normally didn't make anyway. Shortly after the onslaught of the scientific management craze, employers began to institute assembly lines. Here technology substituted for the orders of supervisors. The line or conveyor belt could be set at a speed that would *force* workers to produce more. In fact, less than 10 percent of the labor force in the United States works at assembly-line jobs, but the line has come to stand for everything in factory work that is counter to human initiative and creativity—minute breakdown of jobs into meaningless repetitive motions and a forced pace of work.

In other words, the history of work organization, from preindustrial capitalism and the putting-out system, through factory organization, to scientific management and the assembly line, has been the history of less and less worker control over jobs. Workers have lost control over the place of work, the pace of work, the tools, the final product, the length of the workday, and finally even over their own motions. In return, their major gain has been a shortened workday and workweek.

This is the larger picture from the eighteenth century to the present. A closer look at trends currently underway suggests some reversals of the long-term trend. On the one hand, in many factories, narrowly subdivided jobs, with or without an assembly line, continue to frustrate and anger workers. Repetitive monotonous tasks, paced by machinery and performed in noisy settings, have also invaded the clerical field and reduced it to blue-collar work carried out in street clothes. Some workers have responded by building their life more around their leisure time, by writing off work as a hopelessly unpleasant but necessary evil, by being drunk or stoned on the job, or by demanding more leisure (forty hours pay for thirty hours work). Another response has been to demand a more interesting reorganization of work, in which the workers' control over the production process and the scope of their task would be broadened. Management has sometimes agreed, in hopes of achieving better morale or a higher quality product, especially in plants committed to making fairly high-quality, expensive products, such as the Volvo and Saab auto plants in Sweden.

Often management has been very reluctant to increase workers' control over the job, fearing perhaps that a drop in productivity would occur and also that the change would whet workers' appetites for yet more control, to the point where the plant would become unmanageable. As long as the work force is low-skilled, isolated from each other through subdivided tasks, and transient, management can treat each worker as a replaceable part. Once the workers are skilled, have an overview of the production process, and cooperate with each other, they are more unified and less easily replaced.

New patterns of work organization seem to be hastened by new technologies. Automation and computerization has made office work more like factory work. But it has also had other effects. In some factories, automated industrial control processes have removed workers from the factory floor. They now work as monitors and repairers of the automated equipment. Some people like this work, while others find it frustrating. In any case, automation seems to have widened the scope of factory jobs again, to make work more challenging and crisis-oriented instead of routine and repetitive, and to protect workers from direct contact with noxious chemicals.

Computers have also made possible a partial return to the putting-out system, in which remote terminals can be used to decentralize work and return it to people's homes. This technological capacity so far has been used in fields such as printing to eliminate a highly skilled, highly paid unionized labor force and to replace it with nonunionized part-time workers who are paid less per hour and receive no fringe benefits. The sense of solidarity and shared problems that factory organization fostered among workers are lost in decentralized, computer-based "putting-out" systems. As in the past, technology is being used to lower labor costs and increase management's control over the work process.

What all these trends will add up to is still unclear. Will the labor force become increasingly restless and rebellious, as suggested by the disturbances at the Lordstown Vega plant in recent years, where workers engaged in disruptions and wildcat strikes to protest against management's use of a fast-paced assembly line, semiautomated equipment, and rigid discipline? Will workers be bought off by more leisure time or by job "enrichments"? Will automation make blue-collar work more attractive? Will it encourage white-collar workers to develop unions and a sense of solidarity like factory workers often have? Will it be used to isolate workers from each other in a modern form of the putting-out system? If all these trends occur together, what will be the *net* effect? It is still too early to make predictions.

Overall, however, the organization of production involves larger and larger numbers of people working together in increasingly complicated networks of cooperation. Even when they are no longer physically together (as in the case of people working at widely separated computer terminals), they are still dependent on each other. Farming and white-collar work, as well as manufacturing, have become cooperative and large scale. The coordination of all of these productive activities has become a major activity itself.

The Diffusion of Industrialization

Industrialization spread from England to the continent. By the middle of the nineteenth century, England led the world in industrial production. She produced two-thirds of the world's coal and more than half of its iron and cotton cloth (Landes, 1969:124). But the continental powers had been making efforts to catch up. The state played a much more active role in continental industrialization than it had in Britain. The stimulus to industrialize was the example of Britain.

How long growth could have continued without necessitating a change in technique is another matter. Yet the issue is an idle one, for the continental countries did not have the opportunity to work out their own destinies. The changes across the Channel drastically changed their economic and political situation. For private enterprise, the immediate effects were frightening: traditional domestic industries, wherever they were unprotected, began to smother under the weight of cheap British goods. By the same token, exporters found their competitive position in international trade gravely undermined; and while most were reconciled by this time to seeing English manufactures win a privileged position in overseas markets, they were not prepared to abandon the struggle entirely. Moreover change had its positive attractions; the British had opened a mine of profit for all the world to see.

For the state, British progress was a direct, unavoidable challenge The governments of Europe had long come to look upon economic development as the key to a favourable balance of trade—hence wealth; to large tax revenues—hence power; and to stable employment—hence public order. They had traditionally encouraged enterprise as best they knew, cherishing especially those trades that furnish the means of war. Now they found the entire balance of economic forces upset. Industrialization was, from the start, a political imperative (Landes, 1969:138–139).

In France, the revolution, by wiping away feudal restraints on capitalist enterprise, provided a political and structural base for industrialization. The bourgeoisie had a freer hand; and the state, which involved itself in the economy, did so on behalf of the bourgeoisie.

How did the continental states—France, Belgium, the German principalities—intervene positively in industrialization, other than by merely removing feudal restraints? They provided technical schools, the means of transportation (first waterways and later, in Germany and Austria, railroads) and, above all, capital both in loans and outright gifts. In some areas, like the coal-and-ore-rich German principality of Silesia, the state actually set up mining and smelting establishments. In general, the later the country industrialized, the more the state actively participated in industrialization and the more the industrial enterprises were actually state owned, ranging from Britain, through France and Belgium to western German, Prussia, and Silesia.

Continental technology, although it developed later than British technology, was in some ways more sophisticated. More emphasis was placed on fuel economy. Scientific theories and close cooperation between scientific institutions and productive enterprises developed, in contrast with the more "practical" technological development of Britain.

Another difference between English and continental industrial development was that continental enterprises were less "rationalized" by capitalist standards. Many enterprises were family owned, especially in France, and family ties overlapped and interfered with business relations. The putting-out system survived longer on the continent. Commercial agriculture was in the hands of peasant proprietors in France and western Germany and hence not as efficient nor as rapacious as in England, Prussia, or eastern Europe. Labor discipline was different. Even with the abolition of feudal ties between master and worker, continental employers tended to be more paternalistic, especially in the family enterprises. In England, "the best remedy for insubordination was technological unemployment" (Landes, 1969:190). On the continent, both employers and the state made efforts to limit the number of the unemployed.

At the same time, the continental—especially French—history of revolts and revolutions made the bourgeoisie more afraid of the laboring classes.

By the 1870s, France and Belgium had caught up to England, as did Germany in the 1890s. In some respects, the late developers—especially Germany—surpassed England. As the pioneer industrializing country, Britain had necessarily overcommitted herself to a technology and a physical plant based on coal and iron, and to a laissez-faire state that involved itself relatively little in the actual process of production. When better materials and energy sources were developed in the late nineteenth century, it was easier for the late industrializers to develop them while Britain's capacity for change was hampered.

> The Industrial Revolution in France or Germany was very different from what it was in Britain—and this, not only because of the peculiar circumstances and endowments of each of these countries, but also because they made their moves later and indeed skipped certain moves altogether.... their very lateness now turned to their advantage (Landes, 1969:230–231).

The United States began its major industrializing spurt after the Civil War, and Japan began around the turn of the century. Russia had some beginnings of industrialization before the revolution but little heavy industry till the 1930s. Northern Italy was as industrially developed as the other industrial continental states, but the country as a whole had to cope with the deadweight of the backward south. Eastern Europe and the Scandinavian countries developed some industry, and Spain had a few industrial pockets, whose growth was at least temporarily slowed during the civil war of the 1930s.

By World War II, then, world industrialization had taken the following shape: the European core states were substantially industrialized. Germany, Japan, and the United States, although not in the initial capitalist core, had fully caught up with the core. The Soviet Union was also extensively industrialized. The regions that in the seventeenth century had fallen into the semiperiphery—Italy, eastern Europe, Scandinavia, bits of Spain—were partially industrialized. Latin America, Africa, and Asia (other than Japan) were substantially unindustrialized. They provided raw materials (based on mining and commercial agriculture, often using coerced labor) and a market for finished products. They were affected by the industrialization of the rest of the world but were not themselves industrialized.

At present it is unclear whether these countries will industrialize. Some, like the countries of the western Sudan in Africa, lack natural resources. Others have been forced to let the industrialized countries treat them as raw material sources and find it difficult to break this dependency. As the price of certain raw materials—such as oil or sugar—increases dramatically, these arrangements have actually become profitable for the countries. Nevertheless, their dependency may stand in the way of more even internal development. Often the profits of the export trade are not distributed equitably within the country and are not used to increase the well-being of the population as a whole. Some countries—such as China and Vietnam—are deliberately trying to industrialize only gradually, keeping much of the population agrarian or involved only in light, decentralized industry.

These facts illustrate how countries come to develop unevenly and show why no country's development ever exactly replicates the stages through which other countries have passed. Later developers necessarily face obstacles and enjoy advantages that did not affect their predecessors. Sometimes the early industrializers seized resources and made them unavailable to latecomers. The early industrializers also often turned other areas of the world into colonies or dependent regions, preventing them from embarking an autonomous industrialization. At the same time, however, the later developers were able to learn from the mistakes of their predecessors and to benefit from a direct plunge into more up-to-date technologies—provided, of course, they were able to liberate themselves from exploitation and dependency.

The Second and Third Phases of Industrialization

I've already remarked that one of the most important characteristics of industrial capitalism is the institutionalization of change. Marx pointed up this situation so well in *The Communist Manifesto:*

> Constant revolutionizing of production, uninterrupted disturbance of all social conditions, everlasting uncertainty and agitation distinguish the bourgeois epoch from all earlier ones. All fixed, fast-frozen relations, with their train of ancient and venerable prejudices and opinions, are swept away, all new-formed ones become antiquated before they can ossify. All that is solid melts into air, all that is holy is profaned, and man is at last compelled to face with sober senses, his real conditions of life, and his relations with his kind (Marx & Engels, 1948).

In particular, technological change continued throughout the nineteenth and twentieth centuries. However, it is useful to break this longer period into three subperiods. The first, running from the late eighteenth century to the late nineteenth century, was characterized by the use of coal and iron, by the imposition of the factory system, and by the spread of industrialization throughout the European core states. The second phase, which started in the 1870s and continued to the end of World War II, was characterized by the application of new materials and energy forms. Oil, gas, electricity, and improved steel came into use. Synthetic dyes and textiles were developed. Scientific management, the assembly line, and emphasis on cheap mass production were innovations in the area of the relations of production and distribution. Germany, Japan, the United States, and the Soviet Union became industrial giants. In the third period, which began in the 1940s, nuclear power and sophisticated electronic technology, such as computers and television, were major technological developments. Synthetic fibers, plastics, and jet-powered airplanes are examples of inventions of the previous period that were refined in this period. I have already discussed some of the trends in work organization of the postwar period. During this period, industrial expansion occurred so rapidly that resources were depleted and the natural environment was filled with toxic wastes. These effects of industrialization may ultimately slow down or even terminate industrial expansion.

Changes in industrial processes and work organization were not initiated only by management. During the first phase of industrialization, relations between workers and employers in England and elsewhere were often violent. The second phase began with unrest, in some cases leading to open warfare over control of the political system—as when Paris was seized by the working class in 1871. In some countries, these patterns of conflict continued into the twentieth century. In western Europe and the United States, the revolt of workers tended to be regulated and co-opted. Labor unions helped workers win important demands, such as the shorter workday. They also helped to regulate worker discontent and to channel workers' anger into demands that could be negotiated within the capitalist system. The standard of living, which had dropped in England during early industrialization, began to rise again in the middle of the nineteenth century. With the advent of mass production in the twentieth century, workers became able to purchase a variety of goods. The extension of political participation to propertyless laborers was also generally achieved by the second phase of industrialization. Elections and the party system of the western European and American capitalist countries provided some genuine voice in decision-making as well as outlets for tension and protest that would otherwise have found extralegal expression.

In the next section I shall describe changes in where and how people lived that were caused by the growth of industrial capitalism. These changes include migration to cities and industrial centers, and a sequence of alterations in family structure and population growth.

Urbanization and Changes in Life-Styles

Changes in life-styles accompanied changes in the mode of production. These life-style changes can be broken down into changes in patterns of residence and community structure, changes in family structure, and changes in population characteristics. In fact, however, these changes tended to occur together.

Changes in Patterns of Residence and Community Structure

Urbanization in Europe began in the Middle Ages; or, to be more precise, it began *again* in the Middle Ages, after the long rural interlude that started with the collapse of the Roman Empire. While Europe had some brilliant and creative cities in the late Middle Ages and the transitional period, most Europeans were rural. In the semiperipheral areas, over 90 percent of the population was rural. In the core states, there were more urban residents; but a large majority of the population was rural.

The urbanities often lived in small provincial towns. They were distinct in dress, customs, education, and often ethnicity from the peasantry, but they were not at all like the residents of a modern metropolis or manufacturing city. The urbanites were the gentry with nearby estates; artisans and shopkeepers; middlemen who bought and sold agricultural products; lawyers who handled disputes over land; government officials; and entrepreneurs who managed the putting-out system of the rural craftsmen. In short, the typical town was economically integrated with and dependent on the surrounding countryside.

The middle classes of these towns produced the bourgeois revolutionaries as well as the first industrial capitalists. "These . . . were the towns out of which ardent and ambitious young men came to make revolutions or their first million, or both" (Hobsbawm, 1962:27). In Europe in the late eighteenth century, there were two large cities—London, with a population of a million, and Paris, with about half a million—"and a score or so with a population of 100,000 or more: two in France, two in Germany, perhaps four in Spain, perhaps five in Italy (the Mediterranean was traditionally the home of cities), two in Russia, and one each in Portugal, Poland, Holland, Austria, Ireland, Scotland, and European Turkey" (Hobsbawm, 1962:26–27).

The introduction of the factory meant the concentration of people. In the first half of the nineteenth century in England, and slightly later in other industrializing areas, manufacturing cities and towns appeared. Some of these were older cities converted to industrial centers, others were new urban areas: Manchester, Sheffield, Birmingham, and Leeds in England; Mulhouse, Lille, Lyons, and Rouen in France; and, later, Milan, Turin, the textile towns of Massachusetts, Glasgow, Pittsburgh, Liege, Rotterdam, and so on. In many countries, industry was located in clusters of manufacturing or mining villages rather than in cities. Large cities like London were not industrialized; rather they were primarily commercial, financial, political, and cultural centers.

The concentration of population into manufacturing towns and clusters of manufacturing villages initially meant drops in the standard of living. During the early phase of industrialization, real wages, diet, control over one's work, and the amount of leisure time were reduced as a result of the new mode of production, while mortality rates increased as more and more people became concentrated in the shoddily built, unsanitary towns. Europe experienced repeated cholera epidemics into the 1850s, with the industrial towns being especially hard hit. Although western Europe was undergoing a population boom, the population of the industrial towns did not replace itself.

Engels, a contemporary observer, has described the conditions under which the working classes lived. The city of Manchester, in the northwest of England, was doubtless among the worst in Europe, but it was not unique.

The Old Town of Manchester

Above Ducie Bridge the left bank of the Irk becomes flatter and the right bank of the Irk becomes steeper and so the condition of the houses on both sides of the river becomes worse rather than better. Turning left from the main street which is still Long Millgate, the visitor can easily lose his way. He wanders aimlessly from one court to another. He turns one corner after another through innumerable narrow dirty alleyways and passages, and in only a few minutes he has lost all sense of direction and does not know which way to turn. The area is full of ruined or half-ruined buildings. Some of them are actually uninhabited and that means a great deal in this quarter of the town. In the houses one seldom sees a wooden or a stone floor, while the doors and windows are nearly always broken and badly fitting. And as for the dirt! Everywhere one sees heaps of refuse, garbage and filth. There are stagnant pools instead of gutters and the stench alone is so over-powering that no human being, even partially civilised, would find it bearable to live in such a district. The recently constructed extension of the Leeds railway which crosses the Irk at this point has swept away some of these courts and alleys, but it has thrown open to public gaze some of the others. So it comes about that there is to be found immediately under the railway bridge a court which is even filthier and more revolting than all the others. This is simply because it was formerly so hidden and secluded that it could only be reached with considerable difficulty, [but is now exposed to the human eye]. I thought I knew this district well, but even I would never have found it had not the railway viaduct made a breach in the slums at this point. One walks along a very rough path on the river bank, in between clothes-posts and washing lines to reach a chaotic group of little, one-storied, one-roomed cabins. Most of them have earth floors, and working, living and sleeping all take place in the one room. In such a hole, barely six feet long and five feet wide, I saw two beds—and what beds and bedding!—which filled the room, except for the fireplace and the doorstep. Several of these huts, as far as I could see, were completely empty, although the door was open and the inhabitants were leaning against the door posts. In front of the doors filth and garbage abounded. I could not see the pavement, but from time to time, I felt it was there because my feet scraped it. This whole collection of cattle sheds for human beings was surrounded on two sides by houses and a factory and on a third side by the river. [It was possible to get to this slum by only two routes.] One was the narrow path along the river bank, while the other was a narrow gateway which led to another human rabbit warren which was nearly as badly built and was nearly in such a bad condition as the one I have just described.

Enough of this! All along the Irk slums of this type abound. There is an unplanned and chaotic conglomeration of houses, most of which are more or less unhabitable. The dirtiness of the interiors of these premises is fully in keeping with the filth that surrounds them. How can people dwelling in such places keep clean! There are not even adequate facilities for satisfying the most natural daily needs. There are so few privies that they are either filled up every day or are too far away for those who need to use them. How can these people wash when all that is available is the dirty water of the Irk? Pumps and piped water are to be found only in the better-class districts of the town. Indeed no one can blame these helots of modern civilisation if their homes are no cleaner than the occasional pigsties which are a feature of these slums. There are actually some property owners who are not ashamed to let dwellings such as those which are to be found below Scotland Bridge. Here on the quayside a mere six feet from the water's edge is to be found a row of six or seven cellars, the bottoms of which are at least two feet beneath the low-water level of the Irk. [What can one say of the owner of] the corner house—situated on the opposite bank of the river above Scotland Bridge—who actually lets the upper floor although the premises downstairs are quite uninhabitable, and no attempt has been made to board up the gaps left by the disappearance of doors and windows? This sort of thing is by no means uncommon in this part of Manchester, where, owing to the lack of conveniences, such deserted ground floors are often used by the whole neighbourhood as privies. . . .

This, then, is the Old Town of Manchester. On re-reading my description of the Old Town I must admit that, far from having exaggerated anything, I have not written vividly enough to impress the reader with the filth and dilapidation of a district which is quite unfit for human habitation. The shameful lay-out of the Old Town has made it impossible for the wretched inhabitants to enjoy cleanliness, fresh air, and good health. And such a district of at least twenty to thirty thousand inhabitants lies in the very centre of the second city in England, the most important factory town in the world. It is here that one can see how little space human beings need to move about in, how little air—and what air!—they need to breathe in order to exist, and how few of the decencies of civilisation are really necessary in order to survive. It is true that this is the *Old Town* and Manchester people stress this when their attention is drawn to the revolting character of this hell upon earth. But that is no defence. Everything in this district that arouses our disgust and just indignation is of relatively recent origin and belongs to the industrial age. The two or three hundred houses which survive from the earlier period of Manchester's history have long ago been deserted by their original inhabitants. It is only industry which has crammed them full of the hordes of workers who now live there. It is only the modern industrial age which has built over every scrap of ground between these old houses to provide accommodation for the masses who have migrated from the country districts and from Ireland. It is only the industrial age that has made it possible for the owners of these shacks, fit only for the accommodation of cattle, to let them at high rents for human habitations. It is only modern industry which permits these owners to take advantage of the poverty of the workers, to undermine the health of thousands to enrich themselves. Only industry has made it possible for workers who have barely emerged from a state of serfdom to be again treated as chattels and not as human beings. The workers have been caged in dwellings which are so wretched that no one else will live in them, and they actually pay good money for the privilege of seeing these dilapidated hovels fall to pieces about their ears. Industry alone has been responsible for all this and yet this same industry could not flourish except by degrading and exploiting the workers. It is true that this quarter of the town was orginally built on a poor site, which offered few prospects for satisfactory development. But have either the landowners or the authorities done anything to improve matters when new buildings were erected? Far from adopting any such policy those responsible for recent developments have built houses in every conceivable nook and cranny. Even small passages which were not absolutely necessary have been built over and stopped up. The value of the land rose with the expansion of industry. The more the land rose in value the more furious became the search for new building sites. The health and comfort of the inhabitants were totally ignored, as a result of the determination of landlords to pocket maximum profit. No hovel is so wretched but it will find a worker to rent it because he is too poor to pay for better accommodation.

(Engels, 1958:61-62, 64)

Nevertheless, despite such living conditions in many of the industrial towns, the proportion of the population that was urban steadily increased. By 1850, more than half the population of England was urban (including small towns). In other industrializing areas of the world, urbanization lagged behind England, but it also increased.

Urbanization meant not only the concentration of people in cities but also altered ways of life. A small but increasing proportion of urban people— particularly in the great commercial and political centers—became urbane as well as urban. They developed the wide-ranging tastes, the individualism, and the sophistication of the stereotyped urbanite. Some of these urbanites were the wealthy who could afford to experiment with new life-styles and new entertainments. Under their patronage, experimentation in art, music, and literature began to flourish in the late nineteenth and early twentieth centuries. Fashion changes in art as well as dress took place more frequently than ever before. Their wealth may have been founded on the greed and hard work of their fathers and grandfathers, but the urbanites declared themselves free of these bourgeois virtues. It is this cosmopolitan, playful individualism that some writers have singled out as the hallmark of urbanism (Simmel, 1950).

Poorer people who were uprooted from their rural communities and their peasant and artisan traditions perforce led a less charming life. When trade unions, political movements, or religious sects failed to organize the urban poor into new communities, the resulting individualism was often expressed in ignorance, alcoholism, petty crime, and despair. Urbanization continued throughout the nineteenth century and well into the twentieth century wherever rural people were drawn into industry.

The Population Explosion and the Demographic Transition

Capitalism produced more people as well as more goods. As countries were drawn into the orbit of capitalism, their populations started to grow. Europe was the first region of the world to experience a population explosion. The core states were the first to undergo this steady growth, beginning in the second half of the eighteenth century. The key factor was the drop in the mortality rate. The decline in mortality was due to better sanitation (although, as I've remarked, diseases associated with poor sanitation persisted into the nineteenth century) and more effective distribution and preservation of food, which cut down the number of deaths caused by local famines. Only in the middle of the nineteenth century did modern scientific medicine begin to play a part in the drop in the mortality rate, as vaccination, pasteurization, antiseptic surgery, anesthesia, and so on were invented.

From the core states, the population explosion spread to the peripheral areas of Europe, sometimes with disastrous consequences. Ireland, for example, underwent very rapid population growth incommensurate with the productivity of the agricultural system and the exploitive practices of the English landlords. As the population rose and overwhelmed the food supply, a bad harvest meant starvation. Over a million people starved in the potato famine of the 1840s.

By the end of the nineteenth century, Europeans had become one of the largest segments of world population (See Figure 7).

Figure 7

Percentage of World Population of European Ancestry

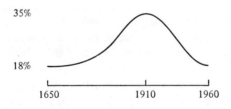

Population-Control Measures.   Europeans developed two solutions to their population problem: birth control and emigration. In the nineteenth century, many couples began to limit the size of their families. At first only infanticide and the primitive methods of birth control available in preindustrial times were used—crude abortion, abstinence, and coitus interruptus (withdrawal before ejaculation). There were some subcultural variations in the choice of these methods. For example, in Ireland, the terrible experience of the potato famine, coupled with a strong Catholic ideology, made late marriage and abstinence the typical population-control measures. Infanticide (including the de facto infanticide of abandoning children in orphanages, where most died) was more prevalent among the desperately poor than among the middle class. More humane birth control became possible with the invention of condoms and diaphragms. The use of contraceptive devices spread despite efforts at official suppression in Protestant as well as Catholic countries.

Since Europeans and people of European descent controlled, either economically or militarily, much of the rest of the world, Europeans could emigrate into more sparsely settled regions. In other words, European population pressure could be relieved because European imperialism made possible the seizure of land from other peoples. Relatively few Europeans emigrated to colonies already densely settled by traditional class societies (India, Indochina, and Indonesia, for example). Europeans also avoided regions with hot tropical climates. Mass emigration took place to temperate regions sparsely populated by hunting and food-gathering bands: North America, Australia, Argentina, southern Africa, and (for the Russians) Siberia. The people who already lived in these places were either killed or confined to reservations.

Meanwhile, European colonialism touched off population explosions in the colonized areas. The same causes that lowered mortality in Europe took effect in the colonies. After World War II, spraying of malarial swamps accelerated these trends in Africa, Asia, and Latin America.

In Europe and countries settled by Europeans, birth rates had dropped with the increased use of birth-control measures. Despite a baby boom following World War II, birth rates remained much lower in these countries than in the rest of the world. Some demographers—people who study population characteristics—believed that the same type of population change that had occurred in Europe might occur elsewhere. Population changes in Europe and North America are summarized in Figure 8.

Figure 8

Population Changes in Europe and North America

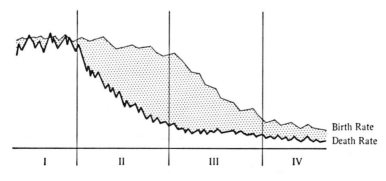

In Phase I of Figure 8, both birth and death rates are high. There is little population increase. In Phase II, the death rate drops but the birth rate remains high. The shaded area indicates population growth, which is large. In Phase III, the birth rate drops. In Phase IV, both the birth and death rates are low. There is little population increase.

The transition from Phase I to Phase II did not require the planning or consent of individuals or couples, but was accomplished by improving city sanitation, by preserving and distributing food more efficiently, by spraying malarial swamps, and by innoculating masses of people against disease. These death-control measures were based on decisions by states, municipalities, or companies. Birth control—the prerequisite for passing from Phase II to Phases III and IV—requires *at present* the agreement and participation of millions of couples or, at least, individual women. So far, no state has been ready to force sterilization on large parts of its population. Most countries of Europe and North America have passed through this demographic transition to the fourth phase. They experienced rapid population growth in the past but now have little or no population growth. Countries in Asia, Africa, and Latin America are generally in Phases II or III. Their mortality rates have dropped but their birth rates remain high; these are areas of rapid population growth. Because of the present world political situation, emigration is not a likely means for relieving population pressure in these countries.

Contrary to popular belief, relatively few countries have *absolute* shortages of food. Food scarcity is primarily a problem of unequal distribution and irrational production. Acreage that should be given over to a diversity of crops for regional or national consumption is devoted to a single cash crop for export. Some of the hungriest regions in the world have been trapped in cash-crop monoculture production: peanuts in Mali, sugar in the Caribbean, coffee and sisal in parts of Latin America, and so on. In other regions, the soil is eroded and forests are destroyed. Food distribution is inefficient and unfair within the country; entrepreneurs are allowed to hoard it and price gouge. Some regions of the world, like parts of Africa, seem simultaneously over-populated and underpopulated. There are too many people for the available food resources although not enough to undertake a more rational diversified labor-intensive agriculture or to provide the necessary labor force for industrial development.

In some countries, population growth may halt only if death rates again climb. Famines, protein deficiency, and sickness are already widespread in parts of Africa and southern Asia. Birth control would be a more rational and humane way to relieve population pressure on scarce resources. However, birth control seems to depend in large part on prior changes in the social structure. In Europe, these changes began when the population became urbanized, when women had to or wanted to work outside the home, and when the family stopped functioning as a source of economic security. As long as the population of underdeveloped countries is largely rural, as long as women are expected to be primarily child bearers, as long as men define masculinity in terms of fathering sons, as long as people believe in religions that preach the immorality of birth control, and as long as there are few institutions other than the family to provide old-age security, couples will continue to have many children. Also, as long as the social structure of these underdeveloped countries is controlled by a small exploitive landowning or managing class or by corporations based in the industrialized world these conditions will not change.

So the vicious cycle continues: increasing population makes industrial and agricultural development difficult because the country has so many mouths to feed; yet until such development takes place, couples need to increase the size of their families to have more help in the fields and to provide a source of support in their old age. For instance, in many countries a son is a vital source of support for his parents. Yet with a child mortality rate of about 50 percent, a couple has to have four to six children to be reasonably sure that they will have a surviving son. Thus, having a large family is a rational decision, at least in the short run. Also, structural changes in the distribution of wealth and the position of women must occur together with the spread of birth-control techniques. China is an example of a nation that has been able to cut into this cycle. After the revolution, the life of the people became more secure and comfortable; they worried less about their old age; their children no longer died; and women moved toward equality. As a consequence, the Chinese limited their family size because it now was a rational action.

Changing Physical Characteristics.   Not only did capitalism change population size, it also changed the physical characteristics of the population. Improved diets made people larger (although not necessarily stronger). For example, in the late eighteenth century, 72 percent of the soldiers in the Italian region of Liguria were under five feet two inches in height (Hobsbawm, 1962:24). Men over five feet eight inches were nicknamed "Colossus" or "Behemoth." In revolutionary France, men five feet three inches or five feet four inches tall were considered of average height.

Heights and weights increased during the nineteenth century and increased rapidly in the twentieth century in Europe and North America. Women began to menstruate at increasingly early ages. The drop in age at first menses occurred first for urban and wealthier populations. This growth in stature and earlier sexual maturation are still underway both in the industrialized countries and among the middle classes in poorer countries. In the latter, marked differences in height and weight according to class position are becoming apparent.

New Life-Styles and Family Patterns

In industrializing countries, urbanization, the factory system, and the political ascendance of the bourgeoisie brought with them new patterns of culture, interaction, and family structure. These developments were by no means simple or unilineal. They were different in form and occurred at different rates for different classes and subcultures.

The most obvious, widespread, and decisive change was in the role played by the family: the family ceased to be a unit of production, and the household ceased to be a production site for urban people of virtually all classes. The place of production and the place of leisure and family life were separated. Different family members might still each contribute to the income of the household, but they did so as separately employed workers not by working together cooperatively. In many middle-class families, a division of activity developed in which women came to be in charge of consumption in the household and men in charge of production at a workplace. Only very recently has the women's movement challenged this arrangement.

Between the end of feudalism and our own day, the size of households has decreased. But this trend has been very gradual and not without reverses. Already in the sixteenth and seventeenth centuries, the households of the poor were reduced to the nuclear family—father, mother, and children—and sometimes only to isolated individuals. This was especially true in England, where the enclosure system tore apart traditional peasant life. Among the middle class, households included not only an extended family—the nuclear family plus grandparents and/or other relatives—but also servants, apprentices, and hangers on. By the early nineteenth century, some of these unrelated residents were disappearing from the household. The factory system reduced the integration of young workers into the households of masters, a practice that had been prevalent in the guild system. By the early twentieth century, servants were disappearing from all but the wealthier households, along with maiden aunts and bachelor uncles. In our own day, even aged parents are gone, sent to live by themselves in communities of the elderly or in nursing homes; such, at any rate, is the ideal promulgated by the media. Households have tended to shrink to a core of one or both parents and their minor children, at least in the urban middle class.

Similar trends seem to be occurring outside of the industrialized core states. As was true in nineteenth-century Europe, people in Asia, Africa, and Latin America who can afford large households prefer to maintain them even in urban areas. The urban poor are forced to be the first to live in smaller households. In addition, the peripheral areas have experienced large amounts of labor migration. Men seeking work have left North Africa, Italy, the Balkans, Spain, and Turkey to find menial jobs in northern Europe. Men have left the rural areas of Africa to work in the cities and in the gold and diamond mines of southern Africa and the copper mines of central Africa. Men have left villages in Bengal and Orissa to eke out a living in the streets of Calcutta. The preponderance of men in the cities and of wives and families left behind in the countryside add personal problems to the already severe economic problems of the developing countries. At an earlier time, similar male migrations took place from Europe and the Orient to the United States as well as within the United States and European countries.

The experience of living in a nuclear family is by no means a typical human experience. On the contrary, it seems most characteristic of the upper and middle strata (i.e., the bourgeoisie and the better-off working class) in the advanced industrial countries. Since the end of feudalism, many people have lived either in larger households, often headed by women, or (particularly men) as isolated individuals, or in all-male barrack arrangements.

A "normal" childhood—the experience of growing up in a child-centered nuclear family—is another experience restricted to the upper and middle strata of the advanced industrial countries. The poorer people of industrial countries and the large masses of people in the peripheral countries, like Europeans of all classes during the transitional period, have conceptions of childhood that are very different from those of middle America. Childhood is a much briefer period of human life for them. Children have had to grow up fast, to go to work as fieldhands, apprentices, or laborers in workshops. Childhood is not thought to be a time of innocence; rather, children are thought of as small incompetent adults. They are not shielded from the adult world of hard labor, violence, or sexuality. Children participate in adult recreation as well as in adult labor. In the past, children wore miniature versions of adult clothing. In many societies, they live in a community filled with adults, in which no special arrangements are made for their development.

At present, there are some trends in the United States and northern Europe toward the complete fragmentation of the family. Capitalism's emphasis on the isolated individual, "freed" from all traditional ties, is reaching its logical extreme. More and more people remain single or return to single life after divorce. Marriages are brittle, and couples often live together on a temporary basis. The birth rate is declining. This brittleness in family structure is partly related to the greater economic independence of women, who now can (and in many cases must) support themselves. The women's movement has given meaning and legitimacy to substructural trends that weaken the nuclear family. The ideology of "freedom," of "doing your own thing," of pursuing "meaningful relationships" has also legitimated and furthered the breakup of the family into its single constituent individuals. It still remains to be seen whether these trends will continue.

New Cities, New Suburbs

In the twentieth century, two new developments have taken place in urbanization. One is the rapid growth of urbanization in the underdeveloped countries. The second is urban sprawl, suburbanization, and the growth of the megalopolis in the industrialized countries.

Urbanization.   Before the presently underdeveloped countries were under-developed—i.e., before they were drawn into the economic sphere of influence of the industrialized countries—they contained cities that were cultural and political centers. These cities were the capitals and the temple cities of the traditional empires and stratified states of Asia and Africa. However, as these regions were drawn into the colonial empires or the commercial spheres of influence of the industrialized countries, the old cities either changed their function or, more frequently, declined in importance and population.

Preeminence passed from the old cultural and political centers to the towns through which trade with the Europeans (or Japanese) was carried on. Calcutta, Singapore, Lagos, Colombo, Rangoon, Port Arthur (in pre-revolutionary China), Aden, Dakar—many of them now major cities in the underdeveloped countries—were trading depots established by Europeans and swollen to monstrous size by floods of people from the hinterlands, peasants uprooted from subsistence farming and seeking a meager living in the new economy. The old centers of the hinterlands—Benin and Timbuktu, Pagan and Mandalay, Kandy, the princely city-states of Java, Fez and Marrakesh, Benares, Shibam in South Arabia—became off-the-beaten-track tourist attractions and romantic names on schoolboys' maps.

The new cities have grown very large without having an industrial base. (It could be argued that cities such as London and Paris are not primarily industrial either, but they are the nerve centers of enormous industrial and commercial empires.) Many people in these new cities are unemployed or underemployed. Often they are not an industrial proletariat; rather they eke out a living as petty traders, as artisans or suppliers of illegal commodities (stolen goods, drugs, prostitution), or as laborers in service work (domestics, restaurant or transportation workers, and so on). The shantytowns in which they live ring the more well-to-do areas of these cities.

The inner cities and attractive suburban areas are occupied by the bourgeoisie—absentee landowners, some industrialists and other entrepreneurs, managers for foreign and local firms, and professionals. A lower middle class of white-collar workers also lives in the central cities and suburbs. The poor live in shacks on the hillsides or in outlying areas that are often without water mains, sewers, paved streets, or other amenities of city life. Sometimes the poor are squatters who have no legal claim to the land they occupy. In South Africa, blacks, Indians, and colored (mixed) people are forced to live in the "locations"—the outlying areas set aside for nonwhites. (This distinction by color and culture is even beginning to appear in France and elsewhere in Europe where laborers from North Africa live in shantytowns—*bidonvilles*—on the outskirts of the great cities.)

In other words, urban growth in underdeveloped countries with only a small industrial base is one of the effects of the division of the world into core industrialized capitalist states and their peripheral areas. This type of urban growth may eventually be remedied. In some countries—the oil rich Arab states, for example—an industrial base is beginning to be established; in other countries—such as China and Vietnam—urbanization is being slowed down by deliberate state policy to avoid the impoverishment of rural areas and the buildup of underemployed masses in the cities.

Urban Sprawl.   The leading twentieth-century trend in North America, Europe, Japan, and other *industrialized* areas is toward the spread of cities into the surrounding countryside. We have already seen how the automobile has been one of the major factors in this urban sprawl. The resistance of many people to high-density living has also led to the growth of suburban areas made up of single-family houses, on small plots of land. Cities have thus spread beyond the legal confines of the original municipality. They are now better identified by the concept *metropolitan area,* which (in the United States) takes in all counties that are economically integrated into the city.

Population growth in the United States has been chiefly in the suburban areas since World War II. The suburbs have received an outflow of white middle-class and better-off working-class people who are fleeing the congestion of the inner city with its—to them—threatening, predominantly black and Latino poor population. These population shifts accompany the move of industry and commercial enterprises into the suburban ring. Virtually no new factories have been built in inner cities since World War II. Suburban shopping centers, office plazas, and industrial parks, all surrounded by acres of parking lots, have shifted the concentration of economic activity in the metropolitan areas. These suburbanizing trends have been accelerated by the American ideological passion for the "new." In Europe, where similar population and economic pressures are at work, but where the ideologies of racism and newness are not such important factors, suburbanization has been less precipitous. In Europe, the suburbs are frequently working-class areas in which factory workers are crowded into cheaply built new high rises.

The federal government, in cooperation with city governments and private developers, has tried to retain some of the commercial and cultural (if not industrial) importance of the central cities. They have tried to attract middle-class residents back to the city and to force lower-income black and Latino peoples away from the city centers. They have also tried to attract businesses to the central cities. The Federal Housing Act of 1949 has been one of the major legal vehicles for this set of goals. This act enabled "urban renewal," the process whereby federal funds were used to buy and clear city land that was then sold to private developers. Urban renewal has been only partially successful from the bourgeois point of view, partly because middle-class people have not been especially attracted to high-density, high-rise, high-rent developments; partly because schools and other public facilities have not kept pace with real estate development; partly because poor people have not accepted their displacement without complaint; and partly because federal funds have run out.

Megalopolis.   Urban sprawl in some areas of North America, Japan, and Europe has produced giant regions of high-density residential, commercial, and industrial use with some scattered open land and farms. These regions are variously called *conurbations* and *megalopolis* ("the giant city"). In satellite photos of the U.S.A., such a high-density area is clearly visible along the eastern seaboard stretching from Boston to Washington. Others seem to be forming in southern California from Los Angeles to San Diego, and along the Great Lakes from Milwaukee to Cleveland. Whether the suburbanization and megalopolistic trends will continue in the face of slowed population growth and increased fuel prices remains to be seen.

Imperialism and Underdevelopment

In this section, I shall discuss the way in which every region of the world has been drawn into a world economy. I shall describe some of the ways in which the United States has maintained its leading position in this world economy. I shall describe the internal structure of underdeveloped countries, and I shall show how ethnic conflicts are by-products of the growth of a world economy.

Definitions

Before beginning this discussion of imperialism and underdevelopment, I would like to define my terms and explain the context in which I am using them.

Imperialism.   According to Williams (1972), imperialism is the situation in which one nation plays or tries to play a controlling and one-sided role in the development of a weaker economy. This way of phrasing the definition focuses on the behavior of individual nations. It might be more useful to suggest that imperialism is the worldwide situation of economic control involving two *groups* of nations, the stronger and the weaker. These correspond roughly to what I have elsewhere referred to as the core or central areas of the world economy and the peripheral areas.

Colonialism.   In colonialism, this control by one nation over another nation is imposed by political and military occupation. The colonized area no longer has an autonomous state or other political institutions nor does it possess an independent means of violence. Thus, all colonialism is a form of imperialism, but not vice versa. For example, the vast holdings of European countries in

Africa between the late nineteenth century and World War II were colonies. Britain's nineteenth-century domination of trade in Latin America was an example of imperialism without colonialism, of economic domination without direct control of the state.

In some forms of colonialism, the colonized area is fully incorporated into the dominant state. For example, France has made *départements* of the Caribbean islands of Martinique and Guadeloupe, giving them the same status as the mainland areas, although ethnically, culturally, and economically these areas are very different from the mainland and have, in fact, been exploited peripheral areas. In other cases (European colonies in Africa and Asia, for instance), no efforts were made to incorporate the regions into the metropole ideologically or politically. By *metropole* I mean the nation-state that creates and dominates the empire.

Underdevelopment.   The term *underdevelopment* describes the condition of the colonized or imperialized area. Underdevelopment does not refer to the traditional nonindustrial society and economy that these areas had before they became peripheral areas of the core states. *Underdevelopment is a new form of economy and society. It has its own distinct economy, class structure, political institutions, and culture. The underdeveloped society is as new a type of society as is the industrial capitalist society, and its emergence is closely tied to the emergence of industrial capitalism.* Underdevelopment is the result of the impact of imperialism on the imperialized areas.

A Brief History of Imperialism

There are four identifiable phases of modern imperialism.

Phase One.   The first phase is marked by the expansion of Europe into the rest of the world. It corresponds to the period during which feudalism collapsed in Europe, modern states appeared, and the bourgeoisie began to assume leadership of the economy. The reader should keep in mind that expansion through trade, plunder, and colonization was one of the solutions to the economic crisis of the fourteenth century. This first phase of imperialism, which was launched by Portugal and Spain, included both commercial ventures and colonies. Colonization was especially active in the Americas.

Phase Two.   After their brilliant beginning, Spain and Portugal fumbled. England recovered the orb of empire. By the middle of the seventeenth century, the second phase of imperialism was under way. This period corresponds to the bourgeoisie's rise to hegemony in the core states and to early industrialization. Imperialism throughout this two-hundred-year period was dominated by England, although not without competition from France and Holland. Europe was beset by a series of small wars between the imperial powers, who no longer fought over ideological religious issues but over territorial ambitions. A number of these wars were fought not on the soil of the metropoles but in the territory of their colonies and other peripheral areas.

While England was busy amassing territory in the British Isles, North America, and Asia, the less industrialized nations of central and eastern Europe were also expanding—not overseas but into their own hinterlands. Poland was gobbled up by her three giant neighbors: Prussia, Austria-Hungary (which had already ingested large parts of the Balkans), and Russia. Russia expanded ever eastward, incorporating Central Asia, Siberia, the Aleutian Islands, and Alaska. But England was the first to use her colonies and her trading empire as the basis of industrialization.

Even as empires expanded, however, they created the conditions for their own weakening. Nationalism and the desire for the institutions of citizenship and parliamentary democracy spread from the core states into the European peripheral areas, first in the North American colonies and then in Italy, eastern Europe, the Balkans, and so on. By the first half of the nineteenth century, eastern and southern Europe was already experiencing movements to drive out the Russian, Austrian, Prussian, and Turkish masters, to restore national languages, and to institute bourgeois democratic political forms. These movements were led by students and other young intellectuals.

Phase Three.   By the middle of the nineteenth century, English domination of overseas imperialism gradually came to an end, and the third phase of imperialism began. This third phase of imperialism corresponds to the diffusion of industrialization throughout western Europe, to the middle period of industrial technology (steel-making, electrification, industrial chemistry, and the use of oil), and to the rise of monopoly capitalism in which production is concentrated in the hands of a small number of giant firms. During this third phase, which lasted until World War II, two developments were particularly important: the colonizing of much of the rest of the world by the core capitalist states of western Europe, including Germany, and the invention of new forms of economic domination without colonization.

In the rush to colonize, almost all of Africa was split up among England, France, Belgium and, dating from an earlier period, Portugal. Germany and Italy also picked up some African colonies. Southern and Southeast Asia were similarly parceled out. Latecomers among the colonial powers found that the more attractive regions had already been seized and that they had to fight to get their share. By the end of the nineteenth century, tension had built up over these claims. A number of small wars were fought by states with rival colonial ambitions—between Japan and Russia over interests in the northwestern Pacific (1904), between the English colonial armies and the Dutch settlers in South Africa (1902), between the Americans and the Spanish over Cuba and the Philippines (1898), and so on. The causes of the two world wars also included these rival claims. In addition to the wars between imperial powers, there were also constant conflicts by the imperial powers against the native peoples. The armies of the imperial powers acted with unbelievable ruthlessness against the peoples of the areas in question; forced labor, punitive massacres, and deliberate extermination were typical practices.

The second major development of this peak period of imperialism—the invention of new forms of economic domination without colonialism—had existed in the early phase of imperialism, when the Portuguese and the mercantile trading companies of the core states had pursued their ends through trade rather than military and political occupation. Now this approach was updated and revitalized. These noncolonial imperialist forms included protectorates (in which the imperial power intervened in the political institutions of the weaker, "protected" state; controlled its foreign affairs; and dominated its economy without, however, establishing a full colonial regime), spheres of influence (regions in which an imperial power enjoyed special or even exclusive trading rights), and the Open Door policy.

The Open Door policy was most explicitly formulated by John Hay, secretary of state in the McKinley administration, in a set of dispatches concerning European interests in China, issued in 1899. The strategy of the Open Door included the principle that American business "shall enjoy perfect equality of treatment for their commerce and navigation" within all of China and soon thereafter also other regions. A second principle was that China (and similar regions) should not be turned into colonies. A third principle was that *loans,* as well as trade, were a key part of the commerce that was to be opened freely to all entrepreneurs (Williams, 1972:51). The reasoning behind these principles was that American businesses were becoming superbly capable of competing with the firms of other countries. If rivalry between the metropoles could be kept on an economic level, U.S. firms were likely to fare well. The expansion of markets of American goods would benefit the country as a whole.

The establishment of colonial administration, on the other hand, was costly and often had to be repressive. To American businessmen, drawing native peoples into the Western way of life through trade was preferable to imposing foreign rule on them. Furthermore, the Open Door policy of economic competition and imperialism without colonialism would avoid wars between the imperial powers. "In a truly perceptive and even noble sense, the makers of the Open Door policy understood that war represented the failure of policy" (Williams, 1972:57). The Open Door policy was given a try in several places before World War II, but the existence of colonial empires prevented it from being the dominant form of imperialism at that time.

Phase Four.   The Open Door policy came into its own in the fourth phase of imperialism, after World War II. The former large imperial powers—Japan, Germany, France, and England (as well as smaller countries like Italy, Belgium, the Netherlands) were in ruins. Their colonial empires were falling apart. The U.S.S.R. contented itself with quickly establishing a sphere of influence in eastern Europe. So the field was finally open for a new imperialism led by the United States. What were the components of this new imperialism?

First, we can briefly describe the objectives of an economic empire:

1. To ensure a supply of raw materials for the metropoles (At present, many of these imports are minerals and oil. The United States is somewhat more self-sufficient than western Europe and Japan in these respects. However, it has been easier to import higher grade or more cheaply extracted foreign raw materials than to develop domestic sources. Until very recently, raw materials have been obtained by American companies on favorable terms.)
2. To develop markets in which to sell the manufactured goods of the metropoles
3. To create outlets for capital, for profitable investments in businesses abroad that are either owned by a native bourgeoisie or established as foreign subsidiaries of multinationals based in the metropoles
4. To benefit from the cheaper labor of the underdeveloped areas

All of these reasons have been aims of imperialism since its inception, in a varying mix. But in the twentieth century, and particularly since World War II, a new overriding goal has become important—the establishment of a favorable climate for maintaining this economic world system.

An empire is under more stress now than in the past. The peoples of the underdeveloped areas are imbued with a spirit of nationalism, a desire for political participation, and a wish for a higher standard of living. However, their increasing populations and the inflated prices of important materials make prosperity less likely for them than before. Population growth, rising expectations, and nationalism are all stresses exported by previous generations of colonial imperialists that now make maintaining an economic empire more difficult. "Native" populations are no longer poorly equipped tribal and traditional warriors. They are organized as nations with armies, often well equipped with weapons provided by industrialized countries, and well versed in guerrilla tactics.

Thus, the imperial wars fought by the French in Indochina and Algeria or by the Americans in Vietnam are conflicts on an altogether different scale from nineteenth-century colonial wars. The latter were usually won fairly quickly by the industrial powers, even when the opposition was as fearless as the Zulus, the Pathans, or the followers of the Mahdi in the Sudan. Furthermore, the rivalry of the large powers, particularly the rivalry between the United States, the Soviet Union, and China, has made conflicts within an empire potentially very volatile. Lacking the coercive power of the colonial administrations, the managers of the modern economic empires have had to resort to far more delicate political and ideological means of preserving order.

What mechanisms have been developed since World War II to cope with these changed circumstances? Let me list a few.

1. *A variety of political and military institutions has been invented to help ensure an area's stability within the American empire without actual occupation of it.* These include: the establishment of puppet regimes, such as that of Nguyen Van Thieu in South Vietnam, propped up by American advisors and military aid; CIA capers, including the creation of organizations to act as clandestine conduits for American funds; and the training of foreign police and military men in American academies, especially for counterinsurgency warfare and repressive social control.

2. *Giving or withholding foreign aid is used effectively to control a country's national policies and form of government.* The U.S. Agency for International Development (AID) and two important international agencies—the International Monetary Fund (IMF), "a major source of short-term loans for deficit countries," and the World Bank (International Bank for Reconstruction and Development), "an important source for long-term funds"—are important vehicles for this carrot-and-stick approach. Many instructive examples of such control are available. For example, Magdoff (1969:128, 137) points out that

aid was withheld or withdrawn in the case of (*a*) Ceylon when it nationalized 63 gasoline stations owned by Esso Standard Eastern and Caltex Ceylon, and (*b*) Peru when a new administration tried to withdraw tax concessions originally granted to the International Petroleum Corporation, a subsidiary of Standard Oil of New Jersey.

Nor did the United States government appreciate the restrictions India wanted to apply to a fertilizer plant investment contemplated by Standard Oil of Indiana. In this case, the weapon was manipulation of the distribution of "food for peace" to hungry India. According to *Forbes Magazine,* "For a long time India insisted that it handle all the distribution of fertilizer produced in that country by U.S. companies and that it also set the price. Standard of Indiana understandably refused to accept these conditions. AID put food shipments to India on a month-to-month basis until the Indian government let Standard of Indiana market its fertilizer at its own prices."

... The simplest element in this operation is to pay off friendly governments and to assist them to stay in power. Often, reading the statistics of government aid agencies is like reading a political barometer. Take the case of AID expenditures in Brazil, shown in Table [2].

What happened before 1964, when AID expenditures dropped so sharply? The United States became increasingly dissatisfied with the economic and political actions of the Goulart regime. What happened in Brazil in 1964? The Goulart government was overthrown by military officers friendly to and trained by the United States, as explained in the statement of the Chairman of the House Foreign Affairs Committee cited above. The data in Table [2] are only one aspect of the spurt in financial aid supplied to the new government: other agencies in addition to AID

Table 2

Expenditures in Brazil by Agency for International Development

Fiscal Year Ending June 30	Expenditures (millions of dollars)
1962	$ 81.8
1963	38.7
1964	15.1
1965	122.1
1966	129.3

SOURCE: Statistics and Reports Division, Agency for International Development, *U.S. Economic Assistance Programs Administered by the Agency for International Development and Predecessor Agencies, April 3, 1943–June 30, 1966*, Washington, D. C., March 30, 1967, p. 28.

were also active. The United States committed itself in 1964 alone to giving and lending over $500 million to the new regime. In addition, as a former high AID official tells us, "multilateral institutions [e.g., World Bank and IMF] were successfully encouraged to supplement this sum."

On the other hand, the World Bank "refused to make any loans to Brazil for several years prior to 1964 mainly because of the unsound financial policies of the government preceding the Branco administration" (Magdoff, 1969:143). Similarly, the World Bank refused loans to Allende's Chile. There is nothing particularly secret or conspiratorial in these decisions. They reflect the fact that IMF and World Bank funds come from capital-rich nations, particularly the United States, and that their decisions, therefore, reflect the interests of these nations (Magdoff, 1969:147).

3. *The new imperialism revolves around an American financial empire.* There have been two major components to this financial network. One was the establishment of the dollar as an international monetary reserve, that is, as an acceptable medium—along with gold, whose price is also defined in dollars—for international payments. Dollar preeminence lasted between the wreck of the West European currencies in World War II and the weakening of the dollar through the costs of the war in Vietnam. The importance of dollars as an international monetary reserve (along with gold) boils down to the following: "In the final analysis—and this becomes painfully apparent on the brink of crisis—the holders of the United States I.O.U.'s can use them only to purchase United States goods at United States prices" (Magdoff, 1969:87). The second

component of the financial network was a banking system. British banking dominated international finance in the nineteenth century. By the end of World War II, this role had shifted to the United States, especially through branch banking and subsidiary corporations that buy into foreign banks (Magdoff, 1969:10).

4. *The new imperialism depends on new developments in technology, especially communications and transportation.* Television and radio spread suitable ideologies, especially the desire for consumer goods—"the revolution of rising expectations"—to all parts of the world. Jet planes and supertankers (among other developments) make possible international business management and shipping (Magdoff, 1969:45). Incidentally, most of the firms involved directly in the economic empire (especially in gathering raw materials) are the large corporations of the monopolistic sector. Many of them use a sophisticated modern technology (of computers, intensive energy use, and so on) and are the basic industries in oil, chemicals, steel, and other fields developed with late nineteenth-century technology and reflecting the onset of monopoly capitalism. Smaller, more competitive industries are less deeply involved in the empire, although some, such as the clothing industry, are also beginning to seek cheaper labor sources overseas.

5. *The new imperialism has a multilevel structure.* There is still a great deal of economic competition between the giants, as there was in the late nineteenth and early twentieth centuries. However, there is also a structure of levels. At the top of the pyramid is the United States. By penetrating the economies of countries in western Europe, the United States indirectly develops access to the former colonial empires of these countries. This multilevel arrangement is particularly evident in banking.

> For example: a Chase Manhattan Bank subsidiary owns 15 percent of the London-based Standard Bank, which in turn has an extensive network of African and Latin American banks; ... a First National City Bank subsidiary has a 40 percent interest in Banque Internationale pour L'Afrique Occidentale, which in turn operates 41 branches in Africa (Magdoff, 1969:79).

Another level of the pyramid is beginning to emerge, a level below the United States and the other developed countries. This level, sometimes referred to as the "subimperialist" countries, includes the more industrialized nations of Africa, Asia, and Latin America, such as Argentina, South Korea, Hong Kong, and Mexico. These countries depend on technology and investment from the imperialist powers, but they in turn produce manufactured goods for and invest in the less developed countries.

6. *The most important ideology of the fourth phase of imperialism has been anticommunism.* The middle classes of the underdeveloped countries, as well as the middle and working classes of the advanced capitalist countries, have been subjected to the argument that socialist revolutions in the under-

developed countries would destroy their way of life and mean their subjugation to the Soviet Union. In the late forties and early fifties, hysterical anticommunism permeated the media. More recently, the ideology has been toned down. Stability and limited reforms have been emphasized as desirable political paths for underdeveloped countries. A modernizing bourgeoisie that would carry out some land reform has been supported by American advisors against the most reactionary elements of the old oligarchy. Of course, when these bourgeois reformers failed to prevent large Socialist movements from becoming powerful, the American state intervened with violence, either through the "dirty tricks" of the CIA or, as in Vietnam and the Dominican Republic, with the direct use of troops.

The fourth phase of imperialism may now be ending. The symptoms are readily visible: the devaluation of the dollar; the ability of the petroleum-exporting nations to raise their prices; the American defeat in Vietnam. The relationship between the developed center and the underdeveloped, dependent periphery may finally be changing. Some of the underdeveloped countries may now be able to resist the domination of the center. They are trying to alter the unequal terms of trade and, in some cases, are ready to use violence to assert their economic as well as their political independence. Their progress to a position of autonomy and economic development is just beginning, however.

Consequences.   Before focusing more closely on the present state of underdeveloped countries, I would like to discuss some of the consequences of the past four stages of imperialism.

The most general consequence of imperalism has been the creation of a world economy. A world economy can be characterized in several ways:

1. It involves specialization *between* nations as well as within nations. Thus, some nations became raw-material providers and sources of cheap labor for plantation agriculture while others became sources of manufactured goods. More recently, the underdeveloped nations have also been furnishing cheap labor for industrial enterprises.
2. Division of labor within the world economy was accompanied by— in fact, was largely the result of—differentiation in power, with the industrialized capitalist nations being able to set the terms of the relationship.
3. The establishment of a world economy has meant that all people have been increasingly drawn into a cash economy. At first, labor in the peripheral areas was largely or partially coerced. Over the centuries, however, more and more labor power was sold as wage labor for cash. With a cash market for labor (or for the products of labor power) came an ideology of wanting more consumer goods.

The world economy brought with it advantages for the proletariat of industrial countries. Although they had to compete with the cheap labor of the underdeveloped, Third World nations, in many respects the working classes of the metropoles benefited from the same arrangements that benefited the bourgeoisie of these countries. Access to cheap raw materials and an opportunity to sell manufactured goods abroad led to economic growth in the metropoles and thus to a rising standard of living.As Engels noted:

> The English proletariat is becoming more and more bourgeois, so that this most bourgeois of all nations is apparently aiming ultimately at the possession of a bourgeois aristocracy and a bourgeois proletariat *as well* as a bourgeoisie. For a nation which exploits the whole world this is of course to a certain extent justifiable (quoted in Hobsbawm, 1967:356).

What was true of the English working class soon became true of the working classes of all the metropoles. Meanwhile, in the United States, overseas expansion, especially along Open Door lines, was repeatedly carried out as a cure for economic depression at home. The policy of expanding markets and investments abroad as a cure for business downswings at home began in the 1890s in the United States and has been pursued ever since. American workers necessarily feel ambivalent about this policy. On the one hand, they suffer from the relocation of industry into underdeveloped countries, where it can take advantage of the low wages of workers in these countries. This practice leads to depressed wages and unemployment at home. On the other hand, American workers (and workers of the other metropoles) have probably enjoyed a higher standard of living because the metropoles have secured such a disproportionate share of the world's resources. The United States, which has about 6 percent of the world's population, uses about 50 percent of the world's nonrenewable natural resources. Although the rewards of this form of exploitation have been reaped by American capitalists, American workers have also benefited from this inequality. In addition, the employment, and hence the prosperity, of American labor has appeared to depend on capitalist drives for markets in the underdeveloped countries. Thus the short-run or even medium-run interest of the working class of the metropoles has been linked to the imperialist expansion of their capitalist class (Ehrenreich, 1974–1975:17).

The Structure of Underdeveloped Countries

A novelist once remarked that happy families are all alike, but unhappy ones differ in their misery. The same is somewhat true of underdeveloped countries. Their structure varies greatly, depending on their resources, their history under colonialism (or another form of imperialism), their geographic location, and the particular position they held in the worldwide division of labor. However, they tend to have some features in common.

1. They have a substantial proportion of the labor force in agriculture. For example, in Brazil and India, more than 60 percent of the labor force is

agricultural. Agriculture is not highly mechanized and, compared with that of many of the metropoles, not very productive.

2. The proportion of the labor force in manufacturing is low. There is only a small industrial base in these countries. Nonagricultural workers tend to be in some kind of service work, such as petty entrepreneurial activity, government white-collar work, and so on—all activities in which little actual wealth is produced.

3. Income and ownership are unevenly distributed. There is a large mass of very poor people, including much of the rural population.

4. There is a small middle class comprised of government officials, the native bourgeoisie, and the managerial and professional employees of foreign enterprises. To an increasing extent, these groups are taking over from the old elite, which was usually composed of landowners. Traditional landowners who use their land rents primarily for personal consumption are generally losing power in the state. They are being replaced by elites of capitalist landowners and other bourgeois groups, as well as by managers and professionals. In some countries—for example, Argentina, Mexico, Uruguay, Chile, Turkey, Taiwan, and Greece—these assorted middle-class groups are fairly substantial parts of the population. In others, they form a tiny stratum. In few cases can they be said to be a hegemonic ruling class like the metropolitan bourgeoisie. Their control over the armed forces is weak, their ideological institutions do not penetrate the mass of the population, and they feel a deep ambivalence over their own identity and relation to the metropoles.

5. Population growth rates are very high.

6. While ideas of citizenship, nationalism, and mobilization by a mass party exist, the organizational network of unions, associations, and so on (either state organized or spontaneous) is weak compared with the organizational networks of industrialized countries.

7. There are many competing belief systems: traditional, Western bourgeois, revolutionary, ethnic, and so on. Although I argued that in advanced industrial capitalist countries diversity in belief systems and subcultures made the social order strong, in the underdeveloped countries diversity seems to stand in the way of economic development. The apathy developed by producers in traditional class societies, and reinforced by their experiences with coerced labor under imperialism, is also an especially serious obstacle (Harris, 1972:483–484).

In many countries, a syncretism of Western and indigenous cultures is taking place. People wear cheap Western clothes—jeans, padded nylon parkas, rubber-thonged sandals, nylon knits—especially in urban areas. In some countries, bilingualism (the native language and the language of the metropole) is common, or a creole is spoken (for example, Haitian French and Jamaican English are almost incomprehensible to speakers of French and English in the metropoles). In some regions with strong musical traditions, such as Africa and the Caribbean islands, Western musical technology—for example, amplified instruments—has made possible vital new forms. Drug use has also been syncretized. Alcohol, marijuana and its variants, and the various opiate derivatives are now used internationally. The flooding of the market with cheap mass-produced goods makes these countries more and more Western in appearance.

8. In some societies, the most dynamic groups in terms of both revolutionary and capitalist potential are ethnic minorities, such as the overseas Chinese who have settled throughout Southeast Asia. However, their minority status keeps them from becoming an effective elite in the society.

9. Urbanization has outstripped the growth of the urban economic base, so that the urban population cannot be drawn into full-time employment. Both urban and rural employment is often part time or seasonal. Under these circumstances, corruption, nepotism, a black market in goods, and other breakdowns of "fair play" represent rational efforts to survive. In other words, the development of norms of neutrality, efficiency, and impartial justice is difficult in an economy of extreme scarcity and underemployment. Who you know and whom you can bribe are not merely shortcuts to making more money; they may become crucial factors in whether an individual or a family can physically survive. (These same factors, of course, also operate in the competitive marginal sectors of the U.S. economy: bribes are common in the New York City housing market; tips to garagemen are necessary for Chicago taxi drivers who want to get a reasonable vehicle for the day. But compared with underdeveloped countries, petty corruption of this rather desperate sort is relatively rarer).

10. Family structure is often different from the nuclear family pattern that has prevailed among the middle class and some of the working class in the metropoles. Both extended families and female-headed households are more common, the latter being especially prevalent among the poor, both in urban areas and in the countrysides from which men have left to find work.

Ethnic Conflict

So far I have discussed three kinds of conflict: class conflict *within* nation-states; wars *between* nations, particularly between the metropoles, over territory and access to resources; and tension *between* the developed metropoles and the underdeveloped areas. The growth of a world economy has also exacerbated ethnic conflict *within* nation-states.

Ethnic conflict was not known in premodern times. On the contrary, the expansion of city-states and ancient empires involved continuing clashes between groups that differed in life-style, language, and physical characteristics. The empires tried to bring "barbarians" into the empire as class groups, forcing them to specialize in some kind of productive or state-related activity as peasants, slaves, or soldiers. The "barbarians" tried to resist this fate, while continuing to plunder the geographical margins of the empire.

Wars of this type were numerous and widespread: between the Chinese and the central Asian tribes; between the Romans and the Huns, the Jews, the Celts, and the Germanic tribes; between the Macedonians and the Greeks; between the Mongols and the Chinese, the Russians, and the Moslems. Two empires would also frequently clash, and with each encounter territory would be gained or lost, and with it, distinct groups of people. Thus the contraction of Byzantium left behind communities of Greeks in the Islamic world. The reconquest of Spain by Christians left pockets of Jews (Marranos) and Moors (Moriscos) who had "converted" to Christianity but who continued to practice their old religions secretly.

While ethnic conflict did not start with the development of a world economy and the growth of modern economic empires, these developments did increase the pace and scope of the processes that caused such conflict. I shall discuss in more detail some of the processes that did help to create ethnic conflict.

Forced Migration of Laborers: Internal Colonies.   One factor was the forced migration of laborers. On the one hand, metropoles needed cheap labor for tropical agriculture (and mining) in sparsely populated or depopulated regions. On the other hand, the metropoles controlled or traded with areas that had large populations. So, a transfer was made. The process began with the African slave trade and continued with the indenturing of laborers for fixed terms of work at very low wage rates. In the eighteenth century, the indentured laborers were Europeans exported to the Americas and Australia, but soon they were replaced by East Indians and Chinese. East Indians became laborers in the Guianas, the Caribbean, the Pacific islands (especially Fiji), Malaysia, and East Africa. The Chinese were exported into Southeast Asia and to North America, where they were an important part of the labor force building the transcontinental railways.

In some regions, these coerced immigrant laborers became a very large ethnic group. Thus, for example, the South American country of Guyana has only a small native population; its two major population groups—blacks and East Indians—were imported by European imperialists. The Caribbean islands and large parts of the mainland of the Americas are populated by the descendants of African slaves. When such a group ends up within the metropole itself —as Afro-Americans have in the United States—speaking of it as an "internal colony" is to some extent justified.

Africans were brought to America to work in what was once a distinctly peripheral area, an agricultural adjunct to Britain and the northeastern United States, that is, the cotton-growing South. The Civil War and the decisions of the postwar decades made the South an integral part of the nation and meant the absorption of its "colonial" population. Blacks in the United States are still forced into precisely the same kinds of jobs that people living in under-developed countries must take: agricultural work (including migrant labor), nonunionized low-paid wage labor in the competitive sector of the economy (such as laundry and restaurant work), some service and clerical jobs, the least attractive jobs in the monopoly industrial sector (sometimes involving danger-ous chemicals or hazardous industrial processes), and marginal and often illegal entrepreneurial and entertainment activities. At present, blacks are forced to perform unpleasant labor, no longer through coercion but through the operation of market forces. *Within the metropole, blacks are forced to perform similar tasks in the national division of labor that underdeveloped countries have been forced to perform within the worldwide division of labor.*

Like the Third World countries, black Americans are generating a grow-ing bourgeoisie and a growing professional and managerial class. The "internal colony" metaphor, of course, can be stretched too far. Black Americans differ from underdeveloped nations in that they have political rights within the metropole (an advantage). On the other hand, however, they lack potential control over the territory of the nation-state and its natural resources (a disadvantage).

Territorial Conquest.   A second way in which ethnic conflict has been gener-ated within the nation-states is through conquest of territory adjoining the metropole. Conflicts between England and her neighbors (or colonies) within the British Isles—Wales, Scotland and, above all, Ireland—is a good example. So is conflict between the Spaniards and the Basques and Catalans. In most of these cases, one ethnic group—the English, the Spaniards—controls the state apparatus or has an overwhelming role in it. The other nationalities are forced to learn the dominant group's language and to accede to its customs. To some extent, the minority peoples are forced into subordinate class posi-tions, and their territory is transformed into an underdeveloped region.

Immigration.   A third type of *intra*state ethnic conflict has been associated with immigration—another trend within the world economy. In the United States, we are accustomed to tension between successive groups of white ethnics. The first arrivals—primarily of British stock—tended to dominate both the corporate sector and the national state. Other groups have been able to climb up the American ladder of success—that is, out of manual labor jobs into bourgeois, petit bourgeois, and professional/managerial jobs—partly be-cause of changes in the economic structure of the country as a whole and partly because they were able to adapt to Anglo standards and behavior.

Three factors largely determine a group's position on the ladder: the structure of the economy at the time of entry (for example, unskilled Latin Americans now find the labor market more discouraging than equally un-skilled Slavs did seventy-five years ago); the time of entry (the longer the group has been here the better off it tends to be); and the "goodness of fit" between the group's culture and the Anglo culture of the state and the corporations (for example, the literate, partially urbanized culture of Eastern Europe Jewish immigrants fit better into the advanced industrial economy of twentieth-century America than did the peasant culture of Polish or Italian immigrants).

A couple of qualifications are necessary here. One is that for historical reasons, it is difficult to distinguish *bourgeois* culture from northern European *ethnic* culture, since northern Europe, particularly England, is also the core area of the spread of industrial capitalism. The existence of a distinctly non-bourgeois WASP culture, that of Appalachians and other poor white Southerners as well as much of the rural population generally, suggests that class is as important a variable in assimilation as is ethnic culture. Being WASP is not automatically a ticket into the middle or upper levels of the social structure, if one happens to be born into the wrong region or into the wrong economic group.

A second qualification that we need to make is that length of stay in the U.S. is an important factor in the group's economic position, not in its own right but as an indicator of other characteristics of the group's entry, namely, the structure of the economy and the amount of cultural hostility the group faced. The latecomers—first the Irish (in the 1840s), then eastern and southern Europeans (Poles, Italians, Jews, Greeks, Czechs, and so on) and Orientals, and most recently Latin Americans and West Indians—have been progressively more distinct physically and culturally from the initial northern European stock. Prejudice combines with a lack of urban-industrial skills and an altered economy to restrict the opportunities of the later immigrants.

Note also that the later the in-migration, the more peripheral the area of origin is within the world economy. The problems that the core states have created for the periphery and semi-periphery are imported from the old country to the new. For example, Sicilian, Polish, or Latin-American immigrants to the United States have been penalized twice by the worldwide division of labor; once because their home country has become a relatively poor peripheral or semiperipheral area that cannot provide them with economic opportunity, and a second time because their background tends to propel them into a less desirable slot within the U.S. economy. *Thus, the patterns of ethnic conflict within the United States become clearer when they are seen as historically related to the rise of the world economy that began in the sixteenth century.*

Settler States.   By *settler state,* I mean a state in which European settlers control the state apparatus, kill or exploit a native labor force, and think of themselves as permanent residents rather than as colonial administrators. When conquest and immigration are coupled, a particularly hostile situation arises. There are a variety of nation-states whose populations are composed of both native peoples and substantial numbers of immigrants of European background. In terms of ethnic mix, settler societies range from those in which the original native population was either small or reduced by genocide (e.g., Argentina, the United States, or Australia) to those in which the settlers are indeed a numerical minority (e.g., South Africa or Rhodesia). Yet in most of these societies, the settlers think of themselves as permanent citizens (not temporarily stationed colonial personnel), and they control the state machinery and the economy. Ethnic lines and class lines overlap almost completely. The whites control the economy and monopolize the good jobs. Their state apparatus is extremely oppressive and heavily based on coercion, including forced relocation, control of movement through passbooks, extensive police forces and prisons, and so on. The white settlers form a fairly cohesive group, often feeling themselves to be in a state of siege. Many no longer have roots in their ancestral country of origin and have little desire to return there.

Specialized Immigrant Minorities. In other societies, immigrants form neither the multiethnic bulk of the population (as in the United States and Argentina) nor a caste in control of the state (as in South Africa and Rhodesia) but a group with a specialized role in the division of labor and often a disadvantaged status in the society. Thus, for instance, Asians (Lebanese and East Indians) in Africa tend to be specialized as merchants and clerical workers. Black Africans, now in control of the state machinery in much of Africa, tend to view them hostilely and, in a number of East African countries, have forced people of Indian descent to emigrate. This has placed a terrible hardship on these people who essentially are now stateless, being excluded from England as the metropole and reluctant to "return" to India, which often they have never seen.

Similarly, the overseas Chinese have been forced into petit bourgeois and clerical slots in Southeast Asia (Vietnam, Malaysia, the Philippines, and Indonesia), where they often become the first victims of outbursts of nationalist rage. A nationalist mob or a demagogue in search of scapegoats finds these groups much more convenient targets than the bourgeoisie of the metropoles, who are too distant and too intellectually abstract a target for many people frustrated by the burden of living in an underdeveloped area.

Different societies represent almost all possible combinations and layerings of these basic sources of ethnic conflict: internal colonies of the descendants of forced laborers; incorporation by conquest of diverse ethnic groups; and immigration of both dominant settler groups and marginal peoples. The important points to keep in mind are the following:

1. *Present ethnic conflicts are the result of the division of labor, control of resources, and migration that are essential aspects of the world economy of the last few centuries.*
2. *For reasons closely related to the growth of the world economy, ethnic and class conflicts have come to overlap to a great degree; thus classes that control resources in the world economy as a whole, and also within a number of nation-states, belong to ethnic groups different from those who do not control these resources.*

Political Modernization

In this section, I shall discuss a number of changes in the superstructure that have accompanied the rise of modern industrial capitalism. Nation-states have become the major way of organizing political activity. The nation-state is legitimated by an ideology of citizenship and political participation.

Throughout the world system, political institutions have undergone changes in the last two centuries. These changes have occurred in the peripheral countries as well as in the core capitalist states. I can best describe the nature of these changes by saying that the masses of the population have entered the political processes of the nation-state. The circumstances of this entrance have differed markedly in the different types of countries. What do I mean by the statement "The masses of the population have entered the political processes of the nation-state"?

The Nation-State

First, the statement asserts that political behavior is now organized by nation-states. Units that were smaller than nation-states, such as tribes or city-states, have been forced to become part of a nation-state. They have been drawn into a larger, more powerful entity. For example, the German principalities were welded into the German nation during the nineteenth century. Likewise Italy was transformed into a nation-state by bringing together scattered smaller states, principalities, and territories controlled by France, Austria, and Spain. In Africa and Asia, similar new units have been created out of the territories of small princely states, tribal groups, city-states, warring kingdoms, and so on. India, for example, is a patchwork of princely domains, tribal regions in the remote hill country, pieces of long-gone empires, and so on; so is Indonesia and the African countries. The territories of tribes and principalities are often preserved in the boundary lines of provinces within the nation.

The building of nation-states has involved not only gluing together small pieces but also breaking apart very large entities. In the process, great empires have disintegrated. Within Europe, the empires had been carved into nation-states by the end of World War I, but the process had started much earlier, with Holland's revolt against Habsburg rule in the late sixteenth century. The process has continued since then, with repeated bursts of national liberation activity in the nineteenth century—in Greece, against the Ottoman Empire; in Latin America, against the Spanish crown; in Italy, against France, Austria, and Spain; and so on. The end of colonial empires in Asia and Africa came in the twenty-year period following World War II. A glance at a globe now shows a large number of nation-states—about 150—as the major territorial units.

A number of other processes underlie nation-building. One is the discovery by the bourgeoisie of the core states in Europe during the sixteenth and seventeenth centuries that a medium-sized country, with a central government and a national (rather than a mercenary) army, was the best political unit for their purposes. These structural developments were translated into the ideology of nationalism.

By including the rest of the world in their economy, the core states unintentionally exported nationalism along with cheap cotton goods and trade beads. The peoples of the colonial empires developed the same beliefs about the virtues of the nation-state that their rulers had. To the colonized people, nationalism seemed to make the same economic good sense that it had for the bourgeoisie of the core states: they came to believe that national independence was a necessary (although probably not sufficient) step toward regaining control of their area's resources. These nationalist considerations appeared first, of course, among the most Westernized people of the colonial empires. Thus nationalism was yet another by-product of the creation of the world economy, and it has been an important ingredient in the efforts of the peripheral areas to free themselves from domination by the center.

Nationalism means more than commitment to a central government. It also has to mean some degree of ethnic homogeneity. After all, what else could define the boundaries of a nation? In the past, in Europe and the Mideast, religion had been an important element of identity and group solidarity. European Catholics felt themselves set apart from the Eastern Orthodox Byzantine Empire and the Islamic world. But by the end of the seventeenth century, religion had ceased to be the dominant source of solidarity in Europe. National identity was emerging.

At first national identity was associated with a national church, but increasingly it was defined by a group of traits, especially language and a sense of shared history. Nationalism came to be based on a complicated cluster of attributes. Language was one of them. In some cases, religion was still a part of national identity. Shared customs or history were rediscovered—or invented. Sometimes even a myth of racial distinctness was created. Residence in an identifiable geographic area was important. To a certain extent, ethnic and national identity could be manipulated to suit the structural realities of the powerful states that were emerging in Europe. Throughout modern history, there has existed a tension between the desire to strengthen the state by annexing new territory and the desire to cleanse the nation of groups that do not fit in ethnically.

The new nations that have emerged since World War II face the same problems of creating a national identity and of strengthening the state by expansion and economic development that were faced earlier by European nations. Many of these new nations have boundaries that were rather arbitrarily imposed by the European powers. Thus, some of these states include more than one ethnic group who then struggle for control of the state machinery of the larger national entity. These struggles take different forms. For example, one ethnic or linguistic group may attempt to impose its language on the nation as a whole, thereby giving an edge to its members in the competition for jobs (illustrated in the dispute over Hindi as a national language in India, favored by the north and opposed by the Dravidian-speaking south). Patronage jobs and other scarce resources are unevenly distributed, depending on which ethnic groups control the state apparatus. Struggle may also be violent, as in the war between Nigeria and Biafra (the seceding region inhabited by the Ibo people).

In other regions, boundary lines have been drawn by colonial powers in such a way that an ethnic group is split between two or more regions. Such is the case of the Somali people. Those who live in Kenya want to secede from Kenya and transfer their region into the state of Somalia.

The disputes between ethnic groups over control of the state apparatus become even more complicated when the ethnic groups are not clearly territorially distinct but occupy the same area. Under these conditions, one ethnic group is frequently forced to occupy a distinct class position as well. Secessionist efforts are not particularly meaningful in such a situation. For example, in Guyana, blacks are more urbanized and tend to be educated and able to acquire white-collar jobs, while the East Indians, descendants of indentured laborers, occupy a more rural and less favorable economic position. Under these circumstances, secession is not a reasonable alternative for settling ethnic conflict.

Issues involving national boundaries, ethnic minorities, and ethnic conflict are endemic throughout the world because, for historical reasons, nation-states do not perfectly match ethnic lines.

So far there are few supranational political entities. The multinationals are supranational, but they must ultimately rely on the nation-states for coercive support. At one time, the Communist party of the Soviet Union had considerable control over the Communist parties in other states, but that situation has largely disappeared. Various international money and capital-distributing and regulating bodies exist as superficially supranational bodies, such as the World Bank and the International Monetary Fund. Ultimately, however, all these supranational entities are dependent on the nation-states for coercive power—that is, for military support.

Political Participation

Second, to say that the masses of the population have entered into the political processes of the nation-state is to assert that some form of political participation has become more widespread. In some cases, this political participation is genuine; people really do participate in making the decisions that affect their lives. In other cases, it is largely a sham; people are mobilized to vote, to participate in rallies, to consume the ideological media, but they do not take part in any decisions. Whether real or sham, this mobilization of people makes the modern nation-state distinctly different from past political institutions in class societies.

I have already mentioned that in primitive egalitarian societies most adults (most males, anyway) participated in political decisions, but that in subsequent class societies the producing masses stood outside the political process and were not expected to take part. In early class societies, people were drawn into the superstructure through religious institutions. The great temples of Egypt and Yucatan and the splendid Gothic cathedrals of Europe attest to this type of participation. With the secularization of society, beginning in the seventeenth century and continuing into the present, the political superstructure—the state—has had to perform the job of integrating the mass of people. We have already discussed two major ways of doing this: the ideological apparatus of schooling and the media, and the mass party.

Mass Parties.   We saw how the history of the mass party began when factions of the bourgeoisie, including its more radical, often petit bourgeois wing, organized to gain hold of the state apparatus. In other words, the roots of the modern mass party are in the *movement organizations* that were created by the bourgeoisie in its struggle to gain control over the state apparatus of the core states during the sixteenth, seventeenth, and eighteenth centuries. The French and American revolutions show us these types of movement organizations in action for the first time.

The growth of the Jeffersonian Democratic-Republicans was an example of the party's development at a slightly later stage, when it was less of a movement and more of an institutionalized organization operating within a legitimate competition for state control. The party structure that grew out of bourgeois movement organizations became the model for subsequent parties, including antibourgeois ones. The Leninist party structure (which I discussed in Chapter 8) provided a new type of core for these parties. Once it had gained power, however, the Leninist core generated a public mass party and auxiliary party-affiliated organizations. In some societies, this process of creating a mass party around the vanguard party core was already begun before the revolution, in the creation of front groups or a "popular front."

Mass parties and mass organizations created by vanguard parties are key features of political modernity. They are the major structural vehicle for integrating the producing strata of society into the existing social order. The actual integration can take many forms, including elections, decision-making meetings, genuine or manipulative efforts to stimulate "citizen imput," and so on.

So when I say that most people have to some extent "entered the political process," I am referring to the increased contact of the mass of people with political parties and the state. Most people have some contact, often fleeting or apathetic, with the party organizations. They are induced to vote, to go to grass-roots meetings, or in some way to care about the organization. The party organization mediates between the mass of people and the state. It legitimates class power and state power, and it brings people into contact with those groups that actually make major decisions in the society. Being able to visit a senator in Washington or to talk to a Party commissar places the average person in a different ideological and even structural position than that occupied by a slave or serf. While many people remain apathetic and cynical, a larger proportion of the people is intensely involved in political life than was involved in premodern class societies. The mass party allows more people to have roles as middle-level people in the organization of the state. (The state apparatus itself, apart from any party structure, has, of course, also grown enormously.)

The ideological concept related to structural participation in mass parties and in the state itself is citizenship. Like nationalism and the modern party, the concept of citizenship emerged with the bourgeois revolutions of the late eighteenth century.

Forms of Political Participation.   Throughout the world, political modernization has taken three major forms: bourgeois democracy, fascism and authoritarianism, and state socialism.

The bourgeois-democratic and fascist states are associated with capitalism as the mode of production. The bourgeois-democratic states are largely the core capitalist states—England, France, the Netherlands, the Scandinavian countries, Belgium, Switzerland—and those states settled by emigrants from the core states—U.S.A., Australia, New Zealand, Canada. They are parliamentary democracies, that is, they have an elected legislative body, and sometimes an elected executive as well. They have two or more parties that compete for elective office. They have fairly firmly established civil liberties, such as freedom of the press, due process of law, and so on. The state appears to be neutral and to represent the public interest, although in fact it acts to stabilize capitalism.

The fascist states are also capitalist but are (or were) generally latecomers to industrialization. In these states, the bourgeoisie has relied very heavily on an authoritarian state to impose its rule on the society. In some fascist states, such as Nazi Germany and Fascist Italy, there was a mass party that seized the state apparatus. In others, such as present-day Chile and Brazil, this mass party is not present. The latter are perhaps more accurately referred to as authoritarian rather than fascist. In fascist and authoritarian states, the state is powerful and repressive. Civil liberties are absent. The state openly supports the bourgeoisie and represses working-class movements and independent unions. The state has a fairly extensive role in stimulating and encouraging the economy. Some fascist states have a corporate ideology in which workers, owners, and professionals are expected to cooperate and each to contribute a distinct and vital activity to the society. In fact, the struggles of the working class are suppressed in this framework. Nazi Germany, Fascist Italy, and prewar Japan are examples of fascist states. Franco's Spain, Salazar's Portugal, and present-day Brazil, Chile, and South Korea also share fascist characteristics, as do a number of other countries.

Socialist states are brought about by revolutionary movements and are characterized by the absence of private ownership of the means of production and by the use of criteria other than profitability in planning economic activities. Socialism has been forced into a nation-state pattern because this is presently the dominant form of political organization. Also, socialist revolutions have often been national revolutions against foreign capitalist domination, which is another reason for nationalism in socialist states. Socialist states are characterized by powerful single parties. Debates and discussion can, in principle, take place within this party, however. Some socialist states also have fairly sophisticated ways of encouraging feedback and debate between the party and the mass of people in the society. Examples of socialist states are the Soviet Union, China, Vietnam, and Cuba.

Many other countries have characteristics of several of these socialist forms. Some countries now like to claim they are socialist when in fact they preserve private enterprise and are more corporatist than socialist. Countries like Sweden are sometimes erroneously seen as socialist because they provide extensive welfare measures and have some nationalized industries.

The ideologues of bourgeois democracies charge that one-party states do not have genuine mass participation in political decisions. State socialist societies counter this charge by asserting that (1) under capitalism, people are barred from making the most important decisions of all, namely, those concerning the means of production, and (2) *intra*party discussion about fundamental economic issues can be more effective in involving people in decision-making than *inter*party competition between parties that are not very different from each other and that fail to raise any very fundamental issues.

Growth of the State Apparatus.   The "entry of the masses into the political process" has occurred not only through party and movement organizations but also through the growth of the state apparatus itself. In all societies, the state apparatus has undertaken the task of stabilizing and unifying the society not only by upholding the ideology and controlling the means of coercion but also by providing services and regulating or managing the economy. Because of this development, the number of people employed by the state has grown enormously. For example, in the United States, government employment accounts for nearly one-third of the labor force. The existence of these large state bureaucracies—the Social Security Administration, the welfare departments and housing agencies, the public school system, and so on—means that many more people are in contact with the state. Sometimes people even believe that this contact is beneficial to them and in the public interest.

In the past, state officials appeared only to gather taxes, impose sentences, and impress men into the army or forced labor. Now the average citizen is in constant and not always unpleasant contact with the state through everything from schools to garbage collection.

The Process of Political Modernization

Political modernization means the entry of the masses into the political process of nation-states, the growth of modern state and party structures, and the formulation of ideological concepts like *nation* and *citizen*. However, different societies have developed very different forms of political modernization. What accounts for the differences?

Three factors are involved. One of them is relatively easy to deal with analytically because it is fairly static: the social order of the society *before* it began to modernize. The other two factors are harder to present because they are dynamic: the timing of the particular society's political modernization relative to changes in its class structure and system of production; and, most important of all, the timing of the society's political modernization relative to the political and economic development of other societies. The constellation of these three factors has produced different forms of political modernization.

The Core States: Bourgeois Democracy.   In the core states, the constellation was as follows: The class structure included a very strong bourgeoisie. The bourgeoisie to some extent saw itself as a revolutionary class. Industrialization occurred before or during political modernization. England, for example, was substantially industrialized before the extension of political rights to most of the population. These countries (and a small number of others, most of them also well industrialized) have ended up as parliamentary democracies with a capitalist mode of production.

The Semiperiphery: Fascism.   The countries of the semiperiphery have taken different routes to political modernity. For instance, German, Italy, and Japan —three industrializers in the middle period—became fascist, at least temporarily. The bourgeoisie in the semiperipheral states lacked the experience of revolution against a prebourgeois state. The state played a very active part in the industrialization of these countries, in some of which there still existed large areas of coerced-labor farming. (Coerced-labor farming had disappeared in England as a result of enclosure; in France, through revolution.)

Because these societies were late industrializers, nationalism—a sense of the need to rapidly catch up—became ideologically important. These societies had to cope with the fact that the core capitalist states had already gobbled up many of the more attractive colonies. Their own expansion brought them into conflict with the core states, for example, German expansion in Europe and Japanese expansion in Southeast Asia. The uncertainty of bourgeois rule, the weakness of bourgeois hegemony, made the bourgeoisie of the semiperipheral states turn to repressive movements that promised tight control over a coercive state apparatus. In the core states, the bourgeoisie had more successfully created ideological and organizational "lines of defense;" consequently, they were more relaxed about their relationship to the working class and the state.

The Periphery: Instability and Authoritarianism.   The countries that were "too late" in industrializing have entered the process of political modernization more recently. They have been greatly hampered in political change by characteristics of their class system. Among these are:
1. The presence of large rural classes (sometimes only recently or partially freed from coerced labor), which are illiterate, culturally conservative, and have little experience in political-action movements, unions, or other politically oriented voluntary associations
2. A weak bourgeoisie, dependent in large part on foreign capital
3. The absence of an urban, industrial working class

Furthermore, these societies have sometimes been carved out of colonial empires along arbitrary boundaries, which has generated ethnic conflict and boundary disputes. Thus, at the level of class structure, the late industrializers lack a hegemonic ruling class. At the level or organizational structure, they lack movements or parties that can mobilize masses of people, particularly the peasants. At the level of ideology, they lack widespread nationalist sentiment, literacy, and the belief in modern—that is, participatory—political forms.

This summary depicts the grimmest aspects of political modernization among underdeveloped countries. Countries beset by these social problems, when combined with a history of exploitation or lack of natural resources, often come to be ruled by a military oligarchy. In the absence of both a hegemonic bourgeoisie and a strong revolutionary Socialist party based on producers (peasants or urban workers), the state apparatus simply is seized by whatever group can muster enough force to grab it. The accompanying ideology is usually nationalist and sometimes superficially socialist (in other cases, as in Brazil or Bolivia, fascist).

Alternatives for the Periphery.   Are there alternatives for the underdeveloped countries? Is there a way of avoiding internal conflict, military coups, political instability, and continued economic domination by the advanced capitalist countries? In a few countries, a native bourgeoisie may be able to use the country's natural resources effectively enough to control the economy and to direct industrialization. In this process, it can become a hegemonic ruling class with an effective ideology and some ability to mobilize the population into modern political institutions, including perhaps both mass parties and parlimentary government. Some of the oil-rich Arab nations may pursue this line of development.

Another route out of the economic and political stagnation of underdevelopment is via Socialist parties with a real commitment to changing class structure, a commitment that many of the self-styled Socialist parties of underdeveloped countries lack. Where is socialism most likely to take hold? The most promising candidates are those societies in which the producing classes are urban or rural wage laborers capable of supporting secular political movements (unions and parties) and uninterested in getting land for subsistence. Chile is an example of a country with a substantial industrial proletariat.

As yet, however, extensive proletariats are exceptional rather than typical features of the social structure of underdeveloped countries. Perhaps an industrial protetariat will become more common as multinational corporations shift factory and office wage work to countries outside the core states. Textile and auto manufacture and raw-materials processing are beginning to take place in Asia (Taiwan, Singapore, South Korea) and Latin America. If these trends continue, these areas will develop modern proletariats, probably accompanied by Socialist movements. These movements will have to combat both the multinationals and the native bourgeoisie. Cuba provides an example of development that can occur in an underdeveloped country with a large proletariat and a revolutionary Socialist movement capable of both ousting foreign capital and seizing power from the indigenous bourgeoisie.

Socialist Revolutions in the Periphery.   Some societies—China and Vietnam —seem to have had socialist revolutions without having developed extensive urban or rural proletariats. There are several possible ways of understanding these cases. One is that the party organization was developed during a war of national liberation against foreign rulers and that the national liberation effort was a prerequisite for mass mobilization. The Japanese invasion during World War II collapsed whatever native bourgeois and nationalist institutions might have developed; thus the field was left open for the Communists to develop the institutions. The mobilization against the foreign invader built a widespread organizational and ideological base for revolution against foreign capital, landowners, the weak native bourgeoisie, and the nationalist quasi-fascist militaristic organization (Chiang Kai-shek's Kuomintang).

World War I seems to have played a similar role in the political history of Russia. Mass mobilization for the war uprouted peasants and created a situation of turmoil and "openness" in which the Communist party could seize state power. In other words, one cannot simply use the internal class structure to predict the political outcome. Internal class structure is only one ingredient in political development. "External" events, such as invasion or war, are important precipitating events for internal political changes. Once such events shake up the social order, the whole society may become "loose" enough for party organization to make a big difference, even if the society is not ready for revolution from the perspective of internal class structure alone. Those who are critical of the kind of state socialism that has developed in the Soviet Union, however, might well argue that this sort of party-imposed socialism, occurring in a war-damaged society and lacking both a large proletarian class base and an industrial productive system, tends to be authoritarian and exploitive of the peasantry. When the party, in its effort to leap over the stage of capitalism, has to undertake the creation of industry and a modern labor force —tasks "normally" carried out by the bourgeoisie—it runs the risk of engaging in precisely the same ruthless behavior that otherwise characterizes the bourgeoisie. China seems to have been able to bypass the stage of capitalism in a more democratic manner than did the Soviet Union.

Summary.   A slightly different way of looking at these processes is to argue that democracy, at least in the form of parliamentary government and civil liberties, is unlikely in the late industrializing nations. In the core capitalist states, these political institutions emerged due to three factors:

1. They were created by the bourgeoisie as a revolutionary class, in an effort to gain control of the royal state apparatus and to use that state apparatus to create a favorable climate for its activities.
2. They were extended to include the industrial proletariat only *after* the bourgeoisie had established its hegemony, used its power to wrest a surplus from the rural population, and proletarianized the work force, at which point the bourgeoisie used parliamentary democracy as a way of integrating the mass of people into the state.
3. They were demanded by proletarians (and radical petit bourgeois), and fought for by these groups in mass movements as an important set of reforms, albeit short of revolution.

All of these conditions are related to the bourgeoisie as a revolutionary class in the core states and to the tension between a hegemonic bourgeoisie and a proletarian class. These circumstances have not been repeated in other societies to any appreciable extent.

In the core states where industrialization preceded (or occurred simultaneously with) political modernization, people had already become urbanized, secularized, and literate. Packed into factories, they had left behind the "idiocy of rural life" and the isolated individualistic competitiveness of the peddler, peasant, or artisan. They had the personal characteristics that could support the institutions of political participation—newspapers, mass political movements, unions, parties, and so on. The bourgeoisie created this situation, largely unwittingly. At present, the Communist parties in the state socialist countries are carrying out the same task of uprooting, collectivizing, secularizing, and politically mobilizing the masses, but in a more planned and intentional fashion than did the bourgeoisie of the core states.

The Ongoing Process of Political Integration

By the way, the process of political modernization and mass entry into political institutions has by no means come to a halt in the core states. Periodically, various minority groups attempt to enter into political decision-making. As I remarked earlier, a "minority" is a group that is largely or wholly excluded from participation in the state apparatus. Historically, women and certain ethnic groups have been the most excluded. For example, the decade of the sixties was a period in the United States during which women and people of African, Latin American, and Asian descent struggled for more participation in decision-making through the state, through parties and movements, and in unions and workplace caucuses. Many people involved in these struggles seemed to believe that their demands could be met within the capitalist mode of production. A few asserted otherwise.

These movements have progressed—although not without reversals—from religiously tinged organizations to more secularized political movements. The career of Malcolm X is an excellent illustration of such progress. Beginning as an adherent of a cultural-nationalist religious movement (the Black Muslims), he came to embrace a more secular black nationalism that recognized the class structure and even the shape of the world economy within which Afro-Americans were imprisoned. In Europe, this process of secularization of movements is further advanced as more people are absorbed into the proletariat. Large numbers of Europeans are involved in the Communist parties, in the left wing of Socialist parties, and in militant labor organizations.

Summary

We have seen the following: how all societies have tended to organize themselves as nation-states; how all have at least begun the process of political modernization, that is, of drawing masses into political participation; how the state has increased its size, the number of its functions, and its penetration into the rest of society; how parties and movements have developed; how national identity and citizenship have become major ideological categories. We also have seen how the particular forms that all the preceding processes took have varied markedly from society to society, depending not only on how each society's class structure was established, but also on how other societies acted on it and on how changes in the society's mode of production and class structure were timed relative to such changes elsewhere in the world.

Proletarianization

In this section, I shall suggest that perhaps the most important change accompanying the rise of industrial capitalism is proletarianization. The fact that more and more people are having to make their living by selling their labor power is a crucial aspect of the relations of production under modern capitalism. In capitalist societies, schools and labor unions have an effect on the conditions under which labor power is sold because they help to reproduce the class structure from generation to generation. Therefore, I shall devote some consideration to these two institutions.

The Process of Proletarianization

Proletarianization is the transformation of a variety of groups into wage or salaried workers who survive by selling their labor power as a commodity in a labor market.[4] Let us now look at the components of this definition.

Transformation of a Variety of Groups. Proletarianization is a process, a type of change that affects groups of individuals. Many *different* kinds of groups are affected, including tribal people, free peasants, serfs, entrepreneurs, artisans, and professionals. The starting places of proletarianization are very different; however, the end of the process is much the same.

For example, a young man raised on an Indian reservation goes to a city and finds a job as a construction worker. The transition is from tribal society (or what is left of it after decimation and deportation) to urban wage labor. To take another example, a woman whose immigrant father was a Sicilian sharecropper on a *latifundium* (a great estate) works as a punch press operator. The transition is from partially coerced labor in a peasant society to wage labor in industrial society. A subsistence farmer in northeastern Brazil becomes a machine tender on a sisal plantation. The daughter of a small restaurant owner in the United States finds a job as a clerical worker for an insurance company. A carpet weaver's daughter in Iran becomes a secretary for an airline. And so on. The transformation is often *inter*generational. It is taking place in most parts of the world. It accompanies the processes of industrialization and urbanization.

Proletarianization in underdeveloped regions. Wage labor can become a major way for workers to make a living, even in societies that are *not* urbanized or industrialized. For example, in Latin America, Africa, and Asia, plantation work is organized as wage labor. Tropical and semitropical products like tea,

---

[4]This definition fails to distinguish between the proletariat in the strict sense of all those persons who create value by their labor (value that is appropriated as surplus value) and the larger grouping of wager earners. In other words, in the strict sense, all proletarians are wage earners but not all wage earners are proletarians. However, because of the similarity in life experiences, I am using the term *proletarian* to refer to all wage earners, whether they produce surplus value or not.

bananas, natural rubber, various fibers, lumber, spices, sugar and other food plants, and so forth are harvested and partially processed by wage laborers in settings that are neither urban nor industrial although they are tied into the economy of industrial capitalist states.

Mine work is also wage labor. Malaysian and Bolivian tin, African and Chilean copper, Jamaican bauxite, South African gold and diamonds, New Caledonian nickel—all are extracted by wage laborers working for large firms that are directly or indirectly tied to the economy of the advanced capitalist countries. Various kinds of new industries are beginning to appear in the underdeveloped countries. They too, are employers of wage labor. Like the plantations and mines, they are tied to the economies of the advanced capitalist countries either as subsidiaries of large corporations, as plants owned directly by these corporations, or as enterprises run by the native bourgeoisie but dependent on distributing companies in the developed countries. For example, food-processing, textile and clothing production, electronics assembly, even auto assembly plants have been started in Asian countries such as South Korea, Taiwan, Malaysia, Singapore, and Hong Kong, and in various Latin American countries.

The new wage laborers in these societies include people recently freed from or pushed out of partially coerced commercial agrarian production (such as debt peonage and sharecropping) and subsistence agriculture. Elsewhere I have dealt with the issue of how population growth and changes in agriculture in underdeveloped countries have led to the displacement of large numbers of people from subsistence farming, transforming them into either landless agricultural laborers or propertyless workers in the cities. Their ranks are joined by urbanites who can no longer survive as artisans or small entrepreneurs. Better educated persons form an extensive white-collar working class of clerks, legal workers, schoolteachers, and minor officials. Many of the underdeveloped countries do not have the economic structure needed to absorb all these workers. Many of the agricultural workers are seasonally unemployed, and the white-collar working class is poorly paid and frequently unemployed. The large households and extended family ties of middle-class people keep the unemployed and underemployed white-collar workers from falling into the poverty that afflicts much of the rest of the population.

Within the advanced capitalist countries there are also hinterland regions, in which proletarianization is associated with the extraction of minerals and the exploitation of a cheap nonunionized labor force. In the United States, for example, Appalachia, Alaska, and the coal-rich areas of the southwestern Indian reservations are forced to function as "resource colonies," furnishing oil, coal, and other raw materials to corporations and populations based in more developed parts of the nation. In the last few decades, the South has provided a more docile nonunionized labor supply for firms that had previously been located in the North. These internal colonies become areas in which rapid shifts from subsistence agriculture or tribal economies (like those of the Indians and Eskimos) to wage labor, occur.

Proletarianization in industrial capitalist countries.   In the advanced capitalist countries, former farmers are a major source of modern proletariats. The transition to proletarianization in industrialized countries has often been accompanied by moves from the rural hinterlands into industrial towns and larger cities. Areas of subsistence farming have lost population. Areas of commercial family farms have lost the most marginal and undercapitalized farmers. The migration of American blacks north and west, beginning in the twenties and continuing into the sixties; the westward journey of the Okies during the Great Depression; the unwilling relocation of Appalachian whites to midwestern manufacturing cities; the depopulation of parts of rural New England—all are geographical manifestations of the search for wage labor as agriculture becomes more and more commercialized, oligopolistic, and mechanized. Some people left the countryside reluctantly, only under the duress of foreclosure during the Depression and the pressures from agribusiness during the sixties and seventies. Others fled the land seeking an easier way of life.

A second major source of wage and salaried workers was the "old middle class"—the petit bourgeois entrepreneurs. Their children tended to find employment in large organizations instead of going into the family business. Some of them had to switch from self-employment to employment because small businesses failed to survive the Depression or the oligopolization of retailing after World War II. "Mom and pop" stores gave way to supermarket chains, nationwide discount stores, and fast-foods restaurants. To some extent, the spirit of entrepreneurship can still be satisfied by owning a franchise in a nationwide chain. Nevertheless, managing the frying of a MacDonald's hamburger (prepared with materials supplied by MacDonald's and made to MacDonald's specifications) is not quite the same as running one's own small business.

The figures in Table 3 help to illustrate the flow of Americans out of subsistence and small commercial farming and urban small businesses into wage and salaried work.

The Labor Market and the Workplace.   The second part of the definition of proletarianization says "wage or salaried workers who survive by selling their labor power as a commodity in a labor market." To be a proletarian means to sell the fixed amount of one's time and effort to an employer. Proletarians, in the strict sense of the word, produce surplus value. In other words, they produce goods that are sold for more than the workers receive in wages. This difference between the market value of the product and the laborers' wages (which includes overhead as well as profit) is the surplus value extracted from the laborers.

In a modern capitalist society, however, most working people experience proletarianized conditions of life even if they do not directly produce surplus value. Thus, whether or not a worker produces goods or services that are sold for profit in the private sector (production of surplus value), he sells his labor power in a labor market. For example, office workers, schoolteachers, state

Table 3

The Proletarianization of the U.S. Labor Force

Year	Wage and Salaried Employees[a]	Self-Employed Entrepreneurs[b]	Salaried Managers and Officials	Total
1780[c]	20.0%	80.0%	—	100.0
1880	62.0	36.9	1.1%	100.0
1890	65.0	33.8	1.2	100.0
1900	67.9	30.8	1.3	100.0
1910	71.9	26.3	1.8	100.0
1920	73.9	23.5	2.6	100.0
1930	76.8	20.3	2.9	100.0
1939	78.2	18.8	3.0	100.0
1950	77.7	17.9	4.4	100.0
1960	80.6	14.1	5.3	100.0
1969	83.6	9.2	7.2	100.0

SOURCE: Reich (1972:175).
NOTE: U.S. labor force is defined as all income recipients who participate directly in economic activity: unpaid family workers have been excluded.
[a]Excluding salaried managers and officials.
[b]Business entrepreneurs, professional practitioners, farmers, and other property owners.
[c]Figures for 1780 are rough estimates. Slaves, who comprised one-fifth of the population, are excluded; white indentured servants are included in the wage and salaried employees category.

employees, and many others who do not produce surplus value in fact share many life conditions with proletarians. They are subject to unemployment and layoffs, to educational channeling during their training period, and to close supervision by management. They share most of the workplace and labor market experiences of proletarians. In this broad sense, the labor force in a modern capitalist society can be said to be proletarianized.

Off the job, however, there is a blurring of class lines in the modern capitalist society. The working class—whether proletarians in the strict sense of the term or the larger bulk of people who experience similar life conditions —are not officially distinct from the economically dominant class in either their legal status or their life-style. The feudal serf lived in a qualitatively different world from the noble or the priest; the slave in Rome or Athens was distinct in every respect from the master. The American factory worker, however, is not necessarily so different from his boss in either outward appearance or the routines of his life. The sharp, all-pervasive differences of earlier class societies persist in American society only on the job. As a citizen and as a consumer, the worker has less power and less money to spend than the manager or the owner, but the differences are quantitative—matters of degree ("more power" or "less power") or likelihood ("more likely to live on Park Avenue" or "less likely to live on Park Avenue")—than qualitative.

This blurring of class differences with respect to off-the-job behavior has softened the impact of mass proletarianization on people in the developed countries. The shortened workday and workweek have increased the amount of the free time, of time outside the productive system. The boss can't tell the workers to step off the sidewalk when he passes by, nor can he forbid them to wear silk shirts, as a noble or slaveowner could. Proletarianization in the last few decades in the developed countries has not been the ruthless process that it was in the days of peasant expropriation and the early factory system. Mass production techniques have given many people access to goods that previously proletarians could not afford. On the job, within the productive system in a narrow sense, class lines are quite apparent; but off the job, class is difficult to identify. To some extent, class lines become more apparent during periods of recession and depression. The power to lay off or to fire—a form of class power—defines class lines clearly. To be unemployed is to be in a position where the inequalities of class have suddenly overflowed the job situation and filled one's whole life.

The media are another factor in the blurring of class consciousness. The media in capitalist society continually tell the worker that he is equal as a citizen and a voter. Many people are disturbed by the contradiction between formal political equality and economic inequality. However, the variety of life-style choices, affluence for large parts of the working class, formal political equality, and the messages of the media reduce class consciousness to some extent.

Proletarianization is experienced not only at the workplace but also in several related institutions—the labor market, schools, and unions. Every experience of selling one's labor power is part of the labor market. For many people, it is a series of humiliations: reading the want ads, being interviewed, seeing "No Help Wanted" signs at the factory gate, getting a haircut for the interview, waiting at unemployment agencies, taking courses one doesn't like in order to become more "marketable," having transcripts sent to potential employers, taking lie detector tests, getting laid off or "pink slipped." More than in any other situation—even the day-to-day job routines—the labor market impresses on the working class its powerlessness and helplessness in an economic situation that it did not create and cannot control.

Some societies have tried to do away with a labor market; China is an example. Various kinds of explicitly political decisions, taking place in local small groups and within the Communist party, are used to allocate labor power. For example, people are selected by their peers and local Party committees to get medical training as "barefoot doctors" (roughly corresponding to medics or public health nurses) or doctors. Labor may be an automatic adjunct of certain positions: for example, university students work in factories during their period of study. Labor may be based on residence: the ablebodied member of a commune—the large collective farms—is expected to work.

Depending on one's ideological bias, one might see these arrangements in different ways—as state and Party coercion limiting the freedom of the individual, or as arrangements that give meaning to human productive effort and assure that all people contribute to the well-being of their compatriots. In any case, there is no unemployment or underemployment. Everyone is assured some role in production. Cash payments have not completely disappeared. There are incentives for working harder and having greater ability. The money paid for such effort or ability can be used to buy small luxuries such as radios. However, just as everyone is expected to work, everyone is provided with at least a minimum level of food, shelter, clothing, free entertainment and recreational facilities, and medical care. The labor market has been largely eliminated. (Most of the other state socialist countries have not gone as far in this direction, and they still have in many sectors hiring practices similar to those in capitalist countries.)

Unions and Schools

In the capitalist countries, two sets of institutions have some effect on the conditions under which labor power is sold: unions and schools. We have discussed unions elsewhere: once as an example of organizational processes, once as an example of movement organizations bringing about major structural reforms, and once as a example of superstructural institutions that help to lubricate the imposition of capitalism on the working class. (Although there seems to be a contradiction, there is truth to both of the last two views of unions. Unions have made labor under the capitalist mode of production less wretched, while at the same time they have smoothed over conflict between owners and producers.)

Another way of looking at unions is to see them as organizations that have tended to improve the conditions under which proletarians sell their labor power. Unions have not attacked the class system directly. They have not made proletarians class conscious in the sense of arousing the desire to become a revolutionary class. In those industries in which workers are unionized, which tend to be the industries of the monopolistic sector, the unions have established better wages and fringe benefits and some protection against the arbitrary exercise of power by supervisors. In return for improving the conditions under which workers sell their labor power, unions have also regularized these transactions and imposed discipline on the workforce by agreeing to fairly long-term contracts, suppressing wildcat strikes, and consenting not to get involved in issues of workplace control that management considers to be its own prerogative.

A second important institution associated with the sale of labor power is the educational system. Elsewhere I have treated schooling as part of the ideological superstructure, as an institution that propagates particular understandings of the world. But it is also useful to see schooling as an institution that channels people into different slots in the labor market. The link between schooling and proletarianization is quite clear, if education is viewed historically. Universal compulsory public schooling began after the Industrial Revolution. It began with the explicit goal of preparing children to be more disciplined and productive workers. It mediates between the family and the productive system. It fulfills this function in several ways:

1. *Training.* Most obviously and benignly, schooling provides different types of training that people will use later on the job. It teaches everything from reading, writing, and ciphering to specialized technical and professional skills.

2. *Certification.* Schools provide certification to insure employers that certain skills and behaviors have been met.

3. *Channeling.* Schooling "cools out" people from the process of upward mobility. Most people would like to have attractive, well-paying jobs. Because of the various tracks, channels, dead ends, and grading practices of the educational system, however, many people are kept from ever trying to reach the desirable slots. This spares employers the trouble of refusing such jobs to people who are "unqualified." In practice, over the last few decades, most people whose parents had the better managerial and professional jobs were themselves able to attain these jobs through the educational system. The growing economy and the expansion of the state and the professions opened up some of these jobs to children of the working class (in the strict sense of the term). Actually, the school system has probably been overrated as a route of mobility. For example, educational attainment, controlled for parental income and test-taking ability, has turned out to be a poor predictor of lifetime earnings. In the fifties and sixties, however, a college degree—often even some college attendance—guaranteed managerial and professional jobs. In the seventies, this route of upward mobility has become much less effective as the available pool of managerial and professional jobs shrank relative to the number of people who wanted them.

Incidentally, in Europe, the school system has been much more openly used to freeze class lines. Entry into higher education and into university-preparatory high schools has been very restricted. Dead-end high school placement and working-class background are very strongly correlated. Dead-end high schools are physically and officially separate from university-oriented ones. There are fewer illusions about the possibility of upward mobility through education.

Education instills attitudes and values that are appropriate to particular slots in the labor market. Working-class schools tend to stress obedience, discipline, and regular habits. Until very recently, the classroom was arranged like a factory, with bolted down desks in straight rows. Individual creativity and self-expression were not particularly encouraged because they were not traits that employers found valuable in factory workers or menial clerical workers.

In the nineteenth century, the school was recognized as explicit preparation for the factory and an important site for imposing docility and regularity on the refractory working class. In working-class high schools and in junior colleges with working-class students, these traditions continue, although in veiled and updated forms. The students are "sold" on the idea of pursuing rather narrow vocational fields because these skills will make them more "marketable." Liberal arts are deemphasized because they are not "relevant" to the needs of employers; science and mathematics are often poorly taught; history and foreign languages are shunned by both the students and administrators. Thus the working class accepts an education that helps to perpetuate dead-end skills and a limited understanding of the social and physical world. It often cooperates in its own preparation for and channeling into "manpower" to meet the demands of employers. The children of the professional and managerial classes tend to receive a more varied, individualized, demanding, and stimulating education.

The hierarchy of tracks is also visible in higher education, in policies such as the state "master plans" that established junior colleges, state colleges, and state universities, each aimed at a different class of clients and each providing a different type of education. The higher institutions in this hierarchy provide more abstract material, more liberal arts courses, and less narrow technical training.

During the 1960s, the schools became the focus of controversies as poorer parents sought to force them to provide better instruction for their children, and as new educational ideas were tested out by teachers. Some of these experiments seemed to be directed toward less physical disciplining for poorer children and less intellectual discipline for middle-class children. In any case, the fit between the school system and the job market is getting more and more strained and unclear. The strains seem apparent in the lack of discipline of younger factory workers as well as in the breakdown of discipline within many urban high schools.[5]

In summary, while upward mobility through the school system is not impossible, it is not the major function of schooling. Aside from providing some substantive training, the major function of the schools is to sort and channel people for the job market and to instill behavior that is suited to the slot for which they are headed.

Proletarianization and Personality

What are the implications of proletarianization for attitudes and personality? In this area, we can see many contradictory trends. On the one hand,

---

[5]See the reading by Andre Gorz on pp. 312–313.

proletarianization—ruthless as the process may be—has freed people from the idiocy of rural life, from the isolation and narrowness of the peasants' world. But sometimes the process led only to shantytowns and slums, to a world even more violent and senseless than the traditional peasant community. Thus for some, proletarianization seemed to produce only apathy, despair, and dehumanization—a culture of poverty. In the long run, however, for more stably employed working people, the working conditions of the proletariat brought about some sense of the collectivity, some unity, and some cooperation. Unlike the peasant, the small entrepreneur, or the self-employed professional, the proletarians cooperated with each other in the production process. This cooperation, along with shared life conditions, often brought about strong solidarity, the basis of working-class movements in all industrialized areas of the world.

Now, however, in the most industrially developed countries, there are also forces at work that could reduce such solidarity. These forces are the decentralization and automation of work, the decreasing length of the workday, a culture of competition in school and the labor market, and the suburban way of life. These trends could produce a more isolated, fragmented, and individualized proletariat. Accompanying these trends is the constant message of the mass media to "do your own thing," to "be an individual," to express your individuality through the endless purchasing of consumer items, and to look out for yourself in a dog-eat-dog world. These images reinforce possessive individualism and competition.

Solidarity is also weakened by management pressures on workers such as teachers, computer programmers, nurses, and many other cultural and technical workers to think of themselves as professionals. The mystique of professionalism reduces solidarity with each other, retards unionization, and cuts off white-collar, cultural, and technical workers from the industrial proletariat. It remains to be seen whether these individualizing trends will create a working class that has the fragmented competitive consciousness that in the past has been characteristic of the petite bourgeoisie.

Epilogue: Socialism or Barbarism

We have seen how capitalism, like all preceding types of society, carries within it the sources of its own collapse. What is the dynamic of this collapse?

Capitalism has to involve growth and expansion. As the working class within the core capitalist states struggles to improve its own conditions, capitalist enterprises must turn in two directions to maintain their profits in the face of these demands for more pay and shorter hours. One way is to increase mechanization and automation, that is, the substitution of nonhuman energy for human labor in the production process, in order to lower labor costs. The second way is to expand capitalist enterprise into the periphery, exploiting the more vulnerable laborers in the underdeveloped areas but, in the process, turning them into a class that comes to resemble the working class of the core areas in its organization and expectations for a higher standard of living.

At this point, the nations of the periphery begin to free themselves from the capitalist center through nationalist and Socialist movements. These movements, such as those in China, Vietnam, Angola, Cuba, and so on, begin to cut off the capitalist states from the supplies of cheap labor and the raw materials that they need to maintain a high level of mechanization. This situation, in turn, generates inflation, higher unemployment, and declining real incomes for the working class in the core states, setting off a new wave of militant labor struggles. Such struggles are now under way in northern Italy, England, and France, and in the United States to a lesser degree.

We are now only in the middle of this process. We cannot predict the exact form it will take, nor can we be certain of the time span. We should not fall into the trap of believing that every downturn of the stock market, every hike in the price of oil, or every fall of a corrupt politician heralds the instant doom of capitalism. This process in its entirety will probably take several decades.

What, then, is the final outcome of the process? There seems to be a race between two opposing forces. On the one hand, the increasing contradictions within capitalism make the working class more aware of the nature of the economic and political system, better organized to take over state power, more aware of the potential of technology, and more ready to take history into its own hands. This possibility is what is meant by socialism. But, on the other hand, the impending collapse of capitalism also generates forces of barbarism —the pressures toward repression and fascism, toward wars between capitalist rivals or between nations of the center and the periphery, toward superstitions and other mystifications, and toward genocide and nuclear war. Since we now have the conceptual tools to understand social change and the organizational tools to shape its course, we should be able to make the transition from capitalism to socialism without the brutalization and despair that were associated with the end of other types of society, such as the fall of Rome or the waning of feudalism. Yet the alternative of barbarism cannot be entirely ruled out.

What is Socialism?

We cannot now predict what socialism could look like. We do not have a blueprint for it. We do know a few things about the transition to socialism, however.

Existing Socialist Societies. One feature of the transition historically has been that all existing socialist societies have had to survive in a hostile environment of capitalist societies. These circumstances have to a greater or lesser degree shaped—and distorted—the priorities of the socialist societies. They have had to fight against invasions and to participate in wars; they have had to engage in the same *realpolitik* as capitalist societies to defend their national interests.

The Soviet Union, as the first socialist state and for many years the only one, has borne the brunt of these problems, first in a civil war accompanied by a foreign invasion, then in World War II. The international situation has been one of the factors that forced the U.S.S.R. to industrialize very rapidly, to continue to give priority to military development, to expand the power of the state apparatus, and to maintain a defensive cultural posture. China, Cuba, and other later arrivals to socialism have faced similar problems, but their transitional experiences have been somewhat eased by the existence of the Soviet Union, both through direct support and by learning from its difficulties. Furthermore, these later arrivals were all to some extent in the periphery or semiperiphery of capitalism before their transition to socialism. Thus they have had to deal with problems of foreign economic domination and underdevelopment. Their period of·transition has also had to be a period of rapid economic development.

For these reasons, the forms of socialism that have developed in these countries do not necessarily provide a blueprint for what socialism might be like in industrially developed nations in a completely socialist world. We can learn from them, but we must do so carefully and critically; we must keep in mind that the historical processes of technological development and growing instability in the capitalist world economy are continually expanding the possibilities for future socialist societies.

The Period of Transition. We also know that the period of transition to socialism is difficult, even if a country embarks on it under circumstances more favorable than those encountered by the Soviet Union in 1917. The period of transition involves the use of state power to suppress the class organizations that seek to restore the old order. The multinational corporations and the privileged strata of owners and managers are unlikely to accept a peaceful transfer of their wealth and power to the working class. A tiny minority of the world's population is likely to resort to armed force to try to regain its hold on the resources and labor of the vast majority. The downfall of Allende's government in Chile as it tried a peaceful transition to socialism shows that the transition can succeed only if the working class and its allies are able and prepared to defend the new society with force.

The period of transition to socialism also brings with it many problems of consciousness. Habits of mind and of life-style that were appropriate in an insecure class society get carried over into the transitional period by many people, not just the old ruling classes. Thus socialist societies have had to cope with black markets in luxury goods, with the accumulation of privileges by state officials, with the desire for power and self-aggrandizement, with the oppression of women, and so on. As we saw in our discussion of human history, these are not traits based in an abstract and unchanging "human nature." They are traits fostered in particular social contexts. However, it would be unrealistic to believe that this cultural and psychological baggage acquired in class societies over centuries will be dropped at the first shot of the socialist revolution. Quite the contrary, these bad habits have to become the focus of a fairly long process of change in consciousness.

We can make a few more positive remarks about socialism. It means above all the operation of an economy for human needs and not for the profit of a small dominant class. It means the end of the appropriation of a surplus by this class for use in its own projects. In socialist society, the means of production are owned by the people as a whole. Wealth produced in a socialist society is either turned over directly to the producers in wages or is returned to them indirectly in projects of development or services (schools, health care, energy resources, and so on). Emphasis in socialist development is on the reduction of great gaps in living standards. The great productive capacity of capitalism makes possible prosperity for all; under capitalism, however, class barriers interfered with the just and rational use of the capacity. Socialism fulfills this productive potential. Socialism means that all people take part in production or other useful activities; there will be neither idle rich nor idle poor. During the transitional stage, there will likely be some disparities in income, disparities based on ability, effort, and the scarcity of certain skills. These disparities cannot disappear overnight, but they should be gradually reduced.

Socialism means planning. We cannot spell out exactly what the groups and units involved in planning would be. In order to maintain an industrial economy with a high level of production, there would have to be national and even international coordination. But some planning could be decentralized to regional or local levels. Opposition to planning in principle is one of the bad habits of mind inculcated in our present society. In fact, capitalist firms and the capitalist state already plan extensively. It is only the subordinate classes that are discouraged from planning both by the media and by their own life conditions. Thus they drift with the vagaries of the capitalist economy and with the demands of the dominant classes. Planning in the best sense means an effort to grasp and direct one's future. In a socialist economy, all people will be able to participate in such planning.

Finally, we can safely predict that socialism means the growth and release of human potentialities of which we can now only dream. We can get a hint of what is possible by comparing feudalism with capitalism. Under feudalism, most people were physically stunted, most were illiterate, most saw their children die in infancy, most were brutalized and dulled. An observer of the Western World in A.D. 1000 would not have been able to imagine a people that was healthy, literate, free from infant mortality, free from superstition.

The existence of many such people now shows that the stultification and apathy of the feudal peasant was not a necessary human condition but only the product of a particular social system. Capitalism has been progressive, a step forward from feudalism; it whispers a promise of prosperity, of political participation, of rational action, of the wise application of science to human needs, of the growth of human potential. In a class system, such a whispered promise cannot be kept at all for many people and only in a distorted way even for the fortunate few. In socialism, the promise must be kept for all.

References

Ehrenreich, John.
1974– "Problems with bringing it back home." New American Movement 6 (December–
1975   January): 17.

Engels, Friedrich.
1958   The Condition of the Working Class in England. Translated and edited by W. O. Henderson and W. H. Chaloner. Stanford, Calif.: Stanford University Press.

Foucault, Michel.
1965   Madness and Civilization: A History of Insanity in the Age of Reason. Translation by Richard Howard. New York: Pantheon Books.

Harris, Marvin.
1971   Culture, Man and Nature. New York: Thomas Crowell.

Hobsbawm, Eric J.
1965   Primitive Rebels. New York: Norton.
1967   Labouring Men. Garden City, N.Y.: Anchor Books.

Huizinga, Johan.
1954   The Waning of the Middle Ages. Garden City, N.Y.: Anchor Books.

Landes, David S.
1969   Unbound Prometheus. New York: Cambridge University Press.

Machiavelli, Nicolo.
1952   The Prince. New York: New American Library.

Magdoff, Harry.
1969   The Age of Imperialism. New York: Monthly Review Press.

Marx, Karl, and Friedrich Engels.
1948   Communist Manifesto. New York: International Publishers.

Moore, Barrington, Jr.
1966   Social Origins of Dictatorship and Democracy. Boston: Beacon Press.

Pirenne, Henri.
1937   Economic and Social History of Medieval Europe. Translation by I. E. Clegg. New York: Harcourt, Brace and World.
1952   Medieval Cities: Their Origins and the Revival of Trade. Translation by Frank D. Halsey. Princeton, N.J.: Princeton University Press.

Reich, Michael.
1972   "Evolution of the United States labor force." Pp. 174–183 in Richard C. Edwards, Michael Reich, and Thomas E. Weisskopf (eds.), The Capitalist System. Englewood Cliffs, N.J.: Prentice-Hall.

Simmel, Georg.
   1950   "The metropolis and mental life," in Kurt H. Wolff (ed.), The Sociology of Georg Simmel. Glencoe, Ill.: Free Press.

Trevor-Roper, Hugh.
   1968   "Religion, the Reformation, and social change," in The Crisis of the Seventeenth Century. New York: Harper and Row.

Wallerstein, Immanuel.
   1974   The Modern World-System: Capitalist Agriculture and the Origins of the European World Economy in the 16th Century. New York: Academic Press.

Williams, William A.
   1972   The Tragedy of American Diplomacy. New York: Dell.

Chapter
13

Methods of
Observing
Large - Scale
Social Change
The analysis of change in whole
societies has usually been based on three types of empirical sources: studies made by
historians, more or less quantitative social indicators, and the accounts of anthropologists.

"SOCIOLOGY IS HISTORY with the hard work left out; history is sociology with
the brains left out" (MacRae, 1956:302). In the first section, I shall tell you
how to benefit from the hard work of the historian. I shall also argue that
historians with brains are by no means rare and often provide the best understanding of social change. The first step is to read the work of historians,
especially those historians with an interest in social history, that is, the history
of institutions and of the lives and experiences of the masses of people rather
than the doings of kings and statesmen (as, for instance, in diplomatic history)
or of intellectuals (as in the history of ideas). Economic history is also useful
because it provides us with information about the mode of production and the
day-to-day activities of most people.

I would like first to suggest some benefits in reading history and some
criteria for evaluating historical studies.

1. The first advantage of historical work is that it is the major source
   of any data dealing with societies that existed prior to the time when
   other social scientists began to collect data regularly. To understand
   the processes of change in these earlier societies and to see how they
   changed into modern states by evolution, revolution, or invasion, we
   must go to historical material.

2. Long-term processes have been much better described by historians than by other social scientists. Historians are trained to think about long-term change and to collect data about it. Most other social scientists are trained to use surveys, participant-observation methods, experiments, and current social indicators in ways that restrict their understanding of change to time spans of, at worst, a few days (as in the one-shot survey) or, at best, a few decades (as in the use of social indicator data collected by the state or large organizations).

3. Historians, more than other social scientists, are attuned to the unique nonrecurrent features of a society or a situation. Therefore, their work serves as antidote to the eagerness of other social scientists to identify "general laws," those statements about social behavior or change processes that hold in all times and places.

4. Historians have been trained to use and evaluate archival data, documents and eyewitness accounts, and other primary sources, while other social scientists have not been trained in this way.

Using the Historian's Data

Here are some criteria for evaluating the work of historians in terms of its usefulness for studying social change. I have formulated these criteria as warnings of what to avoid or to accept only with reservations.

1. Is the historian concerned only with the behavior of elites? Or does he show what kind of consequences this behavior had for other people in the society?

2. Is he inclined to pile up facts and amusing stories? Or does he treat this mass of details according to certain concepts, especially concepts such as class, power, institution, culture contact, social structure, and so on? Does he have a framework that enables him to transcend "the weary process of fact accumulation, plus or minus value judgments" (Jones, 1973:108–109)?

3. Is he inclined to rush into moral judgments about the customs or life-styles of a period? Or does he explain (if not condone) this behavior in terms of the structure of the society?

4. Does he explain beliefs or behavior only in terms of ideas? Or does he seek further explanations of such phenomena in the actual activity and relationship of people?

5. Does the historian portray the society as static and conflict free? Or does he take into account the prevalence of conflict even when social control was rigid and the ruling classes hegemonic? Does he make an effort to present life-styles and ideas that were different from or opposed to that of the ruling class?

Archival Data and Social Indicators

The historian's work, as well as that of many other social scientists interested in change, is based on records of various kinds. These records include eyewitness accounts; the reports of government commissions; statistics collected by public and private bodies, such as actuarial records on births, deaths, and marital status; political and judicial records; sales records; diaries and letters; speeches and leaflets. This material is often buried in government archives, private libraries, obscure provincial collections or journals, or in the files of organizations such as unions and churches. Even if the researcher can gain access to the material, its representativeness and quality are often questionable.

State-level societies generate a fair amount of information about themselves, and this information is a valuable source for the student of change. States tend to develop organizations staffed by experts in information-processing (scribes, priests, accountants, tax auditors, lawyers, archivists, and so on). These information-processing institutions are especially large in the modern state. What types of data do they collect?

1. Data are collected on population characteristics—*demographic* data on population size, age structure, birth and death rates as well as more refined measures of reproduction and death, causes of death, migration within the country and between it and other countries, and so on. Many states collect and publish such data separately and also conduct a *census,* an enumeration of the total population and a documentation of some of its characteristics, on a regular basis.

2. Records are kept of the characteristics of the *labor force*—employment, unemployment, and the distribution of workers into different types of categories. The kinds of categories that are used by the United States government (especially the Department of Labor) include employment by sector (agriculture and related activities, manufacturing, and service) and by occupational type and occupational specialization.

3. Data are collected on the characteristics of the *economy*—the gross national product (the total value of wealth produced); the number and size of productive units (firms in a capitalist economy); income; the extent of poverty; economic growth and the difference in growth rates for different sectors; productivity (output per unit of labor time); inputs and outputs of time, energy, and materials for industries and the economy as a whole; prices and the cost of living; government budgets; and monetary phenomena.

4. The *quality of life* is recorded—the availability of housing, transportation, medical services, recreational facilities, and education; the extent of poverty; the extent of personal well-being as measured by indicators such as suicide or crime rates.

5. The nature of *political participation,* usually in terms of voting behavior or party membership, is recorded.

For the novice user of such material, the best places to begin looking are the reference departments of libraries. Government agencies and some private organizations are also likely repositories. Serious problems arise in using these data as indicators of the conditions of the society, however. The data are often unreliable. Either the circumstances under which they were collected make them poor estimates of the real occurrence of a phenomenon, or, as indicators, the data are often invalid because they fail to tell us much about the condition in which we are really interested, a condition that is more abstract and general than any combination of indicators. Finally, indicators are often based on individuals and completely miss structural features of the society—characteristics of relationships between activities and institutions.

The use of social indicators often makes possible a rigorous quantitative analysis of a situation. For example, the latest fashion in historiography is to subject such data to rigorous quantitative analysis (often using computers). Precision and rigor are commendable, but care must be taken not to substitute quantified data *processing* for careful data *collection.* If careful data collection is lacking, computer analysis will not rescue the material (and, if anything, will give a misleading air of accuracy)—"garbage in, garbage out."

Finally, neither *processing* nor *collection* techniques can substitute for a historical and sociological imagination that places facts into an explanatory framework. Perhaps the greatest danger of all in using social indicators or any characterizations (and especially official quantitative ones) is that we may overwhelm and trivialize our perspective with a mass of "facts." If, however, we use these "facts" within a coherent framework, they can be useful as evidence and as clues to the general condition of the society.

Anthropological Data

Anthropologists trained in describing societies as wholes can provide valuable material for the analysis of change. The importance of ethnography is that it tends to present a society as a whole. Often the society that is described is small and homogenous enough so that one well-trained outside observer can have a good understanding of its whole structure and how it is changing. This overview is much more difficult to master in the large industrial societies. Large complex societies contain so many people, so many subcultures, and so many factors of change that overviews are much harder to construct. Furthermore, the observer generally has grown up on an industrialized society herself and, therefore, has difficulty in not taking parts of it for granted. The small societies typically studied in ethnographies are like laboratories in which to observe structural change.

I do not intend to instruct the reader in how to conduct ethnographic studies. In part, the methodology is much like the participant-observer procedure that I have already described. In part, it can be conveyed only through the field work experience itself, experience that typically is an important and lengthy part of the training of an anthropologist. My main point here is that people interested in social change would do well to *read* good ethnographies, even if they do not produce them themselves. To summarize the advantages of ethnographic study:

1. Ethnographies present societies as wholes, and show how changes can affect the entire structure.
2. Ethnographies give examples of the variety of ways in which "culture contact"—specifically, the inclusion of a small precapitalist society or community into the "world system"—takes place. In other words, a good ethnography should describe how small societies are being swallowed up by the world system of industrial capitalism.

References

Jones, Gareth Stedman.
   1973 "History: The poverty of empiricism." Pp. 96–115 in Robin Blackburn (ed.), Ideology in Social Science. New York: Pantheon Books.

MacRae, Donald G.
   1956 "Some sociological prospects." Transactions of the Third World Congress of Sociology 8:302. Cited in Werner Cahnman and Alvin Boskoff (eds.), Sociology and History. New York: Free Press of Glencoe, 1964, p. 1.

Chapter 14

The Theory
and Practice
of Change In this chapter, I would like to summarize
ways of thinking about change.

HOW PEOPLE CONCEIVE OF CHANGE has consequences for how they evaluate it when it occurs and for how they participate in it. The relatively abstract ways of thinking about change we can call theory; participation in the class struggle itself—action—we can call practice.

Some Principles for Understanding Change

In thinking about social change, we have to be sensitive to the tensions between the need for general abstract principles and the need for grasping the uniqueness of specific historical situations. We have already seen how different types of society have their own laws of motion and their own special characteristics. At the same time, however, we may be able to identify general characteristics of change at a somewhat higher level of abstraction than the laws of motion of specific types of society. Understanding these characteristics of change helps us to see how one type of society is transformed into another type.

I shall identify four such basic characteristics of change.

Quantitative and Qualitative Change

The first characteristic of change is that it really includes two distinct but related kinds of change: quantitative and qualitative.

Quantitative Change.   Quantitative change consists of many small shifts in the behavior and attitudes of a diversity of groups in a society. This kind of change is the product of the interaction, conflict, and negotiation of myriads of people. At some points in time, these interactions are relatively more violent; they are conflict rather than bargaining or agreement. At other times, there is less conflict. Conflict and bargaining often result in consequences that the actors often do not want and fail to anticipate. Changes take place in the "hearts and minds" of the actors and also in their overt behavior. Many changes occur as outcomes of interactions and thus are somewhat removed from the will or motivation of any particular individual.

Ideological change, unlike changes in the mode of production or political institutions, is often best understood as quantitative change because it involves shifts in the consciousness of many separate individuals. For example, in the Chinese Revolution, at first only Party cadres had a Marxist conception of society. Then, through force of circumstances (economic problems, the collapse of the central government, the Japanese invasion), this conception spread to large parts of the Chinese population. They cooperated with the revolutionary forces to carry out the restructuring of Chinese society. Finally, the Marxist conception of society became the standard conception for everyone. However, the propagation of these concepts involved the persuasion of a steadily accumulating number of individuals.

These quantitative changes can be described by the graph in Figure 9. Note that in Phase I, only a few individuals have undergone the ideological change. In Phase II, the ideological change spreads rapidly throughout the population, reaching almost everyone. In Phase III, it reaches the stragglers (leaving some people perhaps untouched).

The units for studying quantitative change tend to be individuals, organizations, or other groups in a society. The imagery that goes with this view is statistical. Aggregates, like molecules in a gas that is being heated, or like individuals changing their behavior and attitudes, are the carriers of change.

Qualitative Change.   Qualitative change is the kind of change that occurs sooner or later when the structure of the whole is abruptly altered. A society has a wholeness to it. It is unified and made coherent by a structure of class relations and relations of power. This structure tends to be relatively stable for relatively long periods of time. A variety of institutions in the society function to preserve the stability of the structure (some authors choose to term the totality of these protective institutions the *state* or *superstructure*).

Many minor changes can be absorbed by these protective institutions. When enough quantitative changes have built up, however, there is a collapse of the whole structure, and a new structure or system emerges. When the new structure appears, the same physical individuals continue to exist. But their interrelationships are completely different. For example, in the seventeenth and eighteenth centuries, French society was gradually changing; agriculture

Figure 9

Spread of Ideological Change

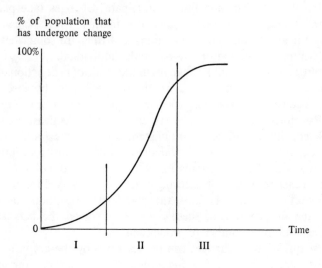

was becoming more commercial, the status of peasants was changing, and a bourgeoisie was emerging. All these changes involved a slow accumulation of small shifts in action, like a steady buildup of water behind a dam. Suddenly the dam broke. The French Revolution was an abrupt and violent transformation of the whole—class structure, political system, and ideology.

We have to be sensitive to how and why quantitative change suddenly adds up to qualitative change in the whole structure. Some quantitative changes are absorbed into the system and seem to produce little qualitative change. This seems especially true of changes in fads and fashions. For example, in the 1960s, some Madison Avenue executives wore long hair and beads and smoked marijuana. These and related changes did not produce the collapse of capitalism, and the structure of private ownership of productive enterprises continued.

In summary, certain types of quantitative change can accumulate to the point of triggering a collapse of the system as a whole—a qualitative change. Such a qualitative or systems change engulfs all aspects of a society, beginning with its mode of production and class structure, but spreading to its political system, its ideology, even its patterns of inter- and intrapersonal behavior.

Totality and Reciprocal Action

Another characteristic of change is that it has to be understood as part of a totality. To understand change, we must always look at it, not in isolation, but in the context of the whole system. Cumulative smaller changes must be studied in relationship to each other; they must be seen as having reciprocal effects on each other. These kinds of smaller quantitative changes must be assessed in relation to change in the system as a whole. Change in parts of a system, in their relationship to each other, transforms the system as a whole.

For example, it is not very useful to study only "changes in the family" or "changes in laws," and so on. Changes in one institution are always related to changes in other institutions and to the configuration of the whole society; the system as a whole changes. Of course, to conduct empirical observation, we may have to focus on one or another institution or group. However, this emphasis should never obscure changes in the whole.

Contradictions

Every system, at its inception, contains potential strains or inconsistencies. As the system develops, these strains become larger and larger until the system collapses. Thus change—dynamism—is built into every system. Contradictions or strains in the system must be understood as a major source of change, even when the actors in the system do not recognize them as such and are not currently engaged in conflict or other consciously motivated behavior concerning these strains. In the long run, people tend to perceive the strains consciously and to act on the basis of their conceptions. The contradictions in a social system are thus transformed into willful conscious action of classes engaged in conflict with each other.

As long as its economy is sound, its ruling class hegemonic, and its producing groups obedient, the society appears to be static, consensual, and viable. Indeed, many class societies *have* remained stable (if not static) for centuries. As long as the population is rural and isolated, the technology primitive and slow changing, political participation limited to a small elite, and the ideology conservative and apathy inducing, the ruling classes can maintain hegemony for long periods of time. Hindu caste society is an excellent example. But when technology is dynamic, the society is eager to expand geographically, the members of the producing class are brought into close contact with each other, the ideology emphasizes secularization and participation, and system-straining changes appear more rapidly. These system-straining changes— "heightening of the contradictions"—do not mean automatic, immediate collapse. But the institutions that are designed to accommodate or suppress change are forced into increasingly elaborate patchwork. In our society, the fiscal strains on the state (the crisis of public funds), the soaring crime rate, the collapse of the urban school systems, the rising price of Third World raw materials, labor unrest and the high rate of strikes—all attest to problems in the superstructural patchwork. These occurrences do not mean that a collapse is going to happen immediately, but they suggest that it may happen within the foreseeable future.

As suggested by the transition from feudalism to capitalism, a collapse of the mode of production may precede by many decades, even centuries, a class revolution to seize the state. Feudalism had ceased to exist as an economic system and the bourgeoisie had become a vital class long before it seized the state. In other words, a collapse of capitalism may well precede a proletarian revolution, and a period of transition may well intervene between the two events.

Dialectical Change: Evolution

The final characteristic of change is the cumulative and nonreversible nature of the system transformations. Every collapse of a system and the emergence of a new system mean the attainment of a new and different level of organization and action. "What is done cannot be undone"; the movie of history cannot be played backwards.

While the processes of change have some similarities in all systems, each system also presents new and unique features. Change is *not* cyclical. In many respects, capitalism is an unprecedented system; its worldwide scope, its particular forms of property and labor, its technology and mass production of goods are key, unique features. Whatever system follows it will necessarily be shaped by the impact of capitalism on human beings and on nature. Many of capitalism's features may be deliberately destroyed, but destruction is different from never having existed in the first place. (Even a nuclear holocaust that "takes us back to the Stone Age" or a total pollution of the environment through industrial wastes would not take us back to a system like the real Stone Age but to a grim, poisoned world, as unprecedented as our own world is now.) History "repeats itself" only in the sense that some processes of change persist. The contents of these processes, the specific behaviors that are changing, are never quite the same. Each new set of behaviors is conditioned by the preceding set.

In summary, small changes pile up until the system collapses. The old system gives way to a new one. The old system drops into the past, never to be revived. However, the new system, already at the moment of its appearance, contains stresses that will slowly enlarge, like cracks in the foundation of a building, until the whole collapses. Yet the process is not cyclical. Growth, decay, and collapse never return us to the initial starting point. Change is spiral rather than cyclical.

Methodology of Practice

The sort of change that I have just outlined requires an appropriate methodology. Various components of change—like change in individuals, in ideologies, in economic systems, and so on—can be studied by using some of the methods that I have described. These are more or less the methods of conventional modern social science. But can a collection of these methods provide the correct way to comprehend how the *totality* of human action has unfolded over time? Is a collection of these methods adequate for understanding qualitative historical changes in the whole structure of human action? Probably not. Relying on a collection of methods leaves us in the position of the blind men touching the elephant: we comprehend the parts but not the whole living creature. These partial methodologies lack built-in ways of changing with changes in the social structure itself. They are static frameworks of concepts and techniques.

An appropriate methodology has to have ways of continually clarifying and sharpening its techniques and concepts. The only appropriate methodology is one that is in constant contact with the events that are pushed up by the contradictions and conflicts inherent in a particular type of society. The methodology must be experimental in that it seeks to affect behavior itself. It must reflect the irreversibility of the course of human history. It must reflect the reflexiveness of human thought, the human ability to comprehend one's own behavior. It must reflect the growing human awareness of human action and human history. This methodology must involve changing as well as interpreting the world of human action.

Riding the White Water

Let me suggest an analogy for this kind of theory and practice. Human history is like a river—sometimes wild, narrow, and swift, sometimes broad and placid, but always moving, always irreversible. The torrent rushes on inevitably, just as the changes in the mode of production and its accompanying structures have unfolded in history. The person who does not understand these currents and plunges into the river unprepared can only hope that luck will save him.

Skilled white-water canoers, equipped with knowledge, can ride the river, avoiding the whirlpools, selecting the channels, and skillfully righting the boat when it capsizes. The most daring and skilled of all can enter the whirlpools themselves, the revolutions in history. The canoers do not alter the river's course, but nonetheless they master it, entering the channels in which they can survive to reach the sea. Their knowledge of the river is theory. Their actual entry into it is practice. Practice sharpens theory, and theory guides practice. Without some prior knowledge of the river, the canoers are doomed to certain failure. But without the act of entering the river, their knowledge would be not only meaningless but less accurate. The act of navigating the river improves knowledge.

Finally, the canoers' equipment is like the organizational vehicles of class struggle. Without the boat, there would only be the desperate lone swimmer, almost certain to die, no matter how clear his understanding of the river's course. The equipment unites the canoers into a team and makes their passage possible. Their control over the equipment—their ability to develop the right organizational forms—is sharpened in their struggles with the river, just as their knowledge is sharpened.

I think this analogy is helpful in thinking about what a methodology should be like. Practice is not a methodology that asserts that the world can be changed in arbitrary ways, by an act of will, regardless of the actual circumstances and the quality of our interpretations of these circumstances. But the methodology of practice does involve judgments about what changes we want. Not all channels of the river are equally navigable. Not all potentials for change in society at a given historical moment are equally desirable.

Need for Participation

Since the contradictions in class structure are the moving force in human history—a perspective that provides the only currently reasonable explanation of the course of that history—the accompanying practice must be one of participation in class struggle. I hope that by now the reader will have a broad enough comprehension of this term to see that these struggles can take many forms and be waged by different strategies, each tested against the course of events. In dull and peaceful times and places, we can develop our theoretical knowledge and organizational equipment in preparation for the more violent times ahead. What precise form these organizational vehicles of class struggle should take now, in a present that is different from the revolutionary periods of the past, is a question that is beyond the scope of this book. Indeed, it cannot fully be answered in books.

This consideration brings me to the question of what you, the individual reader, can do about change. In some cases, you may want to hold up the process of change. You may see change as destroying relationships and structures that are very important to you. Change may come to be a very negative experience: it may mean the loss of your job, the loss of your ethnic heritage, the loss through death or separation of people you care about, the destruction of the community in which you grew up. I have already commented on the fact that many of the large structural transformations of the past brought with them loss of community, hardship, and death.

Unfortunately, we now live in a society in which certain kinds of change are accepted very uncritically. The bulk of the population has little to gain from these changes but seems to lack the ability to resist them. For example, neighborhoods have been destroyed through urban renewal that has been profitable for a small number of real estate developers but for few other people. The ups and downs of the business cycle—inflation, depression, recession—have meant uncertainty and hardships for most people. Planned obsolescence and fads have led to the waste of increasingly scarce resources. The demands of employers have forced people to move from city to city, repeatedly leaving behind friends, so that for many people friendship ties have become increasingly tenuous and meaningless. We are threatened by crimes of violence committed by increasing numbers of desperate and brutalized people. And we look forward to an old age in which we may be separated from our family and friends and hidden away to die alone in a nursing home. We see increasing numbers of people who are stripped of security, of family, of lasting love, of a sense of order, and of the certainty of a peaceful old age.

These kinds of changes rightfully make us want to resist change. They make us conservative in the best sense of the word, in wanting to preserve what is valuable about the past. But resistance to change cannot be piecemeal. The changes that we may deplore are not isolated random events but part of the strains characteristic of the social structure in which we live. We cannot cope with them by a piecemeal effort of patching up the places where the fabric of society is stretching and tearing or by trying to reestablish mythical "good old days," which, in fact, never existed and could certainly not now be created. We cannot play the movie of history backwards. We must have a vision of a transformed social order in which people—all people—can participate in planning the changes that they want.

A Threefold Strategy

To reach this transformed society, each one of us needs to pursue a threefold strategy:

1. At the level of macro social change, we must develop an understanding of what is happening. This understanding includes the following:

   a) Knowledge of what is happening elsewhere in the world beyond our own immediate personal experience

   b) Comprehension of these events, not as isolated incidents in the fragmented form in which they are presented by the media, but as interrelated aspects of a system (which, of course, does *not* mean that they are linked by the conscious purpose of a small clique of conspirators)

   c) A perspective on human behavior that rules out mystical explanations of events and, instead, forthrightly acknowledges that human beings create their own institutions; a perspective that reaffirms faith in the possibility of rational, conscious, humane behavior

d) Development of a sense of how to "seize the time"

2. At the level of individual behavior, participation in change may depend on altering habits and everyday routines. It may depend on breaking through the expectations others have for you, whether these are well intentioned or vicious. It means not accepting "your place" anymore. It means restoring the unity of mind and body. And it means putting aside cynicism and fatalism. The attitudes that "people are basically rotten" and "nothing can ever be changed" are part of an ideology that encourages inaction and passivity.

3. Finally, action for transforming the social order must come through organizations. The lonely hero can only become a martyr, a kamikaze pilot. The Great Refusal to participate in the bankrupt society without working through organizations to change it is a luxury that only a small stratum of intellectuals can enjoy. Most people do not want to be martyrs; nor do the circumstances of their lives—their struggle to survive, to enjoy themselves a little, to live in peace with their family and friends—permit them to "refuse" to participate in an oppressive society. Most people are rational and aware of their situation when they reject the notion of the Great Refusal as unrealistic. For most of us, change must come by working to transform existing institutions, by working for nonreformist reforms, by destroying some existing institutions, and by building new ones. This task cannot be an individualistic effort; it must be a collective one. We cannot go it alone. We must unite in organizations that can build a new society or, to use a different metaphor, that can be the midwives for the birth of a new society. The birth pangs are inevitable. Our task is to ease the delivery, reduce the amount of suffering, and insure the life and health of the infant. There may as yet not be one organization that is best qualified to do this, that is most worthy of your efforts. But there are a large variety of organizations pursuing different strategies and tactics. It is your task to learn more about them.

Bibliography

THE BIBLIOGRAPHY is a small sampling of additional works on social change. It is intended as a supplement to the references, which also can be used as a bibliography. Books were selected for the bibliography because they are interesting general sources on social change or because they provide further information on some specific topics discussed in the text. Most of the books on this list can be understood without advanced specialized training. They should be available in or through college libraries and bookstores.

Part One: Change and the Individual

Included in this section of the bibliography are books dealing with changes in consciousness, the development of new cultures (especially Afro-American culture), the meshing of history and the life cycle in individuals' biographies, and theories of personality change.

Agel, Jerome. *Rough Times.* New York: Ballantine Books, 1973. Readings in radical therapy, stressing practice.
Aries, Philippe. *Centuries of Childhood: A Social History of Family Life.* New York: Random House-Vintage Books, 1965. A history of childhood in Europe since the Middle Ages.
Bastide, Roger. *African Civilizations in the New World.* New York: Harper & Row, 1972. An introduction to Afro-American cultures and how they emerged from the historical situation of slavery.
Brown, Phil. *Radical Psychology.* New York: Harper & Row, 1973. Readings in psychology, with emphasis on theoretical foundations.
Carr, E. H. *Michael Bakunin.* New York: Macmillan, 1937. A biography of the nineteenth-century anarchist.
Deutscher, Isaac. *Stalin.* New York: Oxford University Press, 1949. A biography, with emphasis on Stalin's political rather than his personal life.
Douglass, Frederick. *Narrative of the Life of Frederick Douglass.* Garden City, N.Y.: Dolphin Books, 1963. The autobiography of a slave who fled to freedom and became an abolitionist and political leader.

Erickson, Erik. *Childhood and Society.* New York: Norton, 1950. A classic statement on the relationship between society and individual psychosexual development.

————. *Young Man Luther.* New York: Norton, 1958. A psychoanalytically oriented biography of Martin Luther.

Fanon, Frantz. *The Wretched of the Earth.* Translated by Constance Farrington. New York: Grove Press, 1965. This "great prose poem to violence" describes the transformation of consciousness that accompanies "native" revolts against colonial regimes and, by implication, the transformations that accompany any struggle for liberation.

Freud, Sigmund. *A General Introduction to Psychoanalysis.* Garden City, N.Y.: Doubleday, 1953. A classic.

Genovese, Eugene. *In Red and Black: Marxian Explorations in Southern and Afro-American History.* New York: Random House, 1972. Emphasizes cultural aspects of slavery as well as its political economy.

Gitlin, Todd, and Hollander, Nanci. *Uptown.* New York: Harper & Row, 1970. Life histories and other personal documents of poor whites in Chicago.

Guevara, Che. *Diary.* San Francisco: Ramparts Press, 1968. "Rigorously exact, priceless and detailed information concerning the heroic final months of his life in Bolivia."—Fidel Castro.

Henry, Jules. *Culture Against Man.* New York: Random House, 1963. A critique of American culture and socialization.

Hinton, William. *Fanshen: A Documentary of Revolution in a Chinese Village.* New York: Random House, 1966. A generally sympathetic account of the Chinese Revolution as it affected one village.

Hobsbawm, Eric J. *Bandits.* New York: Dell Books, 1969. Biographies and analysis of folk-hero bandits throughout the world.

Jones, Mary. *Autobiography of Mother Jones.* 3rd ed. Edited by Mary F. Parton. Chicago: C. H. Kerr, 1974. The life history of a labor leader.

Keil, Charles. *Urban Blues.* Chicago: University of Chicago Press, 1966. An analysis of an important part of Afro-American culture.

Keniston, Kenneth. *Young Radicals.* New York: Harcourt Brace & World, 1968. A sympathetic psychological portrait of participants in the antiwar movement in 1967.

Ladner, Joyce. *Tomorrow's Tomorrow.* Garden City, N.Y.: Doubleday, 1971. A study of black women in St. Louis that challenges stereotypes about family structure and socialization.

Laing, R. D. *The Divided Self.* Baltimore: Penguin Books, 1965. An analysis of schizophrenia that makes going mad seem understandable.

Marcuse, Herbert. *Eros and Civilization.* Boston: Beacon Press, 1955. An attempt to link Freud and Marx.

Millett, Kate. *Sexual Politics.* New York: Avon Books, 1969. A feminist attack on present sex roles and the literary traditions that support them.

Montejo, Esteban. *The Autobiography of a Runaway Slave.* New York: Meridian Books, 1969. The life history of a Cuban.

Powers, Thomas. *Diana: The Making of a Terrorist.* Boston: Houghton Mifflin, 1971. A journalistic account of a Weatherwoman's life and death.

Riesman, David. *Faces in the Crowd.* New Haven, Conn.: Yale University Press, 1952. Portraits of young people, with emphasis on the interplay between personality and politics.

Rowbotham, Sheila. *Women, Resistance and Revolution.* New York: Random House, 1974. "A history of women and revolution in the modern world."

Slater, Philip. *The Pursuit of Loneliness.* Boston: Beacon Press, 1970. A criticism of American culture and personality.

Speer, Albert. *Inside the Third Reich.* New York: Macmillan, 1970. An interesting but slightly unreliable political life history of a Nazi minister.

Tart, Charles. *Altered States of Consciousness.* New York: Wiley, 1969. Studies of trance states, meditation, drugs, and hypnosis presented without political consideration; interesting if read critically.

Whitten, Norman E., Jr., and Szwed, John F. *Afro-American Anthropology: Contemporary Perspectives on Theory and Research.* New York: Free Press, 1970. Studies of various aspects of black culture throughout the Americas.

Womack, John. *Zapata.* New York: Random House, 1969. A biography of the Mexican revolutionary.

Woodward, C. Vann. *Tom Watson.* New York: Oxford University Press, 1963. A biography of a Southern populist political rebel and reformer.

Part Two: Organizations and Change

The books in this section of the bibliography are about changes in organizations and institutions, reforms, and the origins and effects of social movements.

Cammett, John. *Antonio Gramsci and the Origins of Italian Communism.* Stanford: Stanford University Press, 1967. Explication of Gramsci's thought and a description of the Communist party in Italy.

Foner, Philip. *History of the Labor Movement in the United States.* New York: International Publishing Co., 1947. A four-volume history of American labor movements from a Communist perspective.

Galbraith, John K. *The New Industrial State.* Boston: Houghton Mifflin, 1967. An interesting but not entirely convincing interpretation of the American economy and the large corporations.

Garner, Roberta Ash. *Social Movements in America.* 2d ed. Chicago: Rand McNally, 1977. A historical treatment of American movements, especially political movements, with a generally Marxist frame of reference.

Hofstadter, Richard. *The Age of Reform.* New York: Random House, 1955. An interpretation of Populist and Progressive movements.

Horn, Joshua. *Away with All Pests: An English Surgeon in the People's China, 1954–1969.* New York: Monthly Review Press, 1971. A personal account of health care in China.

Kornbluh, Joyce. *Rebel Voices.* Ann Arbor: University of Michigan Press, 1964. Anthology of the songs, writings, and cartoons of the Industrial Workers of the World, an anarcho-syndicalist radical American movement.

Lefcourt, Robert. *Law Against People.* New York: Random House, 1971. Essays demystifying the courts and the legal system.

Miles, Michael. *The Radical Probe.* New York: Atheneum Publishers, 1973. An analysis of the student movement in the 1960s.

Oberschall, Anthony. *Social Conflict and Social Movements.* Englewood Cliffs, N.J.: Prentice-Hall, 1973. An analysis of social movements, emphasizing their rational aspects, their origins, and their access to resources.

Perrow, Charles. *Complex Organizations.* Glenview, Ill.: Scott, Foresman, 1972. A good critical introduction to the literature on organizations.

Weber, Max. *The Theory of Social and Economic Organizations.* New York: Oxford University Press, 1947. A classical theoretical statement on organizations.

Weinsteiñ, James. *The Decline of Socialism in America.* New York: Random House, 1967. An attempt to explain the weakening of American socialism after World War I.

Part Three: Large-Scale Change

The books in this section are about changes in modes of production and political behavior. They are about changes in state power and about revolutions. They are about specific aspects of the growth of capitalism and imperialism.

Abendroth, Wolfgang. *A Short History of the European Working Class.* New York: Monthly Review Press, 1972. A history of working-class parties and social movements.

Amin, Samir. *Accumulation on a World Scale: A Critique of the Theory of Underdevelopment.* New York: Monthly Review Press, 1974. A two-volume analysis of the causes of underdevelopment and the inequality inherent in the present international division of labor.

Anderson, Perry. *Lineages of the Absolutist State.* New York: Humanities Press, 1975.

———. *Passages from Antiquity to Feudalism.* New York: Humanities Press, 1975.

Two definitive new works on European history. The scope and brilliance of the analysis are awesome.

Baran, Paul A., and Sweezy, Paul M. *Monopoly Capital.* New York: Monthly Review Press, 1966. An essay on U.S. social and economic order.

Bonachea, Rolando, and Valdes, Nelson P., eds. *Cuba in Revolution.* Garden City, N.Y.: Doubleday Anchor Book, 1972. A reader on Cuba that includes documents and analysis.

Deutscher, Isaac. *The Prophet Armed: Trotsky, 1879–1921.* New York: Oxford University Press, 1954.

————. *The Prophet Unarmed: Trotsky, 1921–1929.* New York: Oxford University Press, 1959.

————. *The Prophet Outcast: Trotsky, 1929–1940.* New York: Oxford University Press, 1963.
The definitive biography of Trotsky, the Russian revolutionary historian, military commander, and arch rival of Stalin. Vintage Books (Random House) has published a three-volume paperback edition of this work.

Dobb, Maurice. *Political Economy and Capitalism.* Westport, Conn.: Greenwood Press, 1972. Essays in Marxist economic theory.

Hobsbawm, Eric J. *Revolutionaries.* New York: New American Library, 1975. Essays on Communists, anarchists, Marxism, and the revolutionary process. Valuable review essays on a number of European Communist parties.

Huberman, Leo. *Man's Worldly Goods: The Story of the Wealth of Nations.* New York: Harper, 1936. A popular version of Marxist economic history.

Hunnius, Gerry, and Garson, G. David, eds. *Workers' Control: A Reader on Labour and Social Change.* New York: Random House-Vintage Books, 1973. A reader on worker participation in industrial decision-making, worker self-management, and strategies for increasing workers' control over production.

Nettl, J. Peter. *The Soviet Achievement.* New York: Harcourt Brace Jovanovich, 1968. A critical but not unsympathetic chronicle of the Soviet Union since the Russian Revolution. Attractively illustrated.

Polanyi, Karl. *The Great Transformation.* Boston: Beacon Press, 1957. On the capitalist market economy and its social effects.

Science for the People. *China: Science Walks on Two Legs.* New York: Avon Books, 1974. A sympathetic account of science, technology, and social organization in China, showing how the entire people have become involved in experimentation and scientific thought.

Underdevelopment and Revolution in Latin America and Elsewhere

Barnet, Richard J. *Intervention and Revolution.* rev. ed. New York: New American Library, 1972. Describes "America's confrontation with insurgent movements." Good case studies of Greece, Lebanon, the Dominican Republic, Vietnam, and several more.

Cockcroft, James D., Frank, Andre G., and Johnson, Dale L. *Dependence and Underdevelopment: Latin America's Political Economy.* Garden City, N.Y.:

Doubleday Anchor Books, 1972. Discussion of underdevelopment as a condition imposed by the international expansion of capitalism.

Etzkowitz, Henry. *Is America Possible?* St. Paul: West Publishing Co., 1974.
———. *Is America Necessary?* St. Paul: West Publishing Co., 1976. Two books of readings that examine various social, political, and economic problems from a conservative, a liberal, and a socialist point of view.

Frank, Andre G. *Capitalism and Underdevelopment in Latin America.* New York: Monthly Review Press, 1969. "Historical studies of Chile and Brazil."

Horowitz, David. *Empire and Revolution: A Radical Interpretation of Contemporary History.* New York: Random House-Vintage Books, 1970. An interpretation of America's role in international affairs.

Stavenhagen, Rodolfo. *Agrarian Problems and Peasant Movements in Latin America.* Garden City, N.Y.: Doubleday Anchor Books, 1970. A reader.

Problems and Prospects in America

Allen, Robert. *Black Awakening in Capitalist America.* Garden City, N.Y.: Doubleday, 1969. Describes black movements from a Marxist perspective.

Blauner, Robert. *Racial Oppression in America.* New York: Harper & Row, 1972. A series of essays mainly on institutional racism, including issues such as jury selection and black studies programs.

Feldstein, Stanley, and Costello, Laurence. *The Ordeal of Assimilation.* Garden City, N.Y.: Doubleday Anchor Books, 1974. "A documentary history of the white working class in the U.S., 1830s–1970s."

Katznelson, Ira, and Kesselman, Mark. *The Politics of Power.* New York: Harcourt Brace Jovanovich, 1975. "A critical introduction to American government."

Mankoff, M. *The Poverty of Progress: The Political Economy of American Social Problems.* New York: Holt, Rinehart and Winston, 1972. A reader on social problems.

Zeitlin, Maurice, ed. *American Society, Inc.* Chicago: Rand McNally, 1970. A reader on political economy, which includes some valuable primary sources such as the Patman Committee Report on banks.

Periodicals

The following periodicals are of interest to the student of social change.

Monthly Review and *Socialist Revolution.* Articles on current issues from Marxist perspectives.

New Left Review. An independent British Marxist journal, featuring analytical essays and excellent background articles on selected nations and issues.

Politics and Society. Essays on the state and political institutions.

Radical America. Primarily descriptive articles on past and present workers' movements in the United States and elsewhere. Emphasizes workplace struggles and labor history.

Working Papers for a New Society. Articles on reforms and social experiments.

Credits and Acknowledgments

ACKNOWLEDGMENT IS MADE to the following for their kind permission to reprint material from copyrighted sources:

Poems on pp. 9 and 262 from *Selected Poems of Bertolt Brecht,* translated by H. R. Hays; copyright, 1947, by Bertolt Brecht and H. R. Hays; renewed, 1975, by Stefan S. Brecht and H. R. Hays. Reprinted by permission of Harcourt Brace Jovanovich, Inc.

Reading on pp. 10–12 from *The Sociological Imagination* by C. Wright Mills. Copyright © 1959 by Oxford University Press, Inc. Reprinted by permission.

Reading on pp. 128–130 from "The Tyranny of Structurelessness" by Jo Freeman. First published in *The Second Wave,* Vol. 2, no. 1, 1972; reprinted in *Ms.,* July 1973, pp. 76–78, 86–89. Reprinted by permission of the author.

Reading on pp. 168–173 from Max Eastman's translation of *The History of the Russian Revolution* by Leon Trotsky. Copyright © by the University of Michigan 1932, 1933, 1960, renewed 1961. All rights reserved.

Quotations on pp. 220–221, 225 from *Culture, Man, and Nature* by Marvin Harris. Copyright © 1971 by Thomas Y. Crowell Company, Inc. By permission.

Reading on pp. 228–229 from *Labor and Monopoly Capital* by Harry Braverman. Copyright © 1974 by Harry Braverman. Reprinted by permission of Monthly Review Press.

Reading on pp. 312–313 from "Domestic Contradictions of Advanced Capitalism," by Andre Gorz, in R. C. Edwards, Michael Reich, and T. E. Weisskopf, *The Capitalist System,* © 1972, pp. 487, 489. Reprinted by permission of Prentice-Hall, Inc., Englewood Cliffs, N.J.

Quotation on pp. 328–329 from *The Modern World System* by I. Wallerstein. Copyright © 1974. Reprinted by permission of Academic Press, Inc.

Reading on pp. 347–349 from *The Condition of the Working Class in England* by Frederick Engels; translated and edited by W. O. Henderson and W. H. Chaloner. Reprinted with the permission of the publishers, Standford University Press. Copyright © 1958 by Basil Blackwell Publisher, Oxford, England.

Table on p. 388 from *The Capitalist System* by R. C. Edwards, Michael Reich, and T. E. Weisskopf, © 1972, p. 175. Reprinted by permission of Prentice-Hall, Inc., Englewood Cliffs, N.J.

Name Index

Subject Index

PRINTED IN U.S.A.